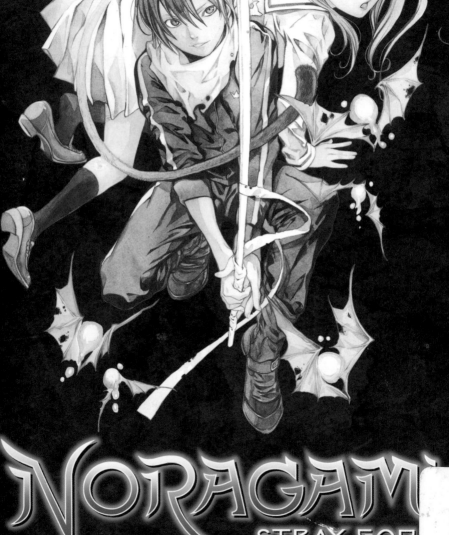

1

ADACHITOKA

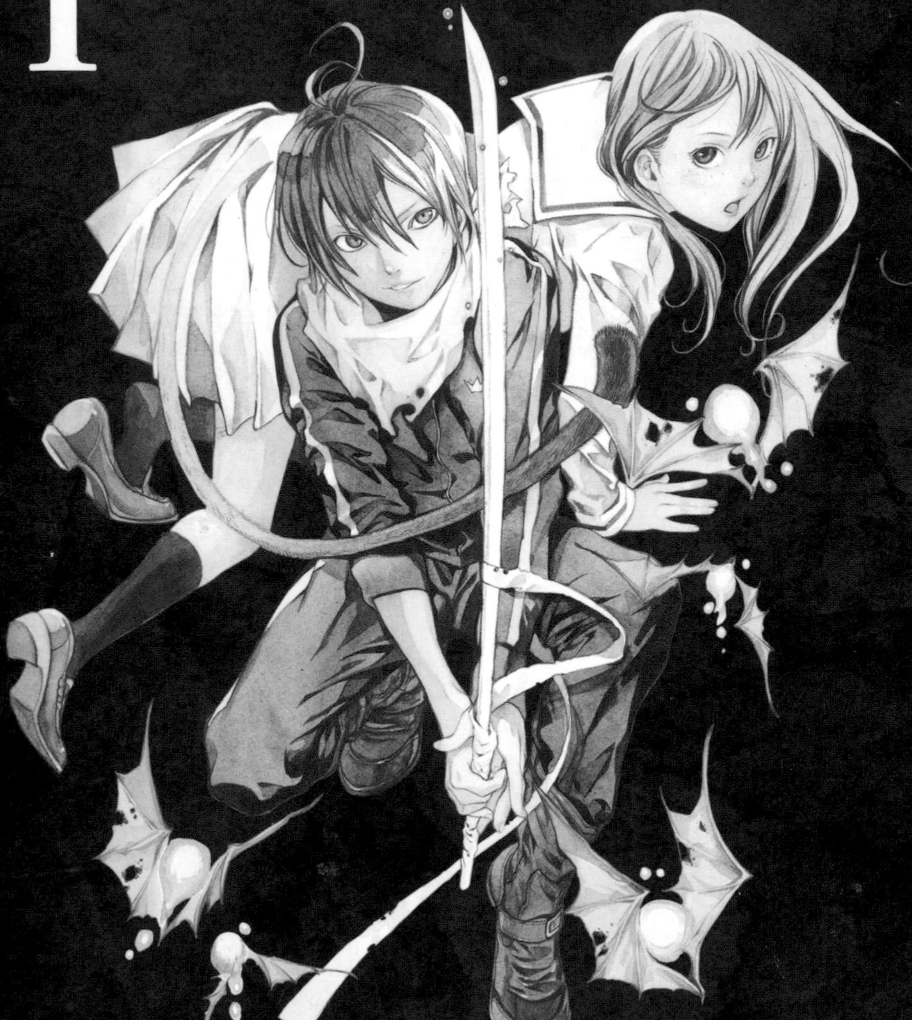

NORAGAMI
STRAY GOD

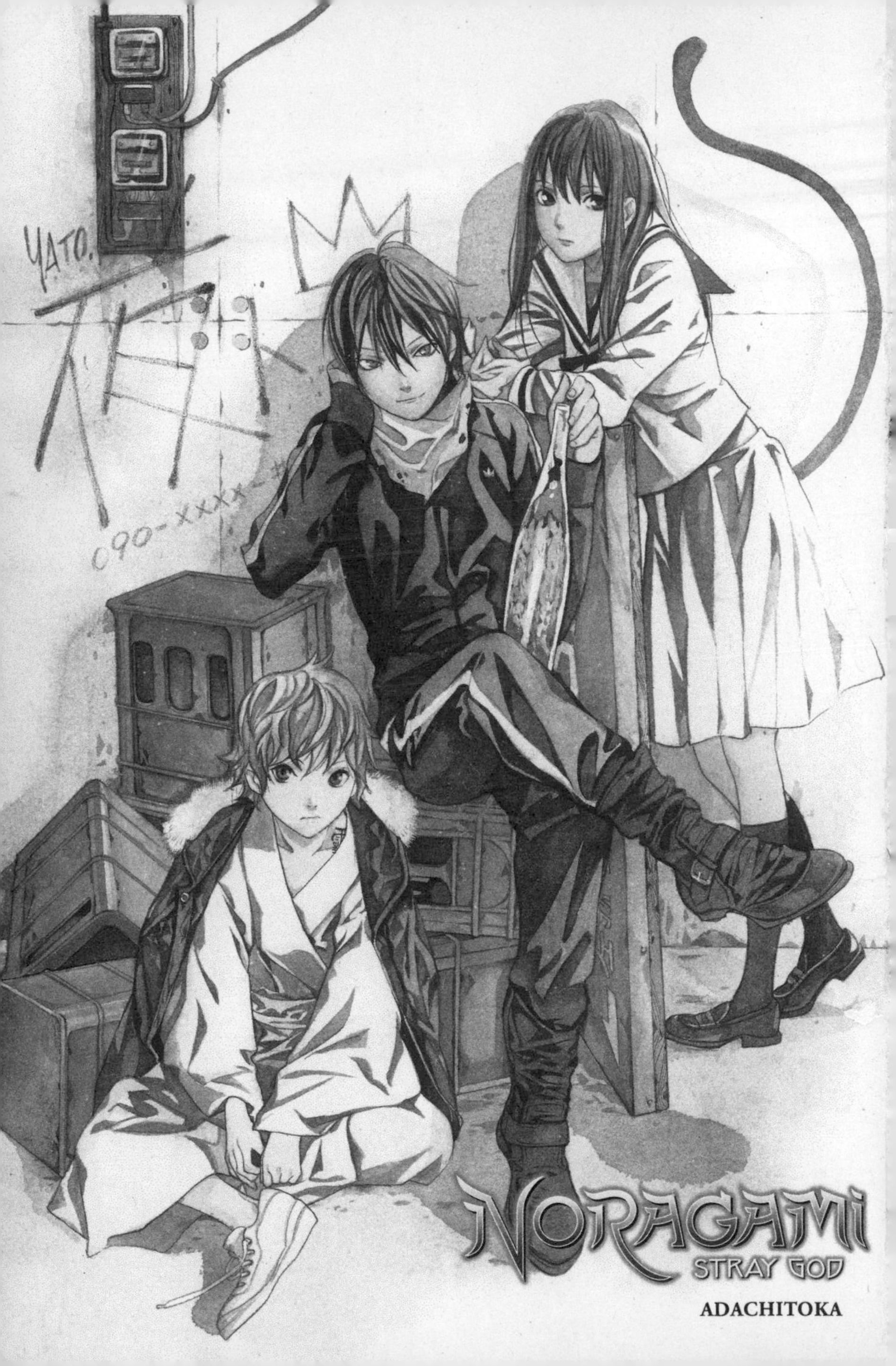
YATO.
090-xxxx-

NORAGAMI
STRAY GOD

ADACHITOKA

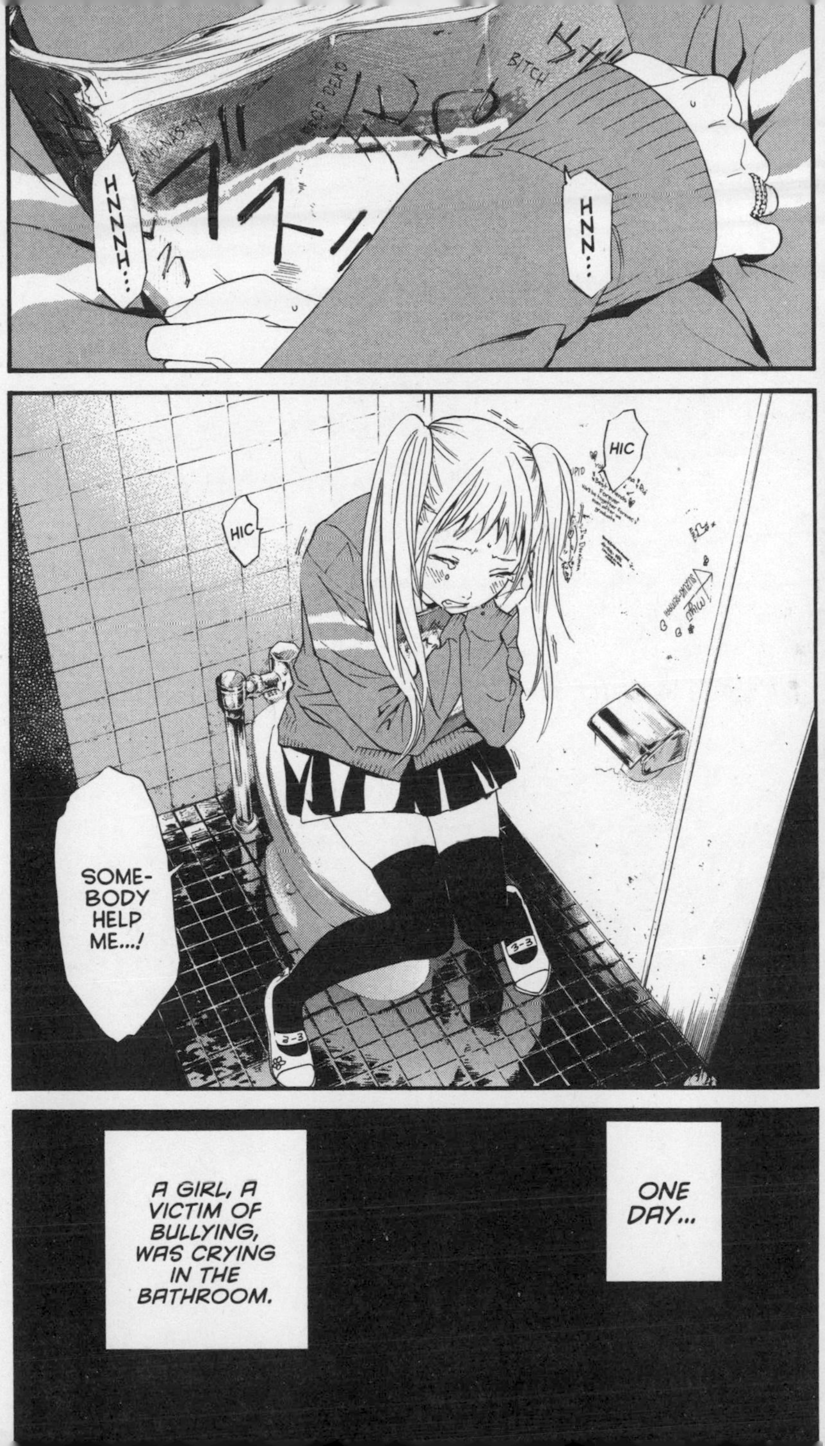
BITCH
DROP DEAD
HNN...
HNNNH...
HIC
HIC
SOME-BODY HELP ME...!
ONE DAY...
A GIRL, A VICTIM OF BULLYING, WAS CRYING IN THE BATHROOM.

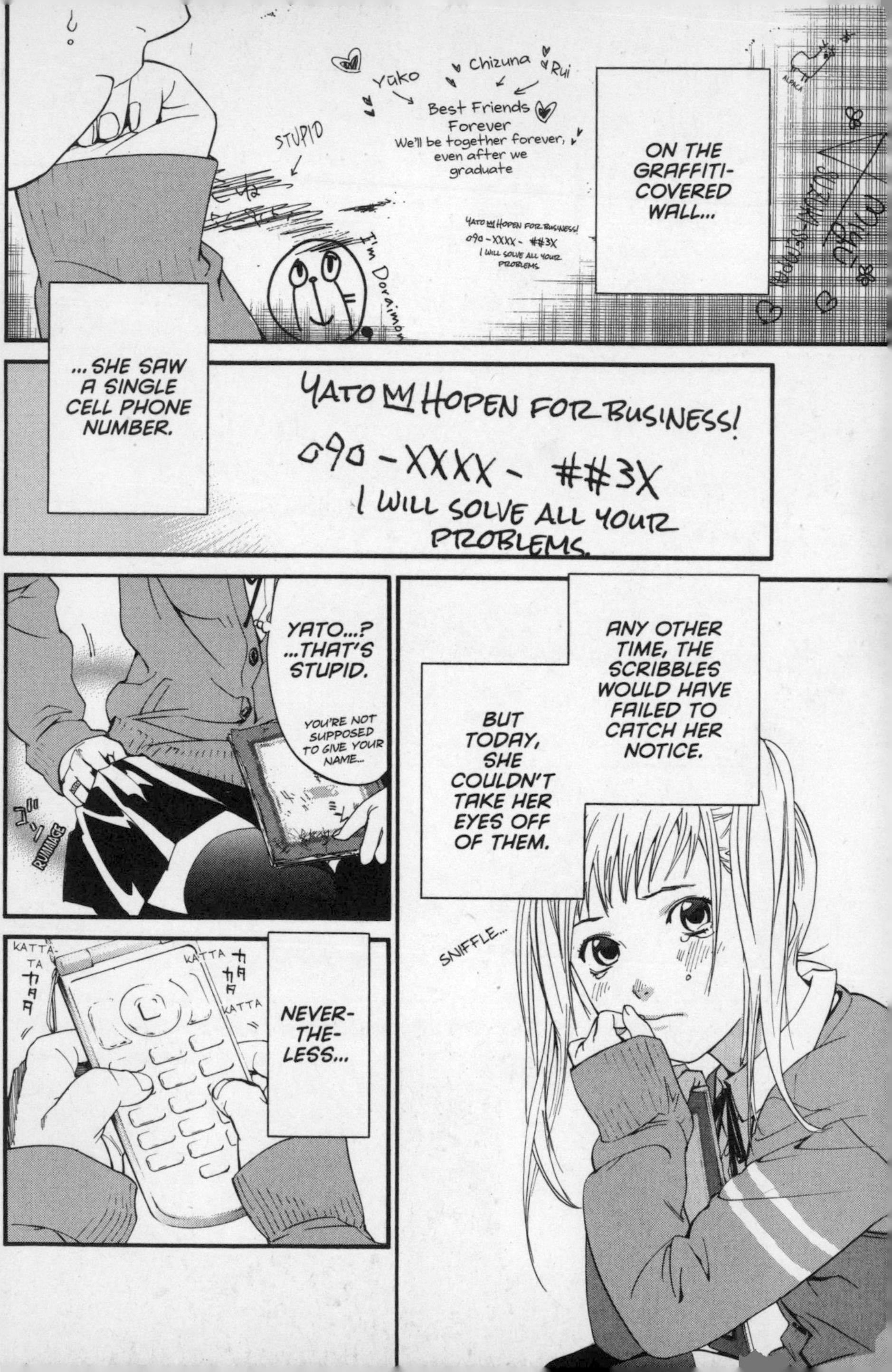
ON THE GRAFFITI-COVERED WALL...
Chizuna
Rui
Yuko
Best Friends Forever
We'll be together forever, even after we graduate
STUPID
I'm Doraimon
Yato Hopen for business!
090-XXXX-##3X
I will solve all your problems.
ALPACA
...SHE SAW A SINGLE CELL PHONE NUMBER.
YATO HOPEN FOR BUSINESS!
090-XXXX- ##3X
I WILL SOLVE ALL YOUR PROBLEMS.
ANY OTHER TIME, THE SCRIBBLES WOULD HAVE FAILED TO CATCH HER NOTICE.
BUT TODAY, SHE COULDN'T TAKE HER EYES OFF OF THEM.
SNIFFLE...
YATO...? ...THAT'S STUPID.
YOU'RE NOT SUPPOSED TO GIVE YOUR NAME...
RUMMAGE
NEVER-THE-LESS...
KATTA KATTA
KATTA-TA

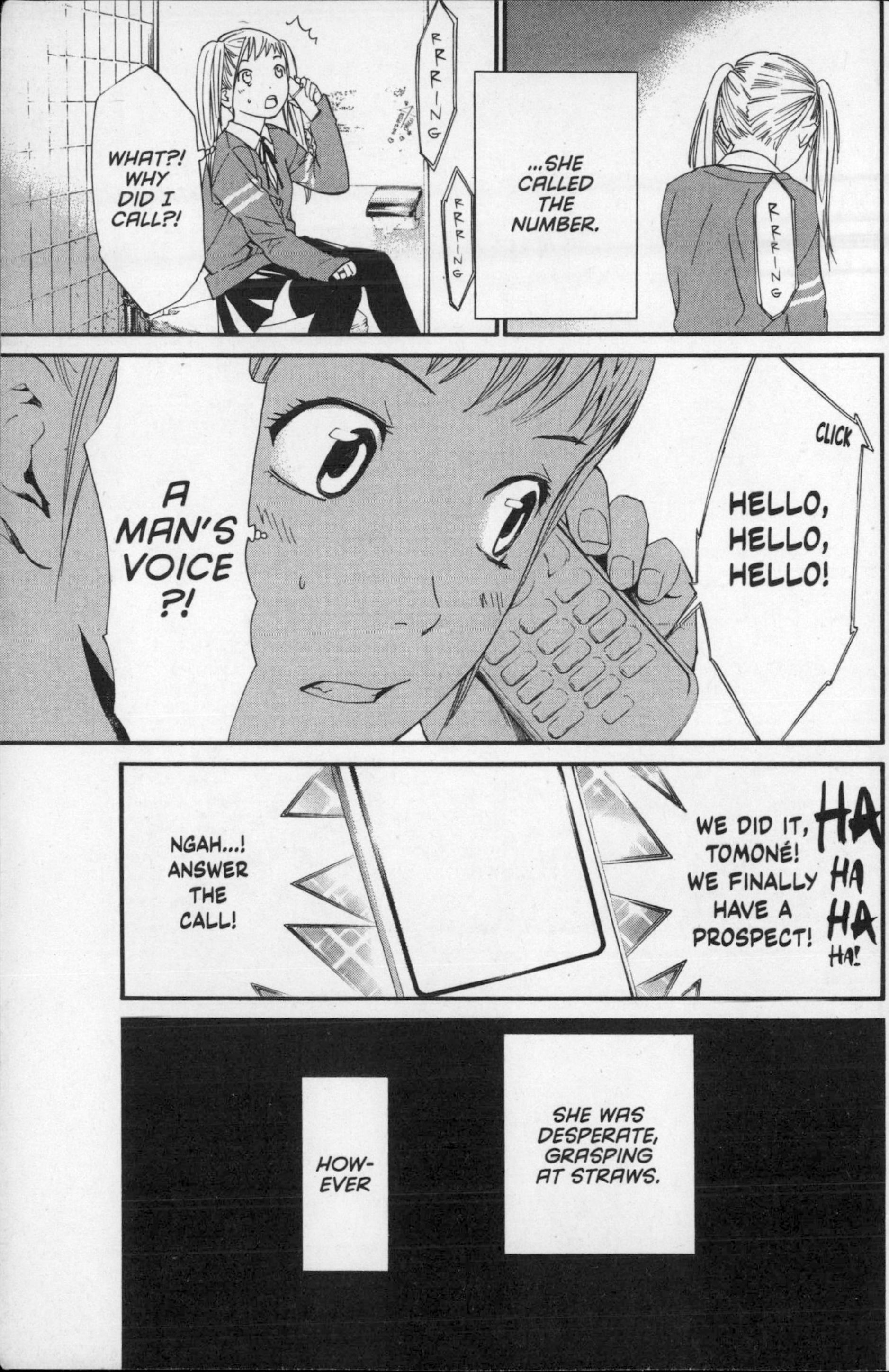
...SHE CALLED THE NUMBER.
RRRING
RRRING
RRRING
WHAT?! WHY DID I CALL?!
CLICK
HELLO, HELLO, HELLO!
A MAN'S VOICE ?!
HA HA HA HA!
WE DID IT, TOMONÉ! WE FINALLY HAVE A PROSPECT!
NGAH...! ANSWER THE CALL!
SHE WAS DESPERATE, GRASPING AT STRAWS.
HOW-EVER

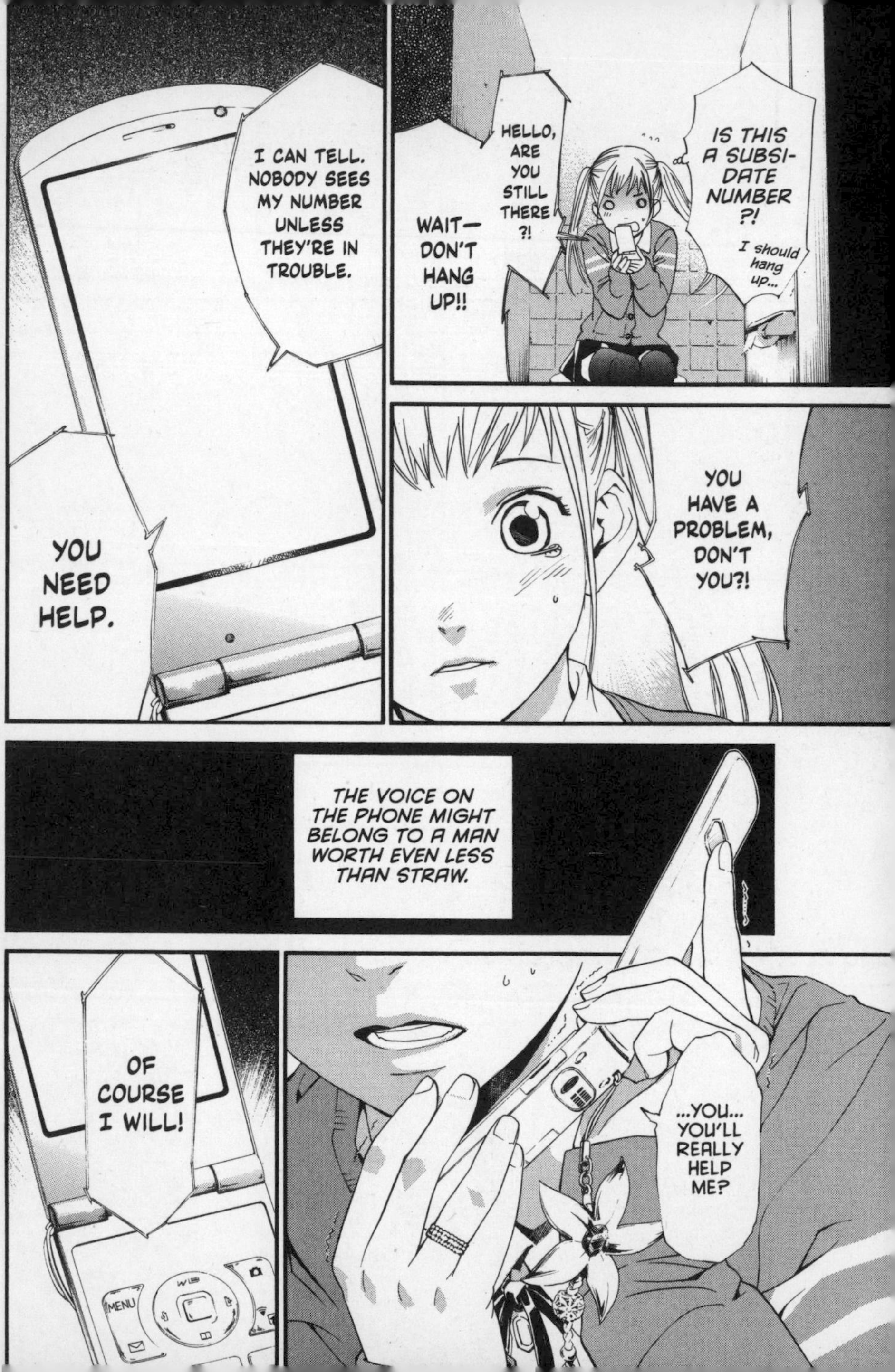
IS THIS A SUBSI-DATE NUMBER?!
I should hang up...
HELLO, ARE YOU STILL THERE?!
WAIT—DON'T HANG UP!!
YOU HAVE A PROBLEM, DON'T YOU?!
I CAN TELL. NOBODY SEES MY NUMBER UNLESS THEY'RE IN TROUBLE.
YOU NEED HELP.
THE VOICE ON THE PHONE MIGHT BELONG TO A MAN WORTH EVEN LESS THAN STRAW.
...YOU... YOU'LL REALLY HELP ME?
OF COURSE I WILL!

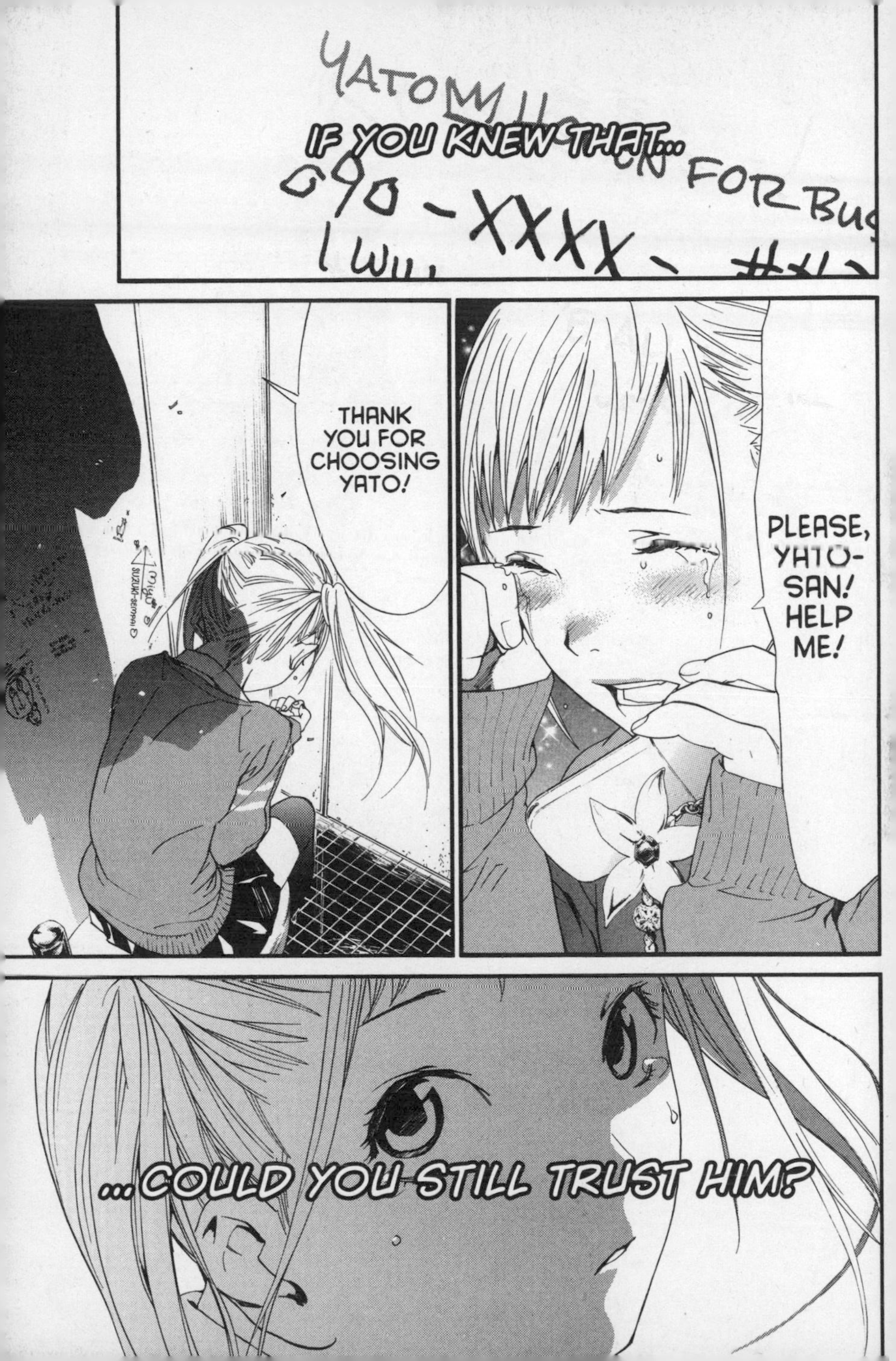
IF YOU KNEW THAT...
PLEASE, YATO-SAN! HELP ME!
THANK YOU FOR CHOOSING YATO!
...COULD YOU STILL TRUST HIM?

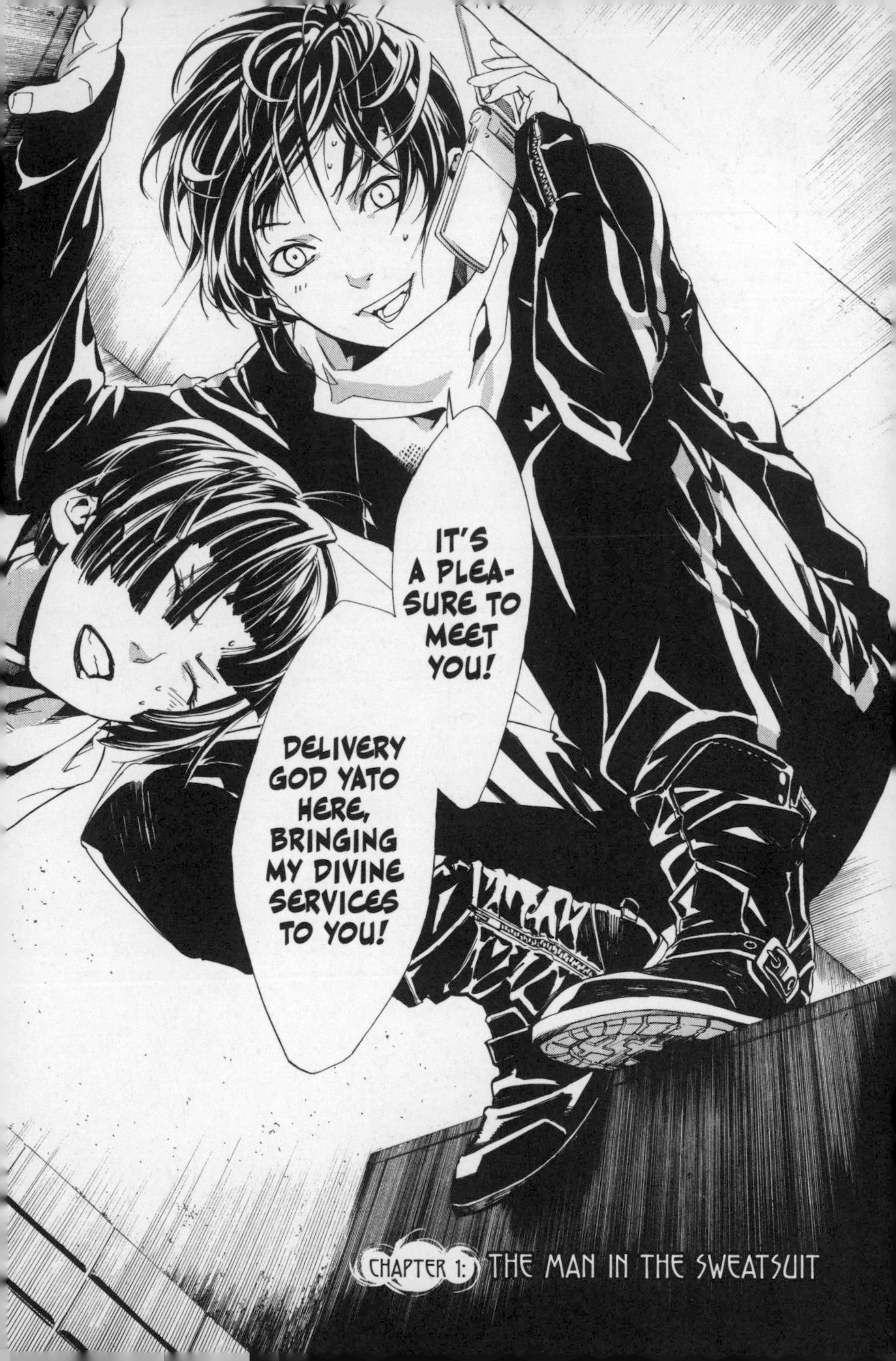
IT'S A PLEASURE TO MEET YOU!
DELIVERY GOD YATO HERE, BRINGING MY DIVINE SERVICES TO YOU!

CHAPTER 1: THE MAN IN THE SWEATSUIT

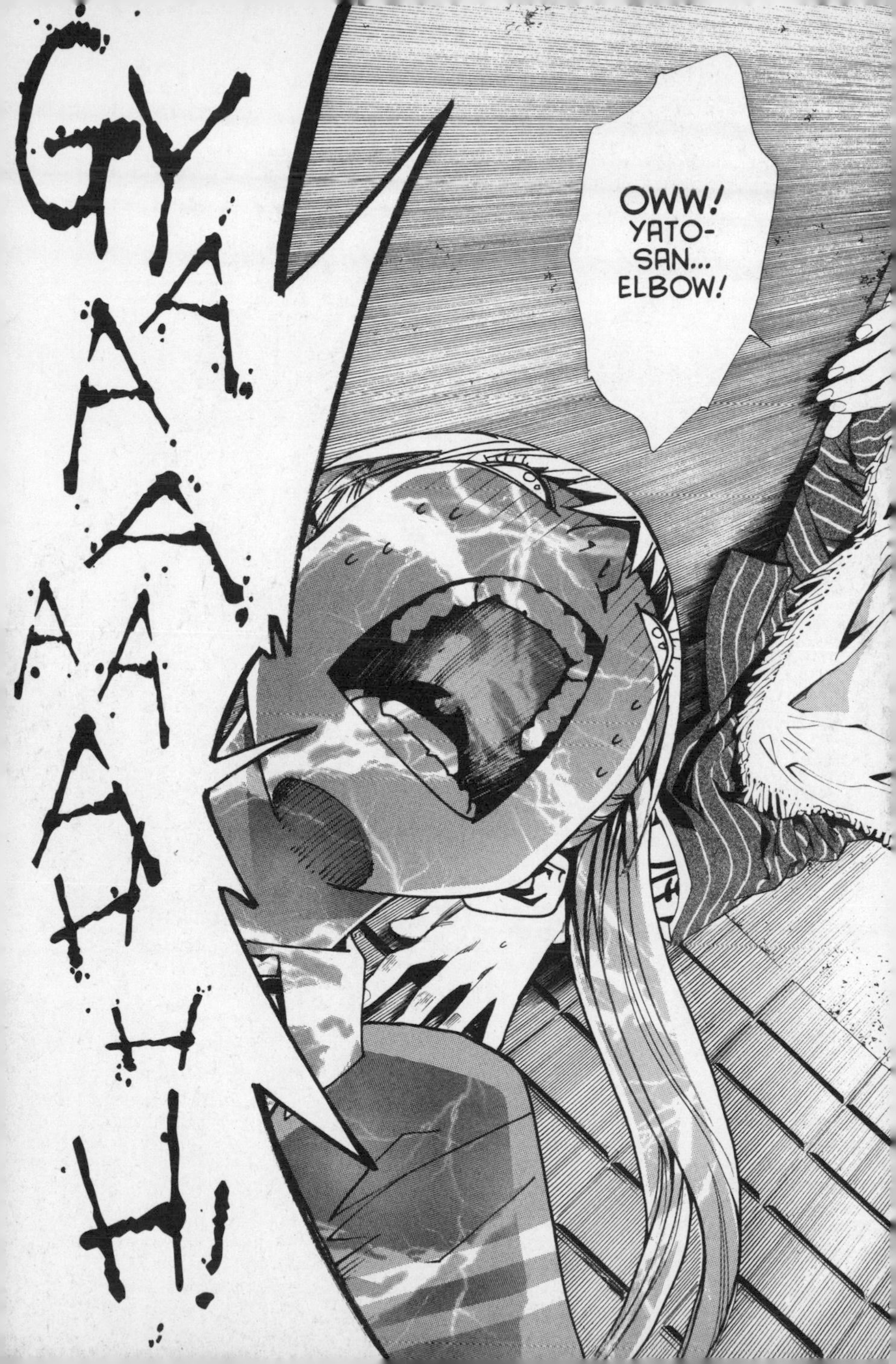
OWW! YATO-SAN... ELBOW!
GYAAAAAAHH!

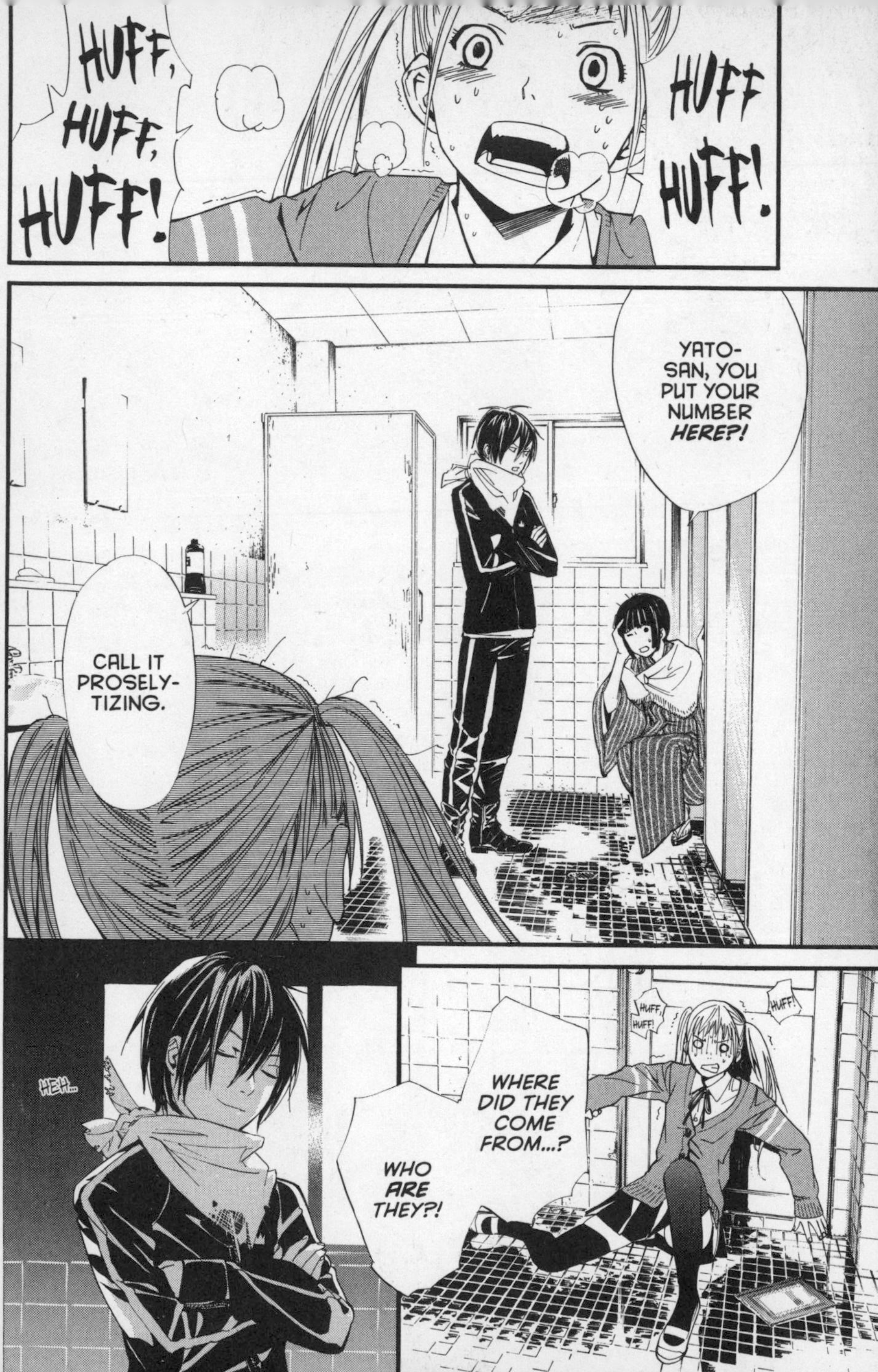
HUFF HUFF!
HUFF, HUFF, HUFF!
YATO-SAN, YOU PUT YOUR NUMBER HERE?!
CALL IT PROSELY-TIZING.
HUFF!
HUFF, HUFF!
WHERE DID THEY COME FROM...?
WHO ARE THEY?!
HEH...

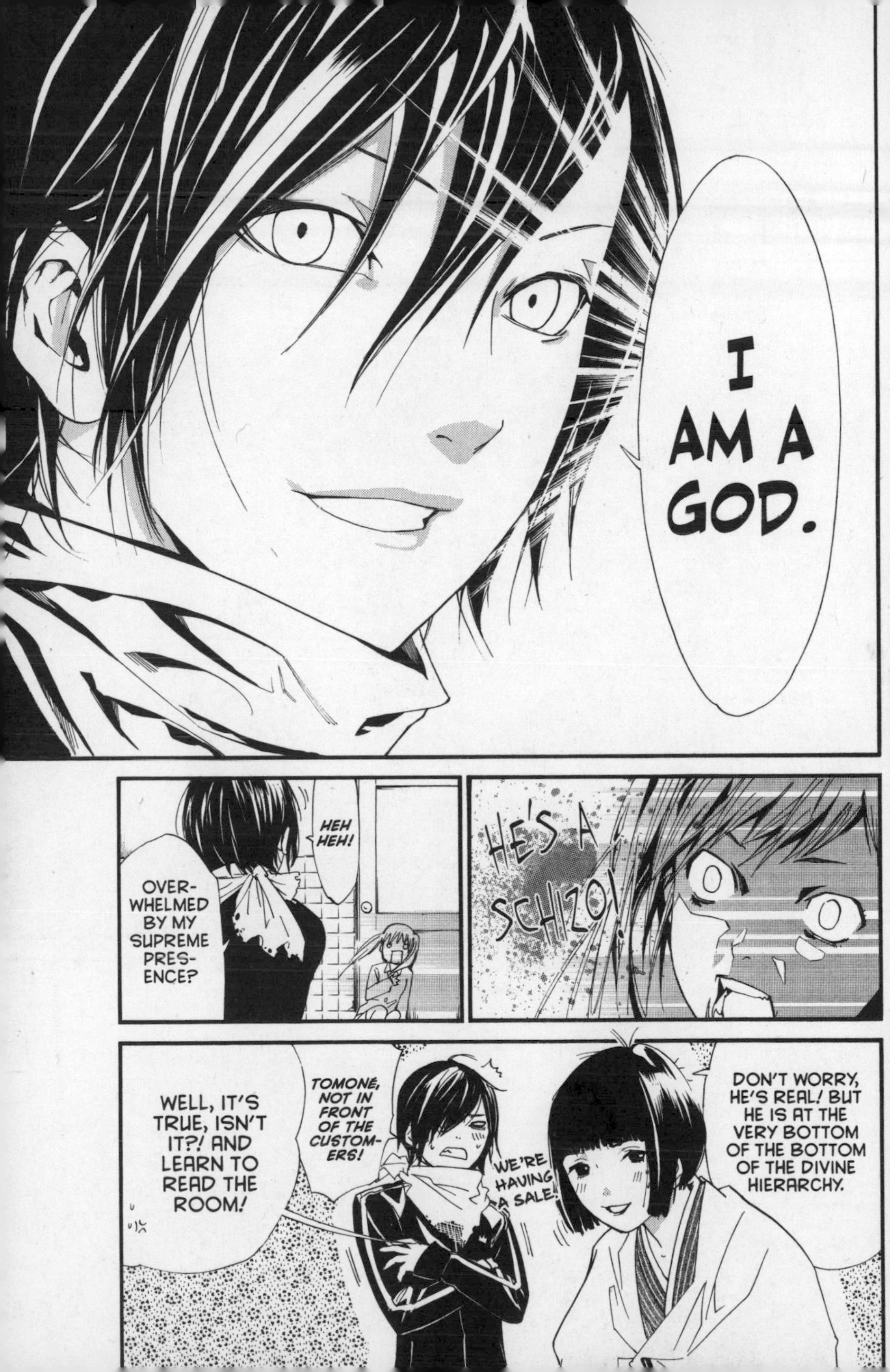
I AM A GOD.
HE'S A SCHIZO!
HEH HEH!
OVERWHELMED BY MY SUPREME PRESENCE?
DON'T WORRY, HE'S REAL! BUT HE IS AT THE VERY BOTTOM OF THE BOTTOM OF THE DIVINE HIERARCHY.
WE'RE HAVING A SALE!
TOMONE, NOT IN FRONT OF THE CUSTOMERS!
WELL, IT'S TRUE, ISN'T IT?! AND LEARN TO READ THE ROOM!

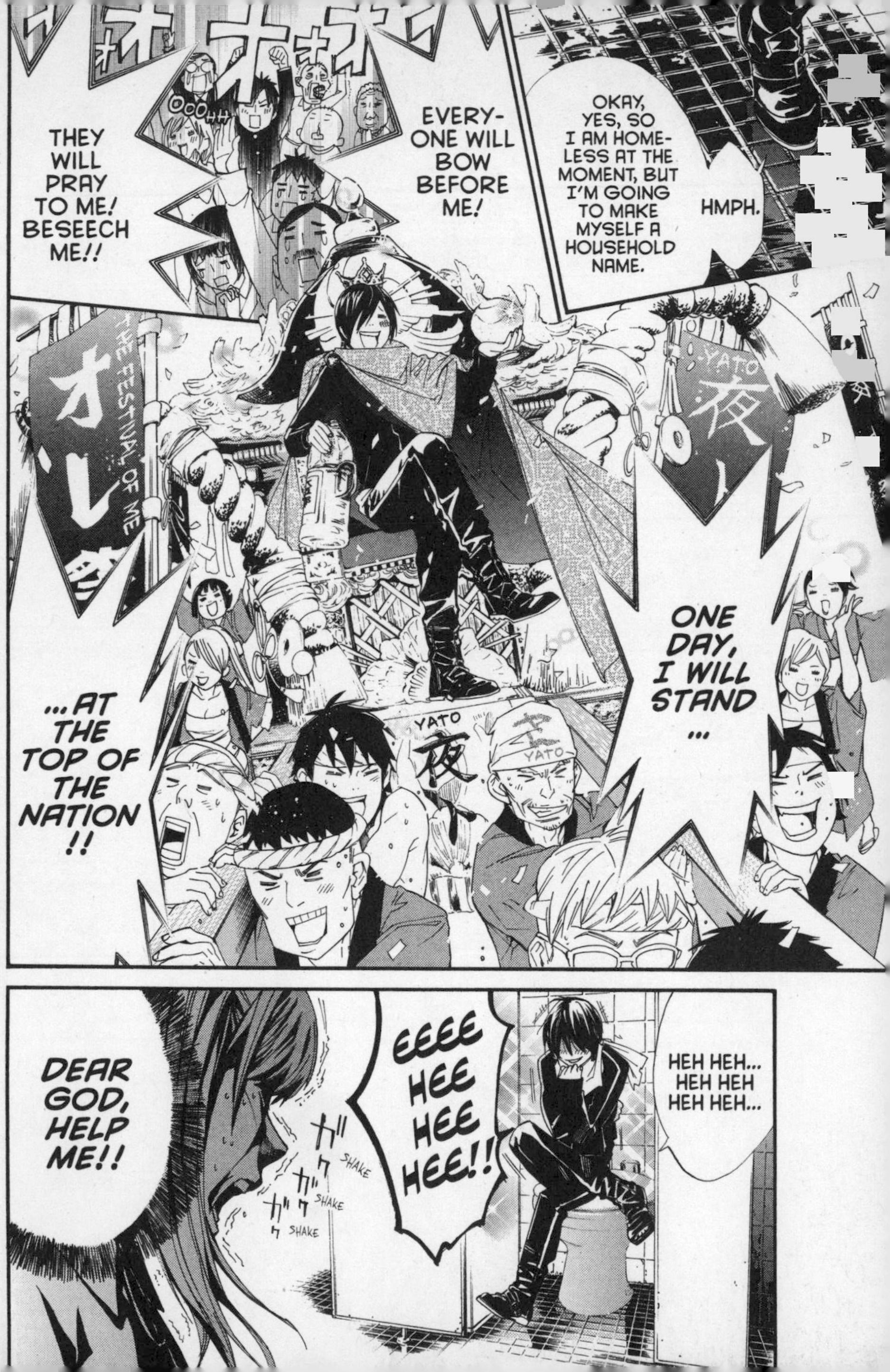
HMPH.
OKAY, YES, SO I AM HOMELESS AT THE MOMENT, BUT I'M GOING TO MAKE MYSELF A HOUSEHOLD NAME.
EVERYONE WILL BOW BEFORE ME!
THEY WILL PRAY TO ME! BESEECH ME!!
OOOHH
YATO
夜
THE FESTIVAL OF ME
ONE DAY, I WILL STAND...
...AT THE TOP OF THE NATION!!
HEH HEH... HEH HEH HEH HEH...
EEEE HEE HEE HEE!!
SHAKE
SHAKE
SHAKE
DEAR GOD, HELP ME!!

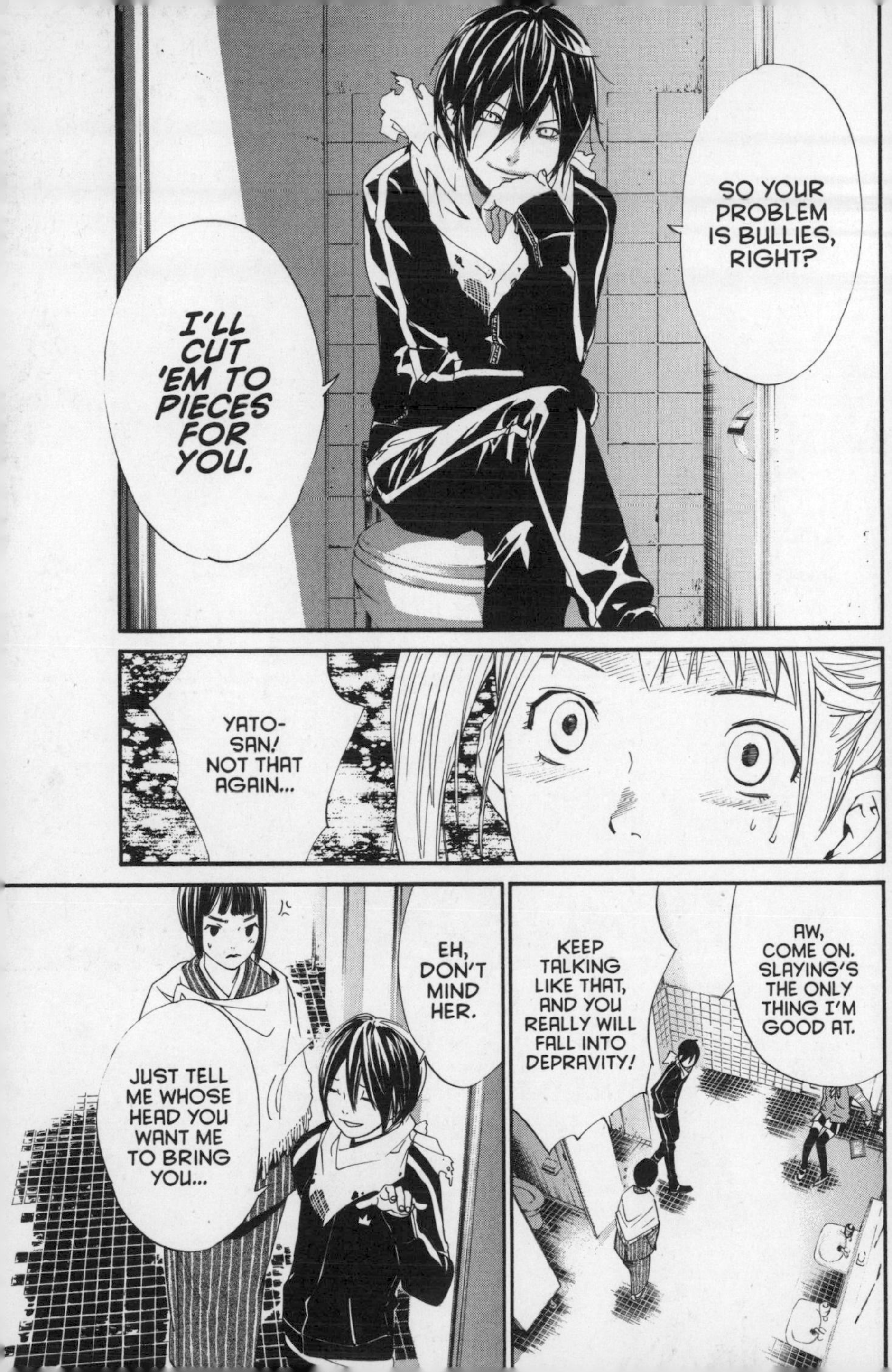
SO YOUR PROBLEM IS BULLIES, RIGHT?
I'LL CUT 'EM TO PIECES FOR YOU.
YATO-SAN! NOT THAT AGAIN...
AW, COME ON. SLAYING'S THE ONLY THING I'M GOOD AT.
KEEP TALKING LIKE THAT, AND YOU REALLY WILL FALL INTO DEPRAVITY!
EH, DON'T MIND HER.
JUST TELL ME WHOSE HEAD YOU WANT ME TO BRING YOU...

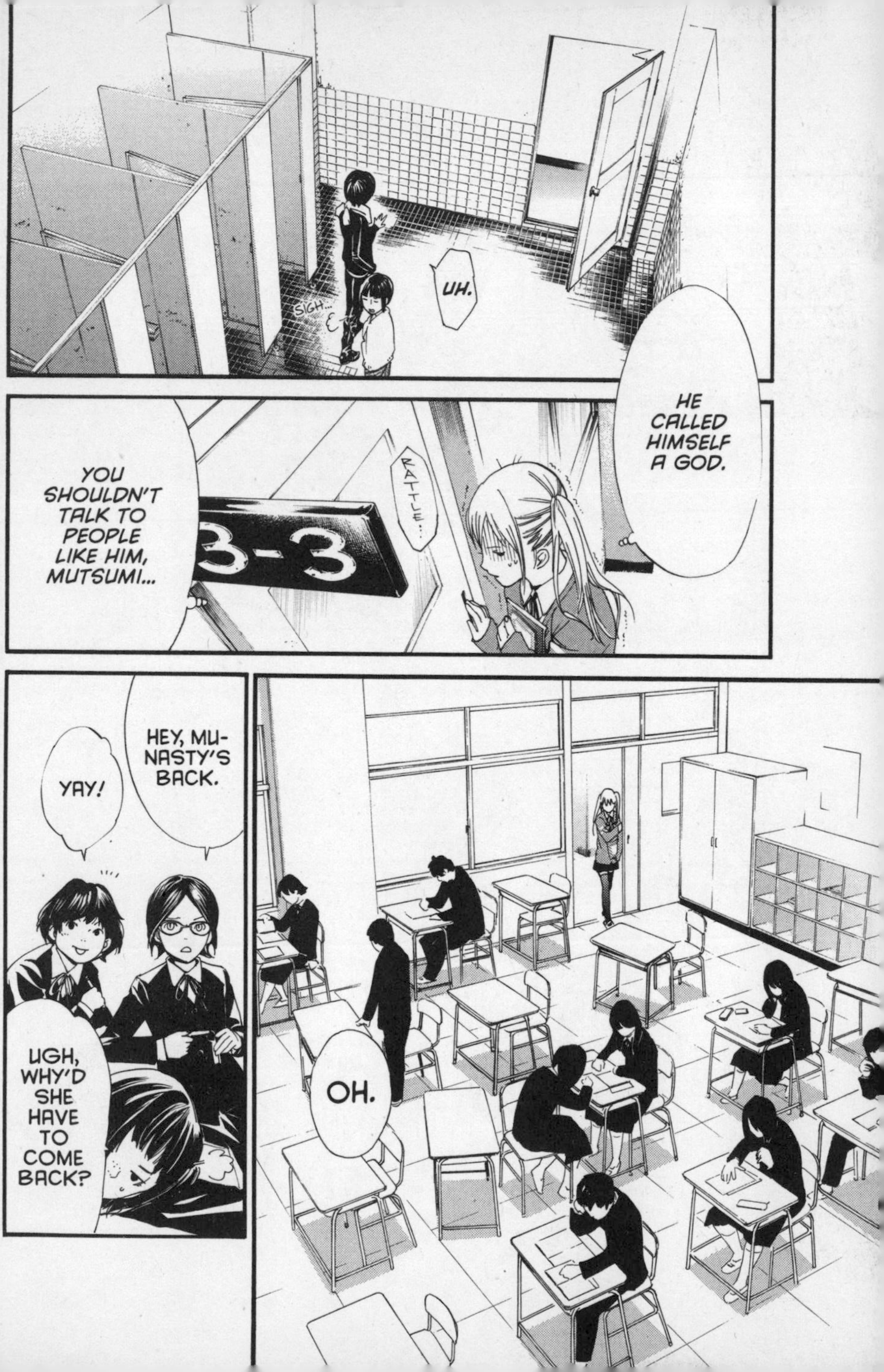
UH.
SIGH...
HE CALLED HIMSELF A GOD.
RATTLE...
3-3
YOU SHOULDN'T TALK TO PEOPLE LIKE HIM, MUTSUMI...
OH.
HEY, MU-NASTY'S BACK.
YAY!
UGH, WHY'D SHE HAVE TO COME BACK?

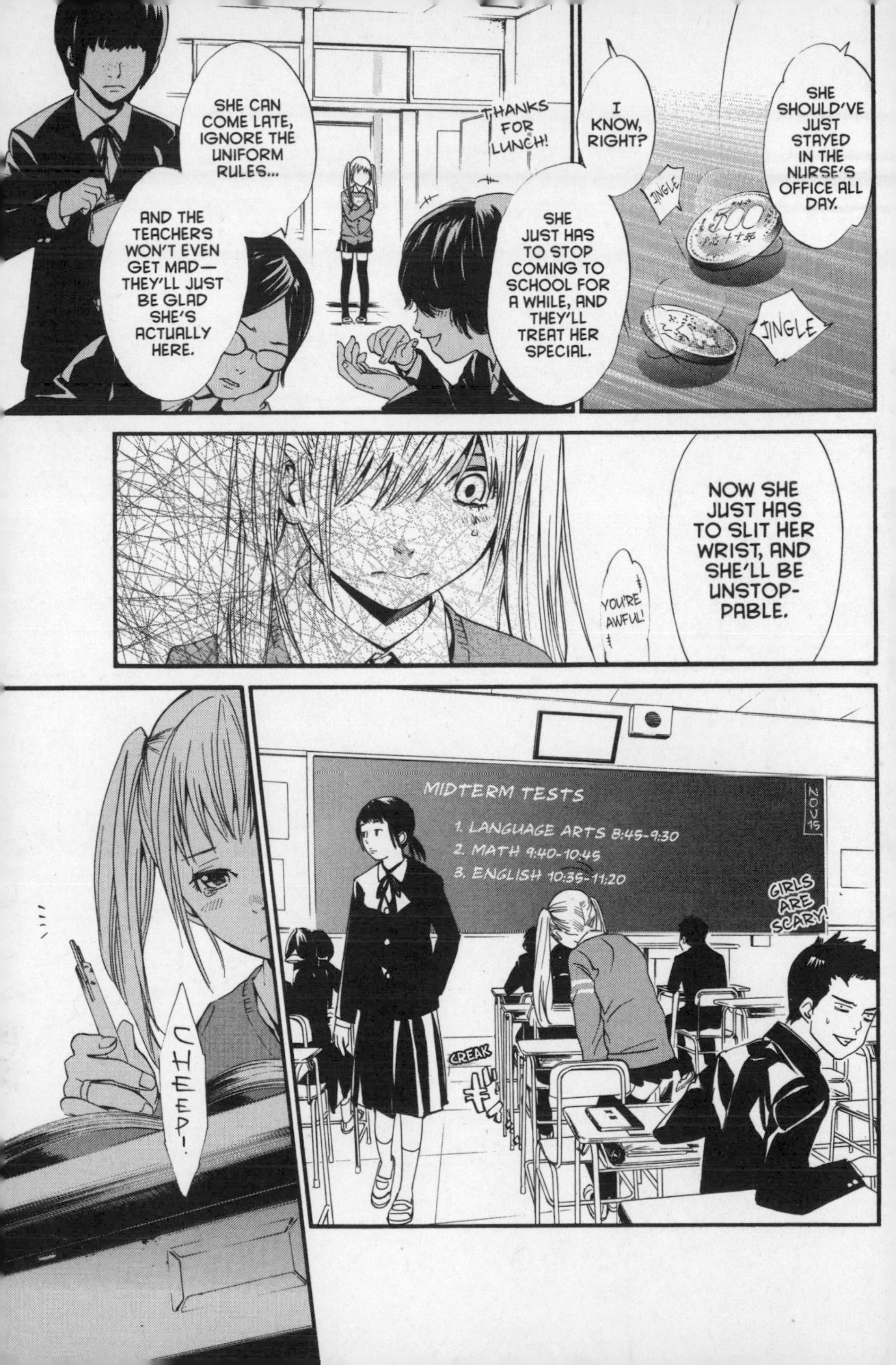
SHE SHOULD'VE JUST STAYED IN THE NURSE'S OFFICE ALL DAY.
JINGLE
JINGLE
I KNOW, RIGHT?
THANKS FOR LUNCH!
SHE JUST HAS TO STOP COMING TO SCHOOL FOR A WHILE, AND THEY'LL TREAT HER SPECIAL.
SHE CAN COME LATE, IGNORE THE UNIFORM RULES...
AND THE TEACHERS WON'T EVEN GET MAD—THEY'LL JUST BE GLAD SHE'S ACTUALLY HERE.
NOW SHE JUST HAS TO SLIT HER WRIST, AND SHE'LL BE UNSTOP-PABLE.
YOU'RE AWFUL!
NOV 15
MIDTERM TESTS
1. LANGUAGE ARTS 8:45-9:30
2. MATH 9:40-10:45
3. ENGLISH 10:35-11:20
GIRLS ARE SCARY!
CREAK
CHEEP!

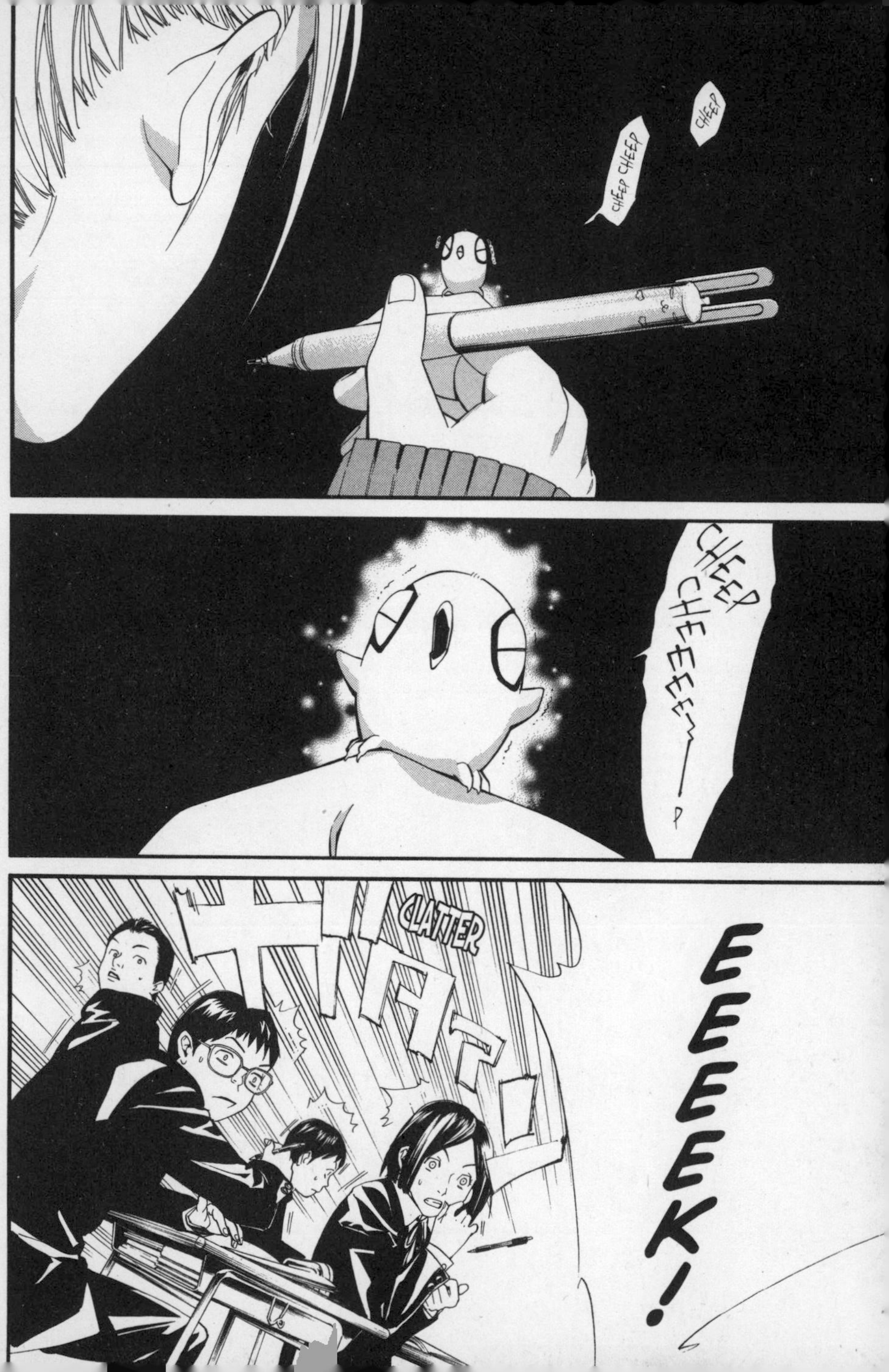
CHEEP
CHEEP CHEEP
CHEEP CHEEEEE—P
CLATTER
EEEEEK!

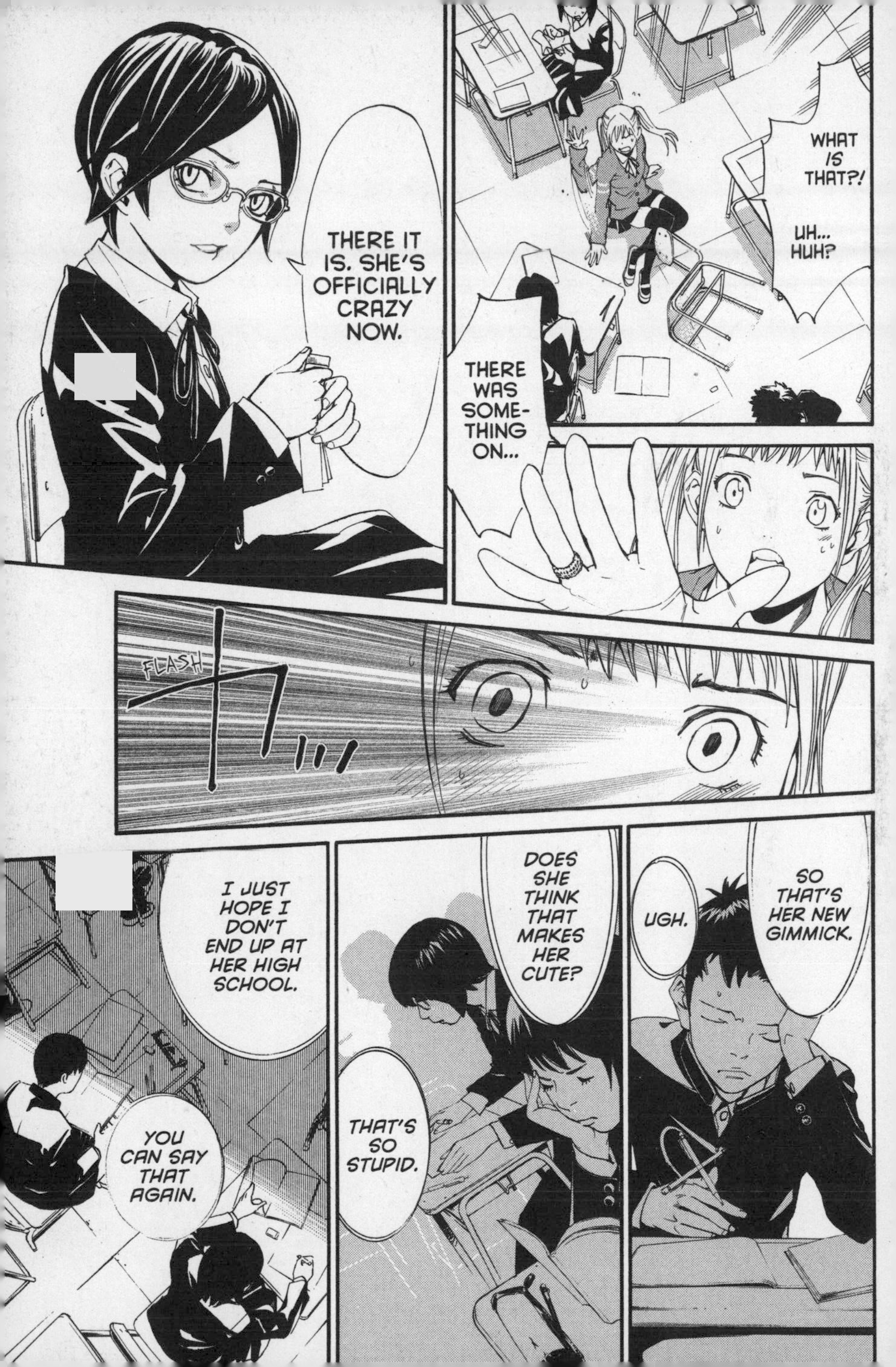
WHAT IS THAT?!
UH... HUH?
THERE WAS SOME-THING ON...
THERE IT IS. SHE'S OFFICIALLY CRAZY NOW.
FLASH
SO THAT'S HER NEW GIMMICK.
UGH.
DOES SHE THINK THAT MAKES HER CUTE?
THAT'S SO STUPID.
I JUST HOPE I DON'T END UP AT HER HIGH SCHOOL.
YOU CAN SAY THAT AGAIN.

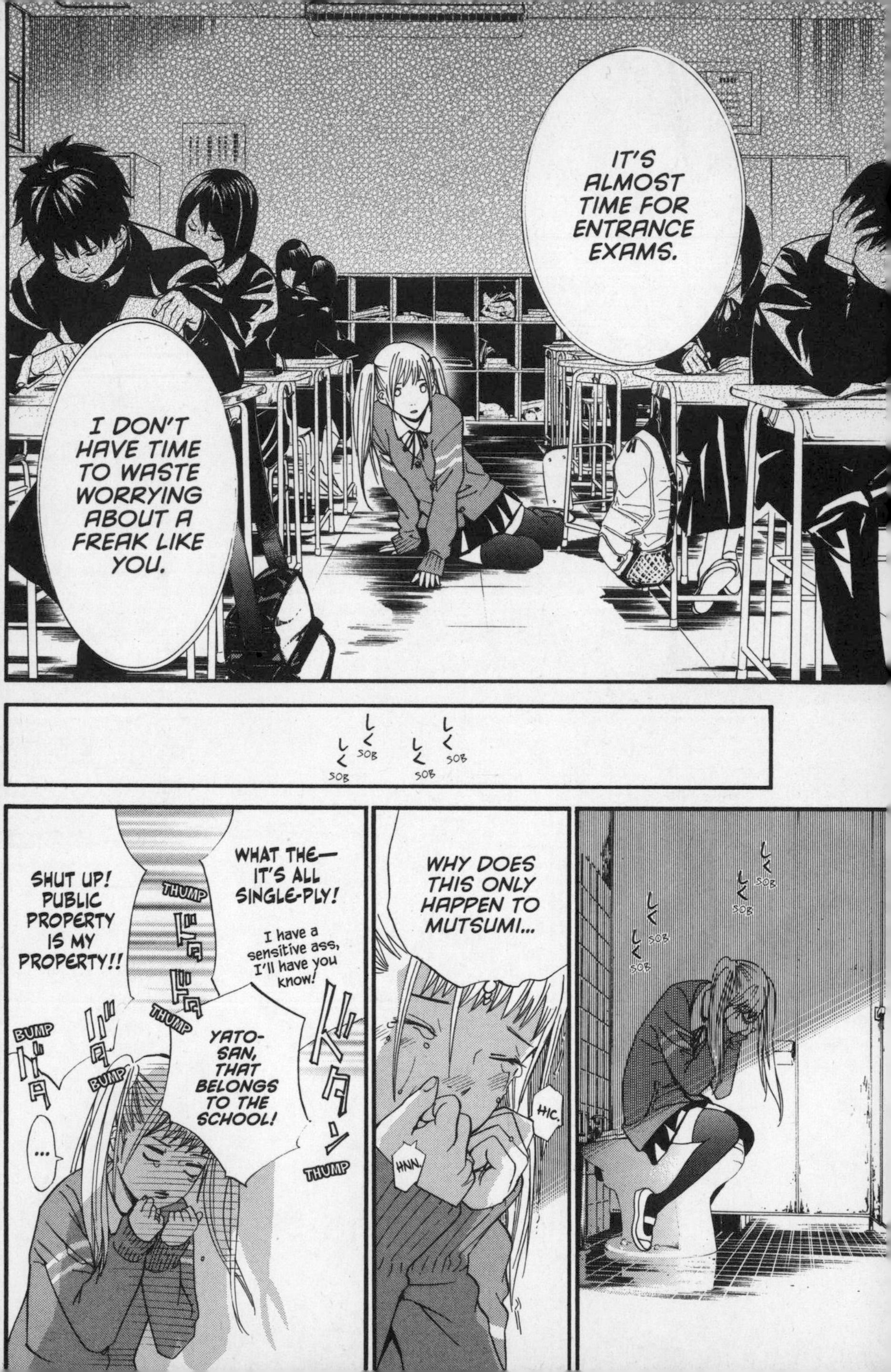
IT'S ALMOST TIME FOR ENTRANCE EXAMS.
I DON'T HAVE TIME TO WASTE WORRYING ABOUT A FREAK LIKE YOU.
SOB SOB SOB SOB
SOB SOB SOB SOB
WHY DOES THIS ONLY HAPPEN TO MUTSUMI...
HIC.
HNN.
WHAT THE— IT'S ALL SINGLE-PLY!
I have a sensitive ass, I'll have you know!
THUMP
SHUT UP! PUBLIC PROPERTY IS MY PROPERTY!!
THUMP
YATO-SAN, THAT BELONGS TO THE SCHOOL!
THUMP
BUMP
BUMP
...

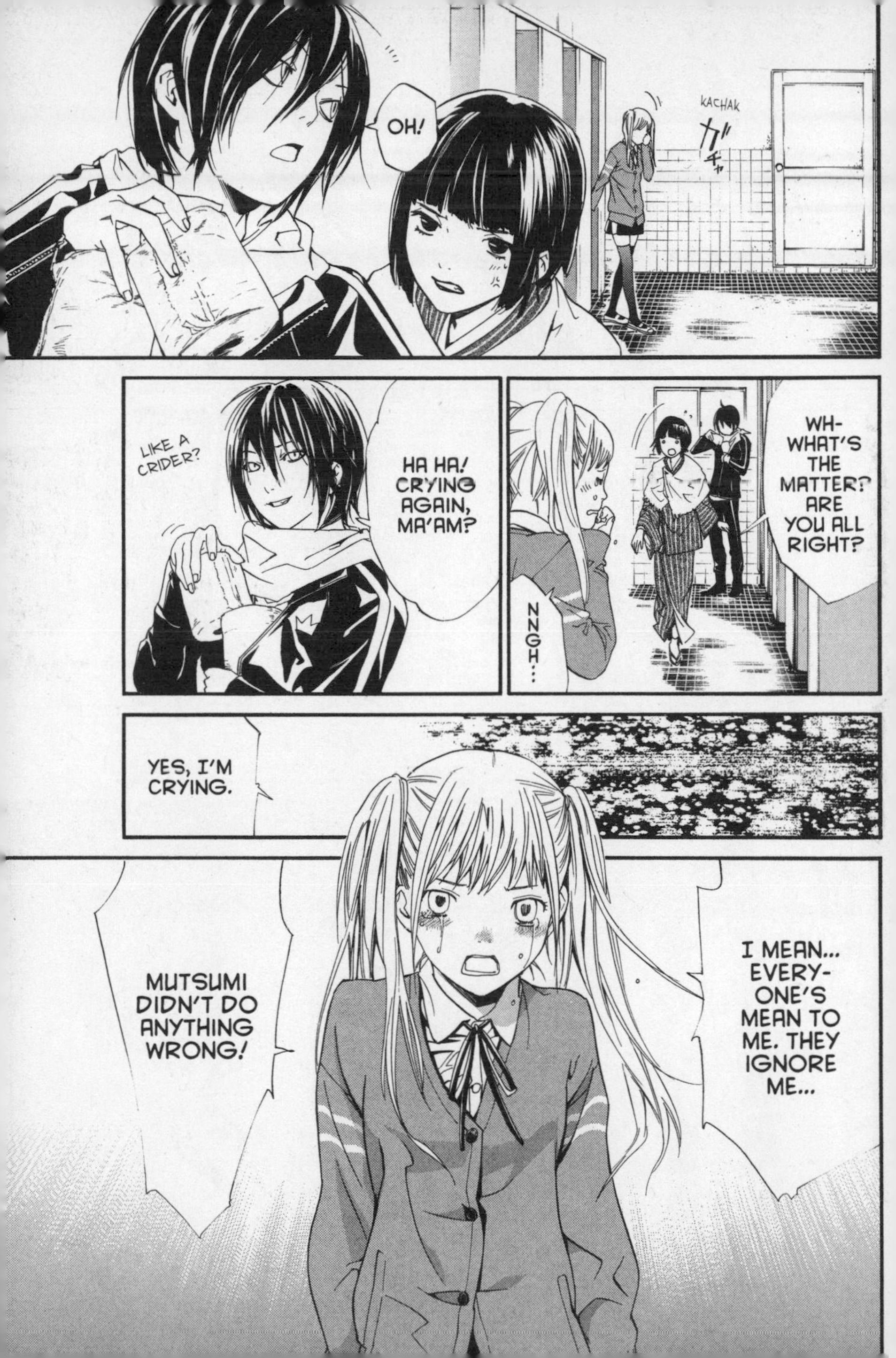
KACHAK
ガチャ
OH!
WH- WHAT'S THE MATTER? ARE YOU ALL RIGHT?
NNGH...
HA HA! CRYING AGAIN, MA'AM?
LIKE A CRIDER?
YES, I'M CRYING.
I MEAN... EVERYONE'S MEAN TO ME. THEY IGNORE ME...
MUTSUMI DIDN'T DO ANYTHING WRONG!

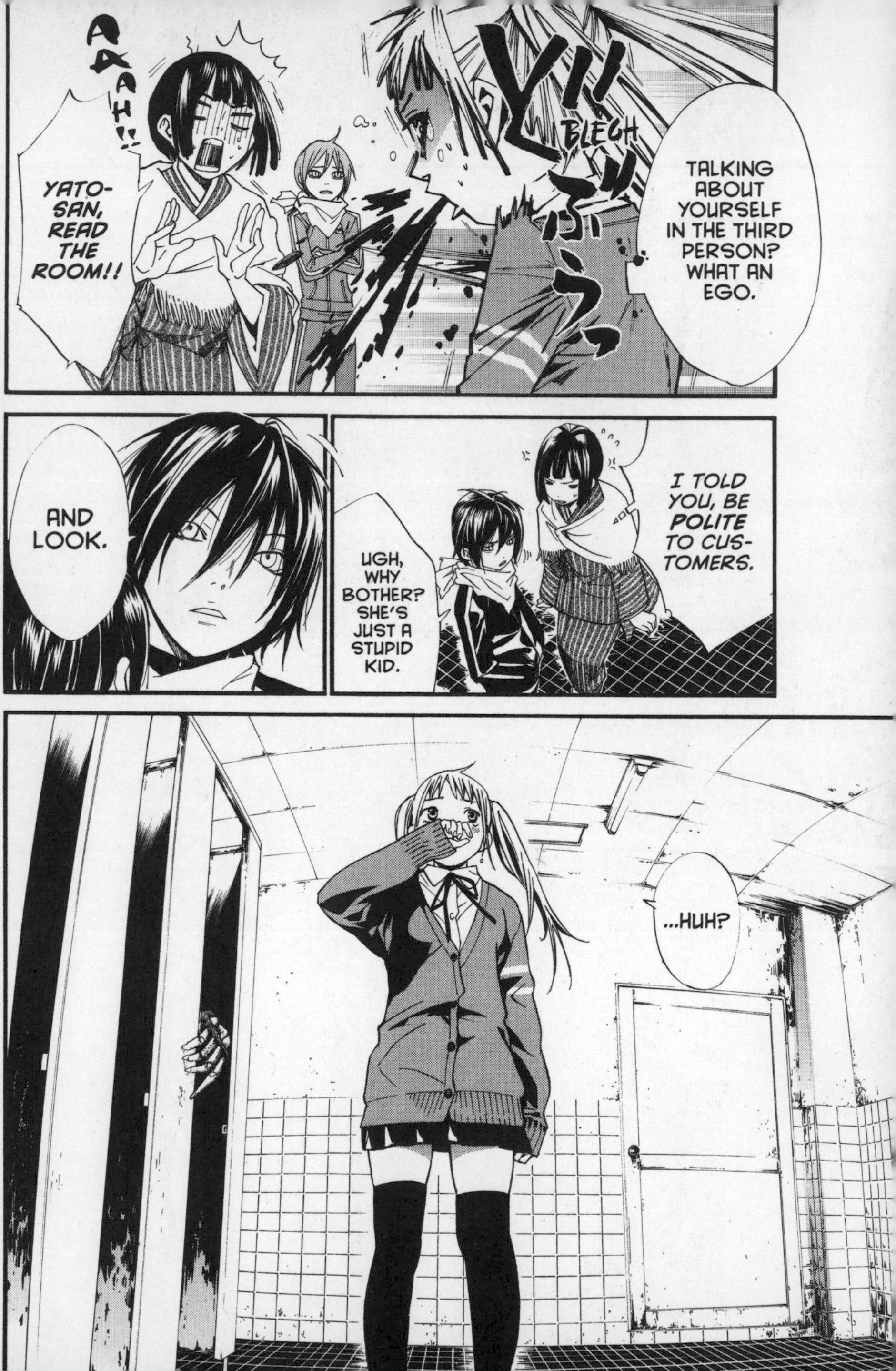
TALKING ABOUT YOURSELF IN THE THIRD PERSON? WHAT AN EGO.
YII
BLECH
AAAH!!
YATO-SAN, READ THE ROOM!!
I TOLD YOU, BE POLITE TO CUSTOMERS.
UGH, WHY BOTHER? SHE'S JUST A STUPID KID.
AND LOOK.
...HUH?

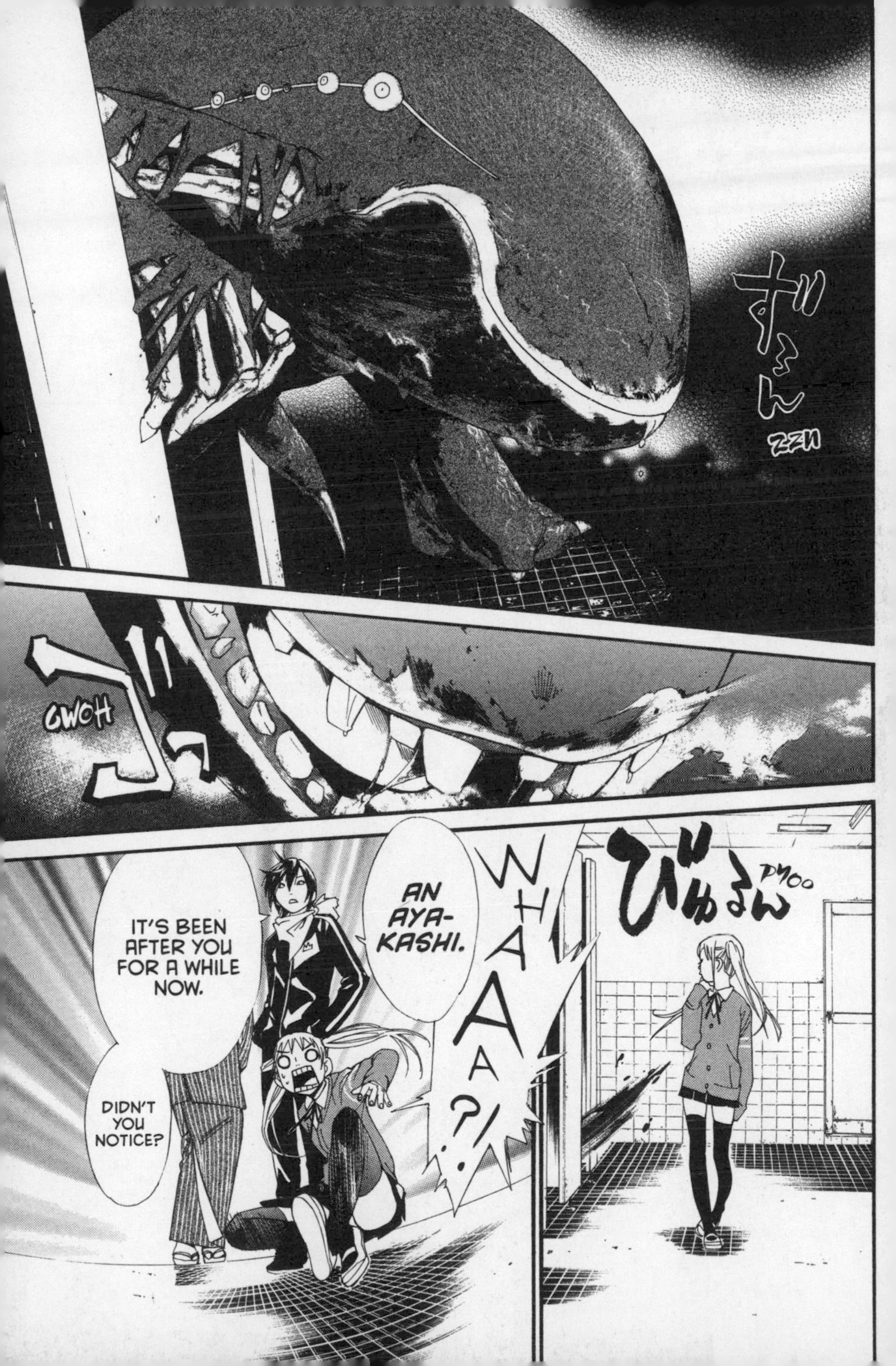

ZZN
GWOH
PYOO
WHAAA?!
AN AYA-KASHI.
IT'S BEEN AFTER YOU FOR A WHILE NOW.
DIDN'T YOU NOTICE?

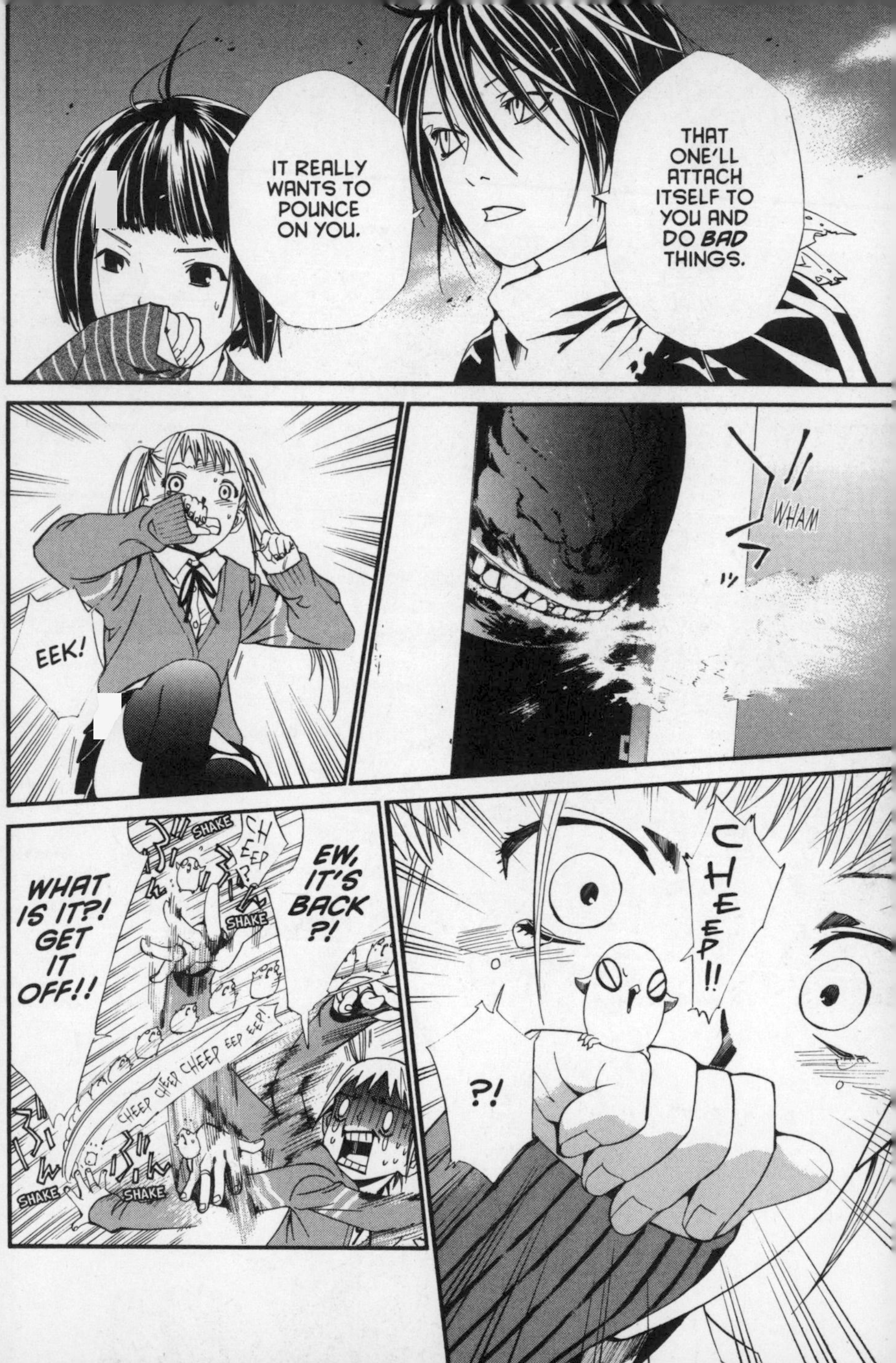
THAT ONE'LL ATTACH ITSELF TO YOU AND DO *BAD* THINGS.
IT REALLY WANTS TO POUNCE ON YOU.
WHAM
EEK!
CHEEP!!
?!
EW, IT'S BACK?!
CHEEP?
SHAKE
SHAKE
WHAT IS IT?! GET IT OFF!!
CHEEP CHEEP CHEEP EEP EEP!
SHAKE
SHAKE

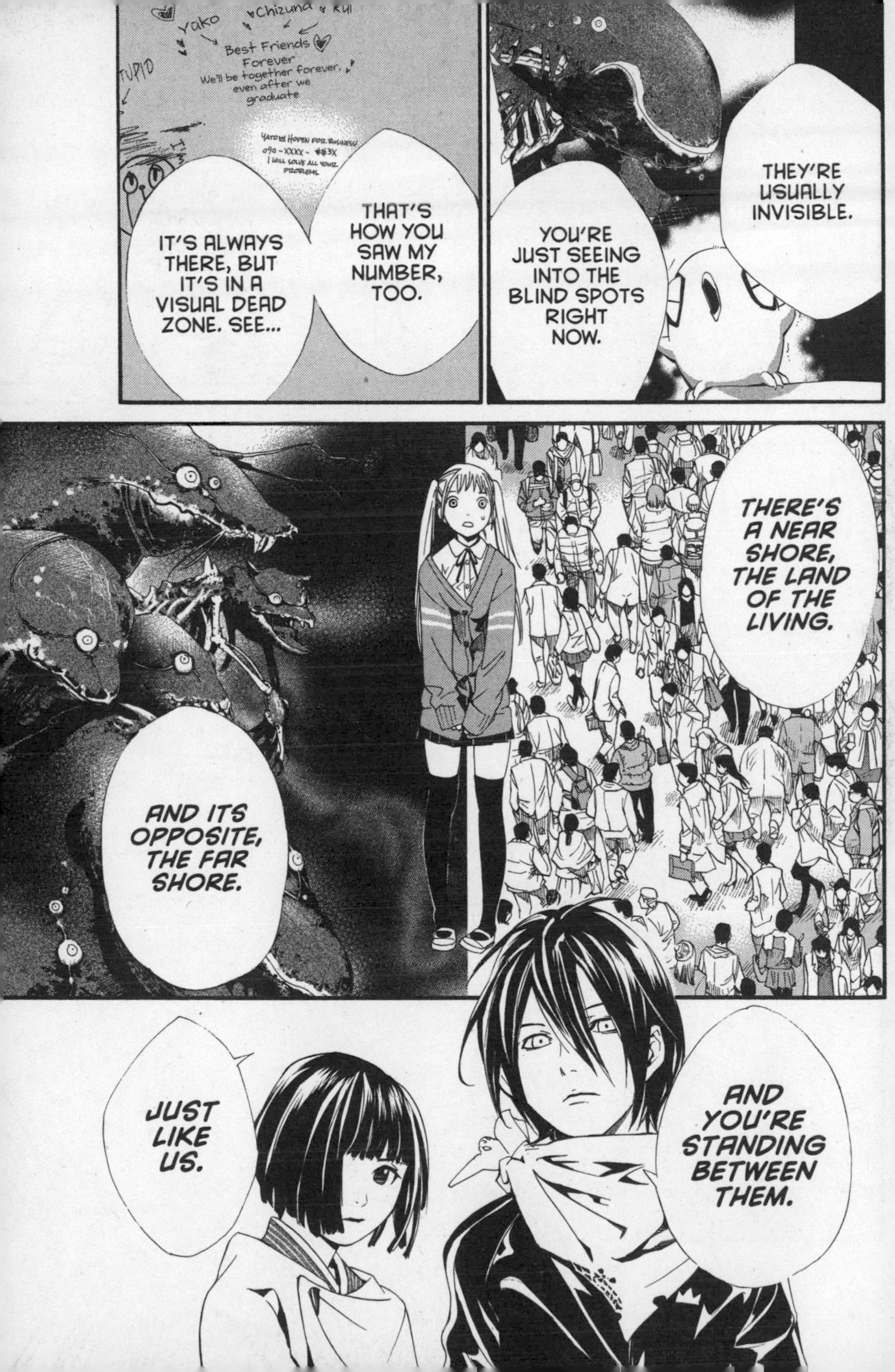
THEY'RE USUALLY INVISIBLE.
YOU'RE JUST SEEING INTO THE BLIND SPOTS RIGHT NOW.
Yako Chizuna Kui
Best Friends Forever
We'll be together forever, even after we graduate
TUPID
YATO HOPEN FOR BUSINESS!
090-XXXX-##3X
I WILL SOLVE ALL YOUR PROBLEMS.
THAT'S HOW YOU SAW MY NUMBER, TOO.
IT'S ALWAYS THERE, BUT IT'S IN A VISUAL DEAD ZONE. SEE...
THERE'S A NEAR SHORE, THE LAND OF THE LIVING.
AND ITS OPPOSITE, THE FAR SHORE.
AND YOU'RE STANDING BETWEEN THEM.
JUST LIKE US.

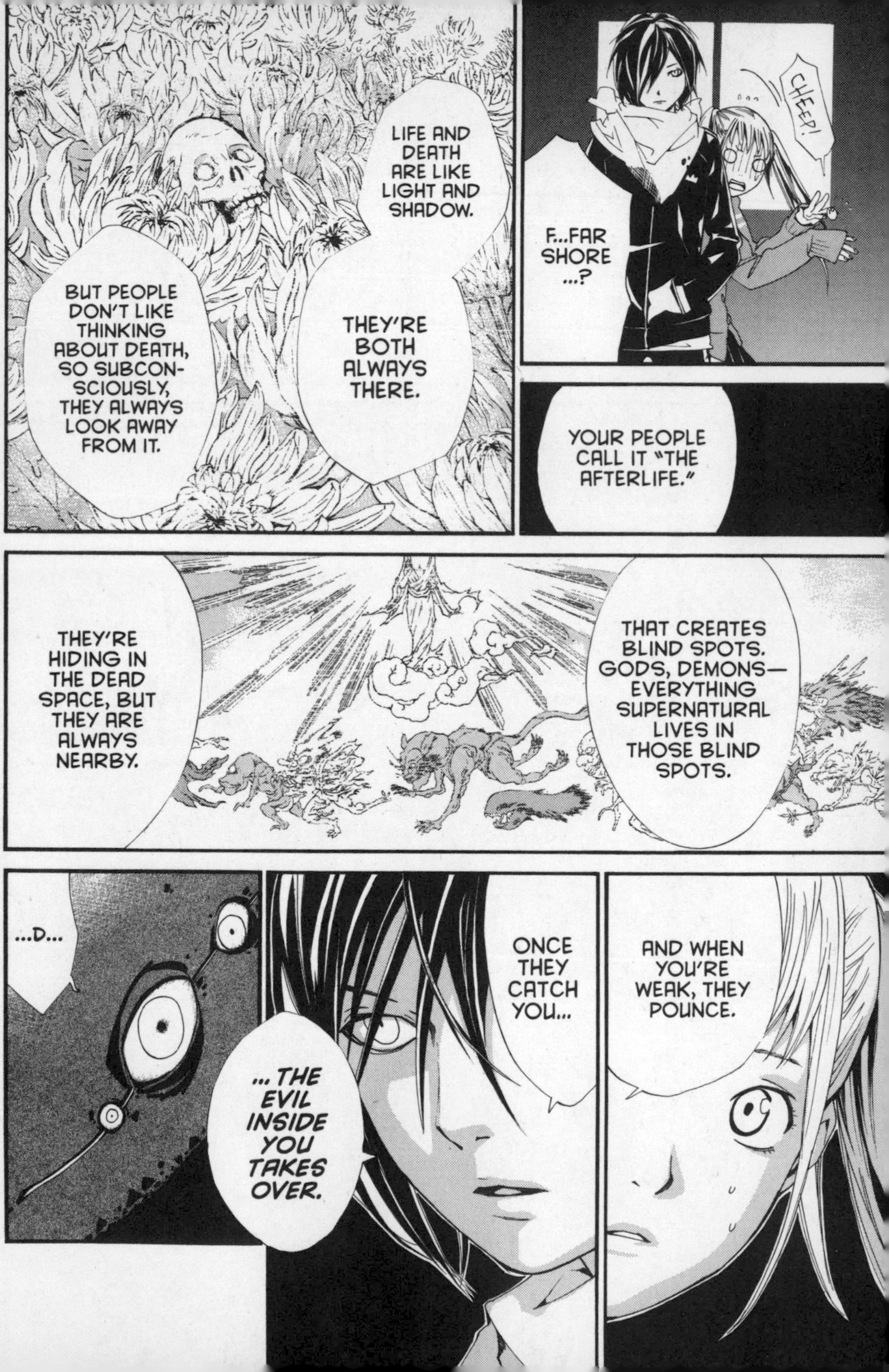
CHEEP!
F...FAR SHORE ...?
YOUR PEOPLE CALL IT "THE AFTERLIFE."
LIFE AND DEATH ARE LIKE LIGHT AND SHADOW.
THEY'RE BOTH ALWAYS THERE.
BUT PEOPLE DON'T LIKE THINKING ABOUT DEATH, SO SUBCON-SCIOUSLY, THEY ALWAYS LOOK AWAY FROM IT.
THAT CREATES BLIND SPOTS. GODS, DEMONS— EVERYTHING SUPERNATURAL LIVES IN THOSE BLIND SPOTS.
THEY'RE HIDING IN THE DEAD SPACE, BUT THEY ARE ALWAYS NEARBY.
AND WHEN YOU'RE WEAK, THEY POUNCE.
ONCE THEY CATCH YOU...
...THE EVIL INSIDE YOU TAKES OVER.
...D...

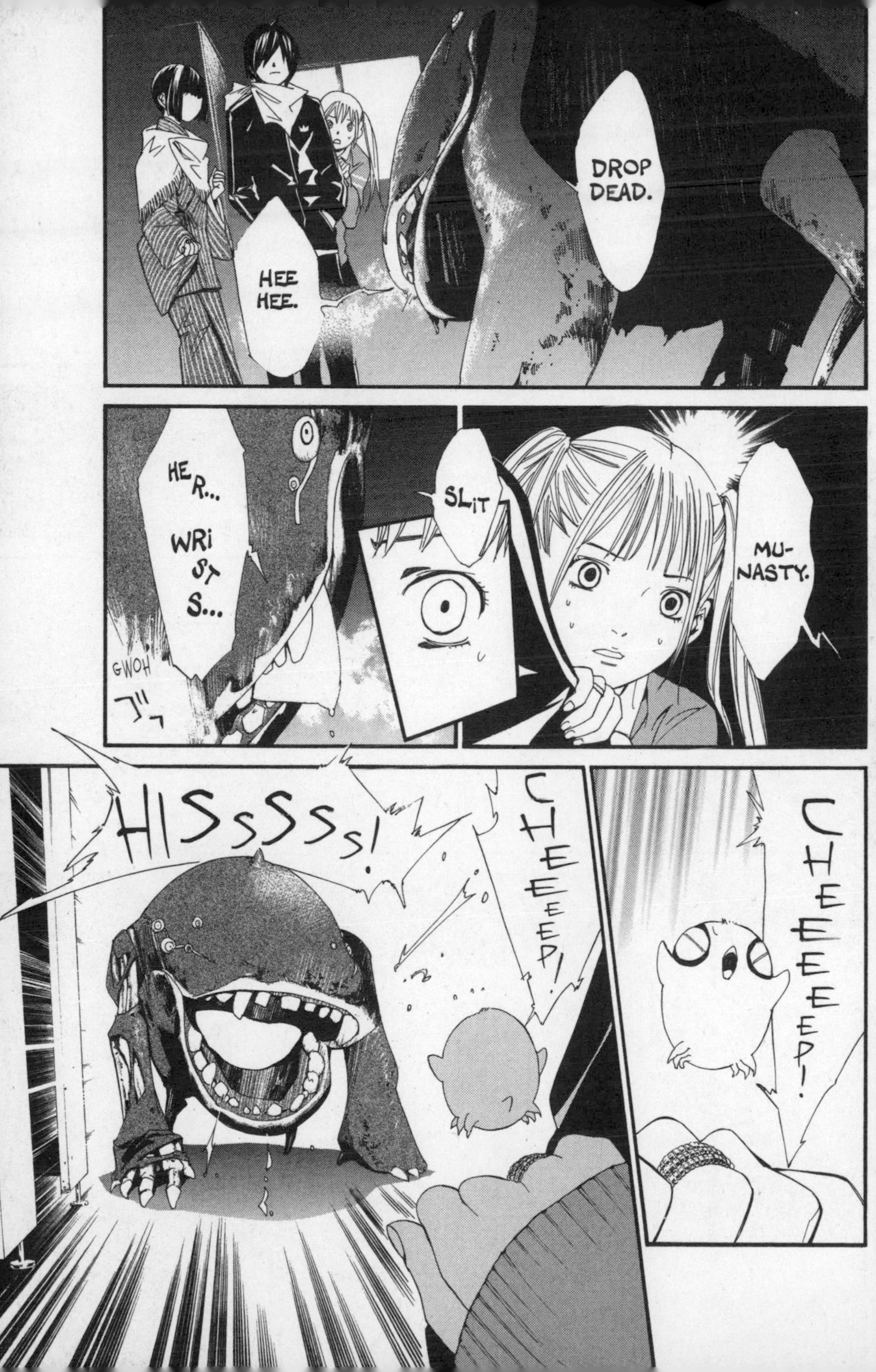
DROP DEAD.
HEE HEE.
MU-NASTY.
SLIT
HER... WRISTS...
GWOH
CHEEEEEEP!
HISSSSS!
CHEEEEP!

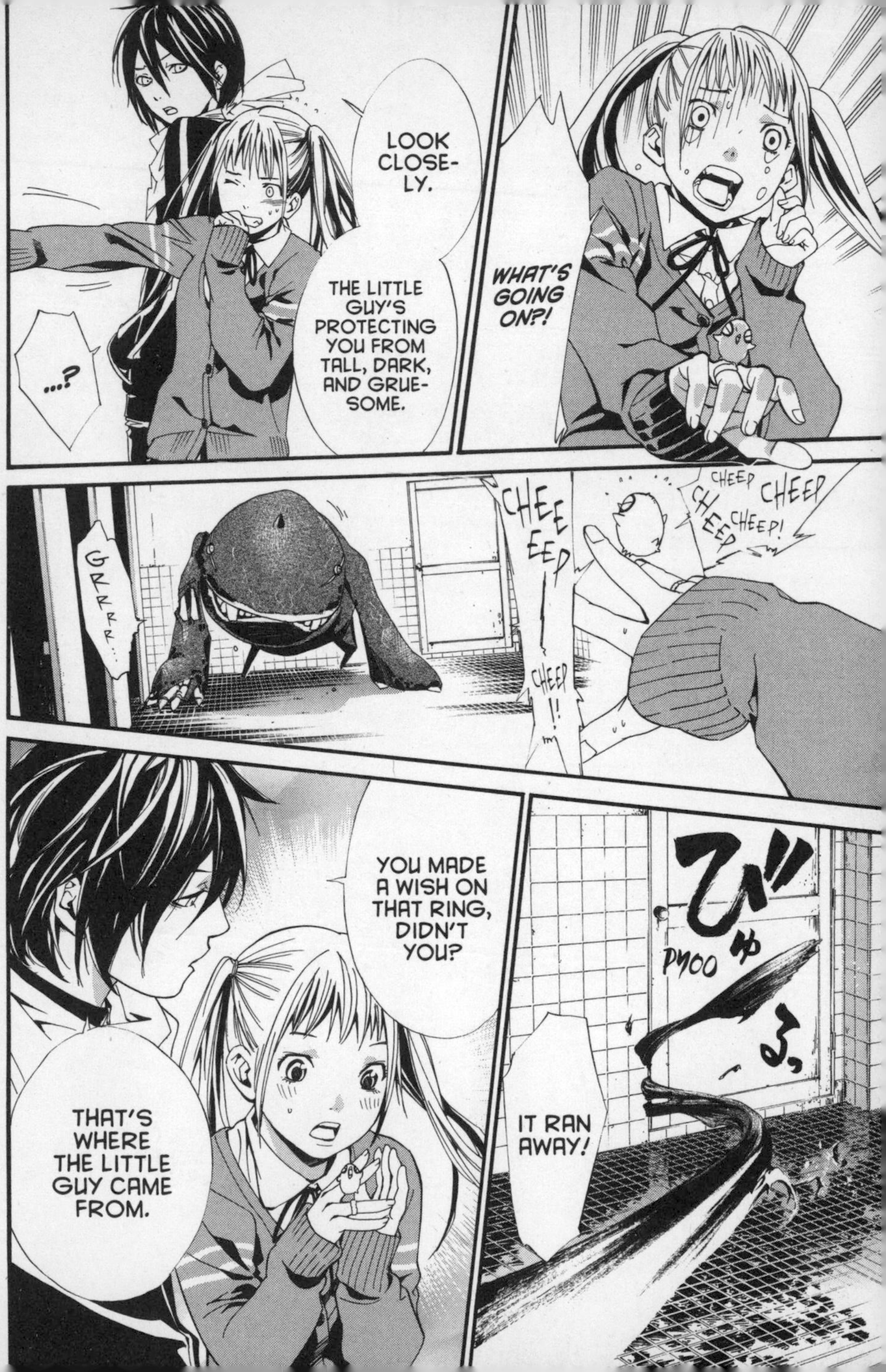
WHAT'S GOING ON?!
LOOK CLOSE-LY.
THE LITTLE GUY'S PROTECTING YOU FROM TALL, DARK, AND GRUE-SOME.
...?
CHEEP CHEEP CHEEP CHEEP!
CHEEEEEP!!
CHEEP!!
GRRRR...
びゅ
PYOO
ふっ
IT RAN AWAY!
YOU MADE A WISH ON THAT RING, DIDN'T YOU?
THAT'S WHERE THE LITTLE GUY CAME FROM.

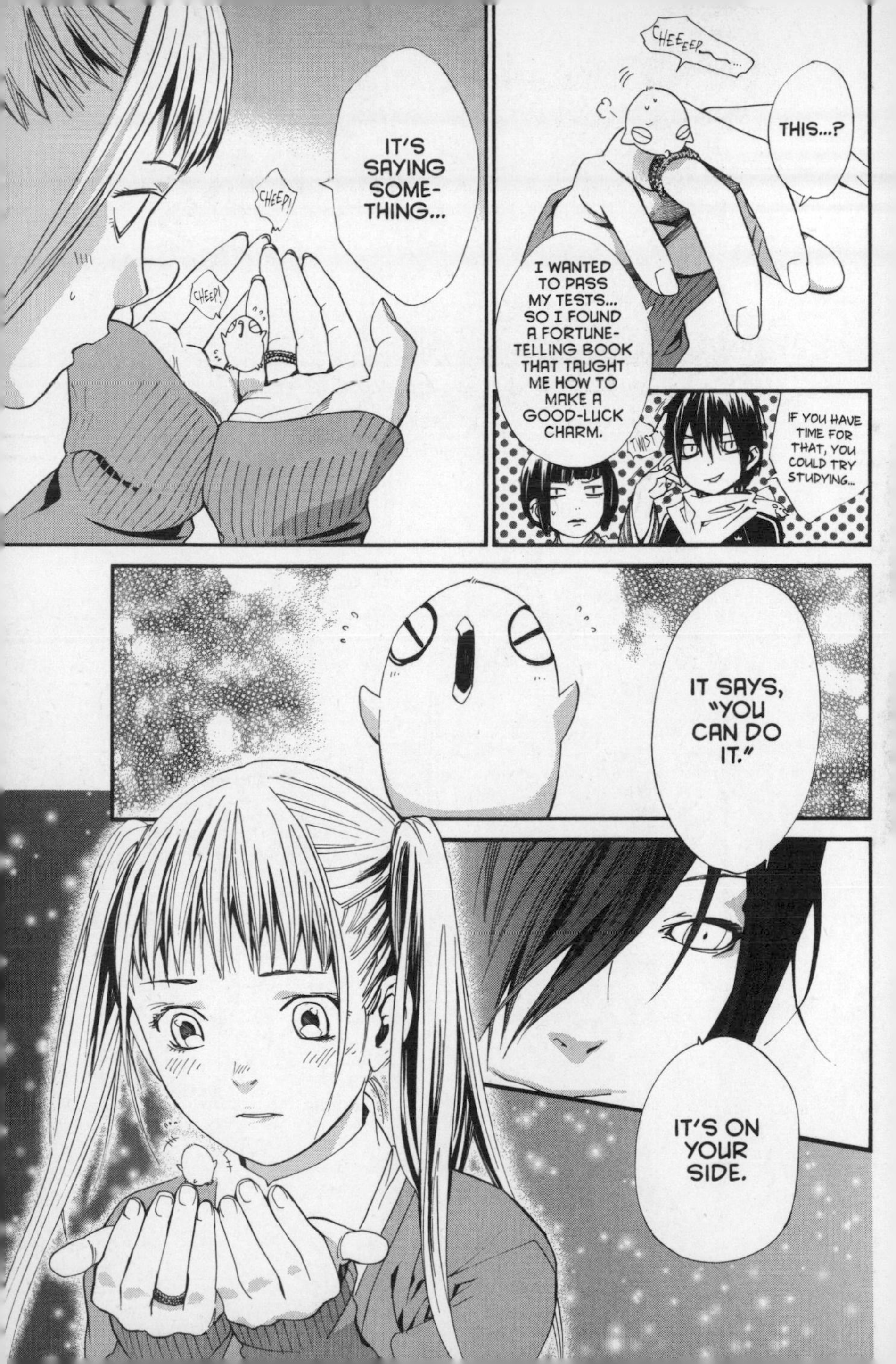
CHEEEEP......
THIS...?
I WANTED TO PASS MY TESTS... SO I FOUND A FORTUNE-TELLING BOOK THAT TAUGHT ME HOW TO MAKE A GOOD-LUCK CHARM.
IF YOU HAVE TIME FOR THAT, YOU COULD TRY STUDYING...
TWIST
IT'S SAYING SOME-THING...
CHEEP!
CHEEP!
IT SAYS, "YOU CAN DO IT."
IT'S ON YOUR SIDE.

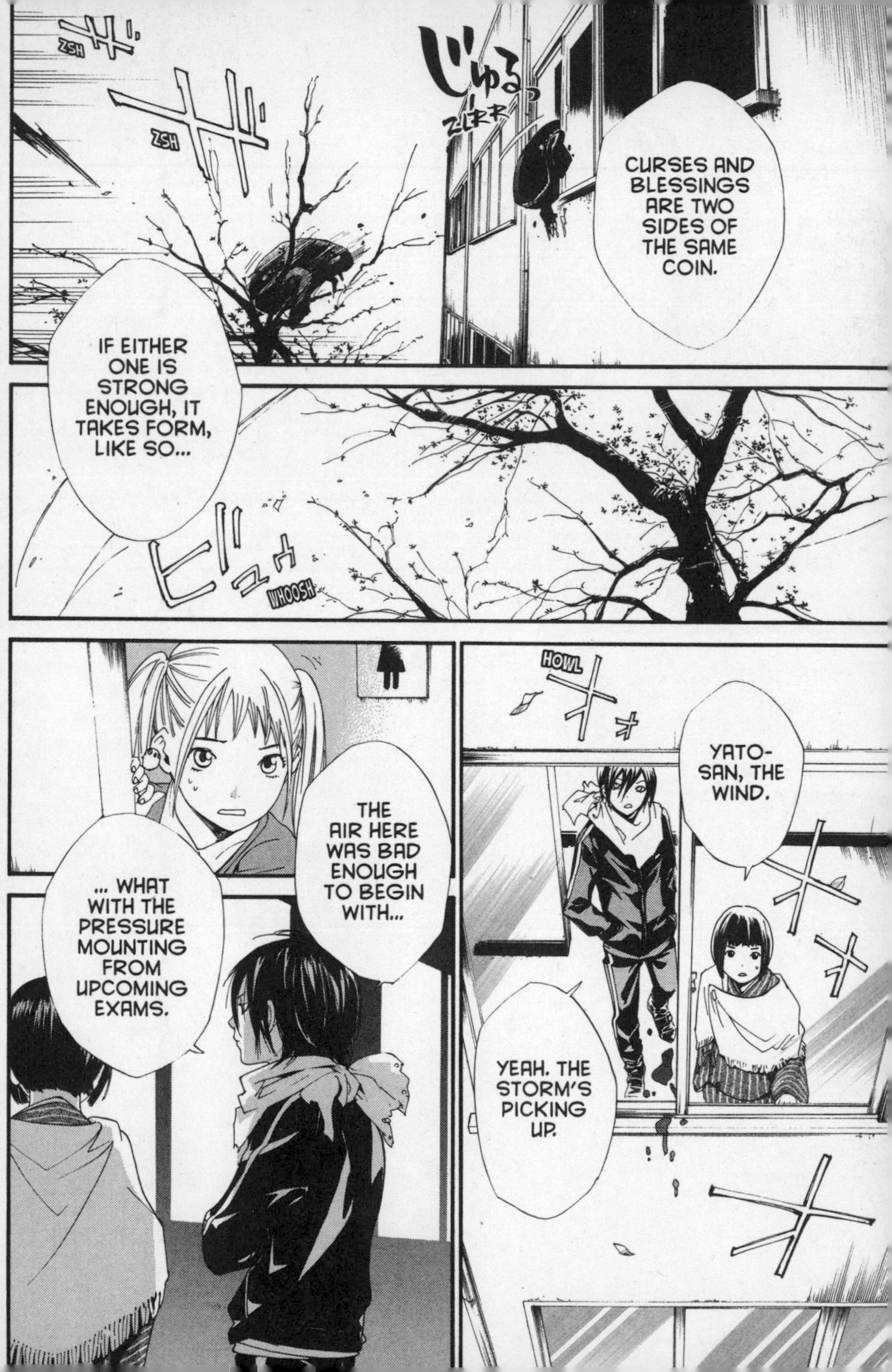
じゅるっ
CURSES AND BLESSINGS ARE TWO SIDES OF THE SAME COIN.
ZSH
ZSH
IF EITHER ONE IS STRONG ENOUGH, IT TAKES FORM, LIKE SO...
ヒュゥ
WHOOSH
HOWL
オォ
YATO-SAN, THE WIND.
YEAH. THE STORM'S PICKING UP.
THE AIR HERE WAS BAD ENOUGH TO BEGIN WITH...
... WHAT WITH THE PRESSURE MOUNTING FROM UPCOMING EXAMS.

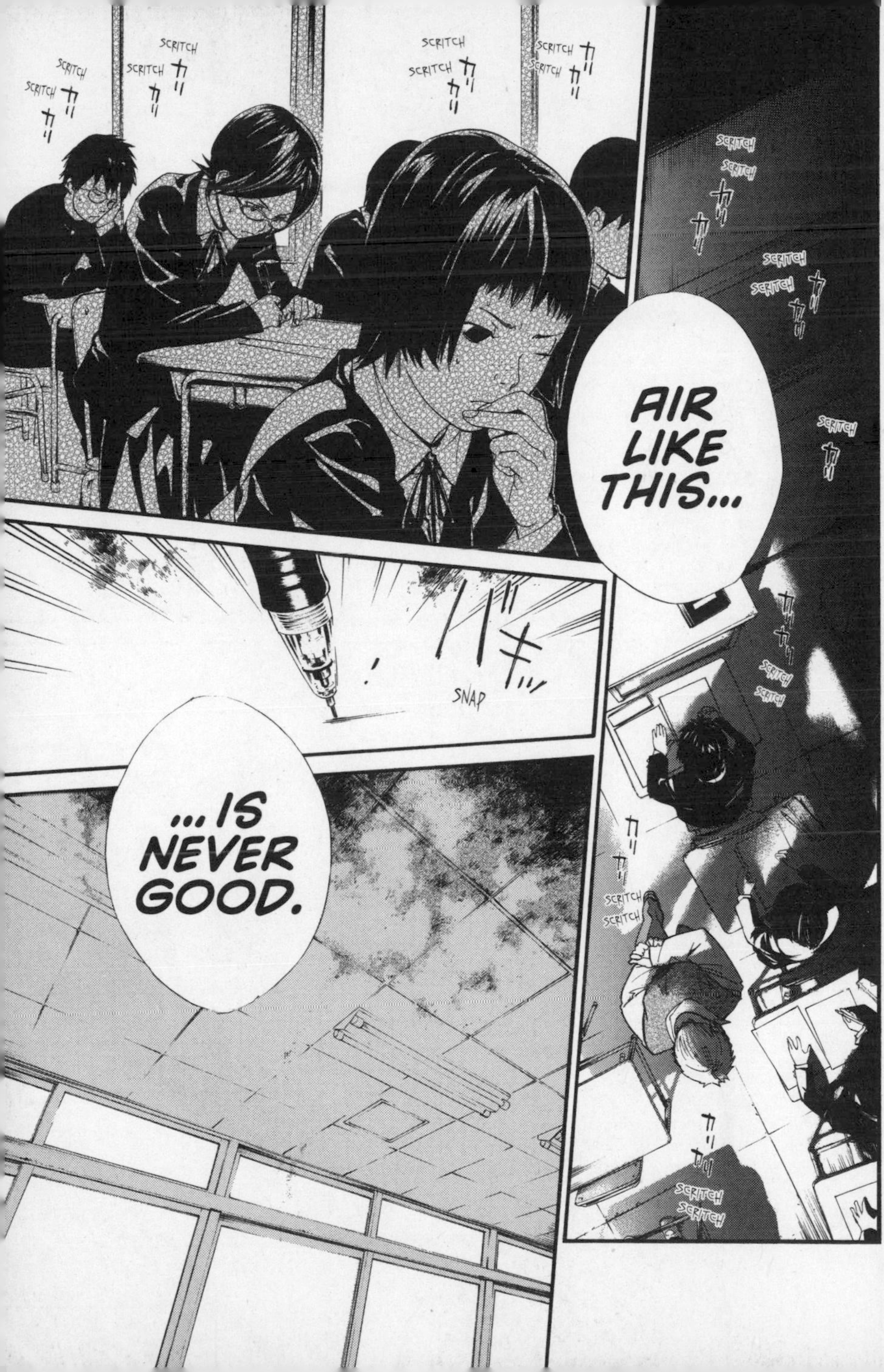
SCRITCH
SCRITCH
SCRITCH
SCRITCH
SCRITCH
AIR LIKE THIS...
SCRITCH
SCRITCH
SCRITCH
SCRITCH
SCRITCH
SCRITCH
SCRITCH
SCRITCH
SCRITCH
SCRITCH
SCRITCH
SCRITCH
SCRITCH
SNAP
...IS NEVER GOOD.

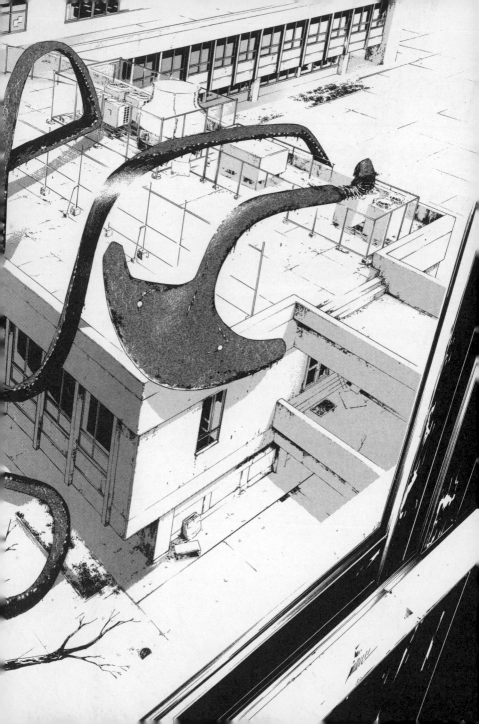

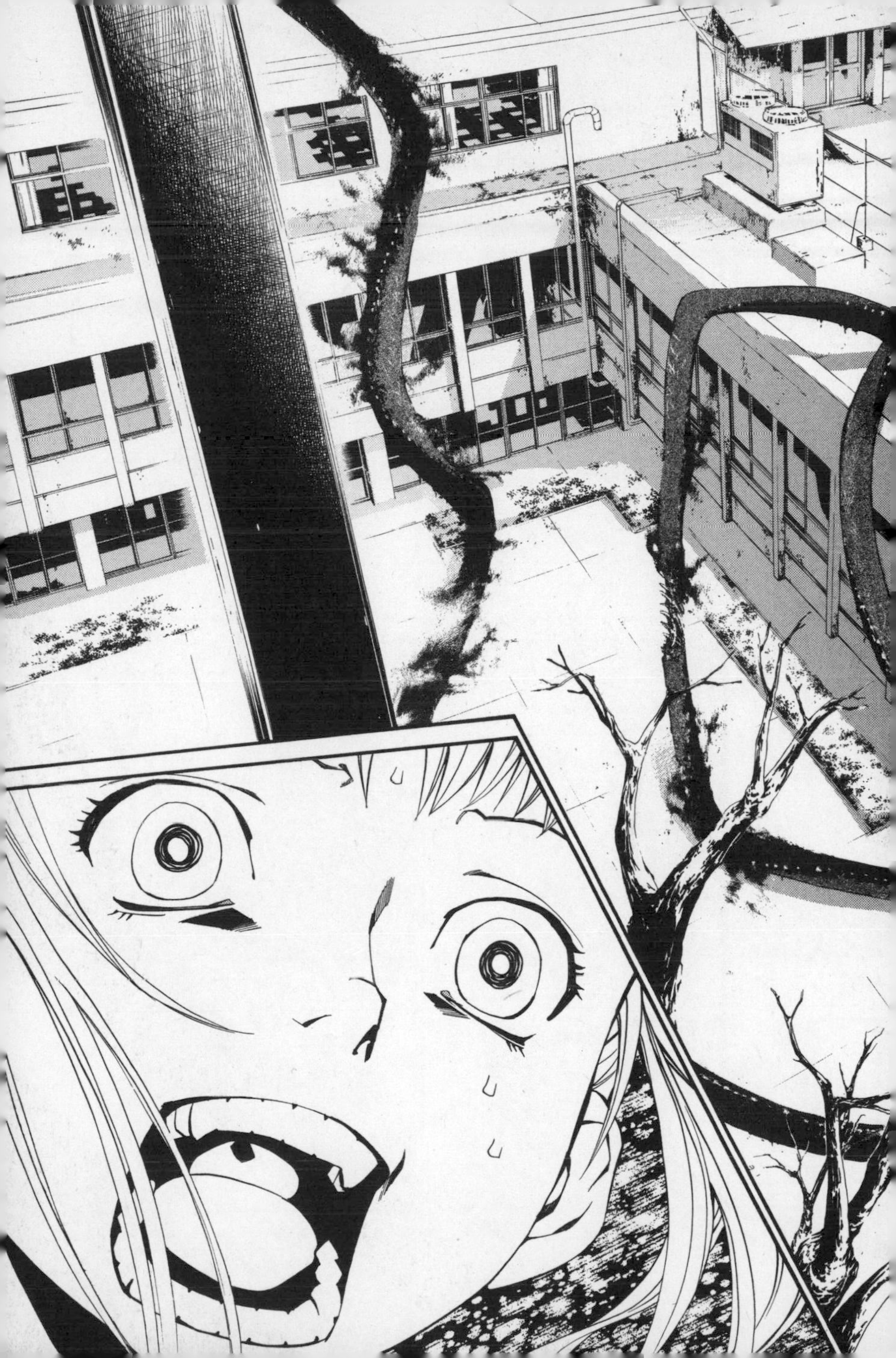

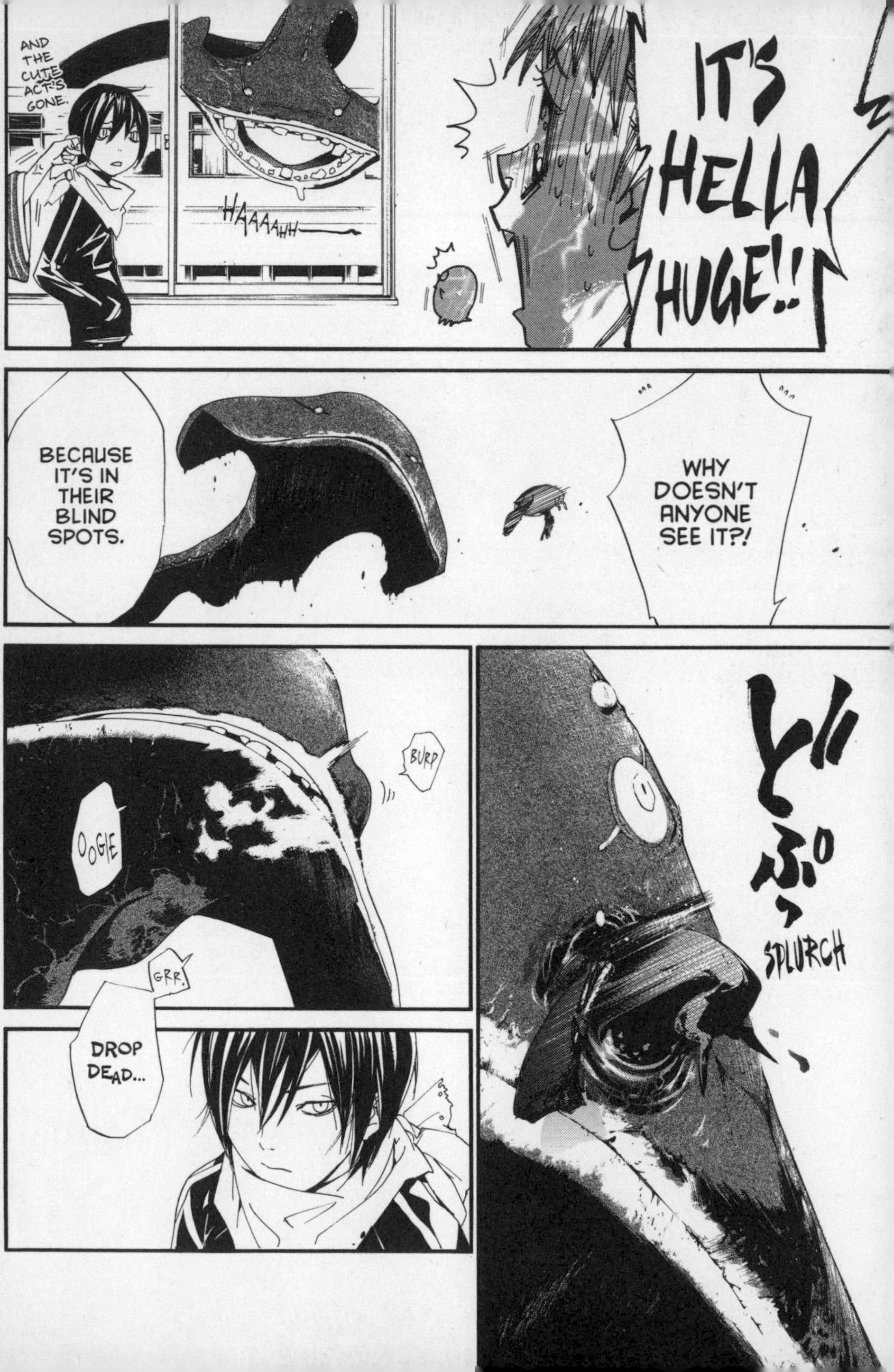
IT'S HELLA HUGE!!
AND THE CUTE ACT'S GONE.
HAAAAHH
WHY DOESN'T ANYONE SEE IT?!
BECAUSE IT'S IN THEIR BLIND SPOTS.
どぷっ
SPLURCH
BURP
OOGIE
GRR
DROP DEAD...

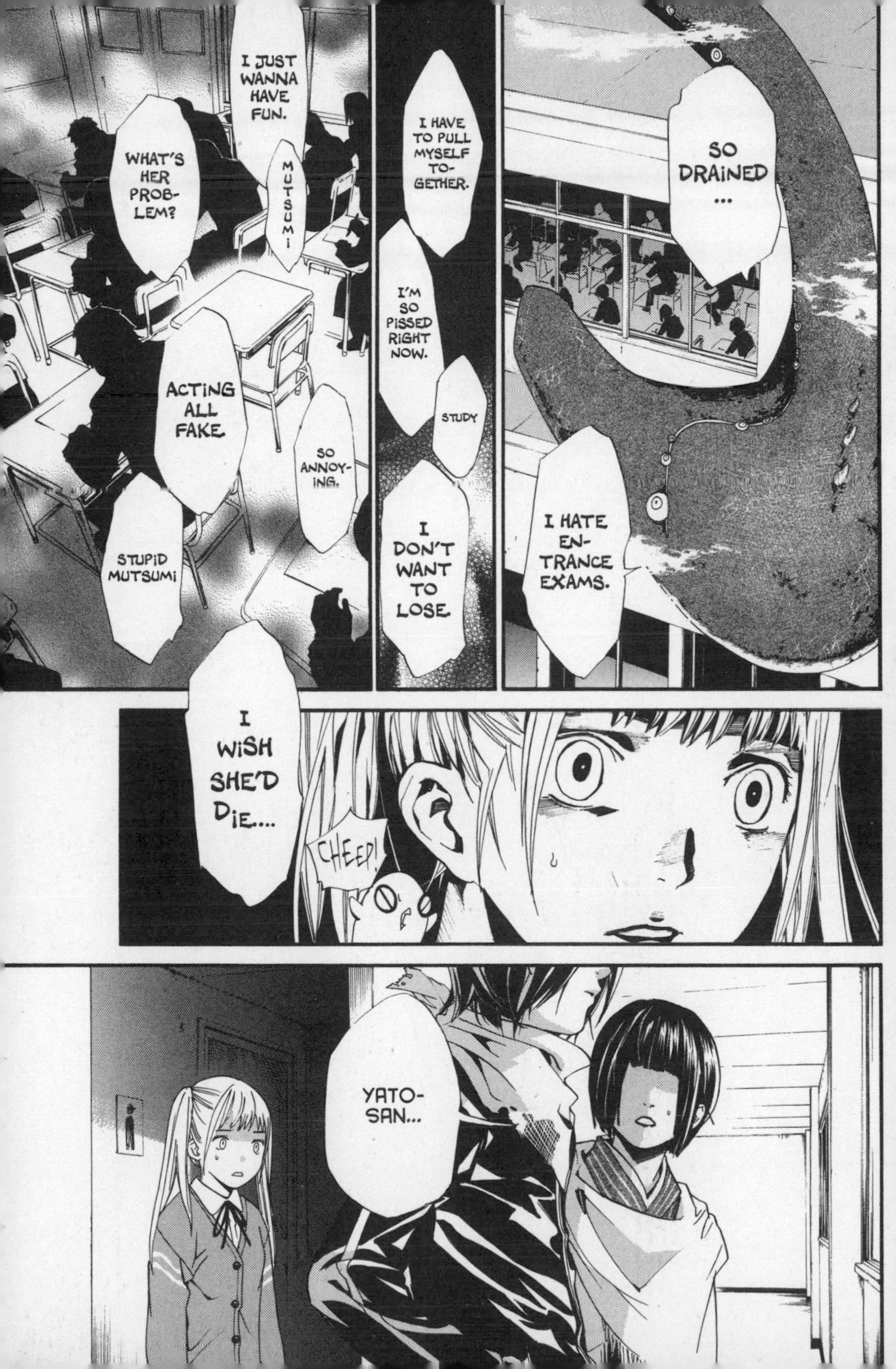
SO DRAINED...
I HATE EN-TRANCE EXAMS.
I HAVE TO PULL MYSELF TO-GETHER.
I'M SO PISSED RIGHT NOW.
STUDY
I DON'T WANT TO LOSE
I JUST WANNA HAVE FUN.
MUTSUMI
WHAT'S HER PROB-LEM?
ACTING ALL FAKE
SO ANNOY-ING.
STUPID MUTSUMI
I WISH SHE'D DIE....
CHEEP!
YATO-SAN...

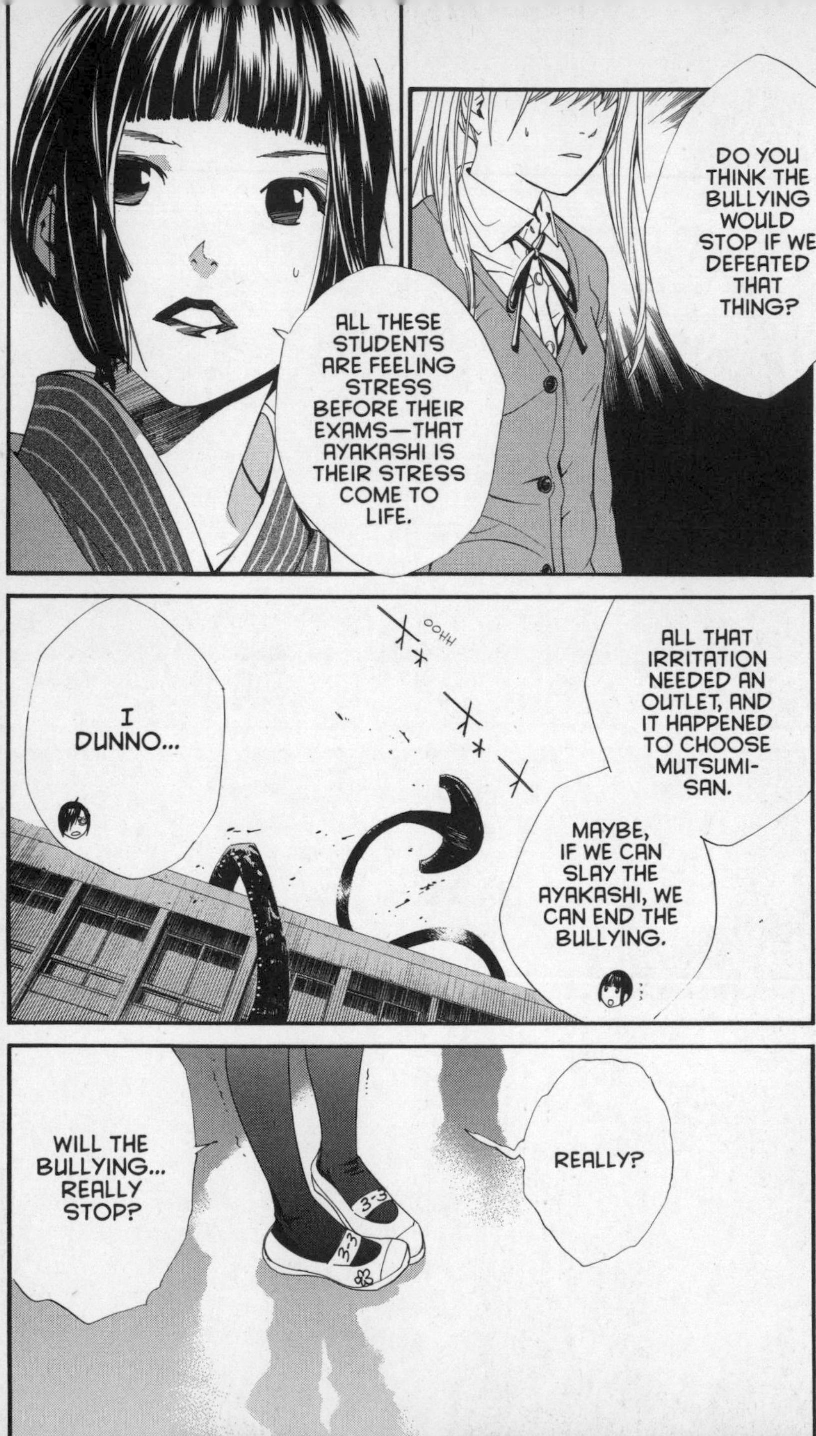
DO YOU THINK THE BULLYING WOULD STOP IF WE DEFEATED THAT THING?
ALL THESE STUDENTS ARE FEELING STRESS BEFORE THEIR EXAMS—THAT AYAKASHI IS THEIR STRESS COME TO LIFE.
ALL THAT IRRITATION NEEDED AN OUTLET, AND IT HAPPENED TO CHOOSE MUTSUMI-SAN.
MAYBE, IF WE CAN SLAY THE AYAKASHI, WE CAN END THE BULLYING.
I DUNNO...
REALLY?
WILL THE BULLYING... REALLY STOP?

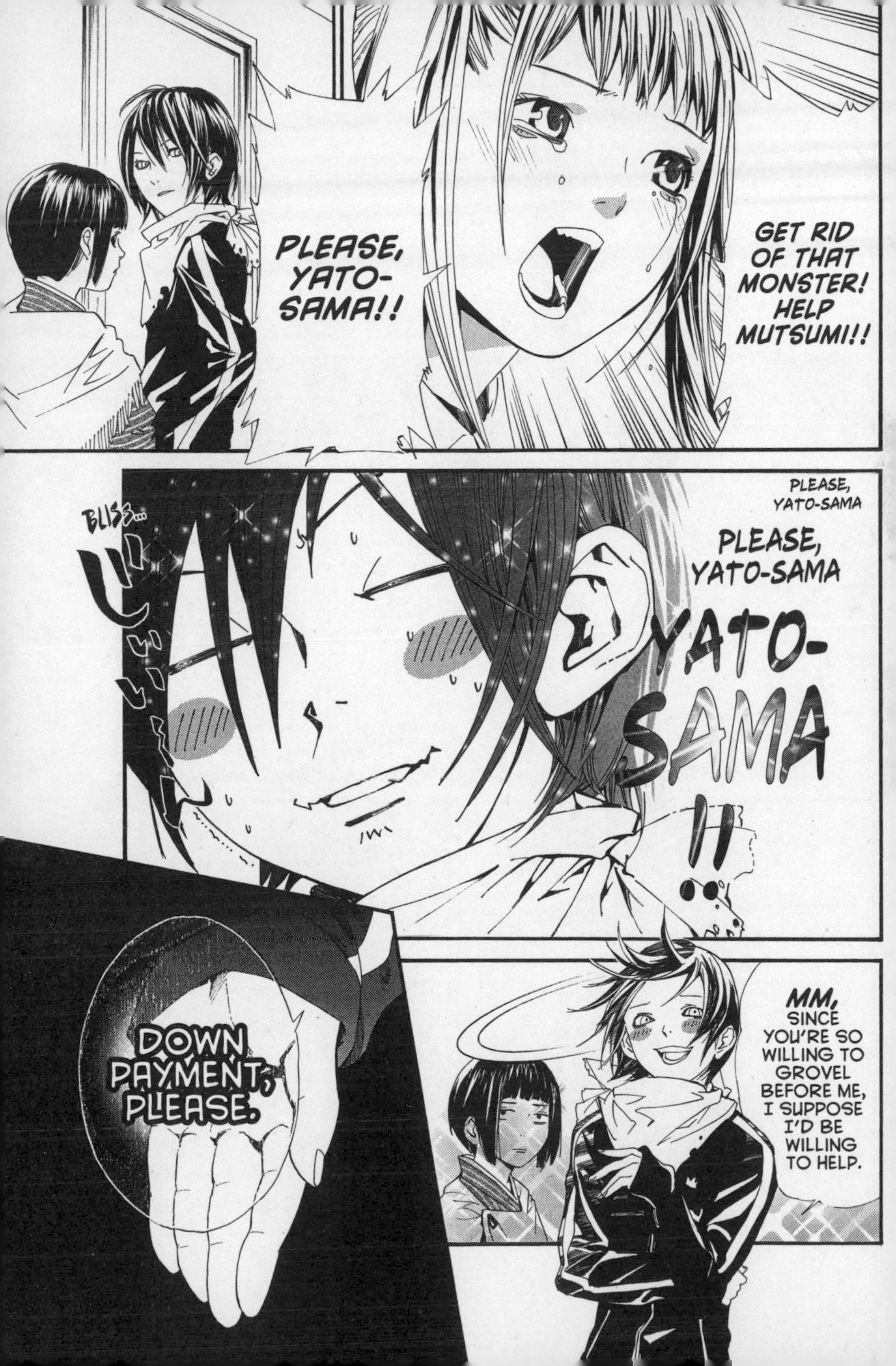
GET RID OF THAT MONSTER! HELP MUTSUMI!!
PLEASE, YATO-SAMA!!
PLEASE, YATO-SAMA
PLEASE, YATO-SAMA
YATO-SAMA!!
BLISS...
MM, SINCE YOU'RE SO WILLING TO GROVEL BEFORE ME, I SUPPOSE I'D BE WILLING TO HELP.
DOWN PAYMENT, PLEASE.

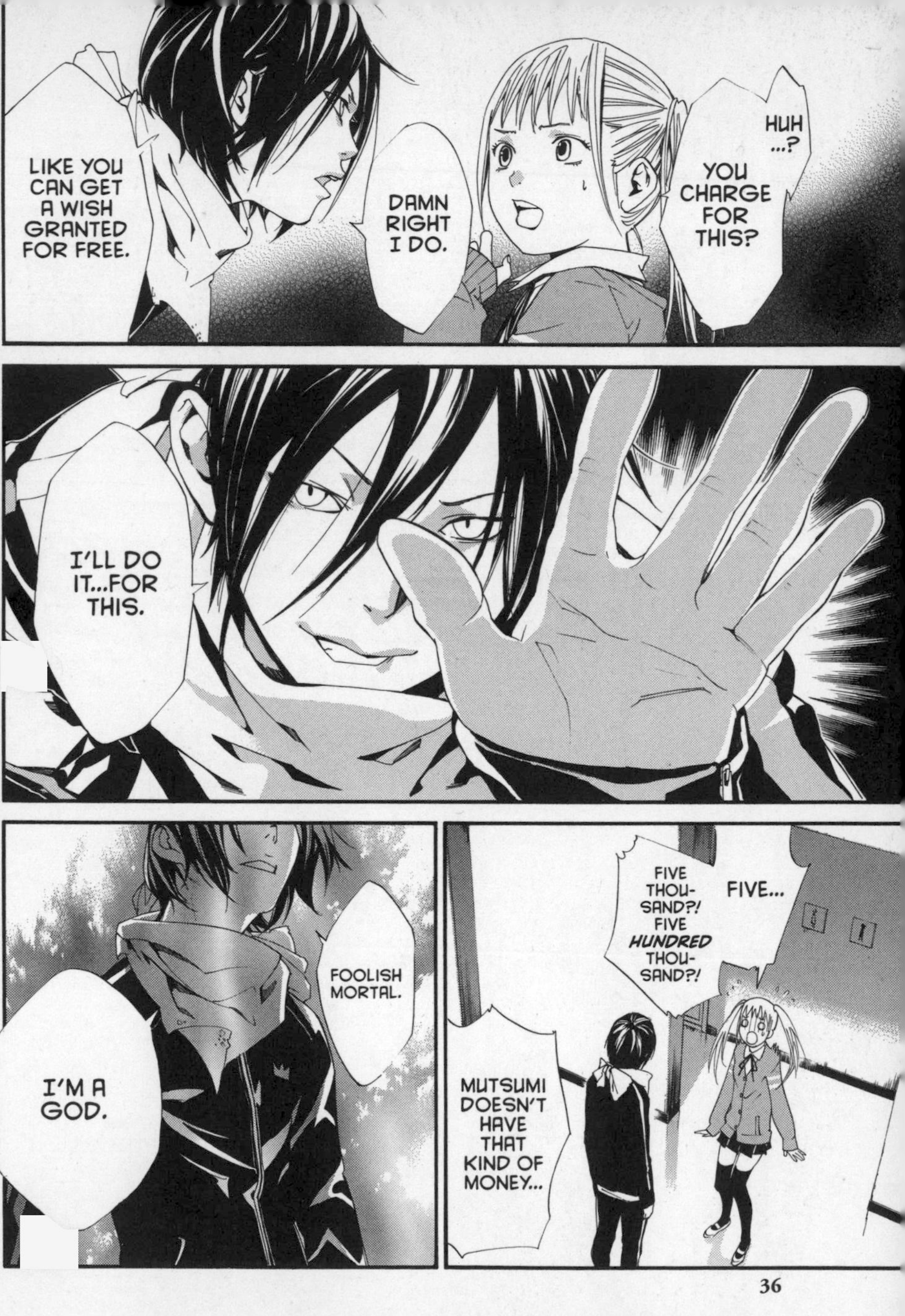
HUH...? YOU CHARGE FOR THIS?
DAMN RIGHT I DO.
LIKE YOU CAN GET A WISH GRANTED FOR FREE.
I'LL DO IT...FOR THIS.
FIVE...
FIVE THOUSAND?! FIVE *HUNDRED* THOUSAND?!
MUTSUMI DOESN'T HAVE THAT KIND OF MONEY...
FOOLISH MORTAL.
I'M A GOD.

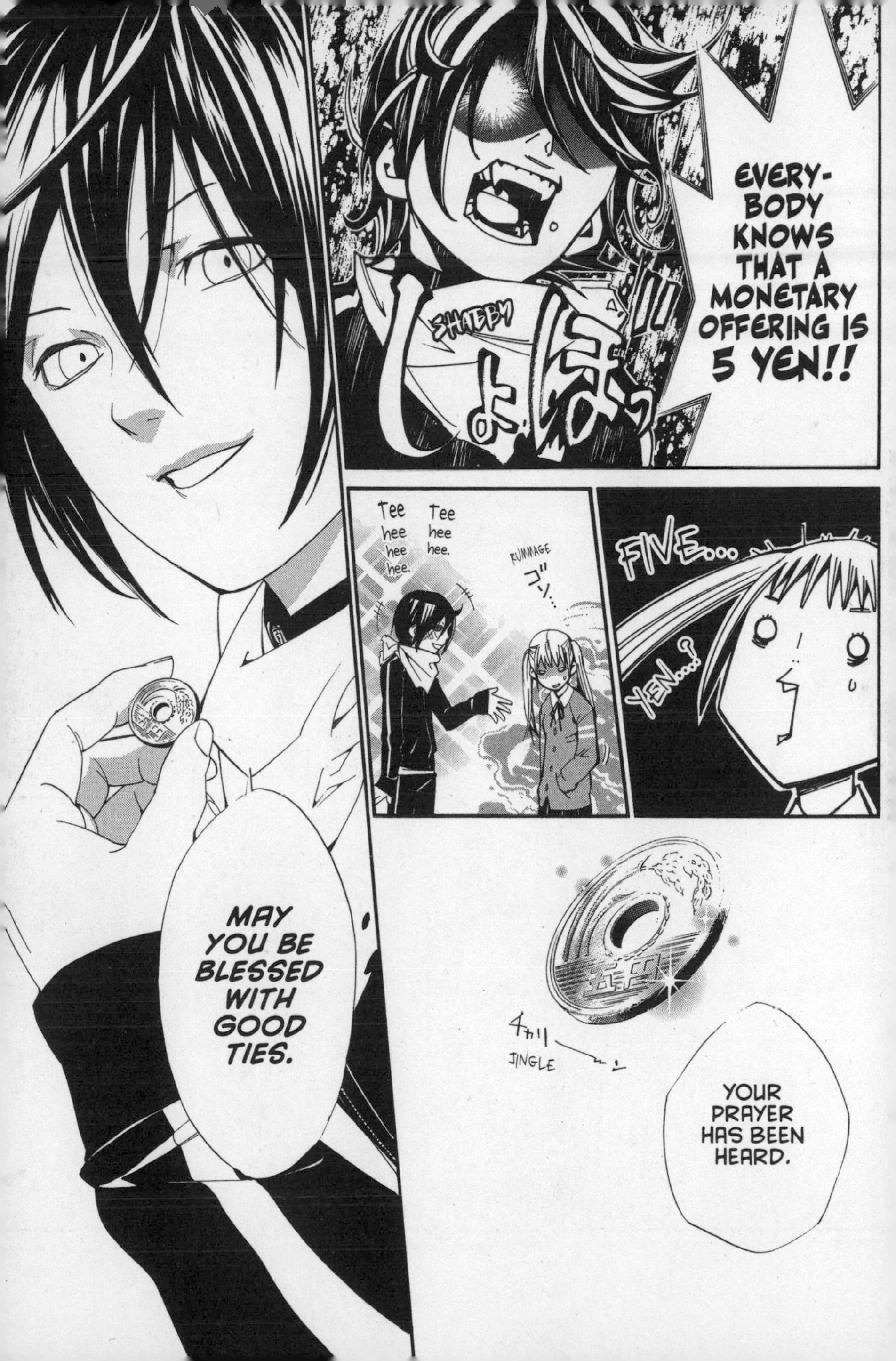
EVERY-BODY KNOWS THAT A MONETARY OFFERING IS 5 YEN!!
SHABBY
FIVE...
YEN...?
Tee hee hee hee.
Tee hee hee.
RUMMAGE
JINGLE
YOUR PRAYER HAS BEEN HEARD.
MAY YOU BE BLESSED WITH GOOD TIES.

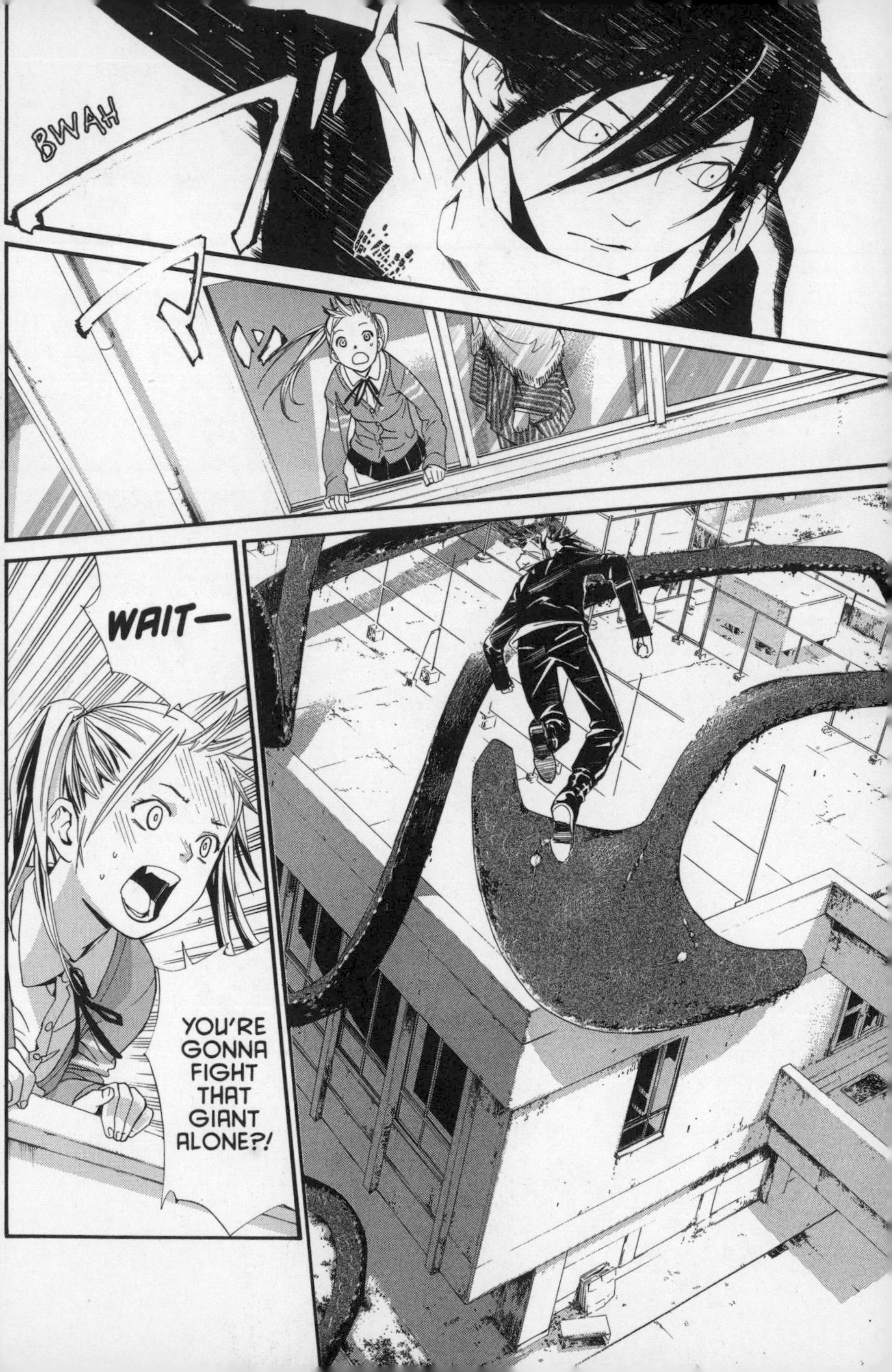
BWAH
WAIT—
YOU'RE GONNA FIGHT THAT GIANT ALONE?!

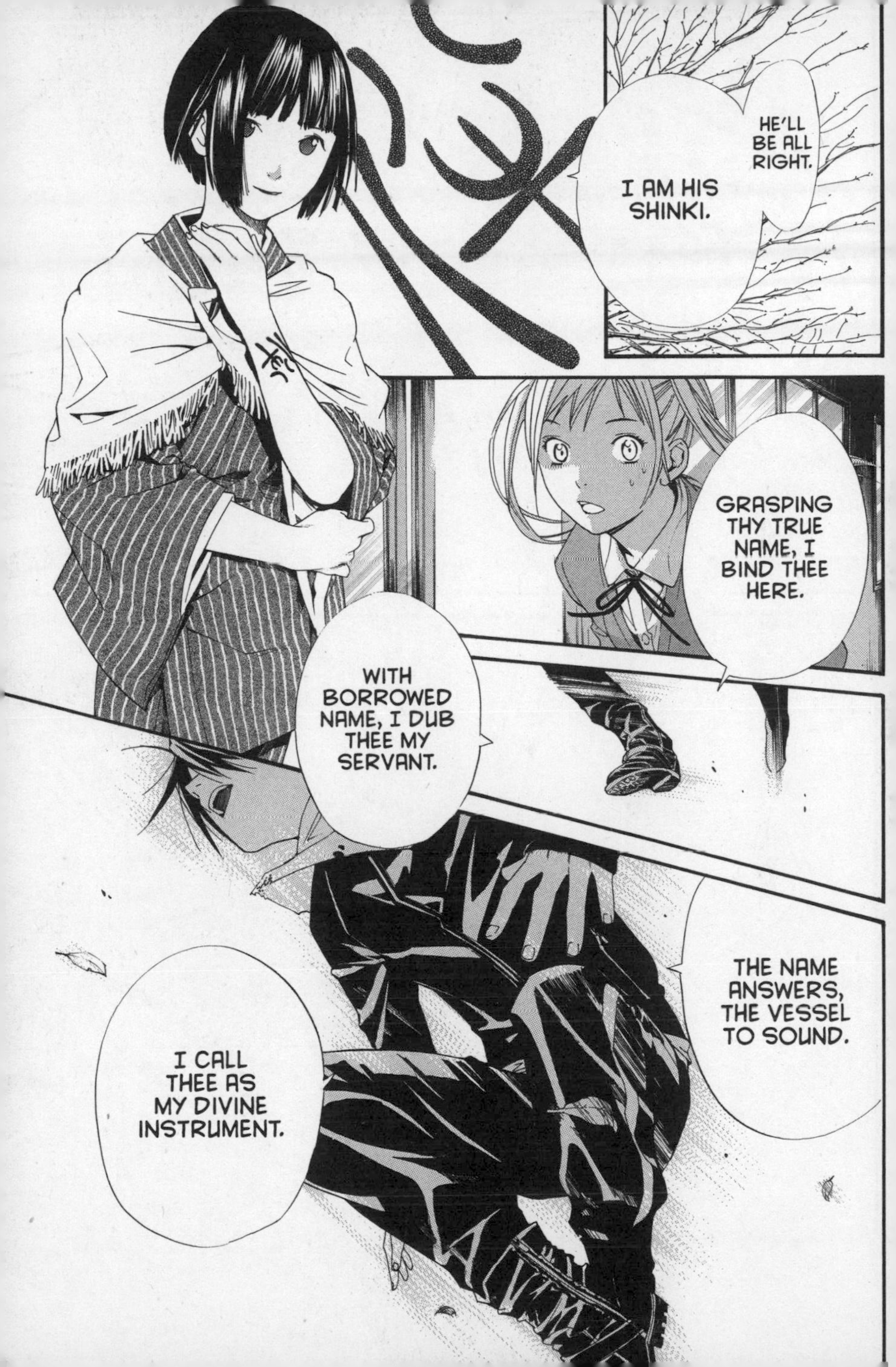
HE'LL BE ALL RIGHT.
I AM HIS SHINKI.
GRASPING THY TRUE NAME, I BIND THEE HERE.
WITH BORROWED NAME, I DUB THEE MY SERVANT.
THE NAME ANSWERS, THE VESSEL TO SOUND.
I CALL THEE AS MY DIVINE INSTRUMENT.

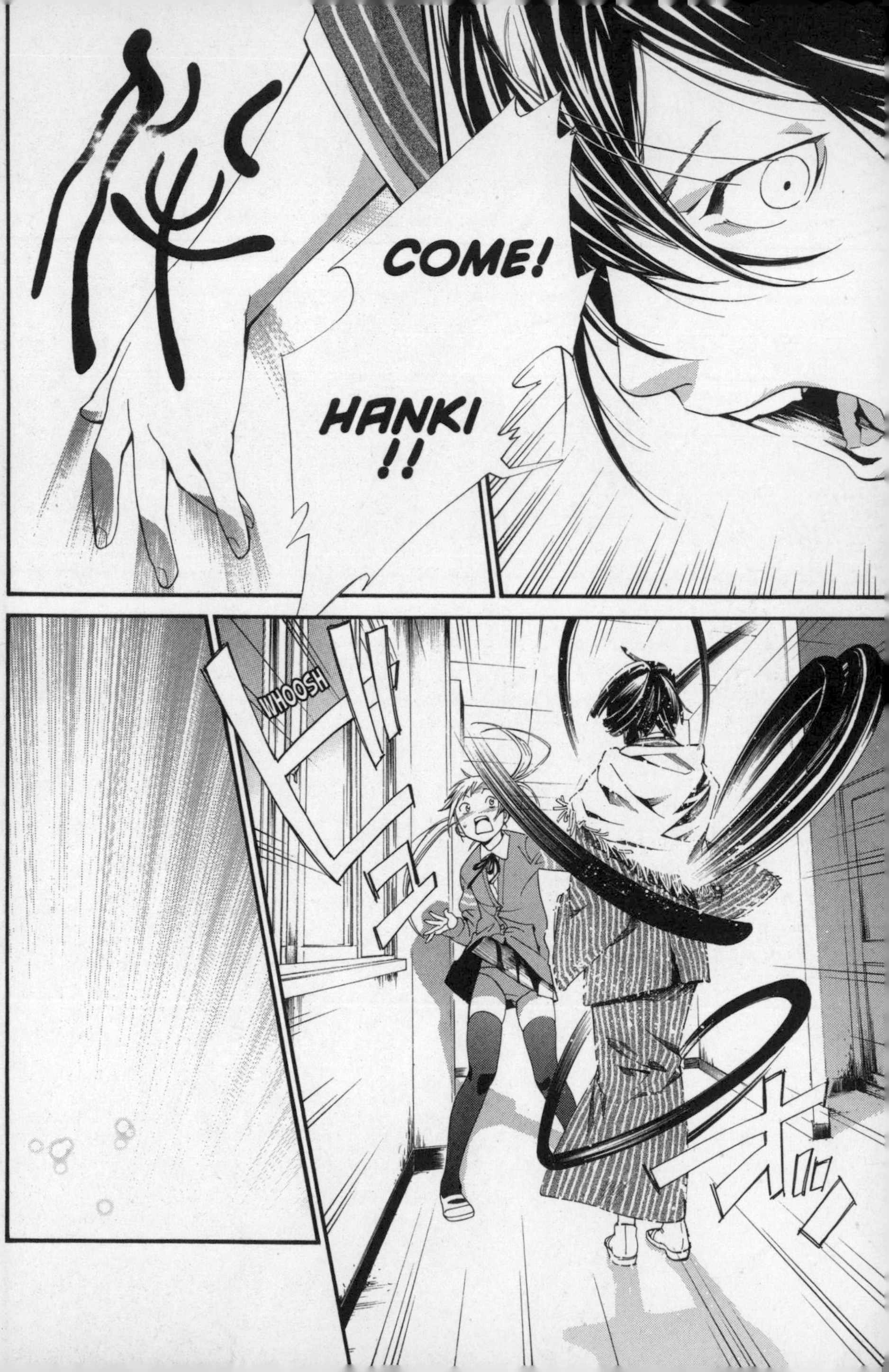
COME!
HANKI !!
WHOOSH

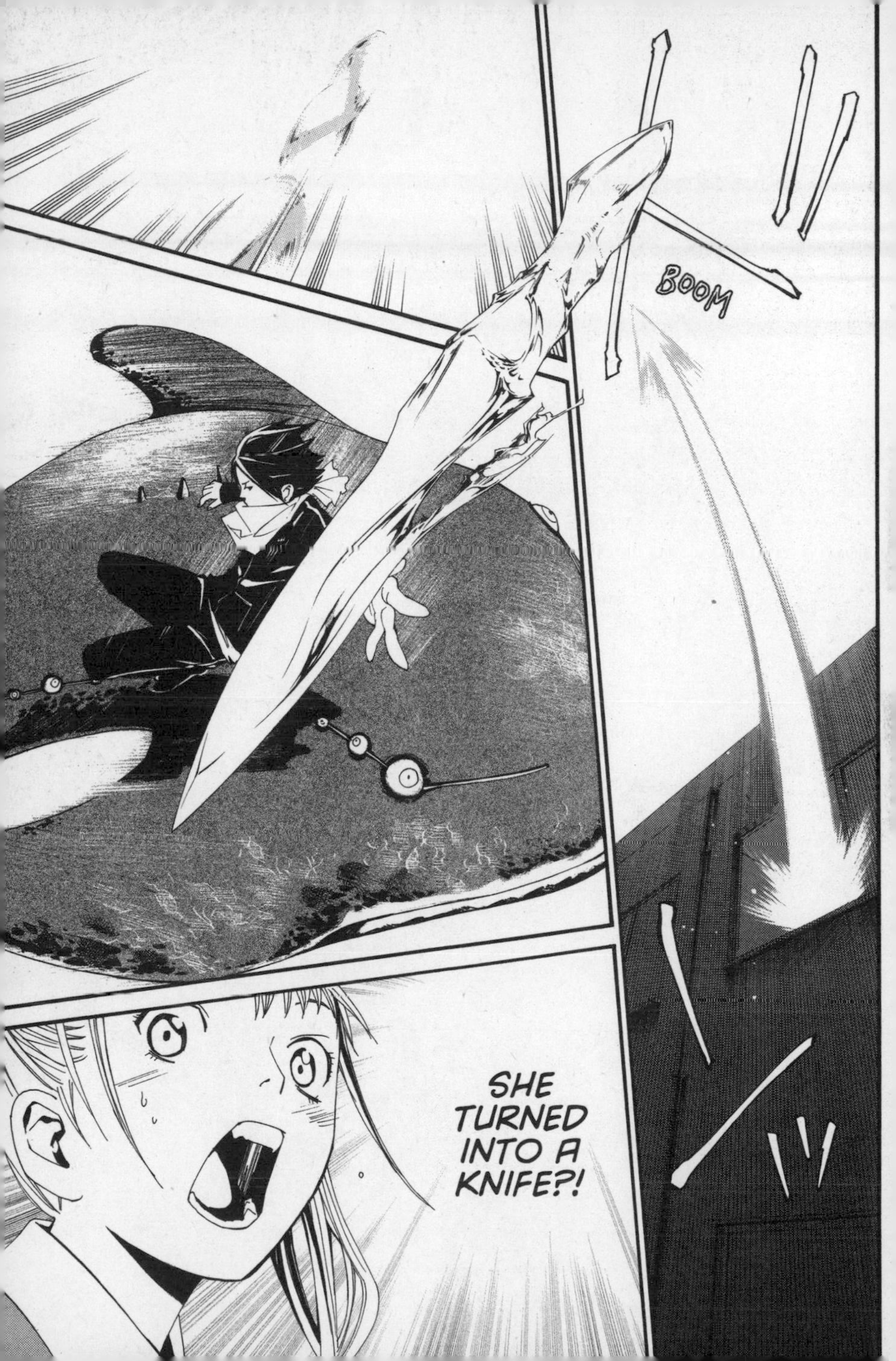
BOOM
SHE TURNED INTO A KNIFE?!

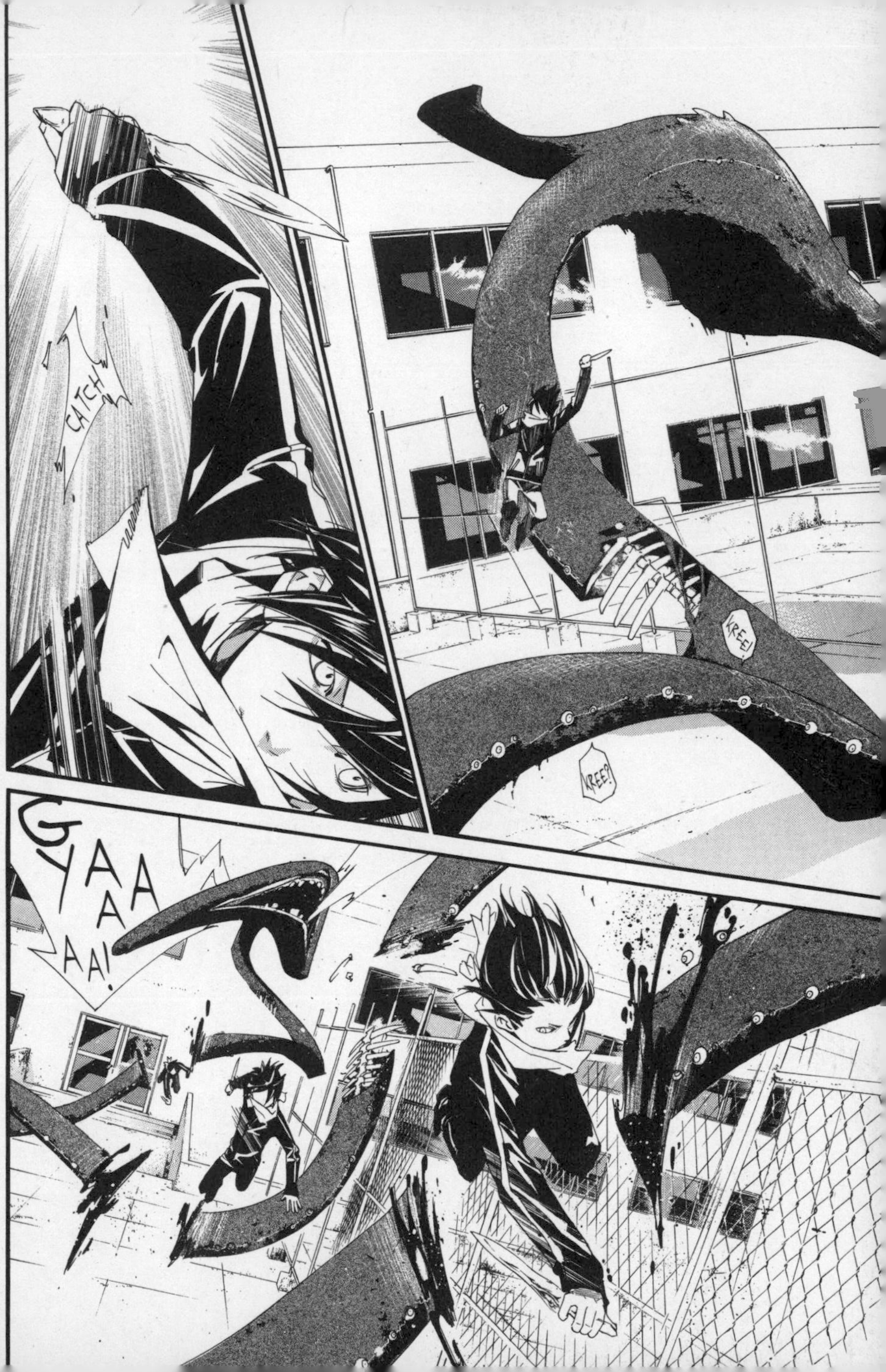
KREE!
KREE?
CATCH
GYAAAAAA!

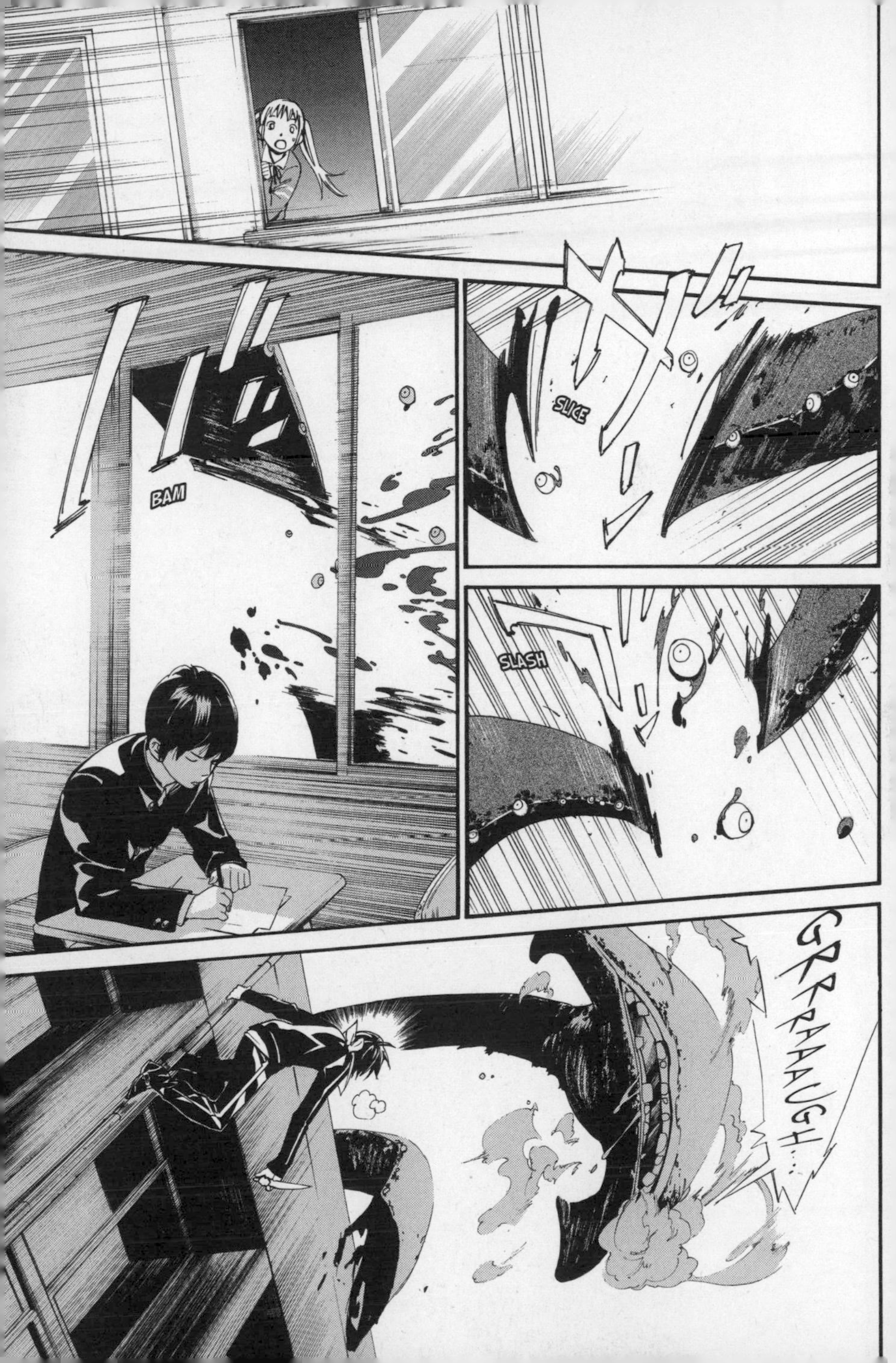
SLICE
SLASH
BAM
GRRAAAUGH...

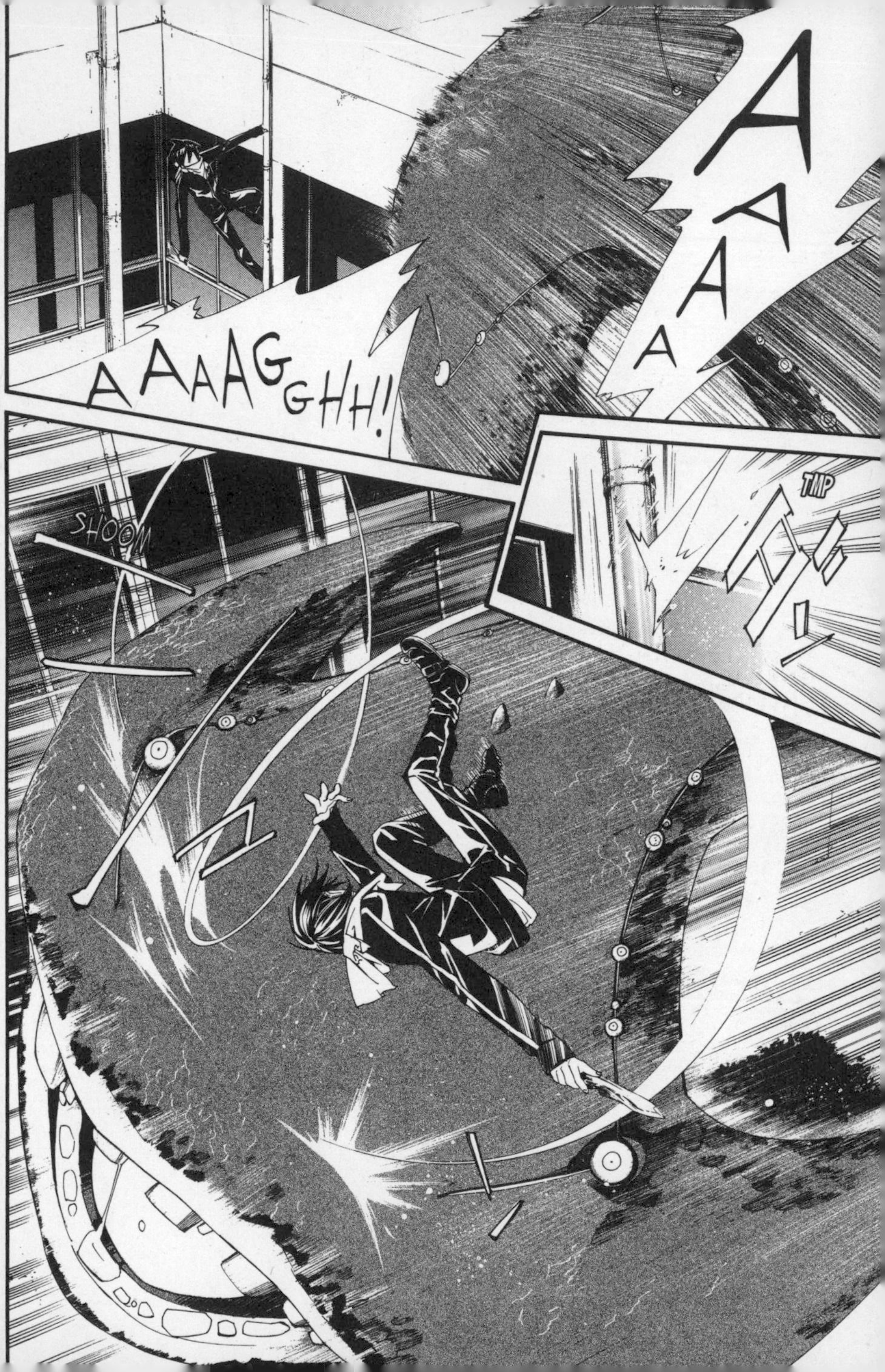
AAAA
AAAAGGHH!!
TMP
SHOOM

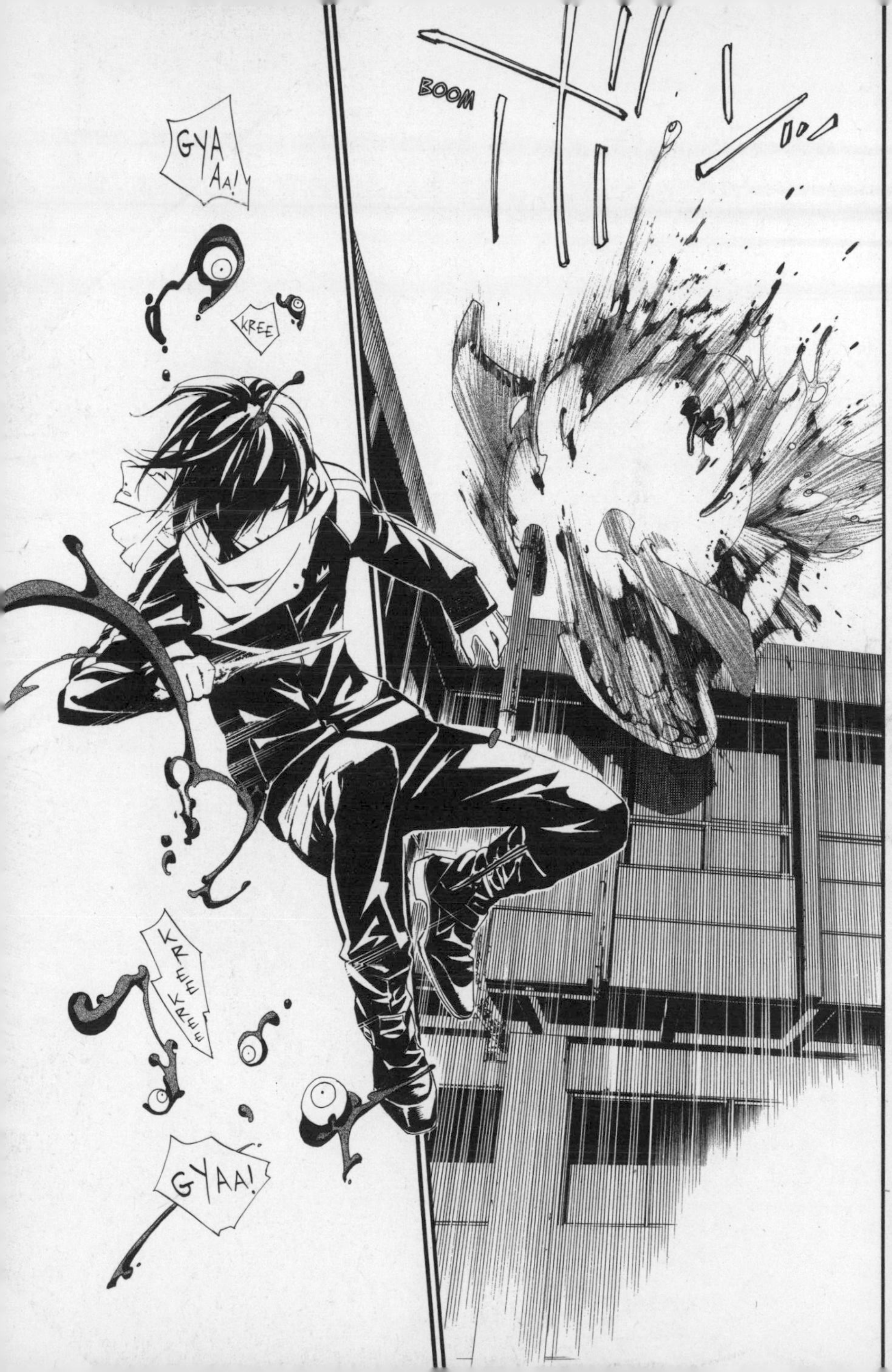
BOOM
GYAAA!
KREE
KREE KREE
GYAA!

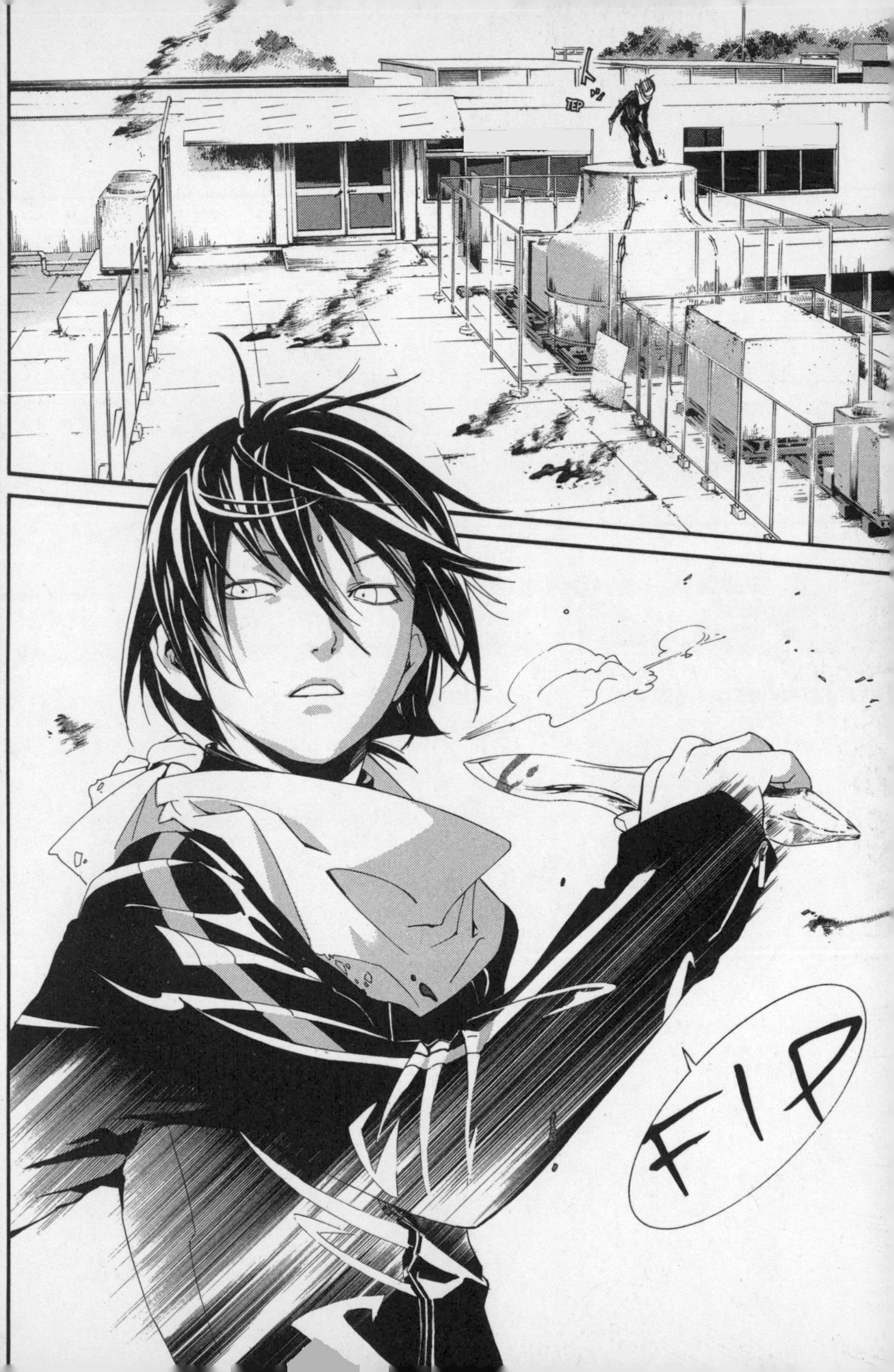
TEP
FIP

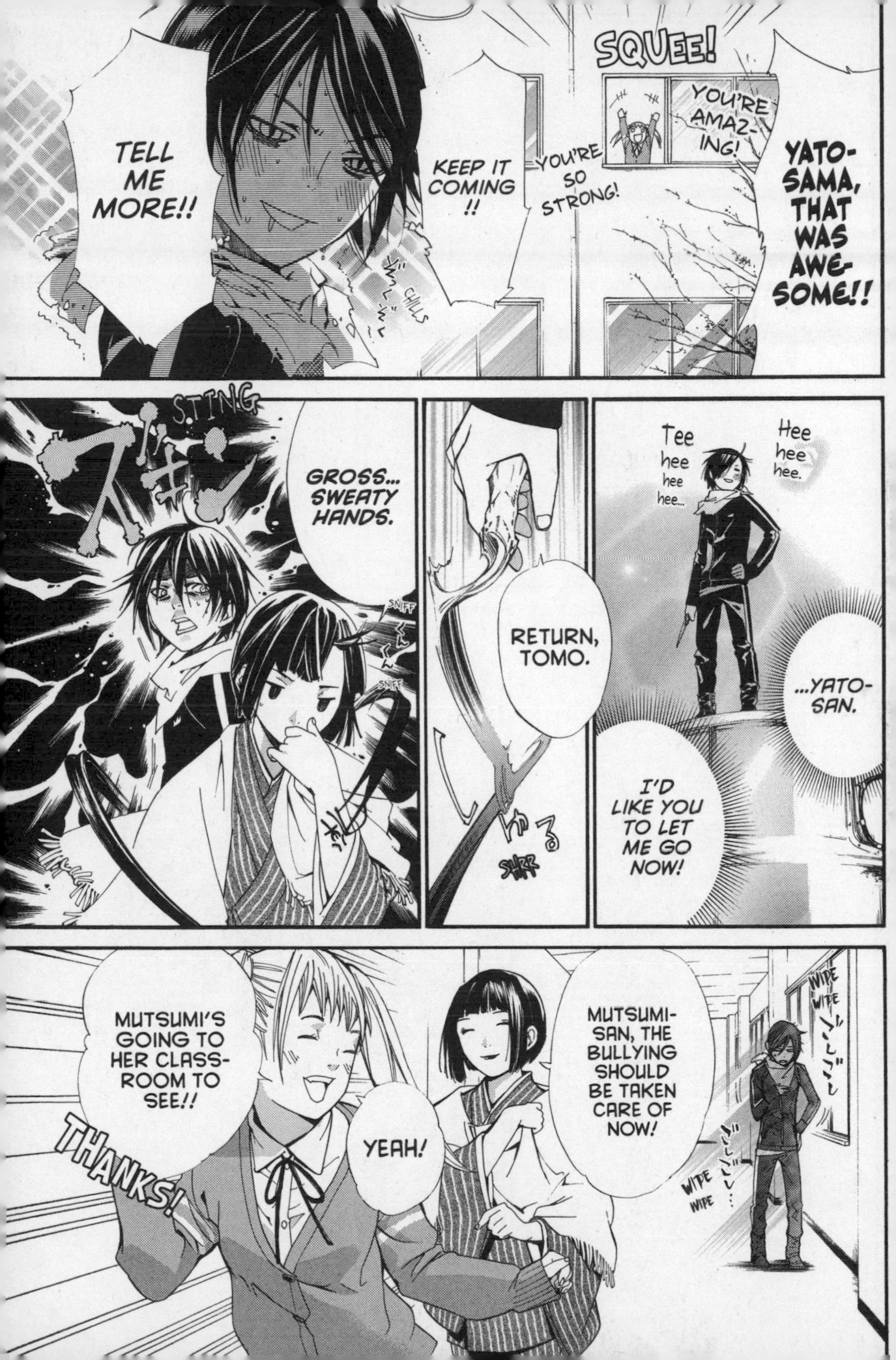
YATO-SAMA, THAT WAS AWE-SOME!!
SQUEE!
YOU'RE AMAZ-ING!
YOU'RE SO STRONG!
KEEP IT COMING!!
CHILLS
TELL ME MORE!!
Hee hee hee.
Tee hee hee hee...
...YATO-SAN.
I'D LIKE YOU TO LET ME GO NOW!
RETURN, TOMO.
SHRR
STING
GROSS... SWEATY HANDS.
SNIFF
SNIFF
WIPE WIPE
WIPE WIPE
MUTSUMI-SAN, THE BULLYING SHOULD BE TAKEN CARE OF NOW!
YEAH!
MUTSUMI'S GOING TO HER CLASS-ROOM TO SEE!!
THANKS!

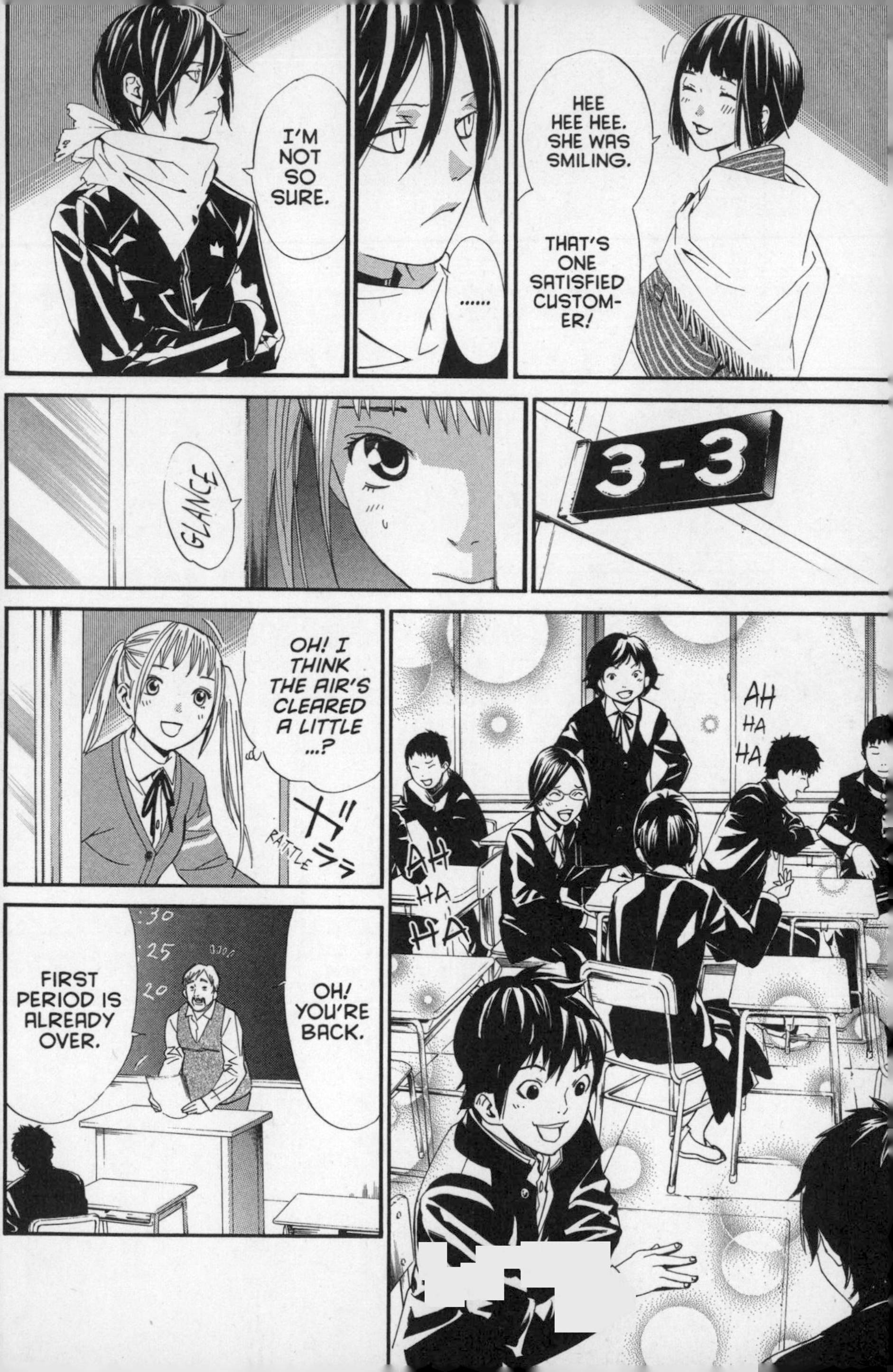
HEE HEE HEE. SHE WAS SMILING.
THAT'S ONE SATISFIED CUSTOM-ER!
......
I'M NOT SO SURE.
3-3
GLANCE
AH HA HA
AH HA HA
OH! I THINK THE AIR'S CLEARED A LITTLE ...?
RATTLE
OH! YOU'RE BACK.
FIRST PERIOD IS ALREADY OVER.

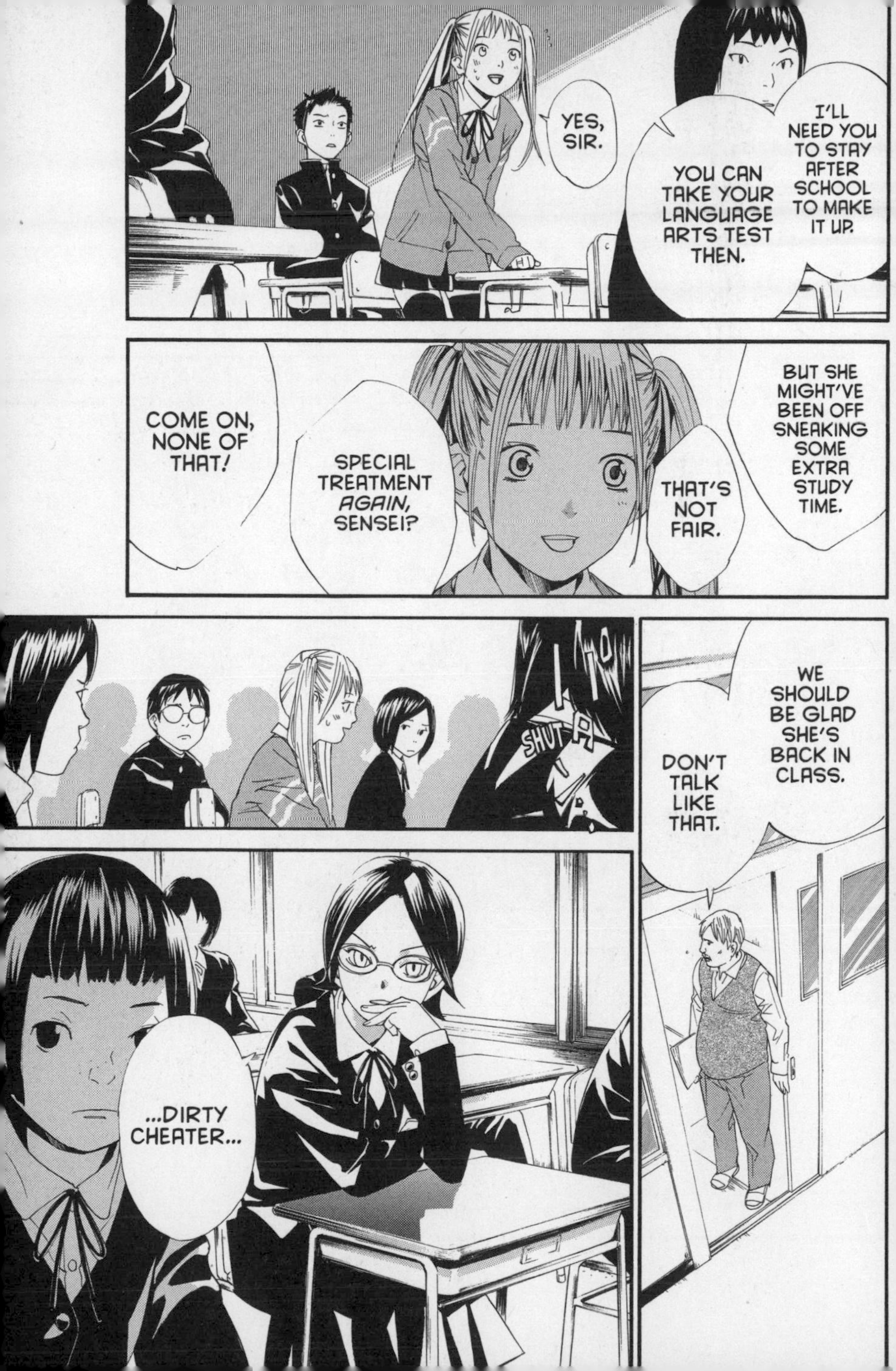
I'LL NEED YOU TO STAY AFTER SCHOOL TO MAKE IT UP.
YOU CAN TAKE YOUR LANGUAGE ARTS TEST THEN.
YES, SIR.
BUT SHE MIGHT'VE BEEN OFF SNEAKING SOME EXTRA STUDY TIME.
THAT'S NOT FAIR.
SPECIAL TREATMENT *AGAIN*, SENSEI?
COME ON, NONE OF THAT!
WE SHOULD BE GLAD SHE'S BACK IN CLASS.
DON'T TALK LIKE THAT.
SHUT
...DIRTY CHEATER...

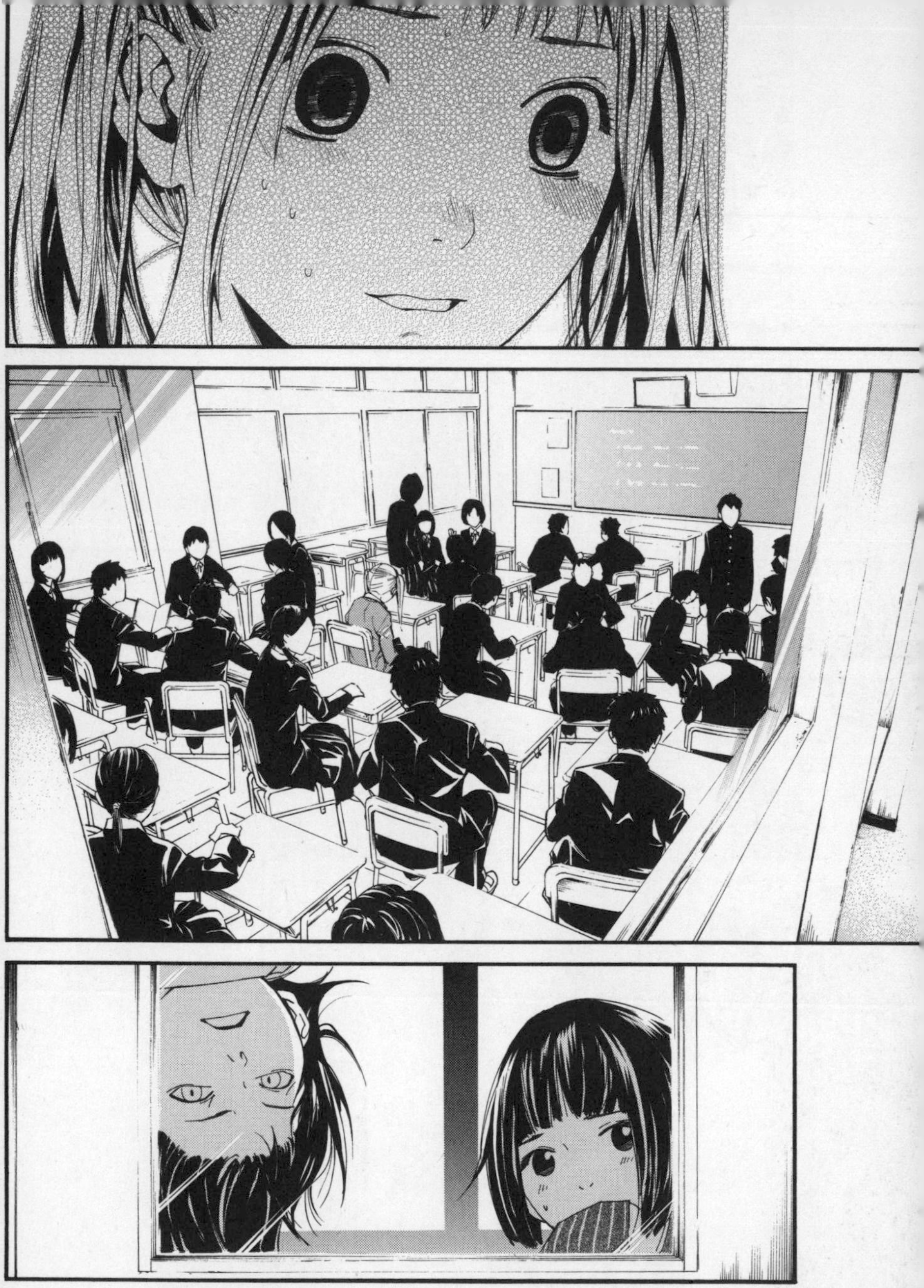

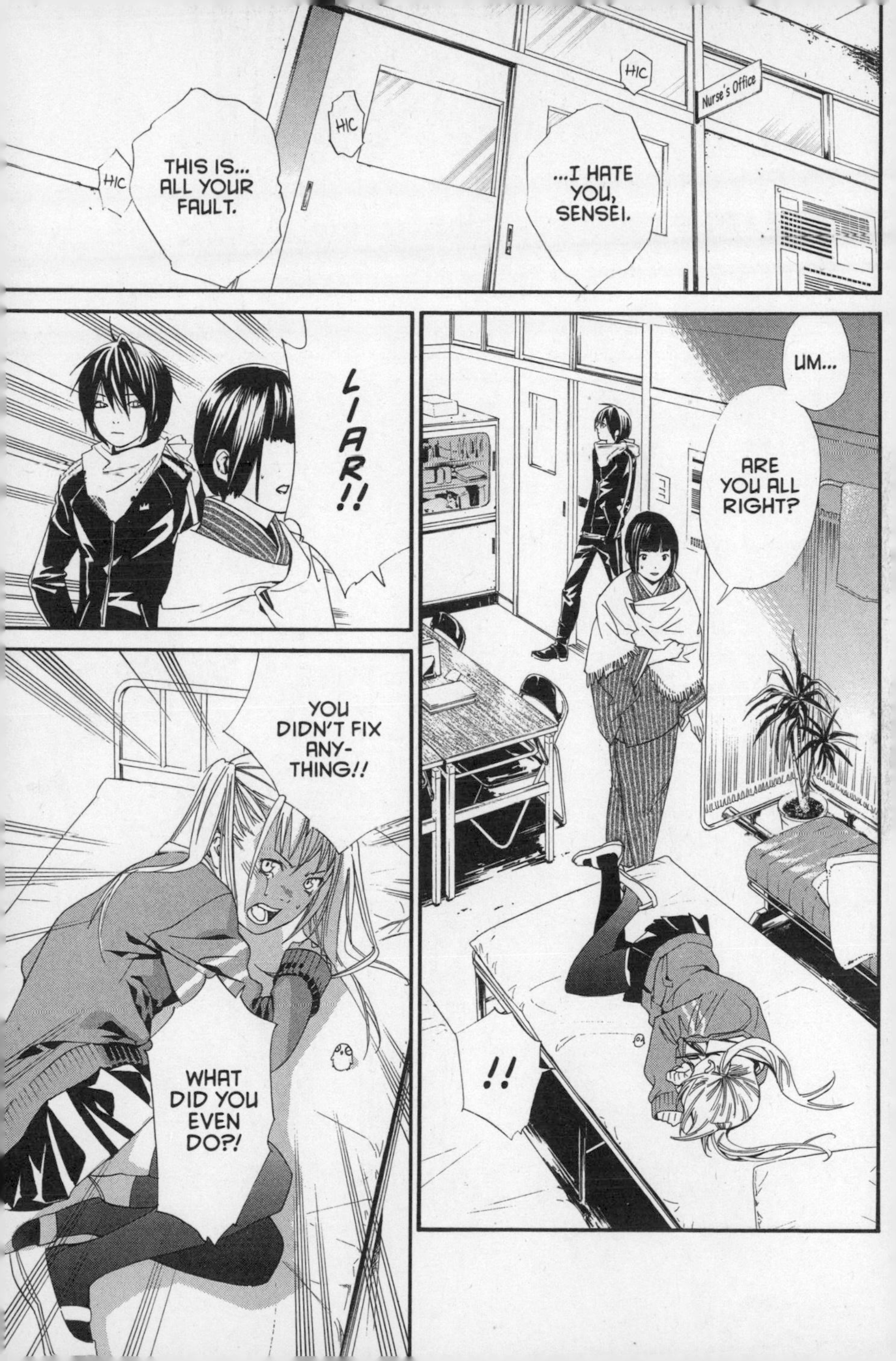
Nurse's Office
HIC
...I HATE YOU, SENSEI.
HIC
THIS IS... ALL YOUR FAULT.
HIC
UM...
ARE YOU ALL RIGHT?
!!
LIAR!!
YOU DIDN'T FIX ANY-THING!!
WHAT DID YOU EVEN DO?!

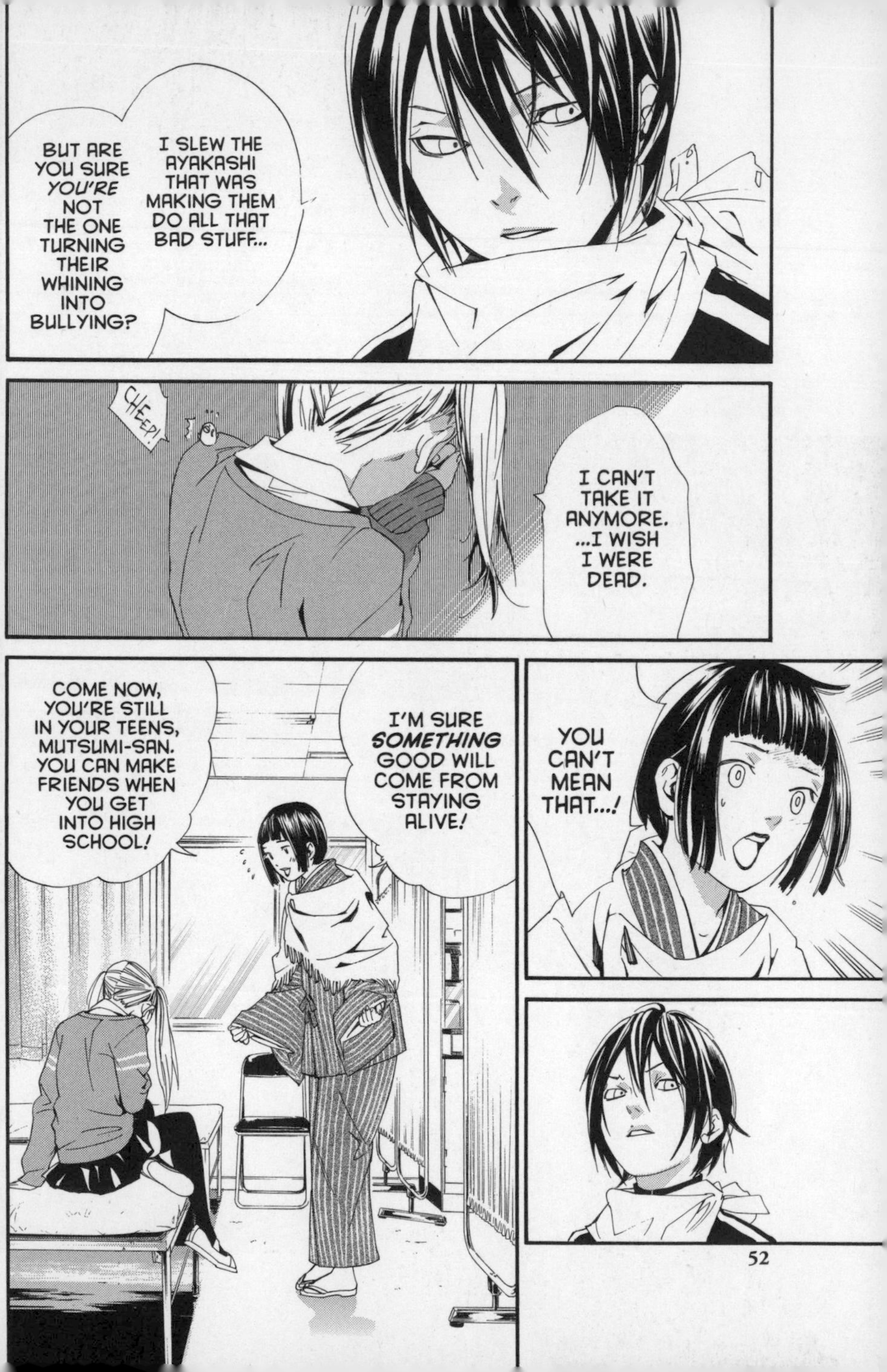
I SLEW THE AYAKASHI THAT WAS MAKING THEM DO ALL THAT BAD STUFF...
BUT ARE YOU SURE *YOU'RE* NOT THE ONE TURNING THEIR WHINING INTO BULLYING?
I CAN'T TAKE IT ANYMORE. ...I WISH I WERE DEAD.
CHEEP!
YOU CAN'T MEAN THAT...!
I'M SURE *SOMETHING* GOOD WILL COME FROM STAYING ALIVE!
COME NOW, YOU'RE STILL IN YOUR TEENS, MUTSUMI-SAN. YOU CAN MAKE FRIENDS WHEN YOU GET INTO HIGH SCHOOL!

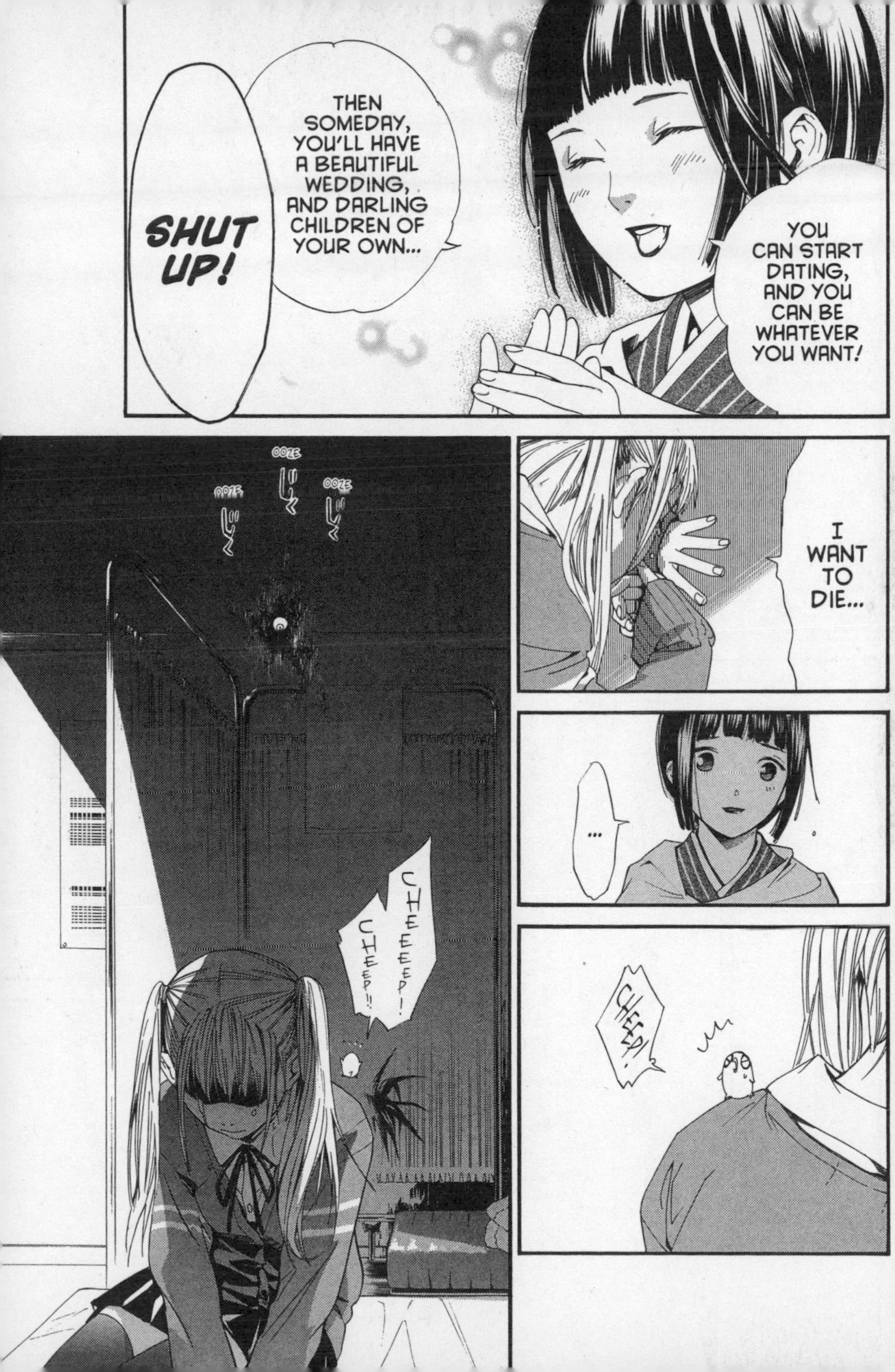
YOU CAN START DATING, AND YOU CAN BE WHATEVER YOU WANT!
THEN SOMEDAY, YOU'LL HAVE A BEAUTIFUL WEDDING, AND DARLING CHILDREN OF YOUR OWN...
SHUT UP!
I WANT TO DIE...
...
CHEEP!
OOZE
OOZE
OOZE
CHEEEEEP!
CHEEP!!

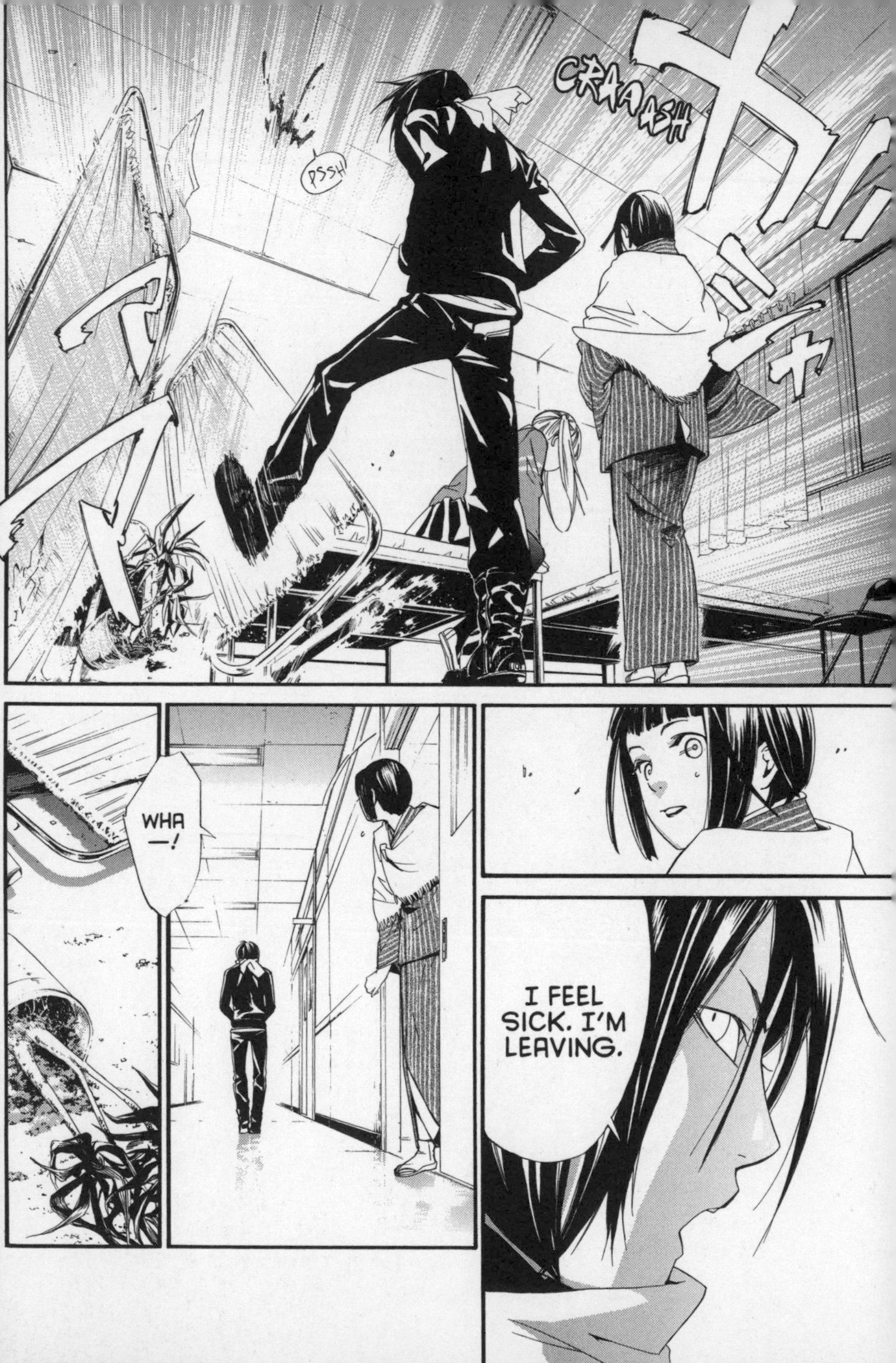
CRAAASH
PSSH!
I FEEL SICK. I'M LEAVING.
WHA—!

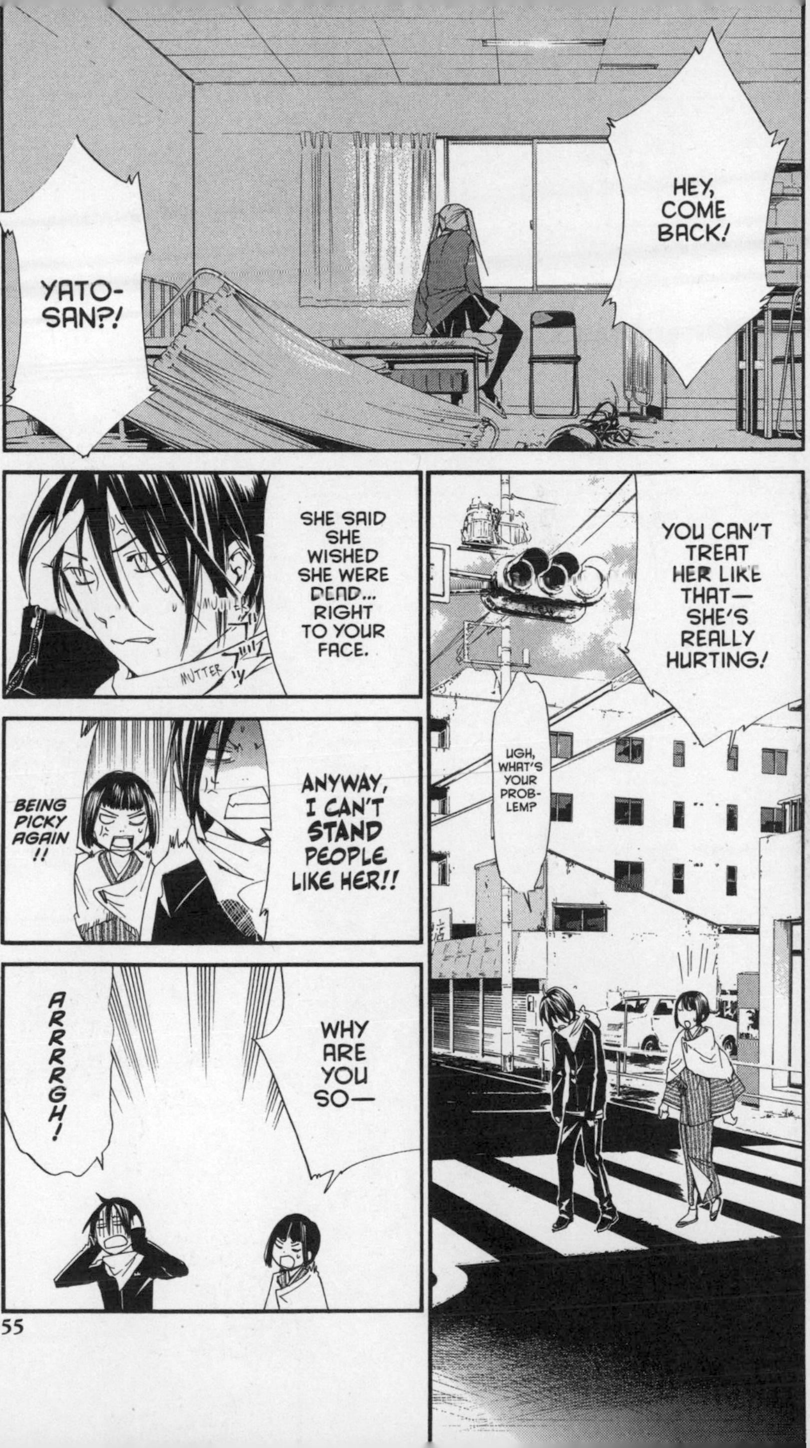
HEY, COME BACK!
YATO-SAN?!
YOU CAN'T TREAT HER LIKE THAT—SHE'S REALLY HURTING!
UGH, WHAT'S YOUR PROBLEM?
SHE SAID SHE WISHED SHE WERE DEAD... RIGHT TO YOUR FACE.
MUTTER
MUTTER
ANYWAY, I CAN'T STAND PEOPLE LIKE HER!!
BEING PICKY AGAIN!!
WHY ARE YOU SO—
ARRRRGH!

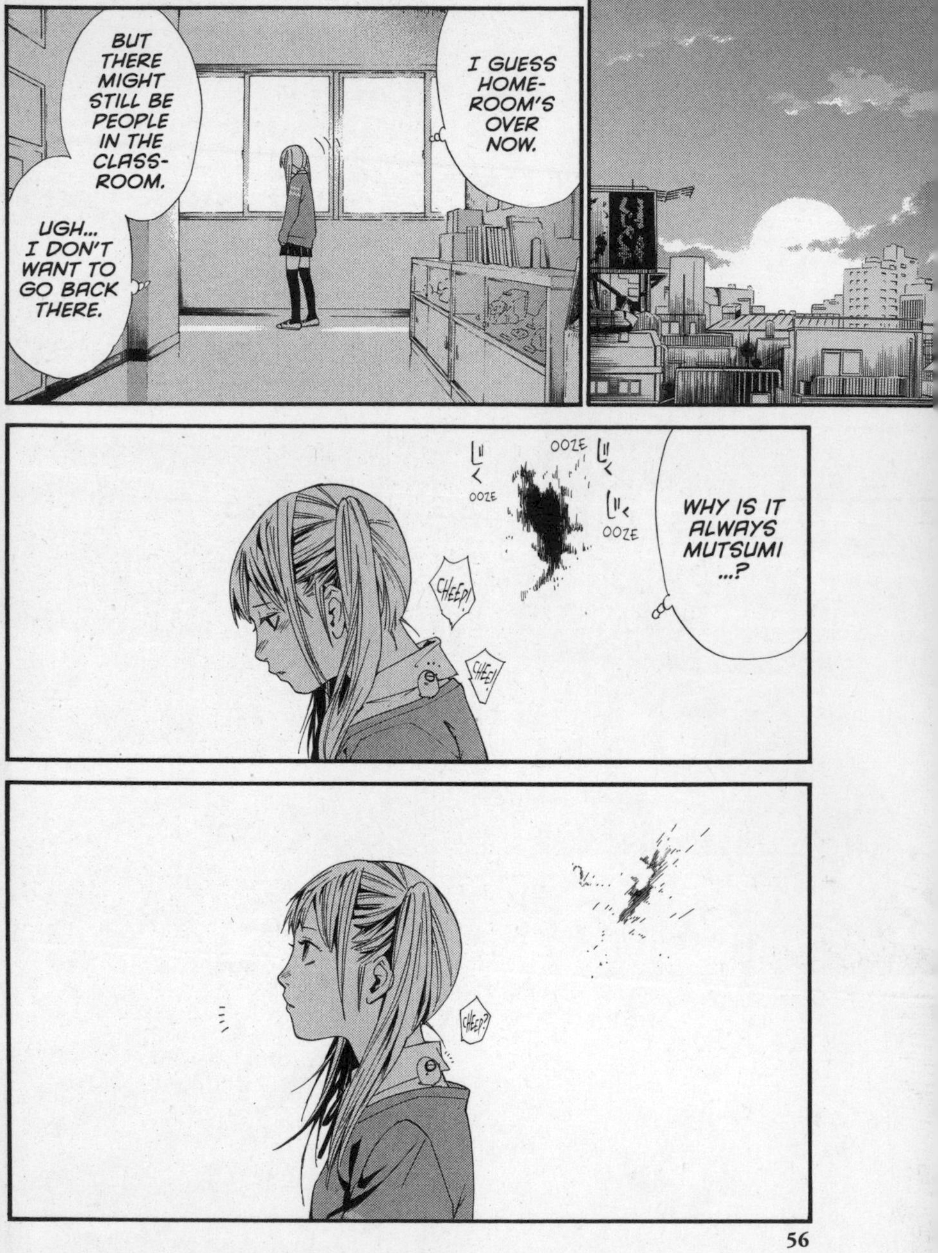
I GUESS HOME-ROOM'S OVER NOW.
BUT THERE MIGHT STILL BE PEOPLE IN THE CLASS-ROOM.
UGH... I DON'T WANT TO GO BACK THERE.
WHY IS IT ALWAYS MUTSUMI ...?
OOZE
OOZE
OOZE
CHEEP!
CHEE!
CHEEP?

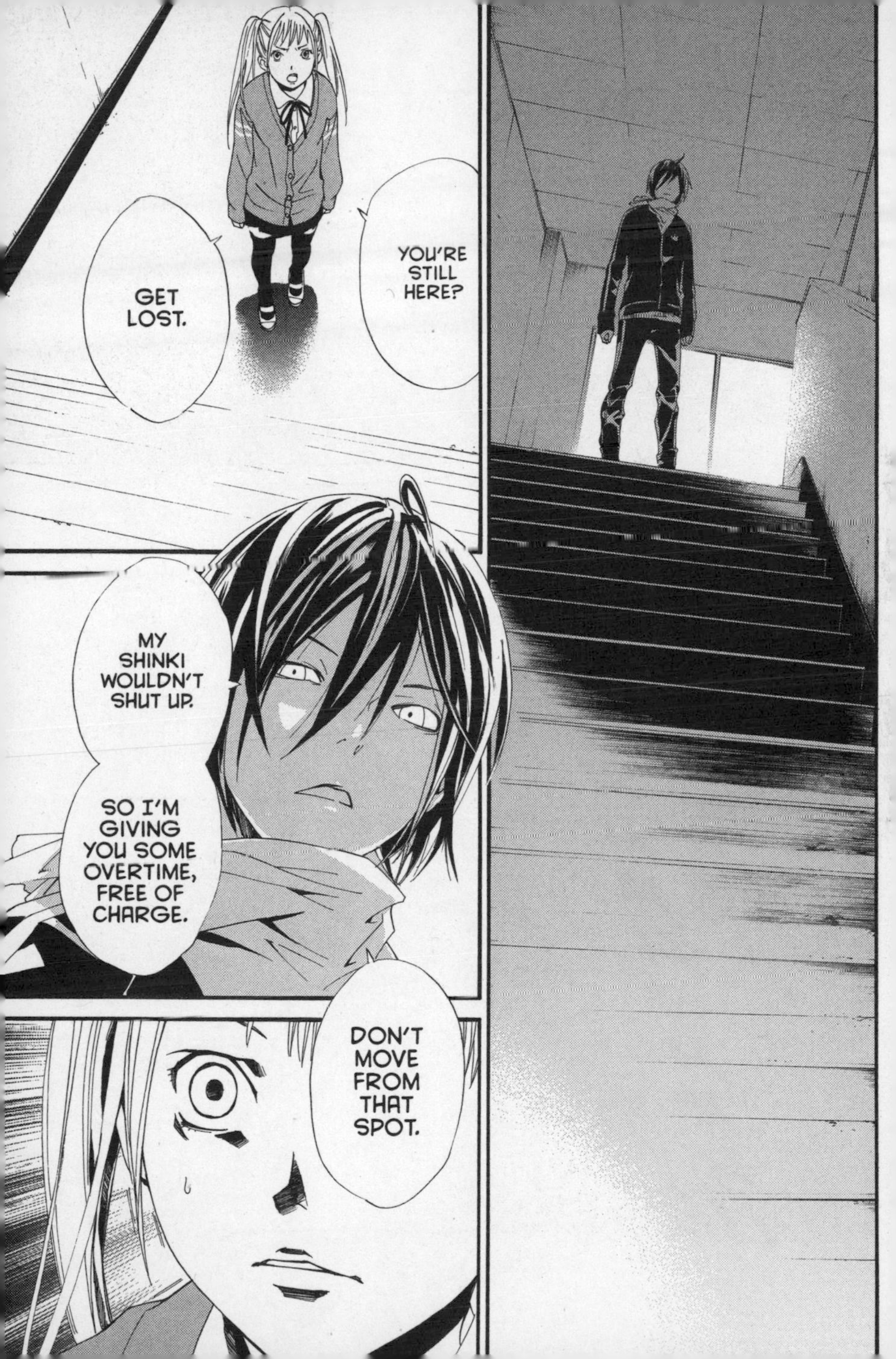
YOU'RE STILL HERE?
GET LOST.
MY SHINKI WOULDN'T SHUT UP.
SO I'M GIVING YOU SOME OVERTIME, FREE OF CHARGE.
DON'T MOVE FROM THAT SPOT.

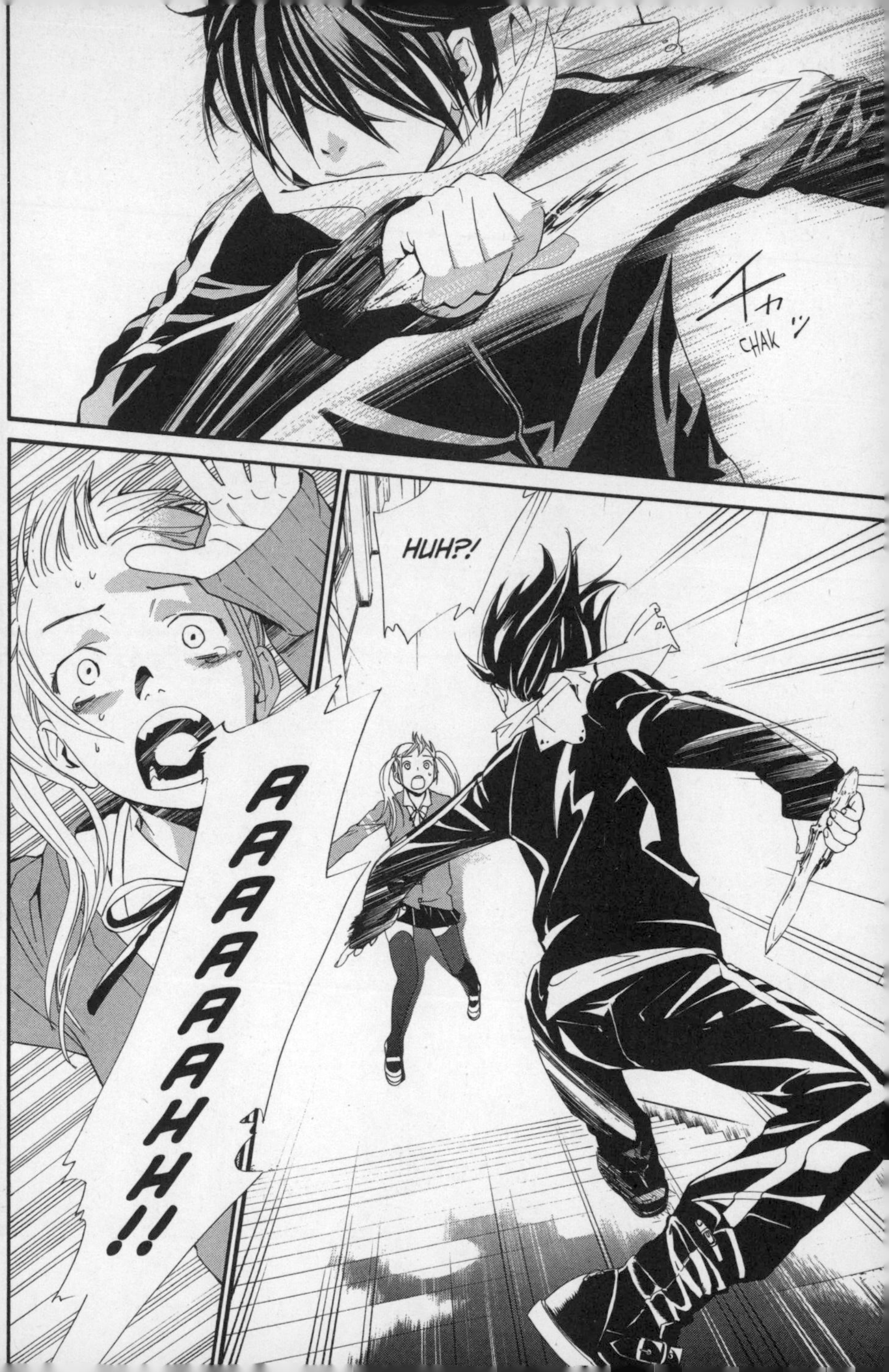

チャッ
CHAK
HUH?!
AAAAAAHH!!

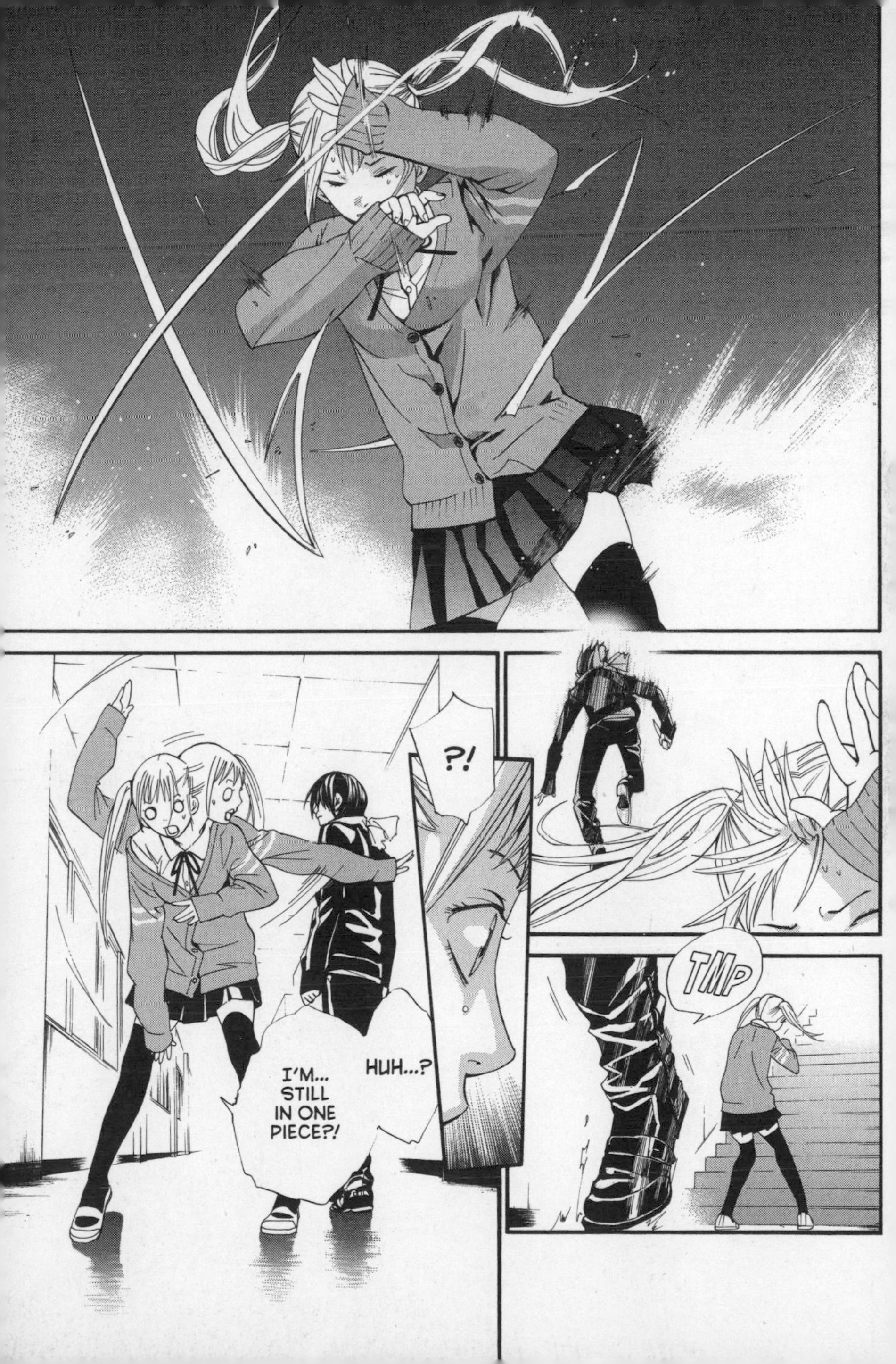
TMP
?!
HUH...?
I'M... STILL IN ONE PIECE?!

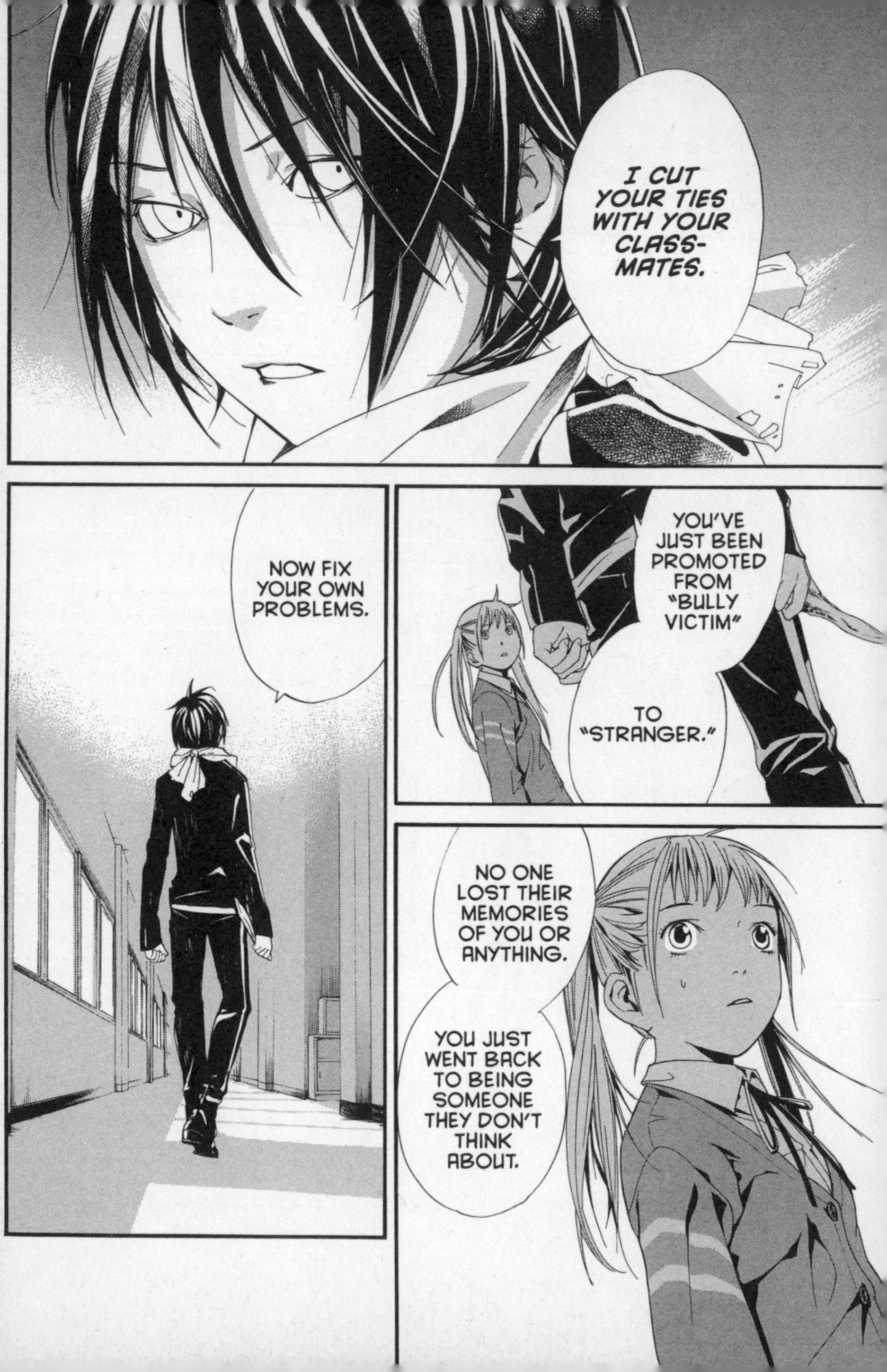
I CUT YOUR TIES WITH YOUR CLASS-MATES.
YOU'VE JUST BEEN PROMOTED FROM "BULLY VICTIM"
TO "STRANGER."
NO ONE LOST THEIR MEMORIES OF YOU OR ANYTHING.
YOU JUST WENT BACK TO BEING SOMEONE THEY DON'T THINK ABOUT.
NOW FIX YOUR OWN PROBLEMS.

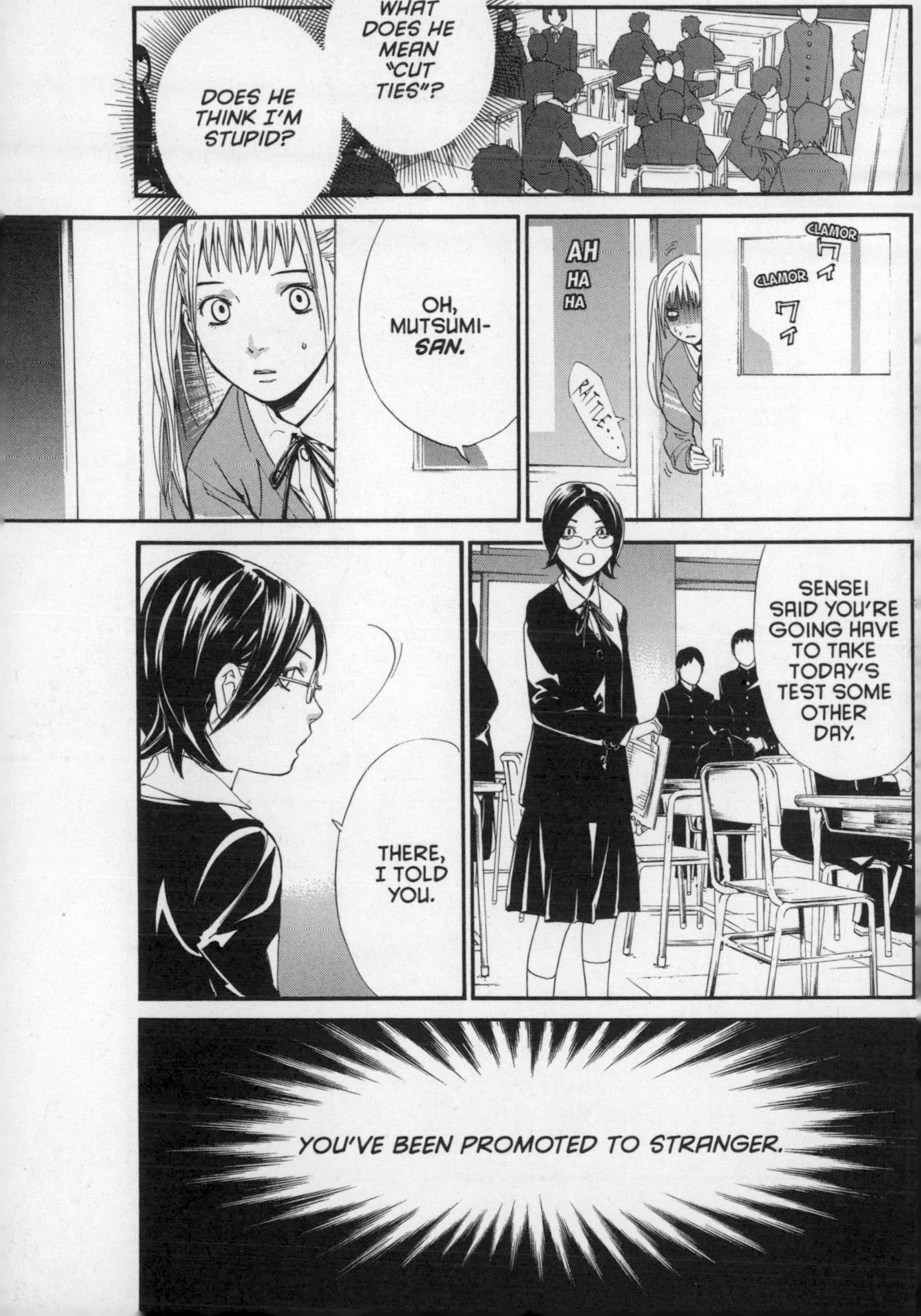
WHAT DOES HE MEAN "CUT TIES"?
DOES HE THINK I'M STUPID?
CLAMOR
CLAMOR
AH HA HA
RATTLE...
OH, MUTSUMI-SAN.
SENSEI SAID YOU'RE GOING HAVE TO TAKE TODAY'S TEST SOME OTHER DAY.
THERE, I TOLD YOU.
YOU'VE BEEN PROMOTED TO STRANGER.

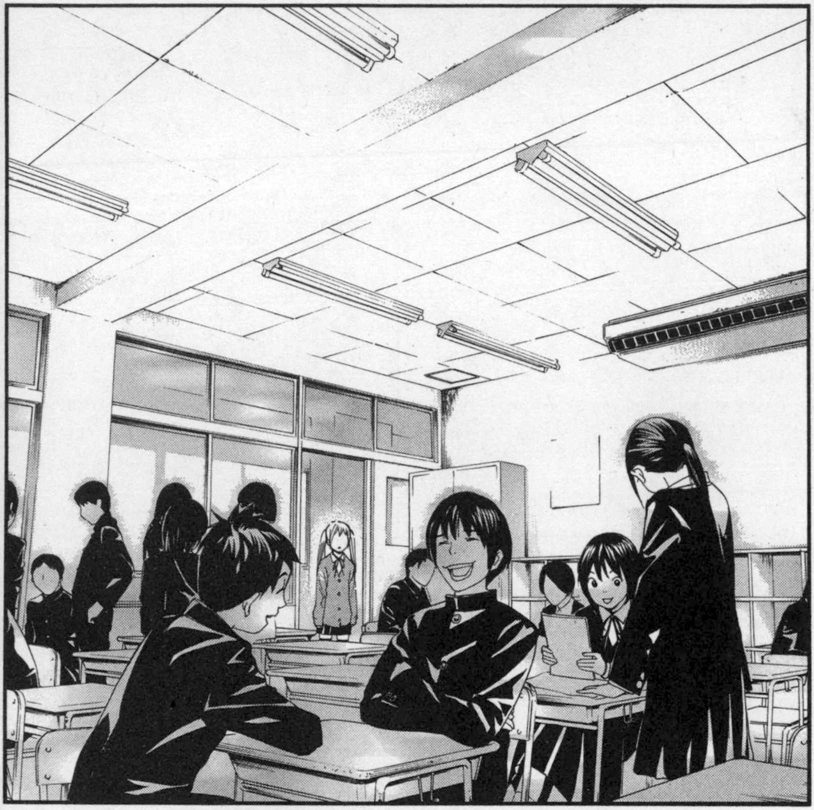
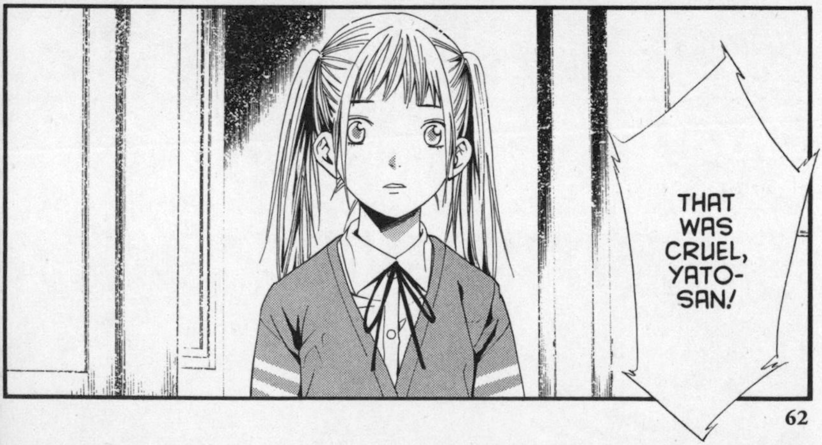
THAT WAS CRUEL, YATO-SAN!

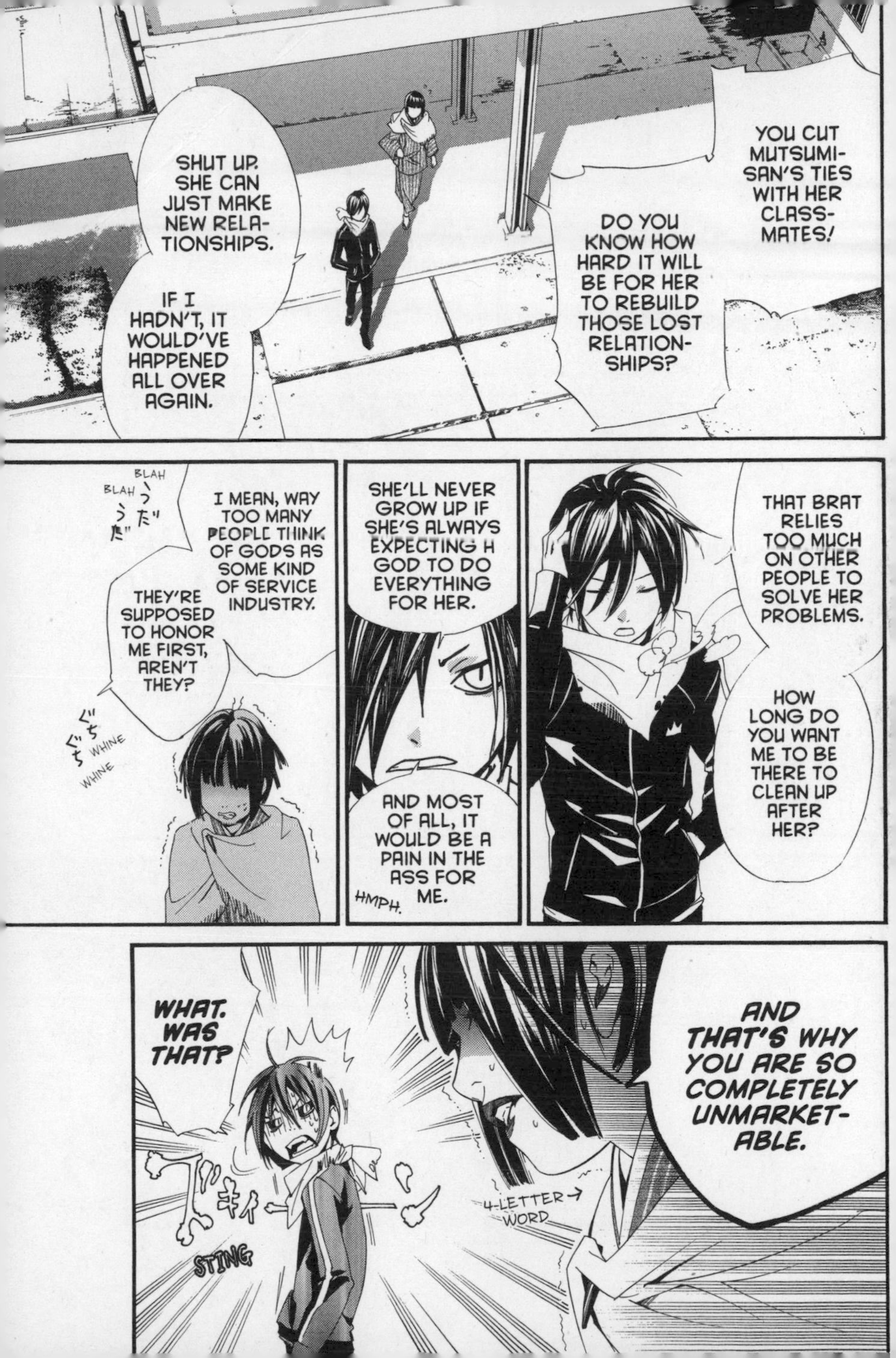
YOU CUT MUTSUMI-SAN'S TIES WITH HER CLASS-MATES!
DO YOU KNOW HOW HARD IT WILL BE FOR HER TO REBUILD THOSE LOST RELATION-SHIPS?
SHUT UP. SHE CAN JUST MAKE NEW RELA-TIONSHIPS.
IF I HADN'T, IT WOULD'VE HAPPENED ALL OVER AGAIN.
THAT BRAT RELIES TOO MUCH ON OTHER PEOPLE TO SOLVE HER PROBLEMS.
HOW LONG DO YOU WANT ME TO BE THERE TO CLEAN UP AFTER HER?
SHE'LL NEVER GROW UP IF SHE'S ALWAYS EXPECTING A GOD TO DO EVERYTHING FOR HER.
AND MOST OF ALL, IT WOULD BE A PAIN IN THE ASS FOR ME.
HMPH.
うだうだ BLAH BLAH
I MEAN, WAY TOO MANY PEOPLE THINK OF GODS AS SOME KIND OF SERVICE INDUSTRY.
THEY'RE SUPPOSED TO HONOR ME FIRST, AREN'T THEY?
ぐちぐち WHINE WHINE
AND THAT'S WHY YOU ARE SO COMPLETELY UNMARKET-ABLE.
4-LETTER WORD
WHAT. WAS THAT?
STING

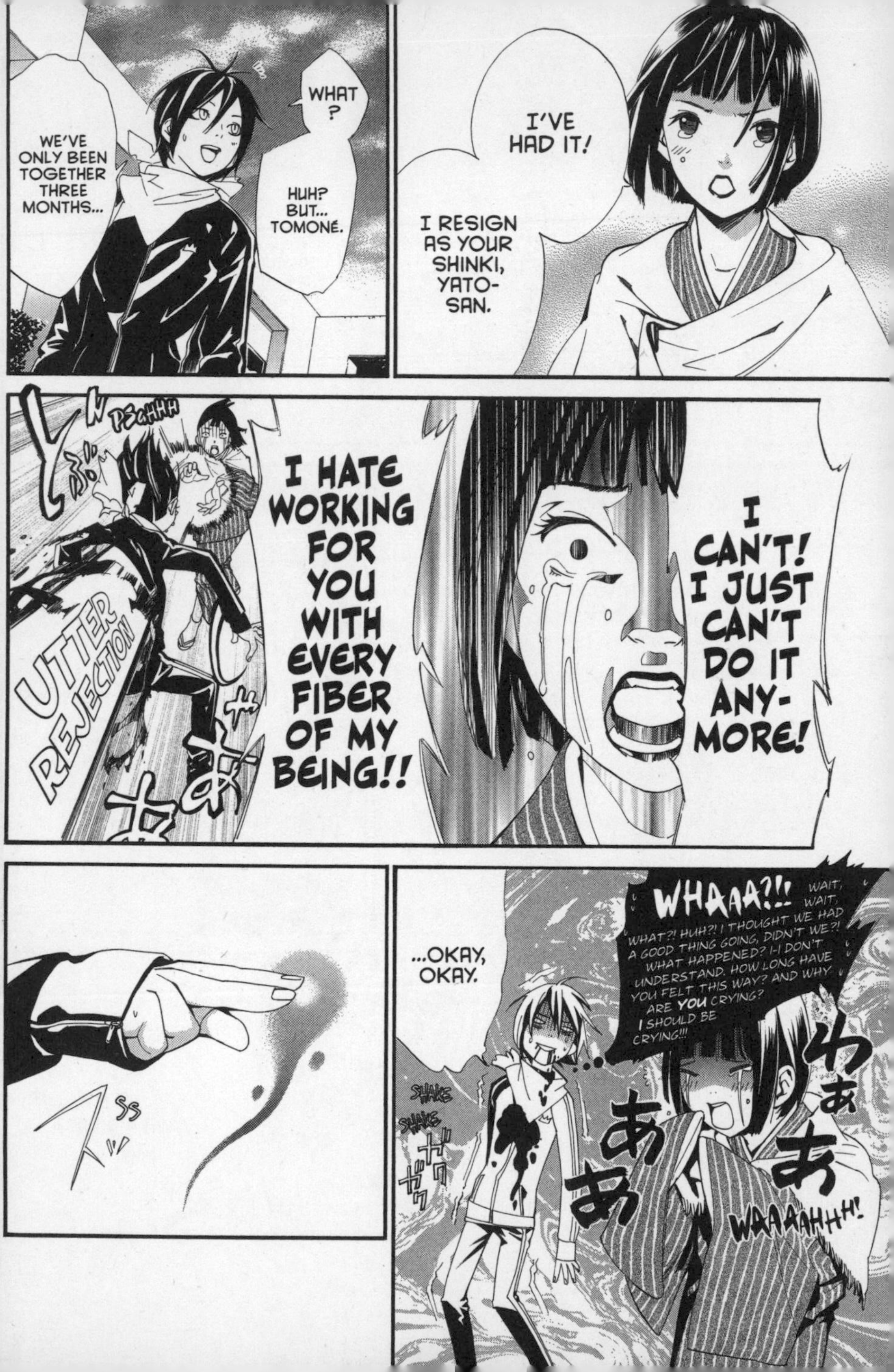
I'VE HAD IT!
I RESIGN AS YOUR SHINKI, YATO-SAN.
WHAT?
HUH? BUT... TOMONÉ.
WE'VE ONLY BEEN TOGETHER THREE MONTHS...
I CAN'T! I JUST CAN'T DO IT ANY-MORE!
I HATE WORKING FOR YOU WITH EVERY FIBER OF MY BEING!!
PEAHHH
UTTER REJECTION
WHAAA?!! WAIT, WAIT, WHAT?! HUH?! I THOUGHT WE HAD A GOOD THING GOING, DIDN'T WE?! WHAT HAPPENED? I-I DON'T UNDERSTAND. HOW LONG HAVE YOU FELT THIS WAY? AND WHY ARE YOU CRYING? I SHOULD BE CRYING!!!
...OKAY, OKAY.
SHAKE
SHAKE
WAAAAHHH!
SS

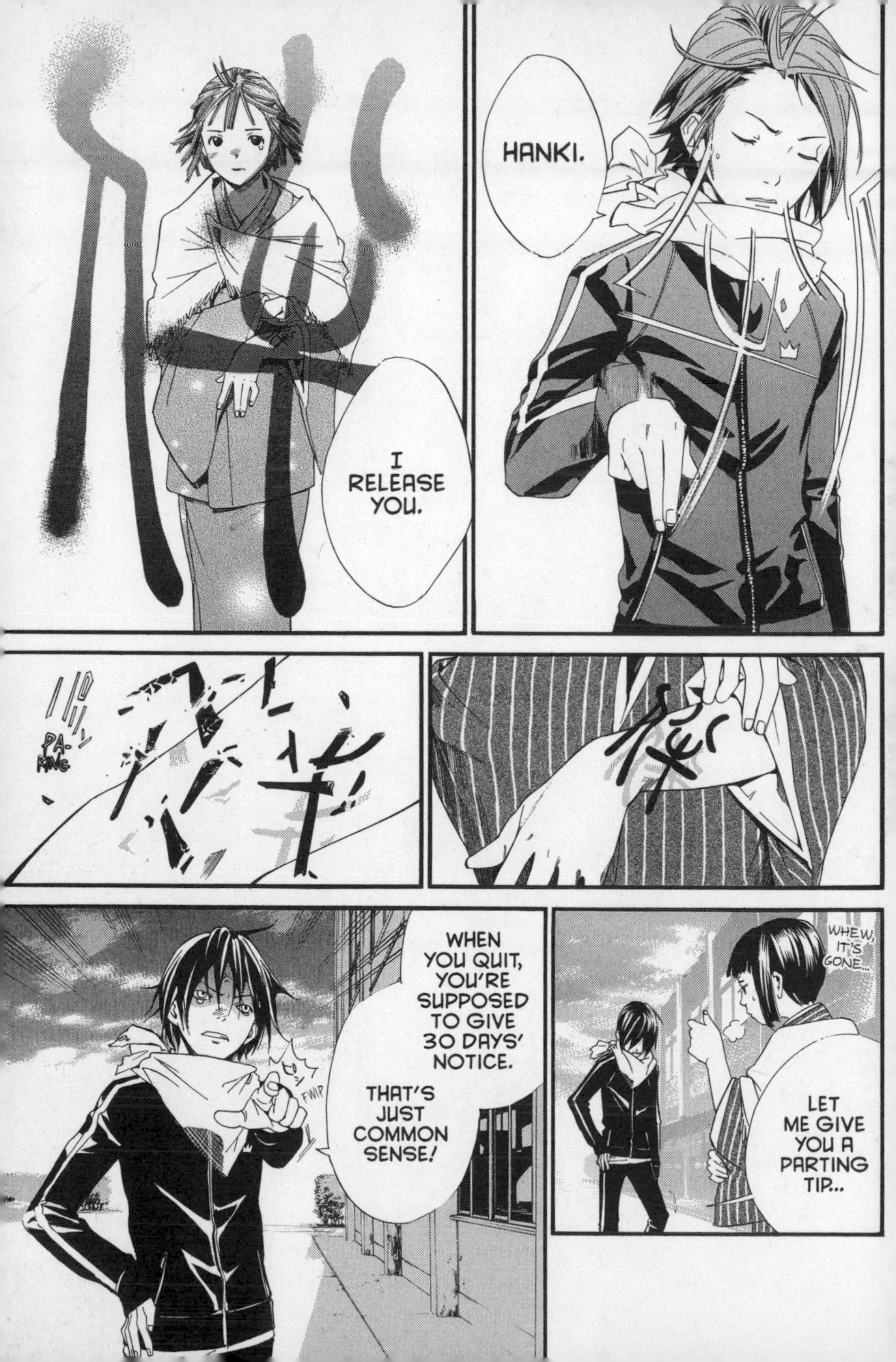
HANKI.
I RELEASE YOU.
PA-KING
WHEW, IT'S GONE...
LET ME GIVE YOU A PARTING TIP...
WHEN YOU QUIT, YOU'RE SUPPOSED TO GIVE 30 DAYS' NOTICE.
THAT'S JUST COMMON SENSE!
FWIP

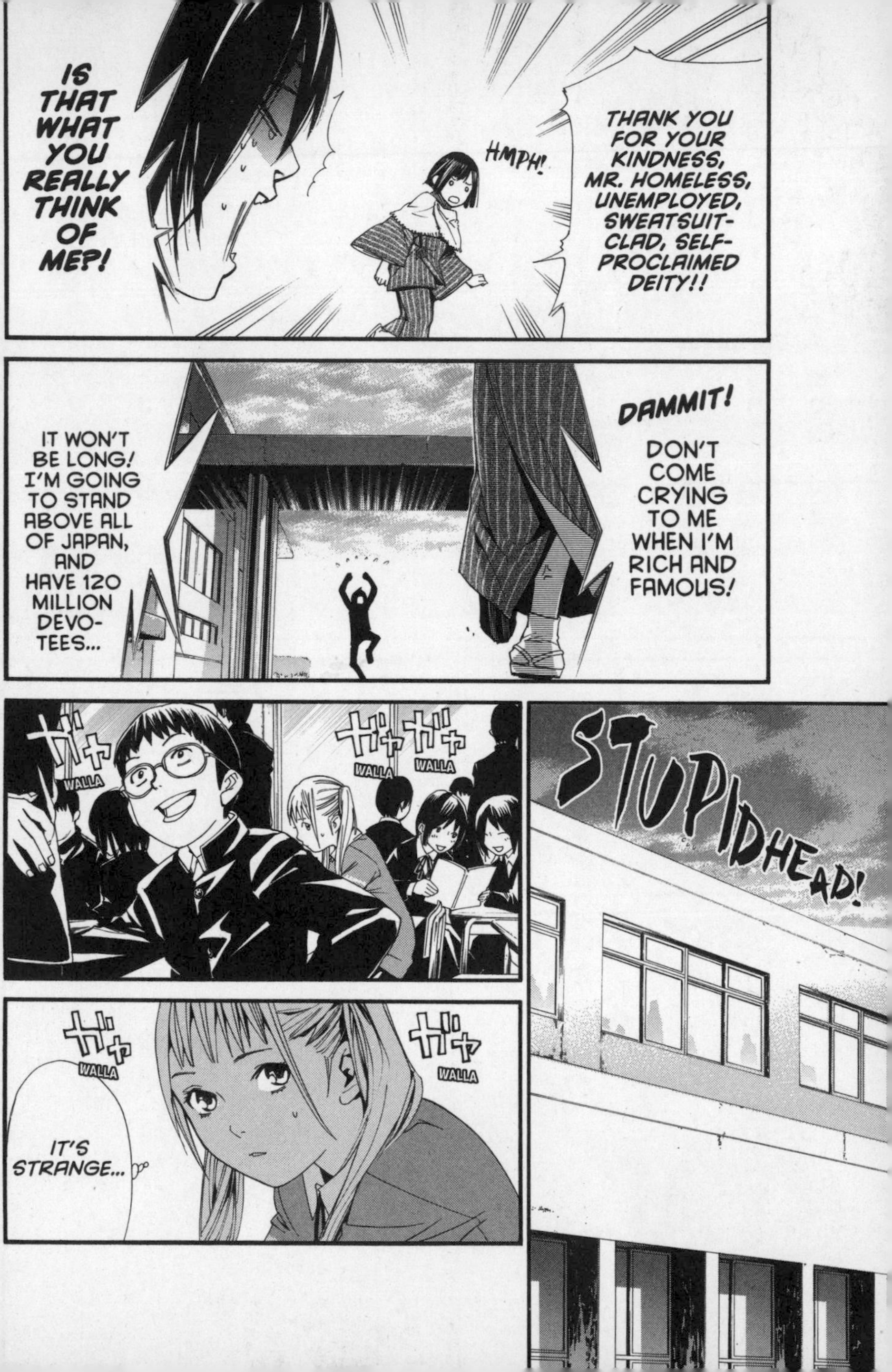
THANK YOU FOR YOUR KINDNESS, MR. HOMELESS, UNEMPLOYED, SWEATSUIT-CLAD, SELF-PROCLAIMED DEITY!!
HMPH!
IS THAT WHAT YOU REALLY THINK OF ME?!
DAMMIT!
DON'T COME CRYING TO ME WHEN I'M RICH AND FAMOUS!
IT WON'T BE LONG! I'M GOING TO STAND ABOVE ALL OF JAPAN, AND HAVE 120 MILLION DEVOTEES...
STUPIDHEAD!
ガヤガヤ
WALLA WALLA
ガヤ
WALLA
ガヤ
WALLA
ガヤ
WALLA
IT'S STRANGE...

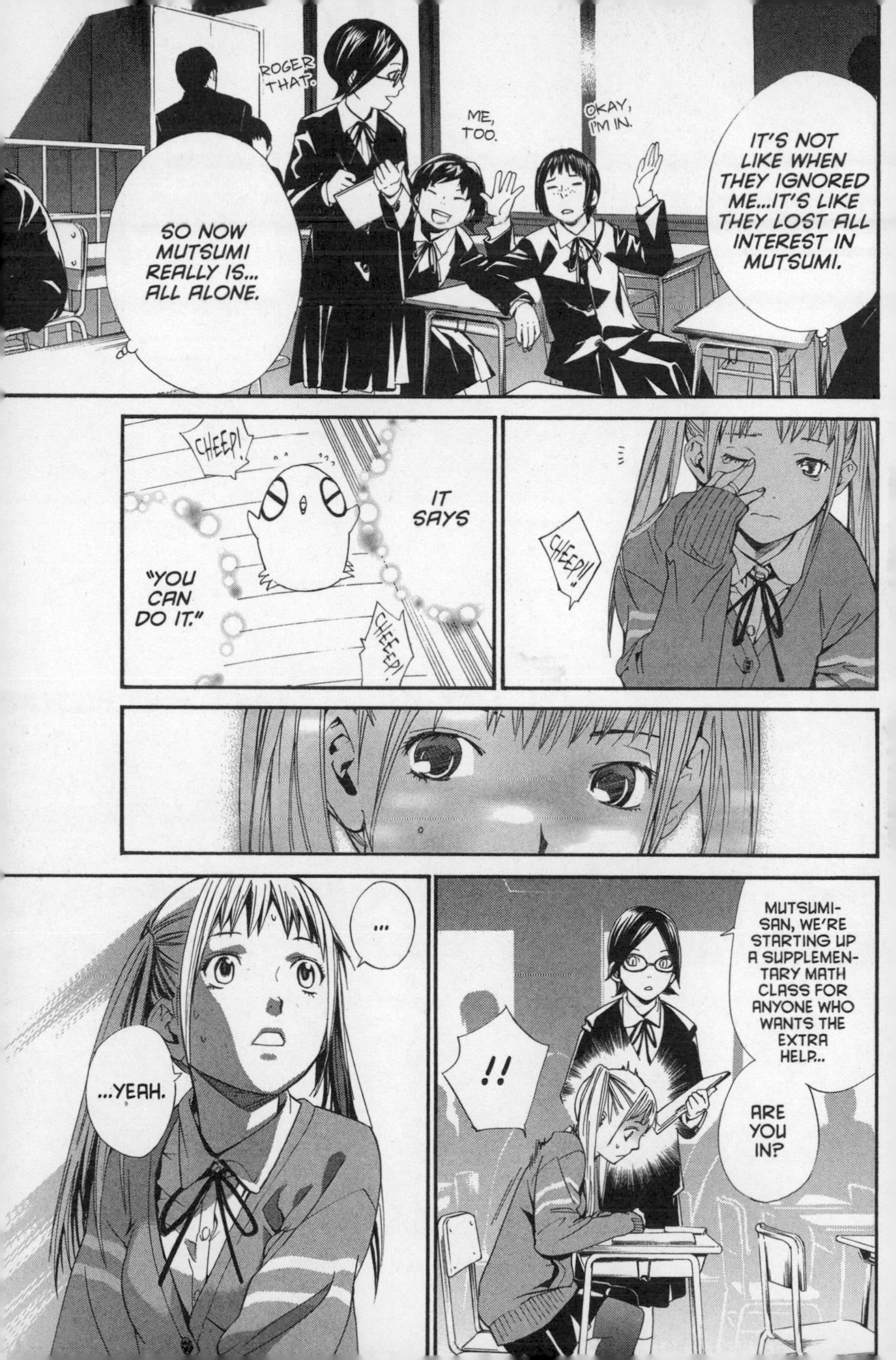
IT'S NOT LIKE WHEN THEY IGNORED ME...IT'S LIKE THEY LOST ALL INTEREST IN MUTSUMI.
OKAY, I'M IN.
ME, TOO.
ROGER THAT.
SO NOW MUTSUMI REALLY IS... ALL ALONE.
CHEEP!!
CHEEP!
IT SAYS
"YOU CAN DO IT."
CHEEEP!
MUTSUMI-SAN, WE'RE STARTING UP A SUPPLEMENTARY MATH CLASS FOR ANYONE WHO WANTS THE EXTRA HELP...
ARE YOU IN?
!!
...
...YEAH.

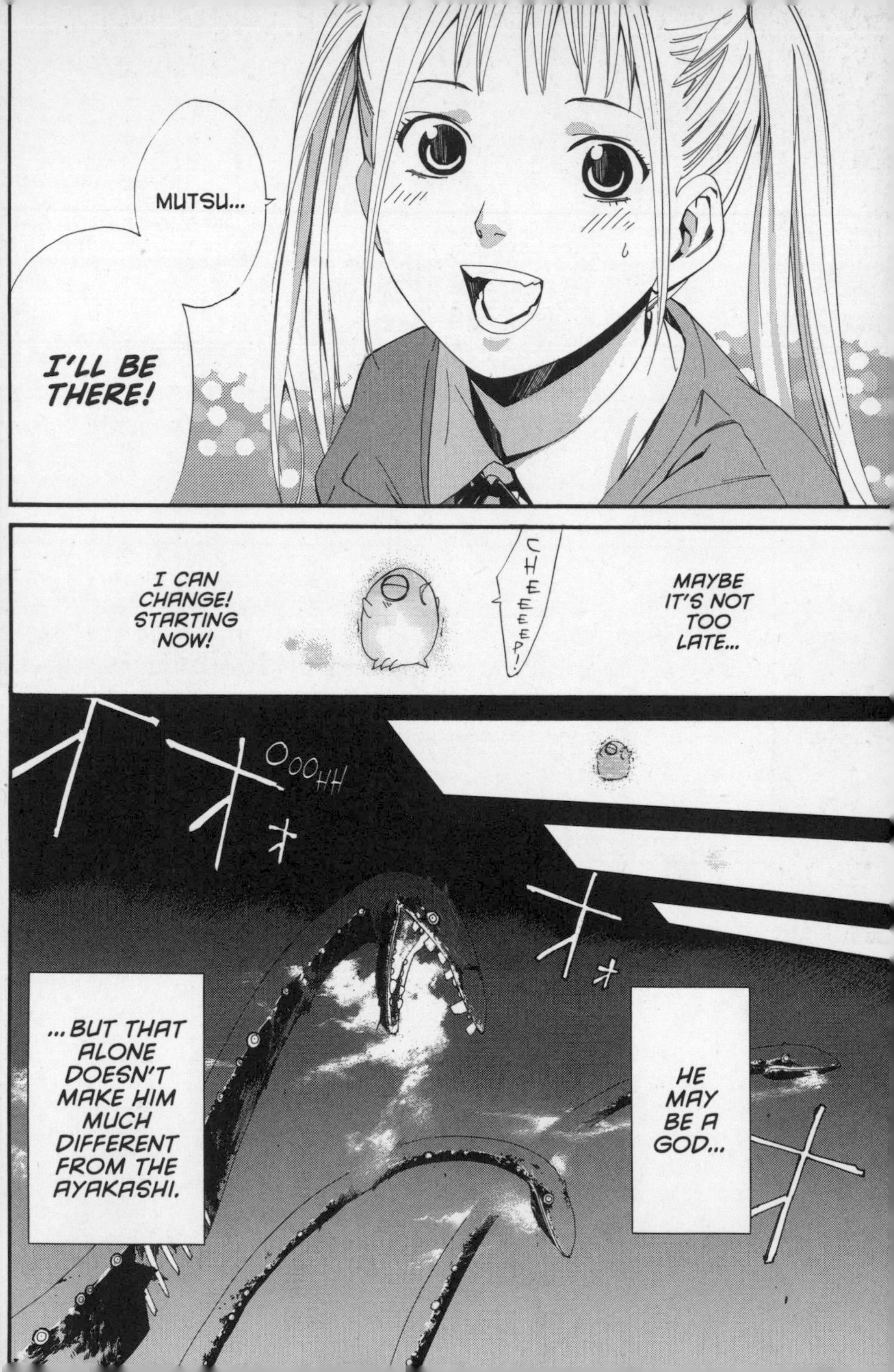
MUTSU...
I'LL BE THERE!
MAYBE IT'S NOT TOO LATE...
CHEEEEP!
I CAN CHANGE! STARTING NOW!
OOOHH
HE MAY BE A GOD...
...BUT THAT ALONE DOESN'T MAKE HIM MUCH DIFFERENT FROM THE AYAKASHI.

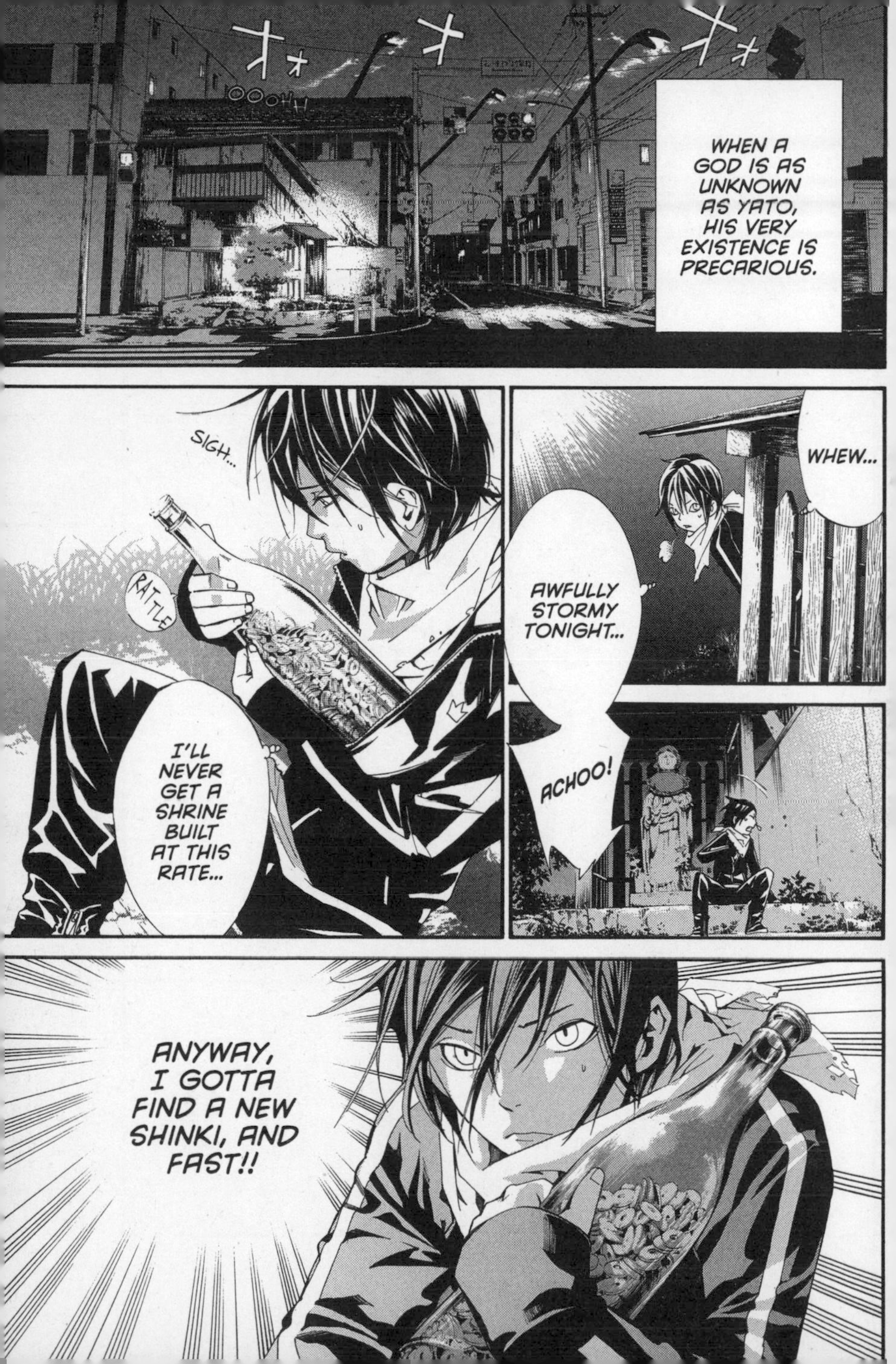
WHEN A GOD IS AS UNKNOWN AS YATO, HIS VERY EXISTENCE IS PRECARIOUS.
OOOHH
WHEW...
AWFULLY STORMY TONIGHT...
ACHOO!
SIGH...
RATTLE
I'LL NEVER GET A SHRINE BUILT AT THIS RATE...
ANYWAY, I GOTTA FIND A NEW SHINKI, AND FAST!!

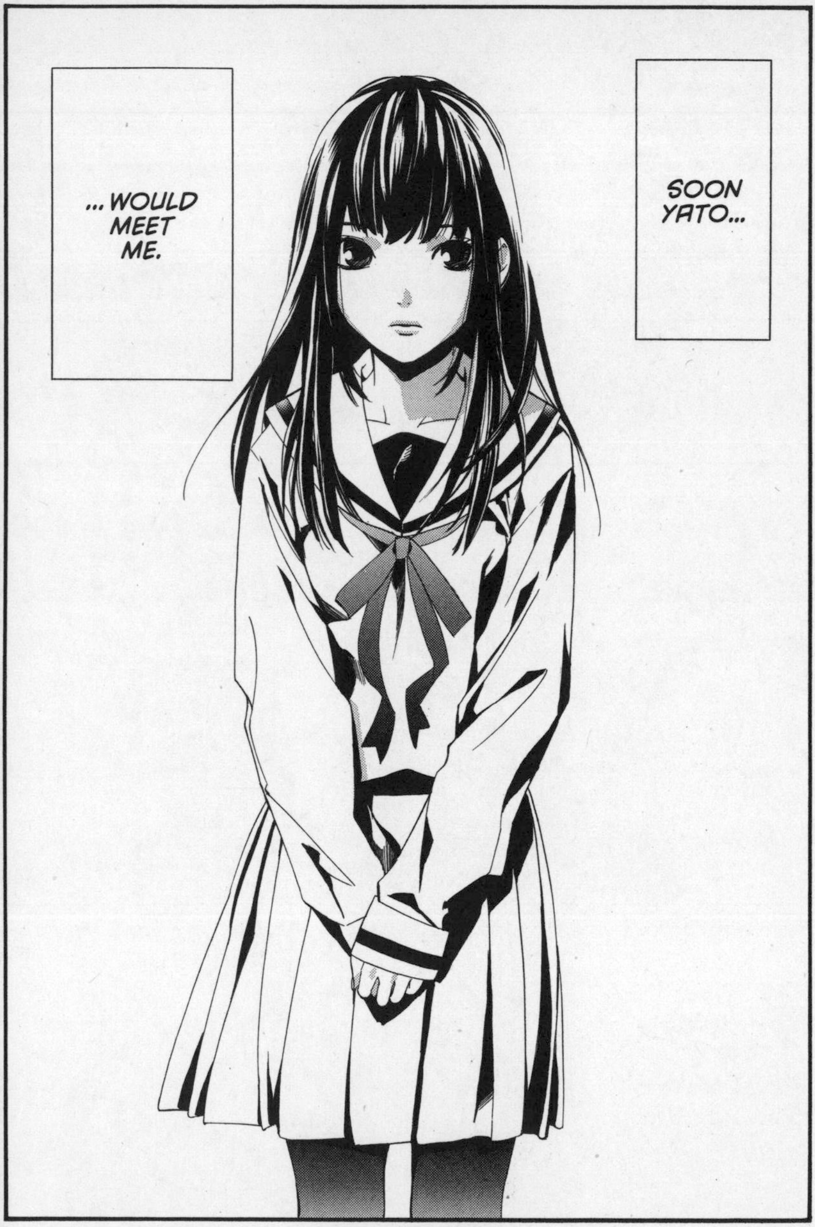
SOON YATO...
...WOULD MEET ME.

CHAPTER 1 / END

野

皂

神

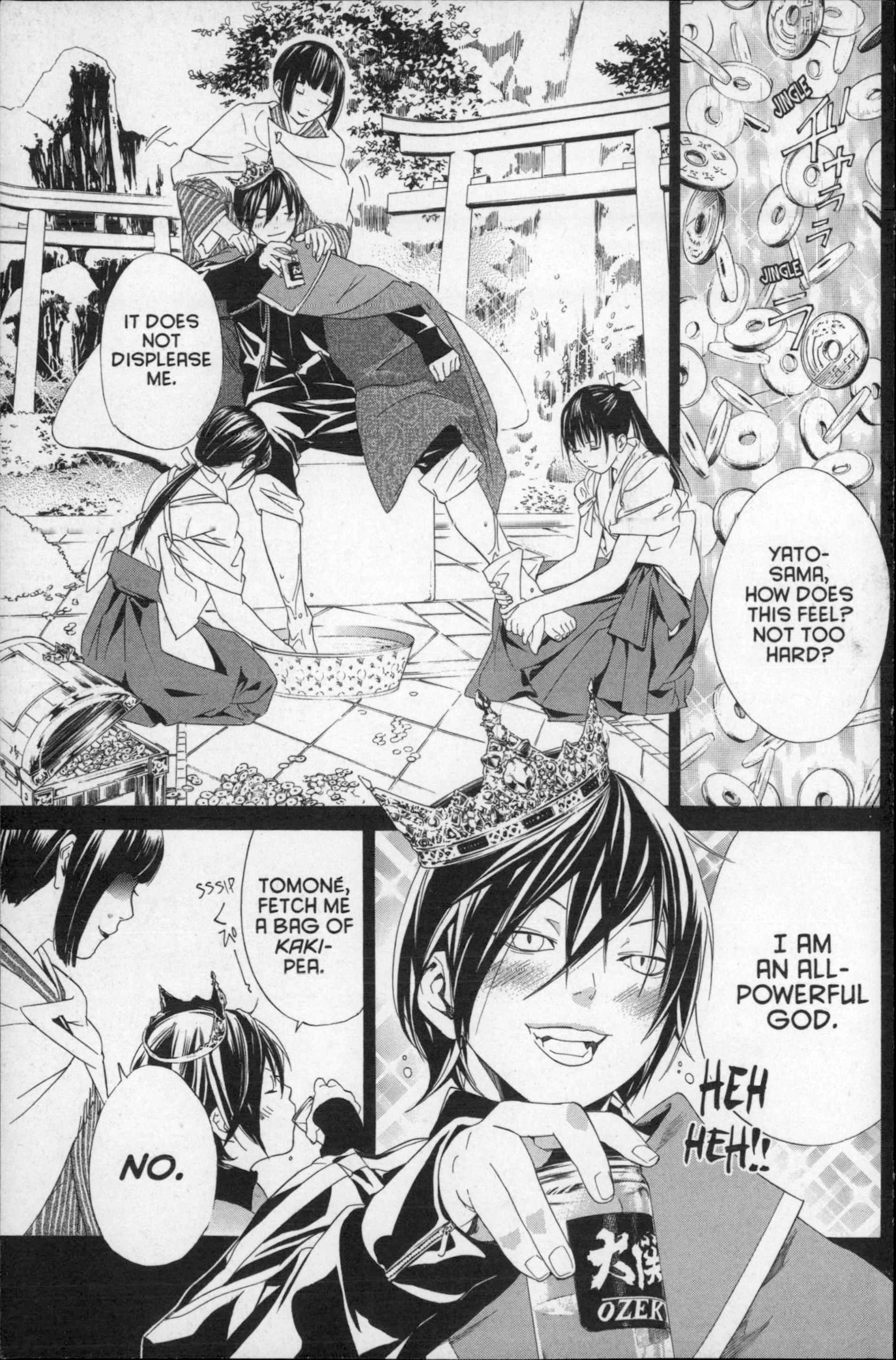
JINGLE
JINGLE
YATO-SAMA, HOW DOES THIS FEEL? NOT TOO HARD?
IT DOES NOT DISPLEASE ME.
I AM AN ALL-POWERFUL GOD.
HEH HEH!!
TOMONÉ, FETCH ME A BAG OF *KAKI-PEA*.
SSSIP
NO.

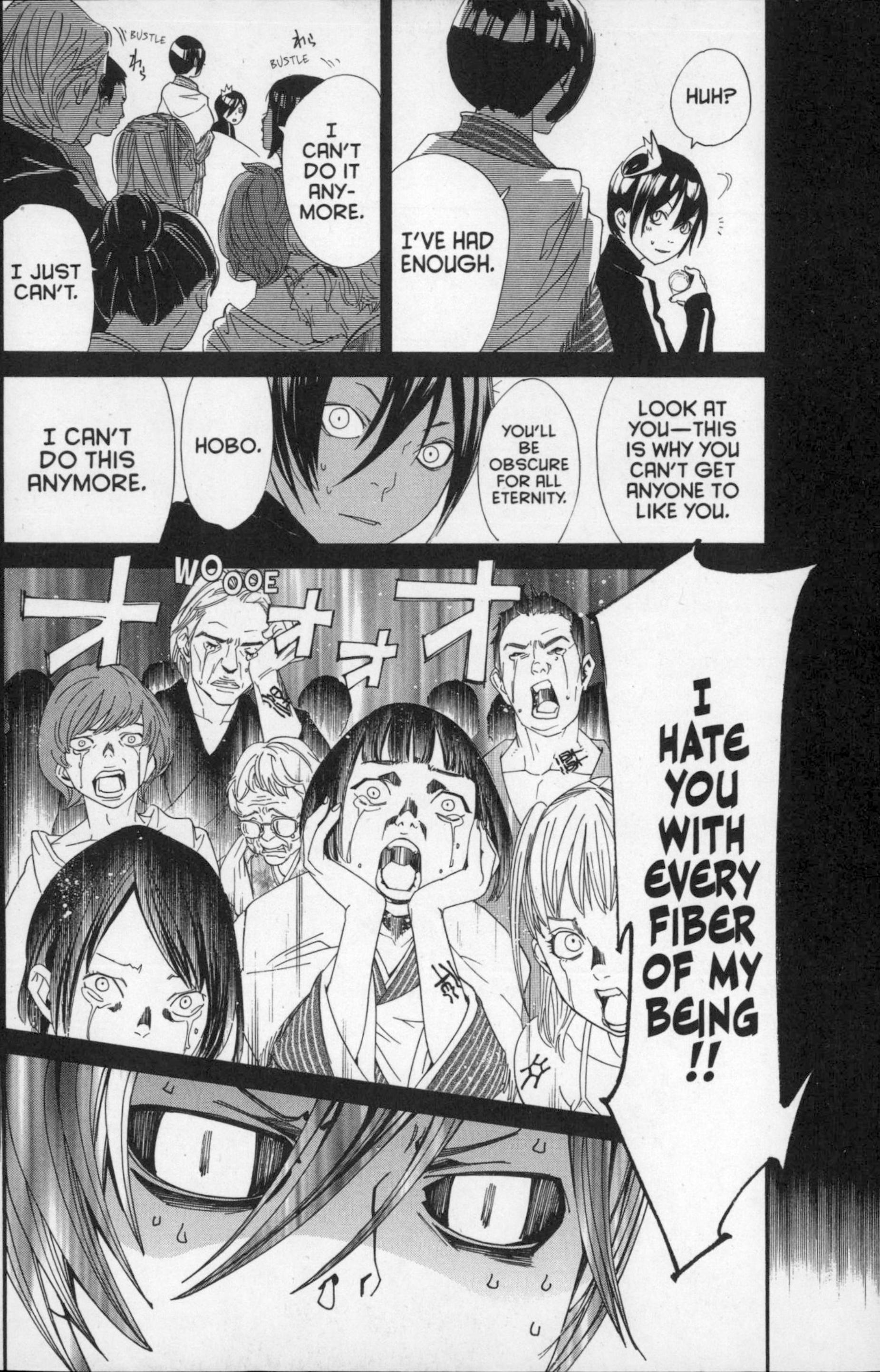
HUH?
I'VE HAD ENOUGH.
BUSTLE
BUSTLE
I CAN'T DO IT ANYMORE.
I JUST CAN'T.
LOOK AT YOU—THIS IS WHY YOU CAN'T GET ANYONE TO LIKE YOU.
YOU'LL BE OBSCURE FOR ALL ETERNITY.
HOBO.
I CAN'T DO THIS ANYMORE.
I HATE YOU WITH EVERY FIBER OF MY BEING!!
WOOOE

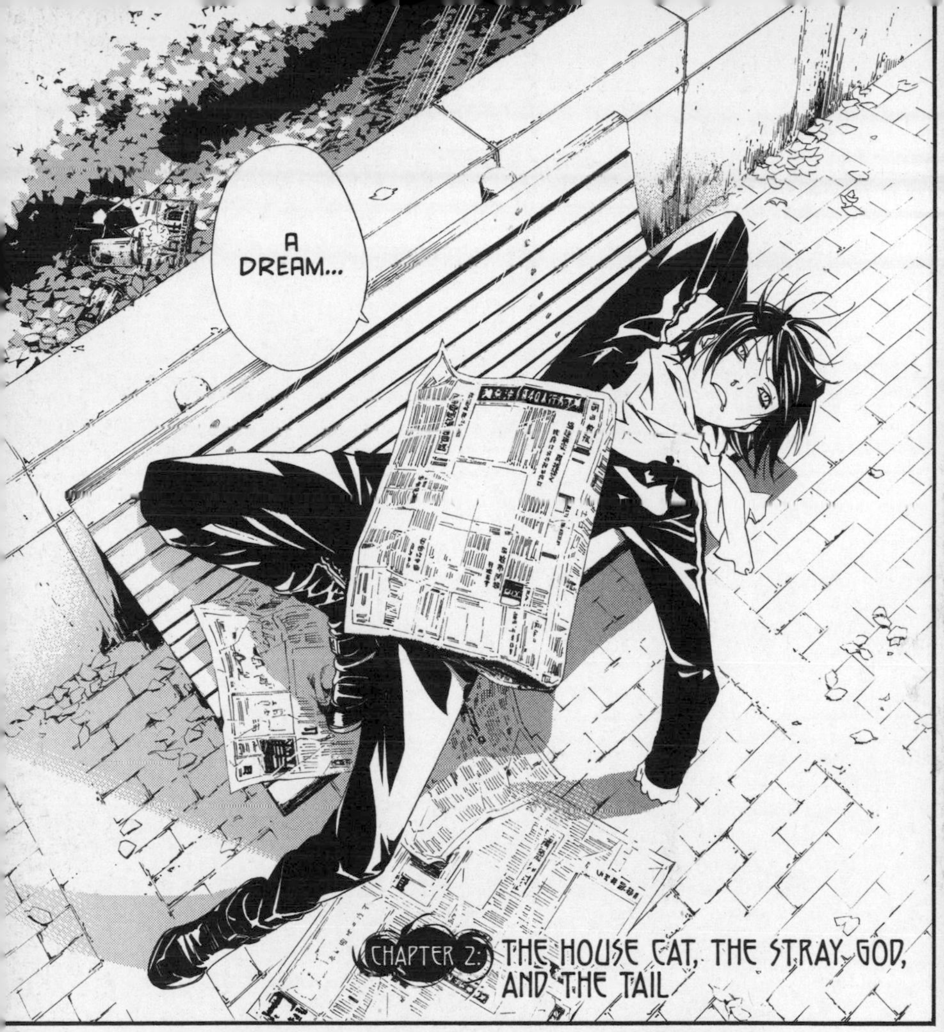
A DREAM...
CHAPTER 2: THE HOUSE CAT, THE STRAY GOD, AND THE TAIL

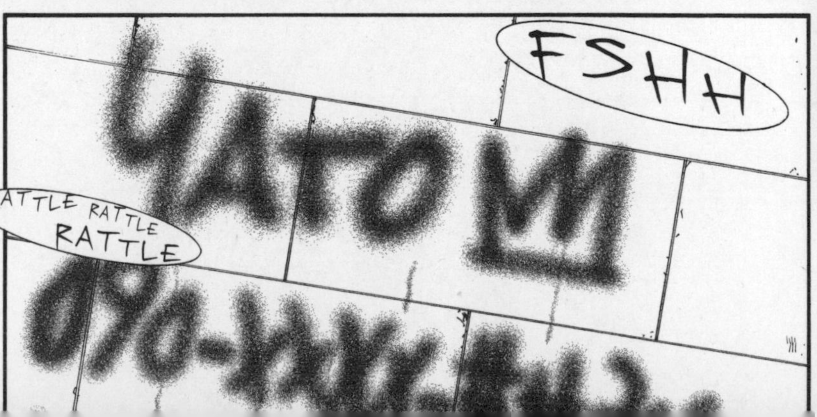
FSHH
RATTLE RATTLE RATTLE

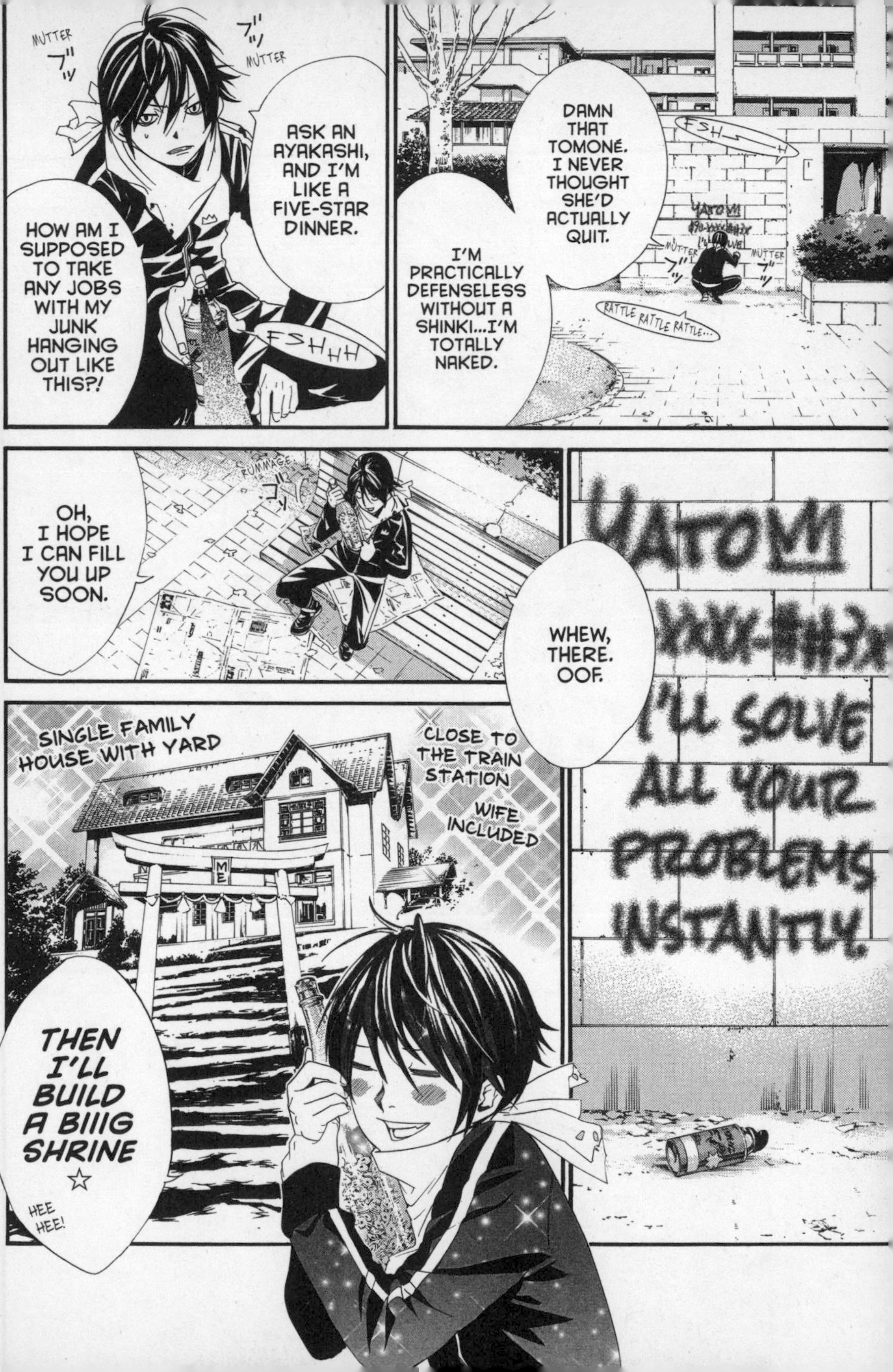
FSH
DAMN THAT TOMONÉ. I NEVER THOUGHT SHE'D ACTUALLY QUIT.
MUTTER
MUTTER
I'M PRACTICALLY DEFENSELESS WITHOUT A SHINKI...I'M TOTALLY NAKED.
RATTLE RATTLE RATTLE...
MUTTER
MUTTER
ASK AN AYAKASHI, AND I'M LIKE A FIVE-STAR DINNER.
HOW AM I SUPPOSED TO TAKE ANY JOBS WITH MY JUNK HANGING OUT LIKE THIS?!
FSHHH
YATO
I'LL SOLVE ALL YOUR PROBLEMS INSTANTLY.
WHEW, THERE. OOF.
RUMMAGE
OH, I HOPE I CAN FILL YOU UP SOON.
CLOSE TO THE TRAIN STATION
WIFE INCLUDED
SINGLE FAMILY HOUSE WITH YARD
ME
THEN I'LL BUILD A BIIIG SHRINE ☆
HEE HEE!

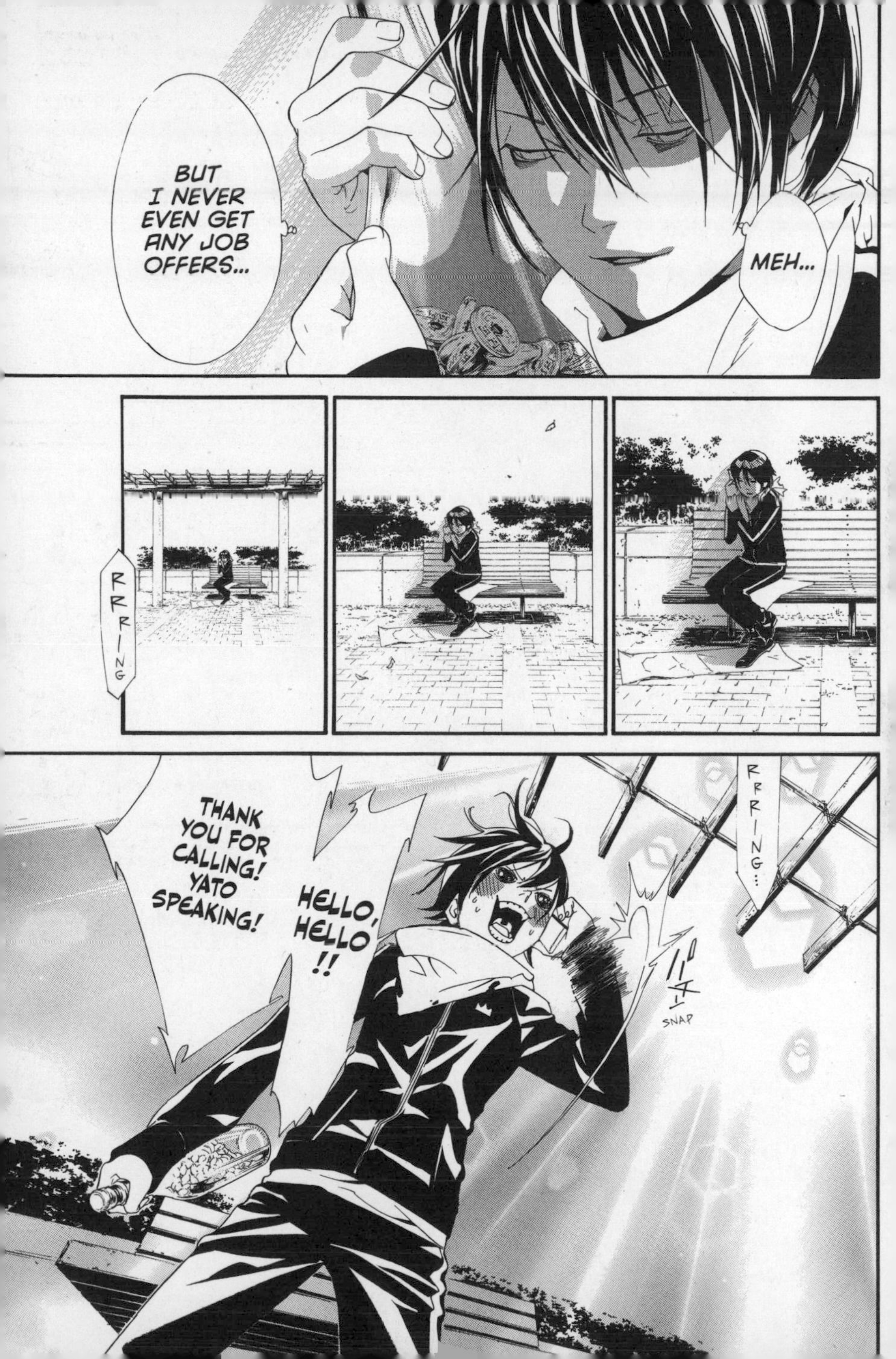
MEH...
BUT I NEVER EVEN GET ANY JOB OFFERS...
RRRING
RRRING...
SNAP
HELLO, HELLO!!
THANK YOU FOR CALLING! YATO SPEAKING!

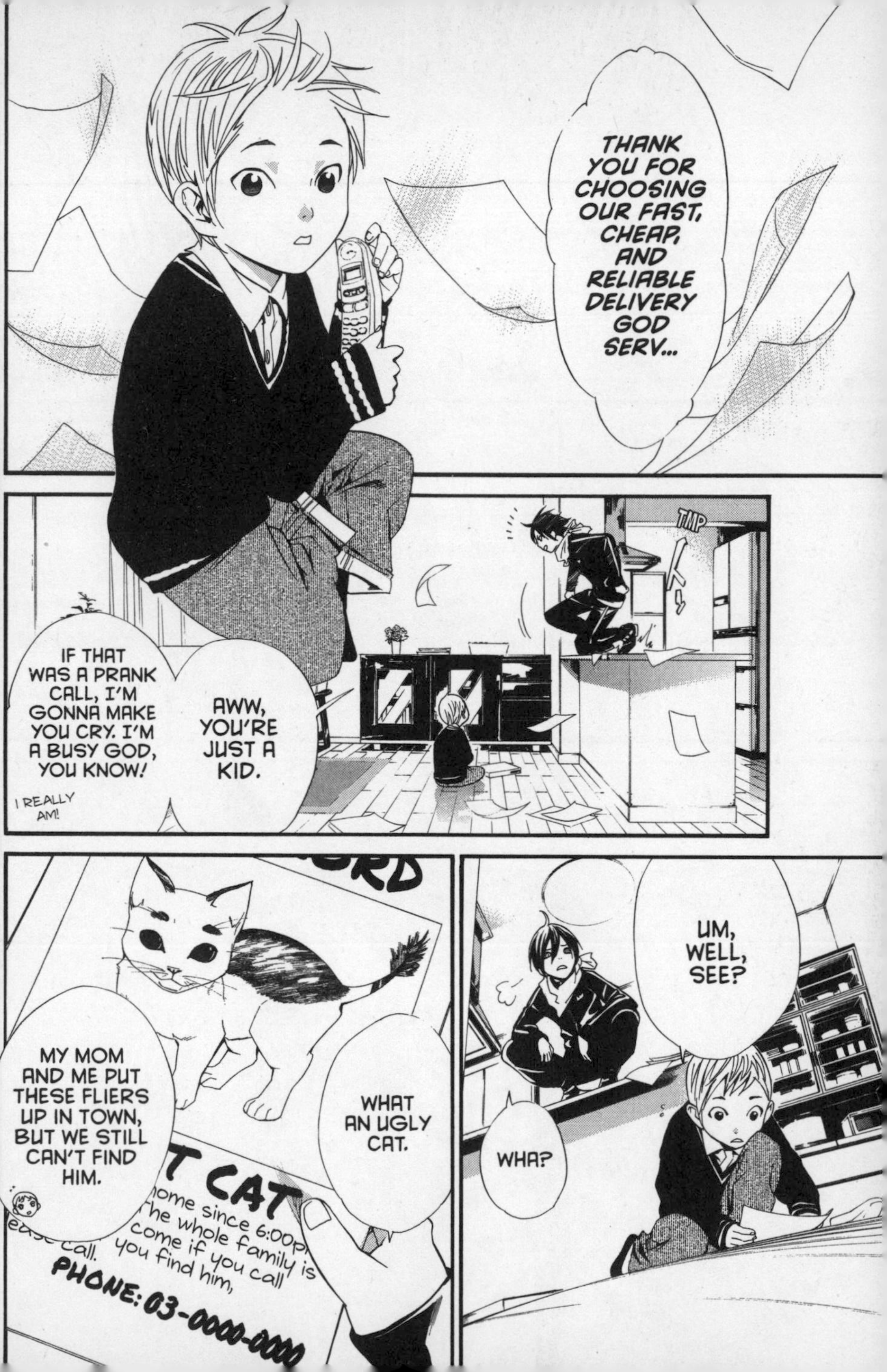
THANK YOU FOR CHOOSING OUR FAST, CHEAP, AND RELIABLE DELIVERY GOD SERV...
TMP
AWW, YOU'RE JUST A KID.
IF THAT WAS A PRANK CALL, I'M GONNA MAKE YOU CRY. I'M A BUSY GOD, YOU KNOW!
I REALLY AM!
UM, WELL, SEE?
WHA?
WHAT AN UGLY CAT.
MY MOM AND ME PUT THESE FLIERS UP IN TOWN, BUT WE STILL CAN'T FIND HIM.
CAT
PHONE: 03-0000-0000

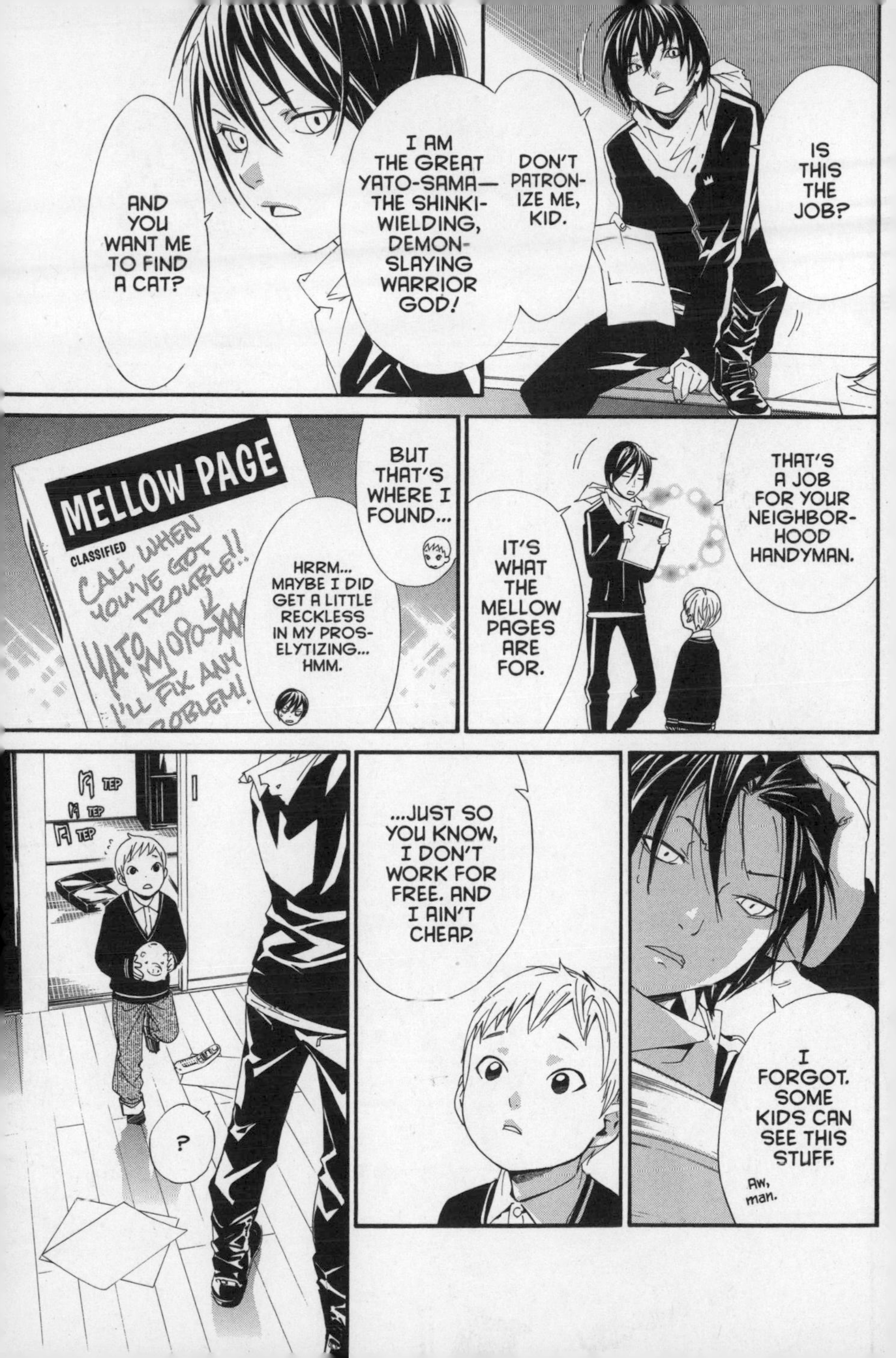
IS THIS THE JOB?
DON'T PATRON-IZE ME, KID.
I AM THE GREAT YATO-SAMA— THE SHINKI-WIELDING, DEMON-SLAYING WARRIOR GOD!
AND YOU WANT ME TO FIND A CAT?
THAT'S A JOB FOR YOUR NEIGHBOR-HOOD HANDYMAN.
IT'S WHAT THE MELLOW PAGES ARE FOR.
BUT THAT'S WHERE I FOUND...
HRRM... MAYBE I DID GET A LITTLE RECKLESS IN MY PROS-ELYTIZING... HMM.
MELLOW PAGE
CLASSIFIED
CALL WHEN YOU'VE GOT TROUBLE!!
YATO
I'LL FIX ANY
I FORGOT. SOME KIDS CAN SEE THIS STUFF.
Aw, man.
...JUST SO YOU KNOW, I DON'T WORK FOR FREE. AND I AIN'T CHEAP.
TEP
TEP
TEP
?

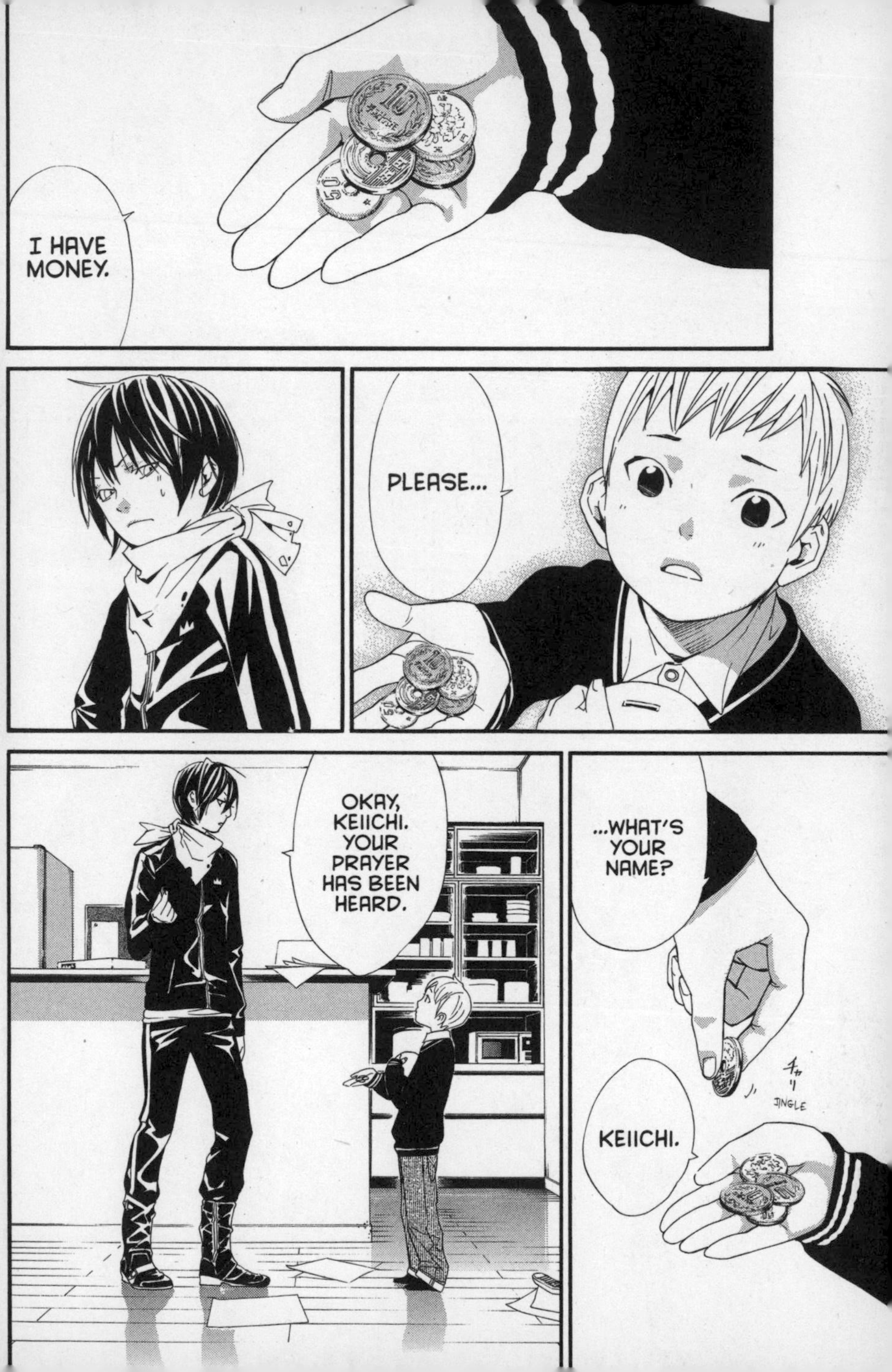
I HAVE MONEY.
PLEASE...
...WHAT'S YOUR NAME?
KEIICHI.
JINGLE
OKAY, KEIICHI. YOUR PRAYER HAS BEEN HEARD.

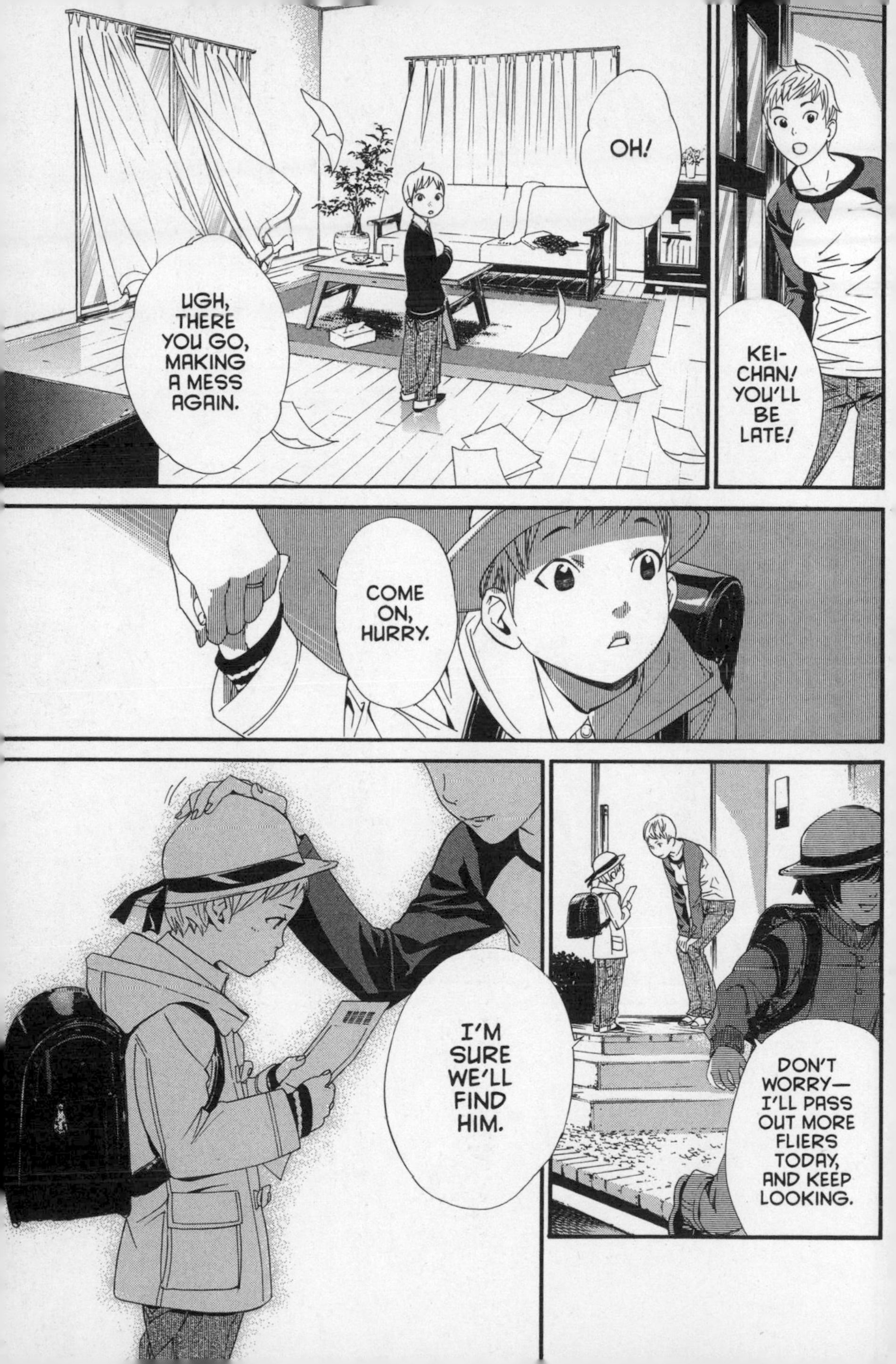
KEI-CHAN! YOU'LL BE LATE!
OH!
UGH, THERE YOU GO, MAKING A MESS AGAIN.
COME ON, HURRY.
DON'T WORRY—I'LL PASS OUT MORE FLIERS TODAY, AND KEEP LOOKING.
I'M SURE WE'LL FIND HIM.

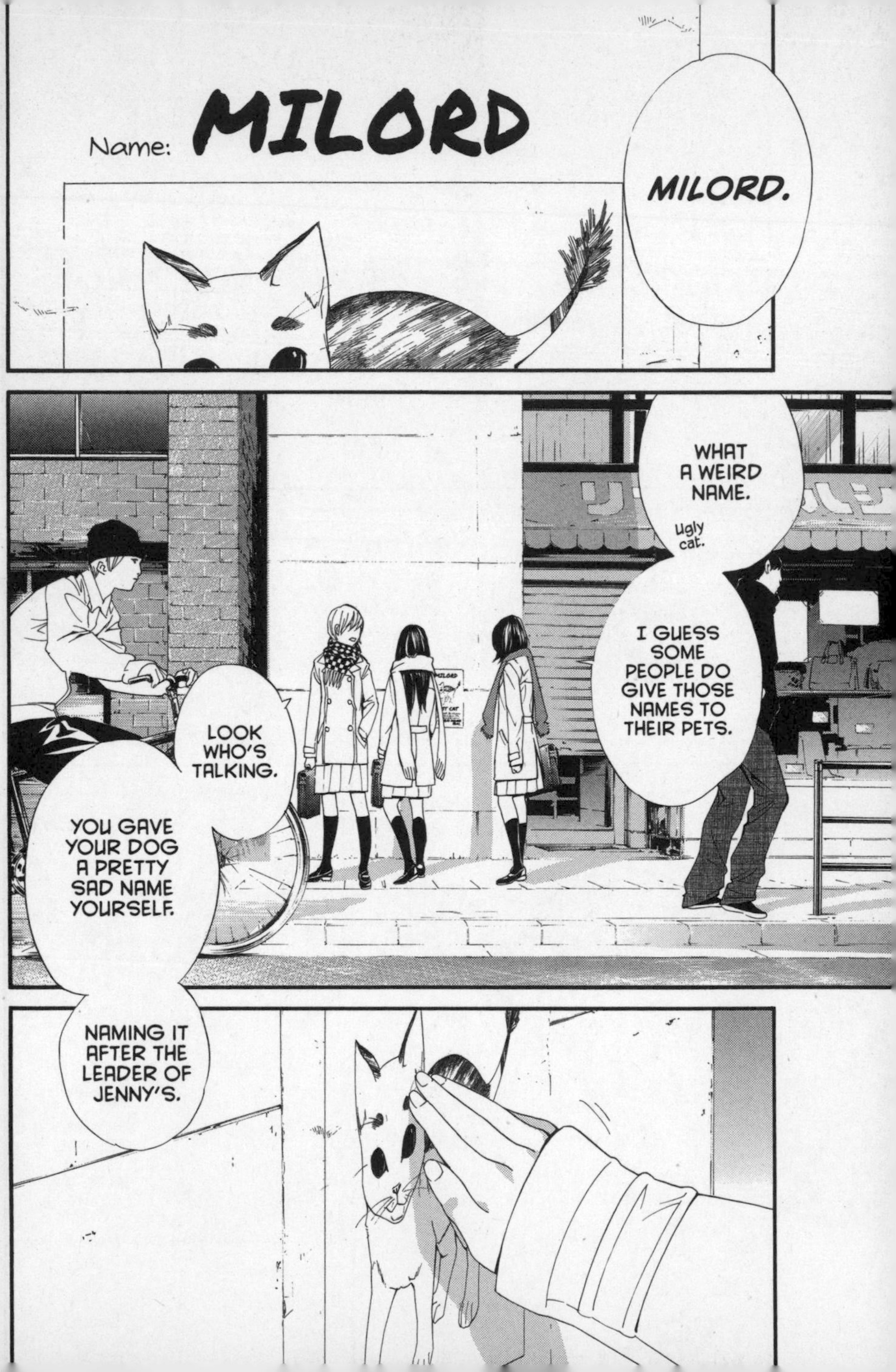
MILORD.
Name: MILORD
WHAT A WEIRD NAME.
Ugly cat.
I GUESS SOME PEOPLE DO GIVE THOSE NAMES TO THEIR PETS.
LOOK WHO'S TALKING.
YOU GAVE YOUR DOG A PRETTY SAD NAME YOURSELF.
NAMING IT AFTER THE LEADER OF JENNY'S.

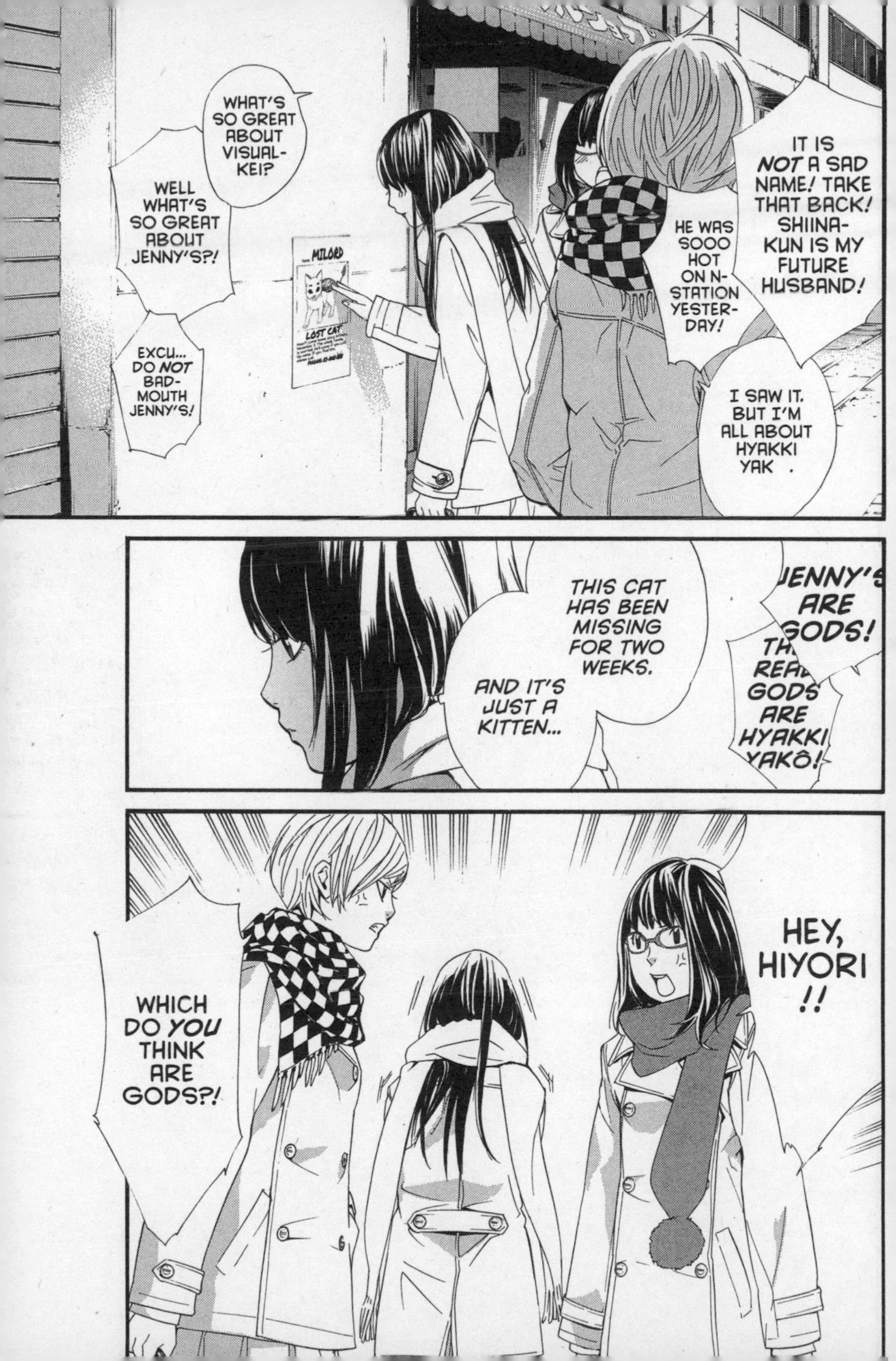
IT IS *NOT* A SAD NAME! TAKE THAT BACK! SHIINA-KUN IS MY FUTURE HUSBAND!
HE WAS SOOO HOT ON N-STATION YESTER-DAY!
I SAW IT. BUT I'M ALL ABOUT HYAKKI YAK .
WHAT'S SO GREAT ABOUT VISUAL-KEI?
WELL WHAT'S SO GREAT ABOUT JENNY'S?!
MILORD
LOST CAT
EXCU... DO *NOT* BAD-MOUTH JENNY'S!
JENNY'S ARE GODS!
THE REAL GODS ARE HYAKKI YAKÔ!
THIS CAT HAS BEEN MISSING FOR TWO WEEKS.
AND IT'S JUST A KITTEN...
HEY, HIYORI!!
WHICH DO *YOU* THINK ARE GODS?!

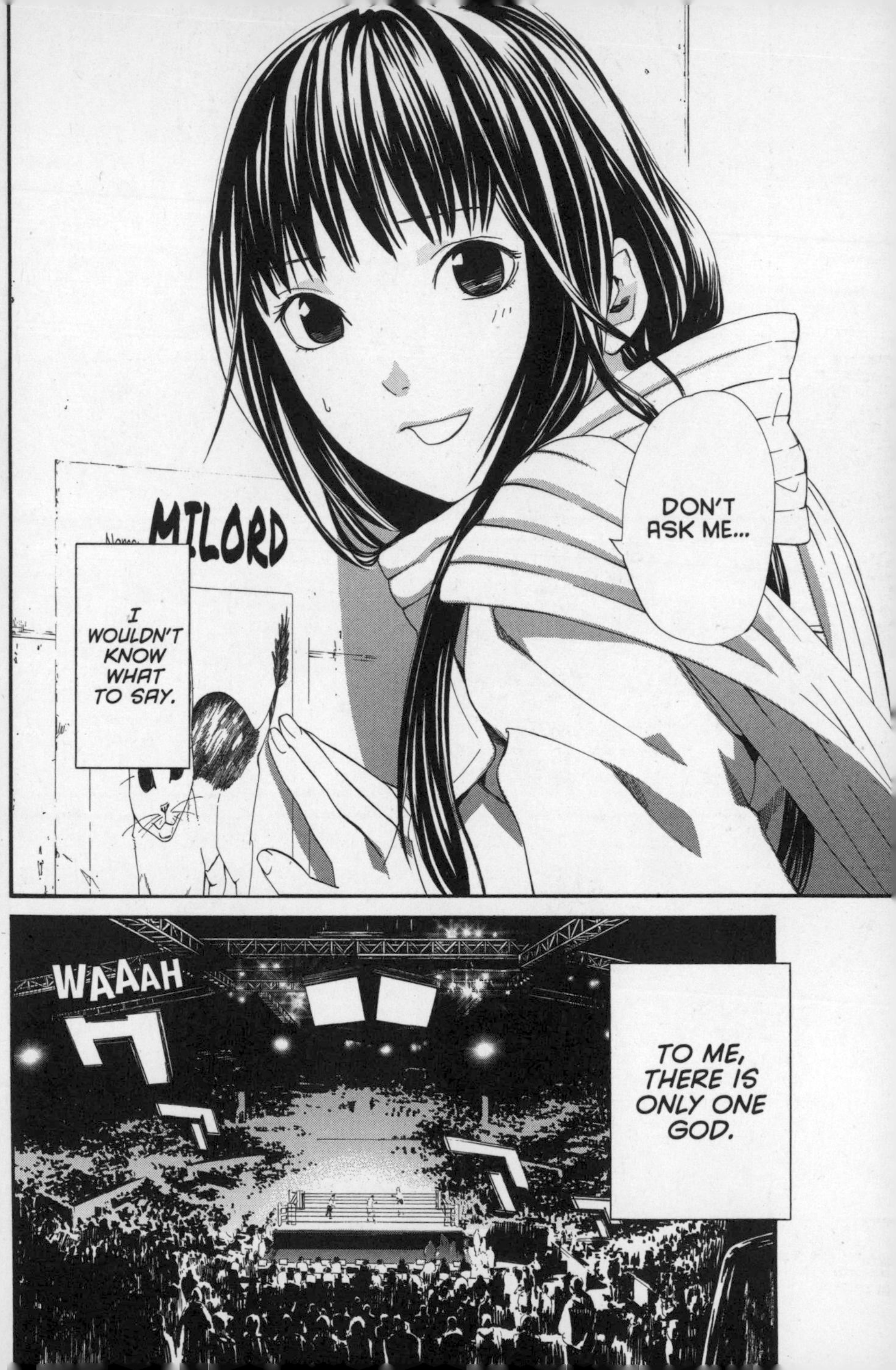
DON'T ASK ME...
MILORD
I WOULDN'T KNOW WHAT TO SAY.
TO ME, THERE IS ONLY ONE GOD.
WAAAH

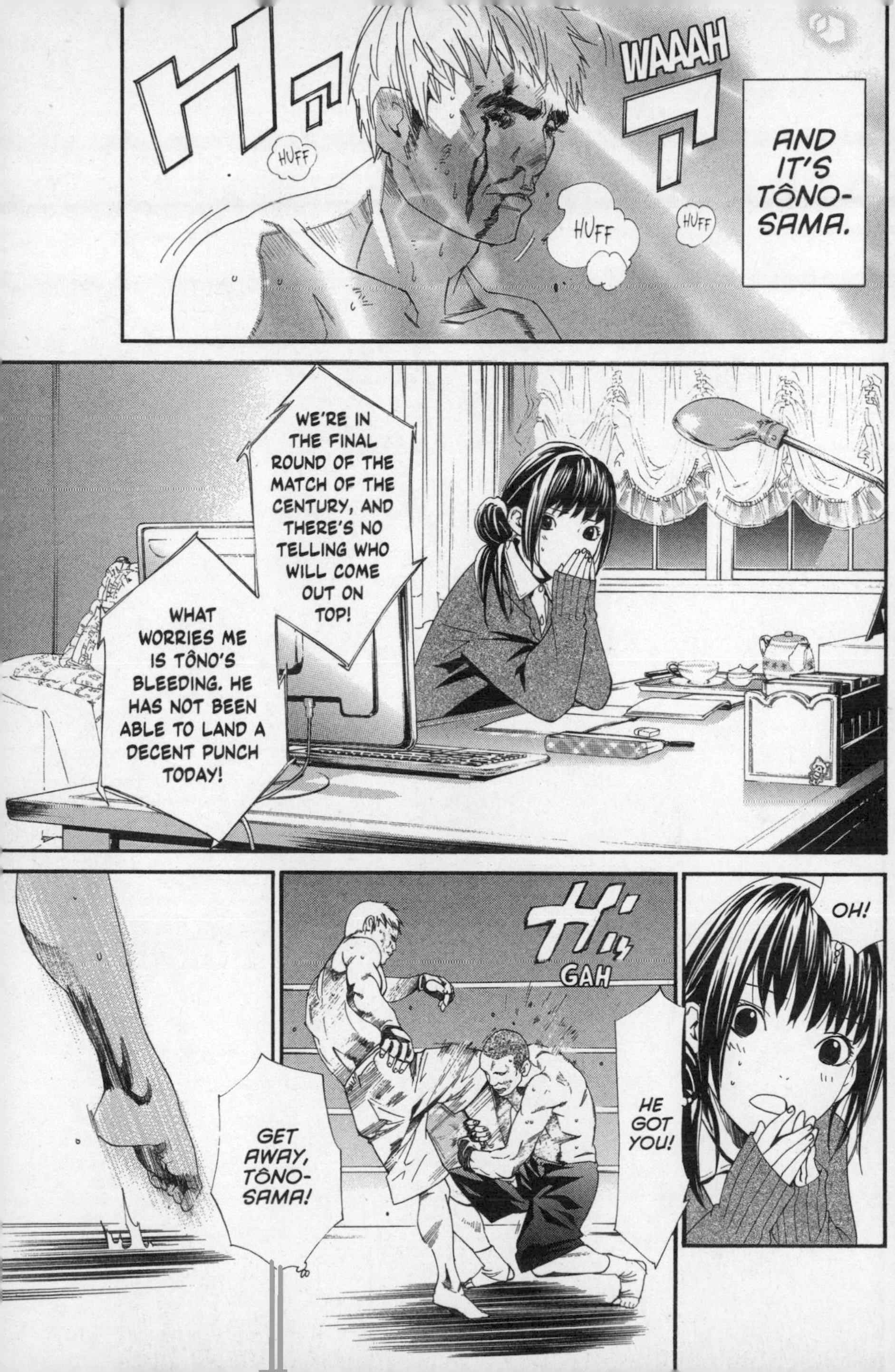
AND IT'S TÔNO-SAMA.
WAAAH
HUFF
HUFF
HUFF
WE'RE IN THE FINAL ROUND OF THE MATCH OF THE CENTURY, AND THERE'S NO TELLING WHO WILL COME OUT ON TOP!
WHAT WORRIES ME IS TÔNO'S BLEEDING. HE HAS NOT BEEN ABLE TO LAND A DECENT PUNCH TODAY!
OH!
HE GOT YOU!
GAH
GET AWAY, TÔNO-SAMA!

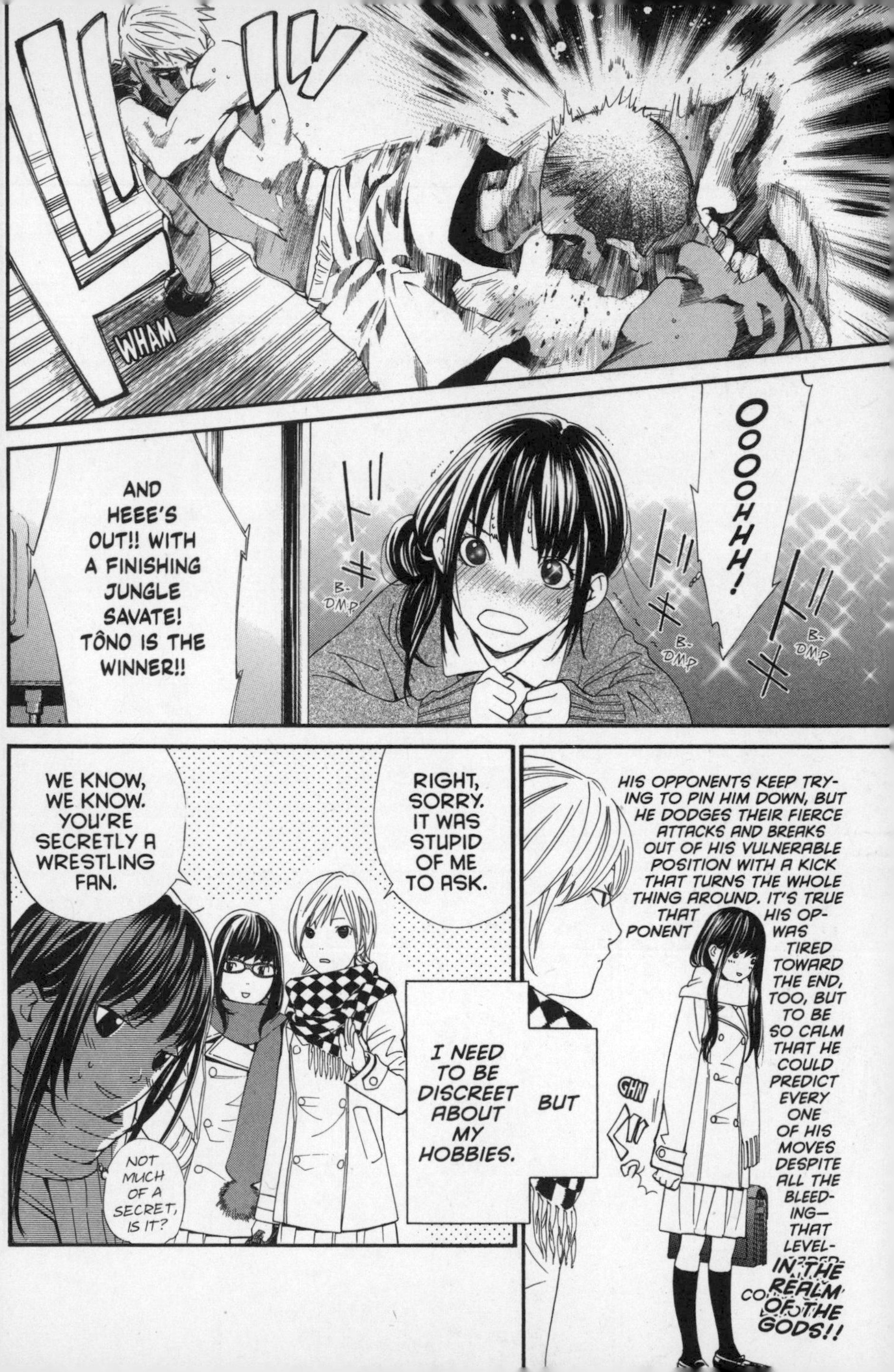
WHAM
OOOOOHHH!
B-DMP
B-DMP
B-DMP
AND HEEE'S OUT!! WITH A FINISHING JUNGLE SAVATE! TÔNO IS THE WINNER!!
HIS OPPONENTS KEEP TRYING TO PIN HIM DOWN, BUT HE DODGES THEIR FIERCE ATTACKS AND BREAKS OUT OF HIS VULNERABLE POSITION WITH A KICK THAT TURNS THE WHOLE THING AROUND. IT'S TRUE THAT HIS OPPONENT WAS TIRED TOWARD THE END, TOO, BUT TO BE SO CALM THAT HE COULD PREDICT EVERY ONE OF HIS MOVES DESPITE ALL THE BLEEDING—THAT LEVEL-
IN THE REALM OF THE GODS!!
GHN
BUT
I NEED TO BE DISCREET ABOUT MY HOBBIES.
RIGHT, SORRY. IT WAS STUPID OF ME TO ASK.
WE KNOW, WE KNOW. YOU'RE SECRETLY A WRESTLING FAN.
NOT MUCH OF A SECRET, IS IT?

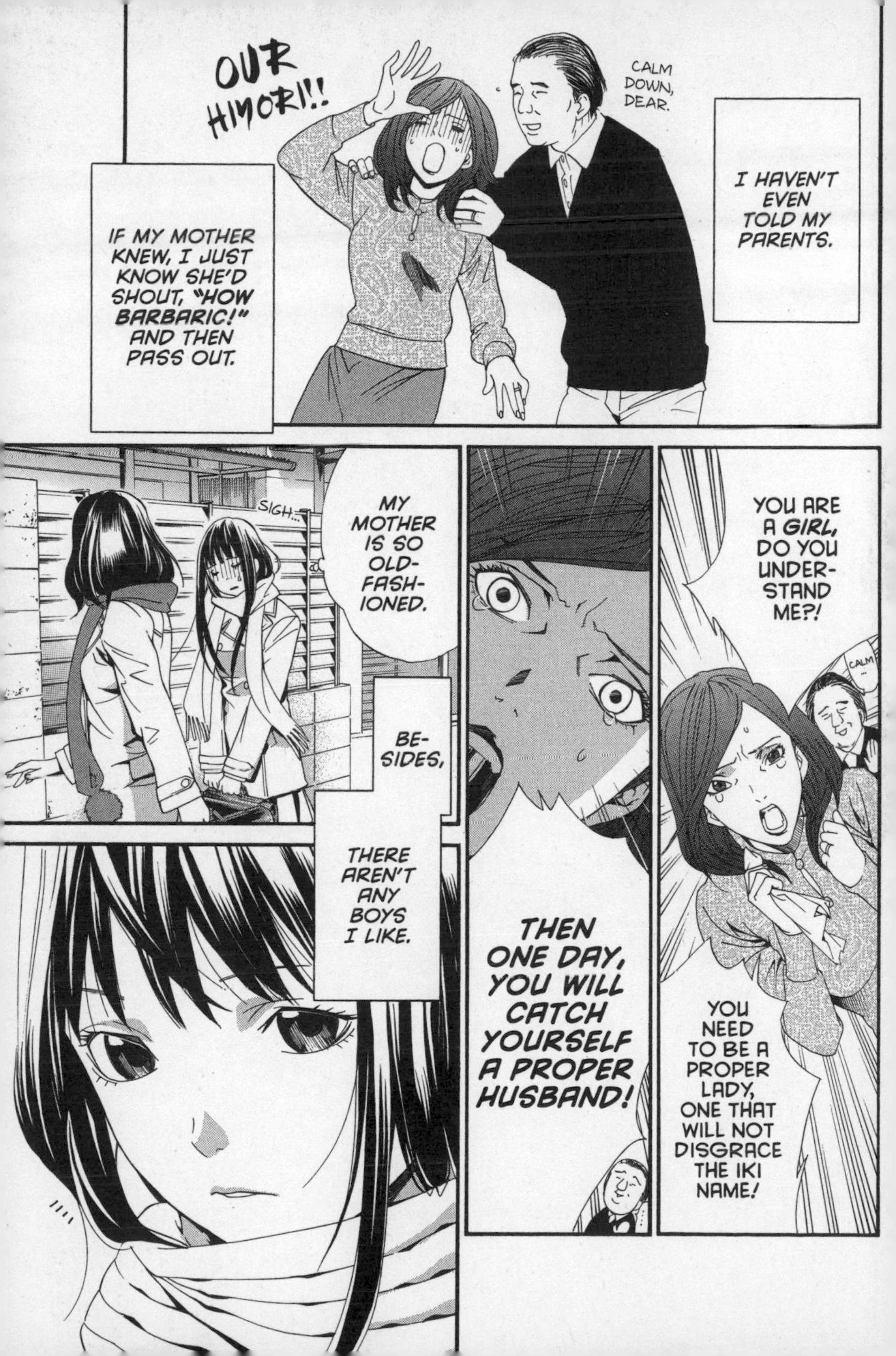
I HAVEN'T EVEN TOLD MY PARENTS.
CALM DOWN, DEAR.
OUR HIYORI!!
IF MY MOTHER KNEW, I JUST KNOW SHE'D SHOUT, "HOW BARBARIC!" AND THEN PASS OUT.
YOU ARE A *GIRL*, DO YOU UNDER-STAND ME?!
CALM...
YOU NEED TO BE A PROPER LADY, ONE THAT WILL NOT DISGRACE THE IKI NAME!
THEN ONE DAY, YOU WILL CATCH YOURSELF A PROPER HUSBAND!
MY MOTHER IS SO OLD-FASHIONED.
SIGH...
BE-SIDES,
THERE AREN'T ANY BOYS I LIKE.

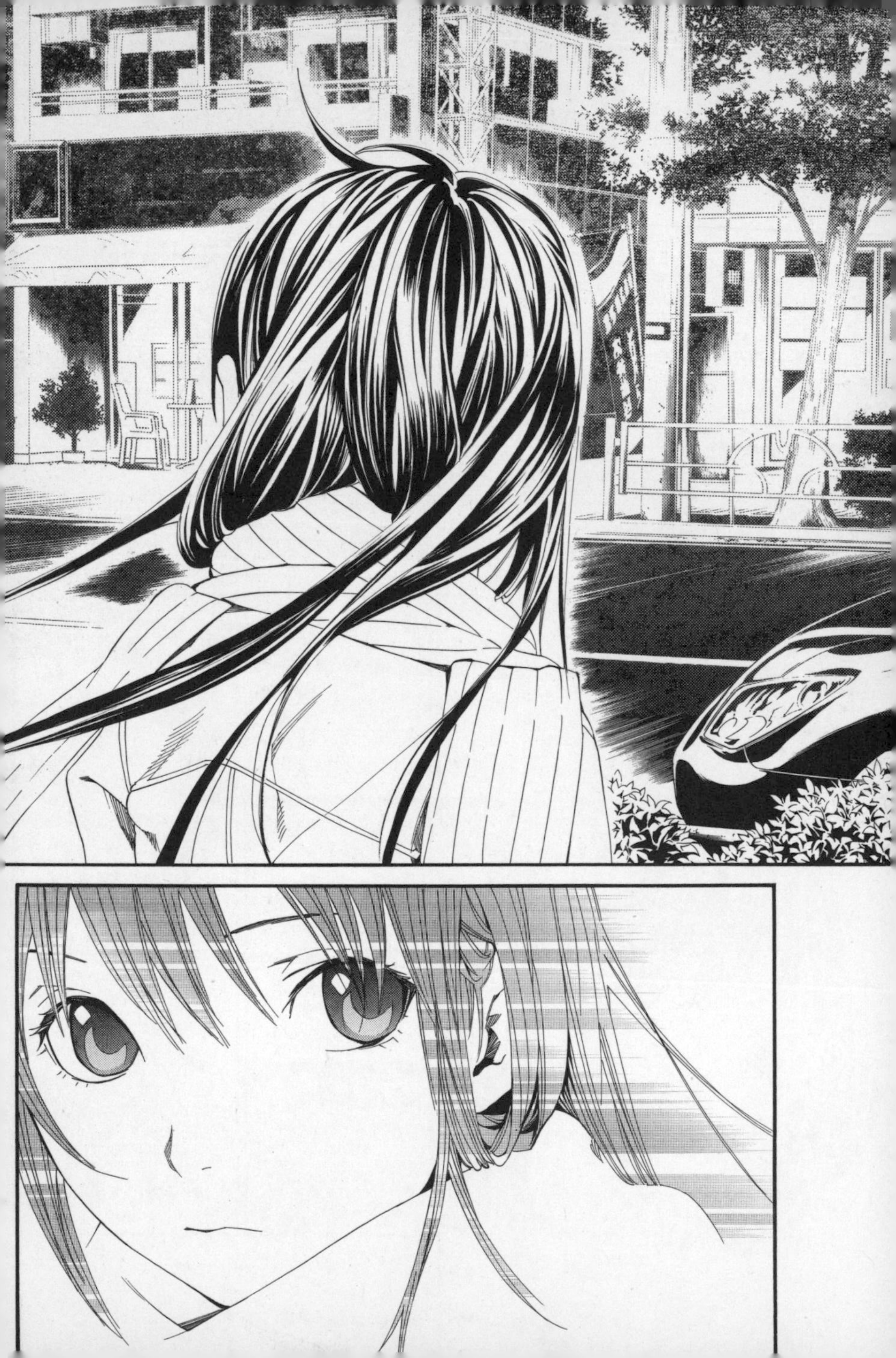

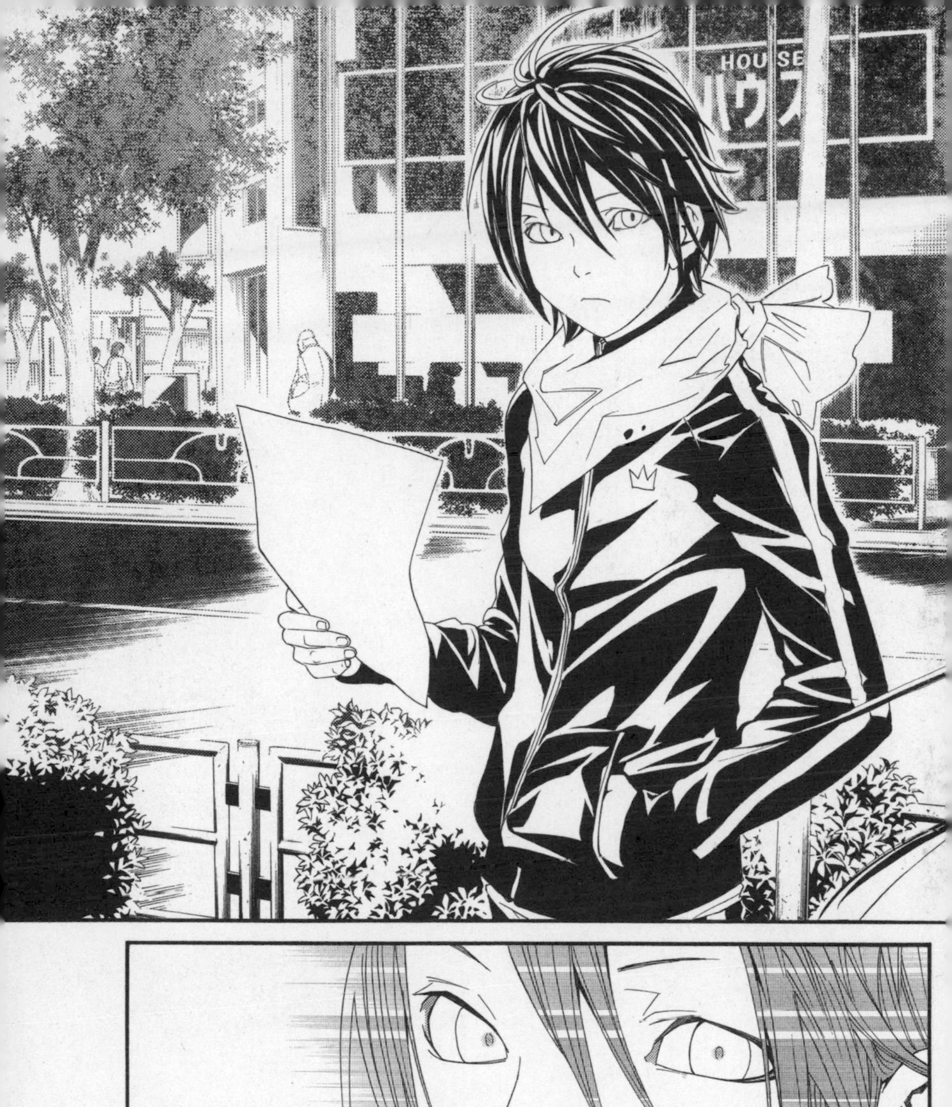
HOUSE
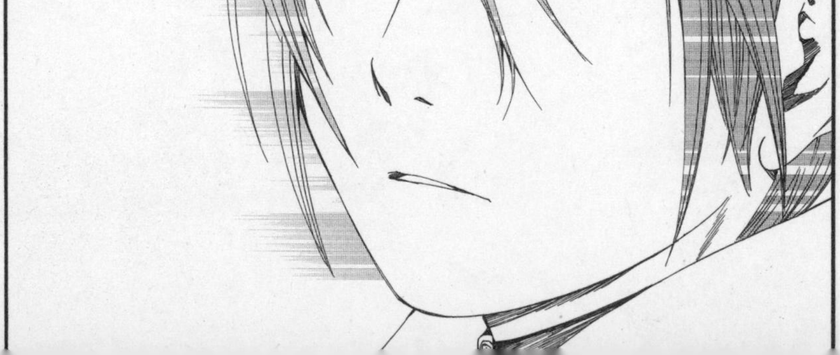

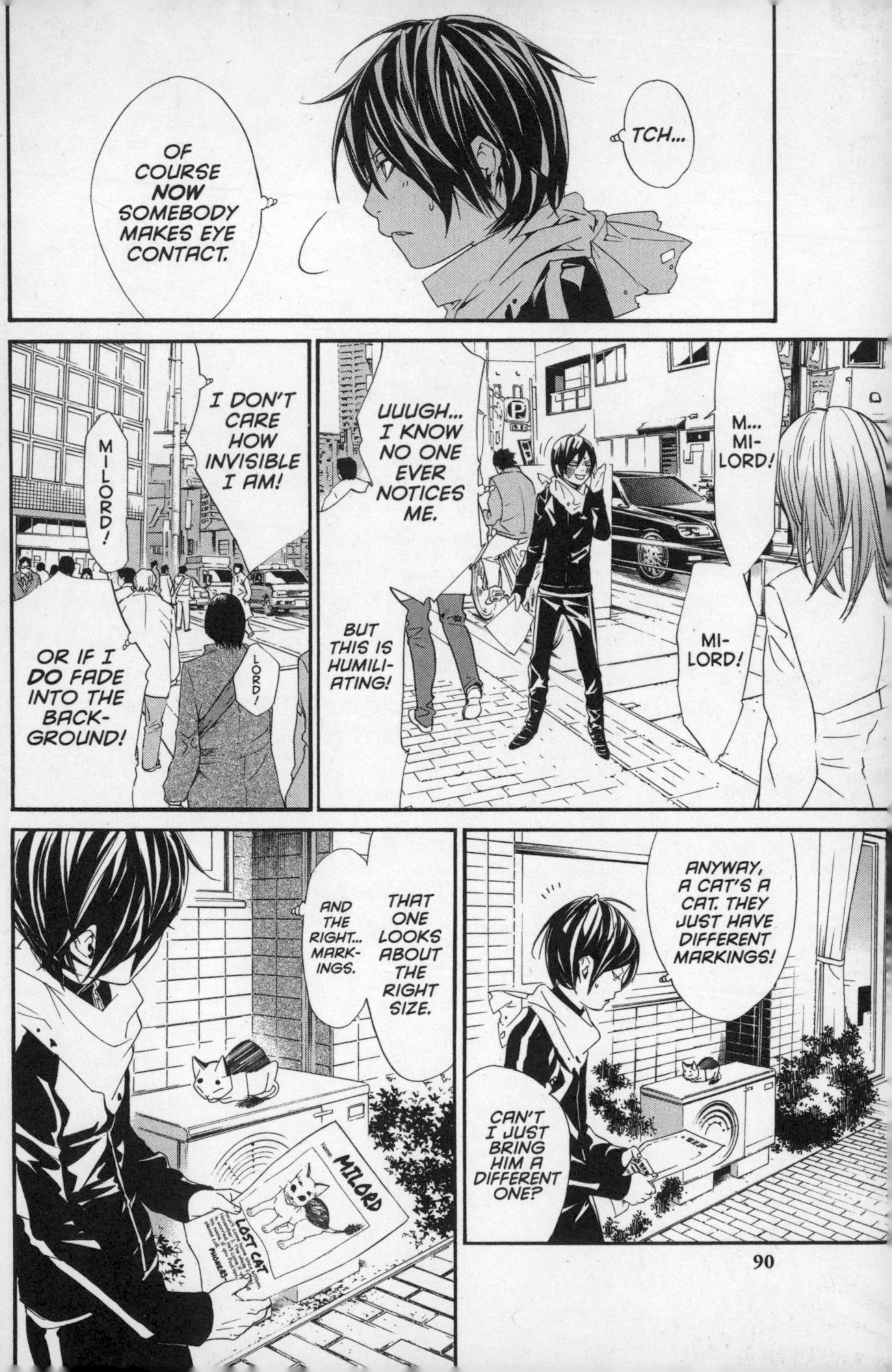
TCH...
OF COURSE NOW SOMEBODY MAKES EYE CONTACT.
M... MI-LORD!
MI-LORD!
UUUGH... I KNOW NO ONE EVER NOTICES ME.
BUT THIS IS HUMILI-ATING!
I DON'T CARE HOW INVISIBLE I AM!
MILORD!
LORD!
OR IF I DO FADE INTO THE BACK-GROUND!
ANYWAY, A CAT'S A CAT. THEY JUST HAVE DIFFERENT MARKINGS!
CAN'T I JUST BRING HIM A DIFFERENT ONE?
THAT ONE LOOKS ABOUT THE RIGHT SIZE.
AND THE RIGHT... MARK-INGS.
MILORD
LOST CAT

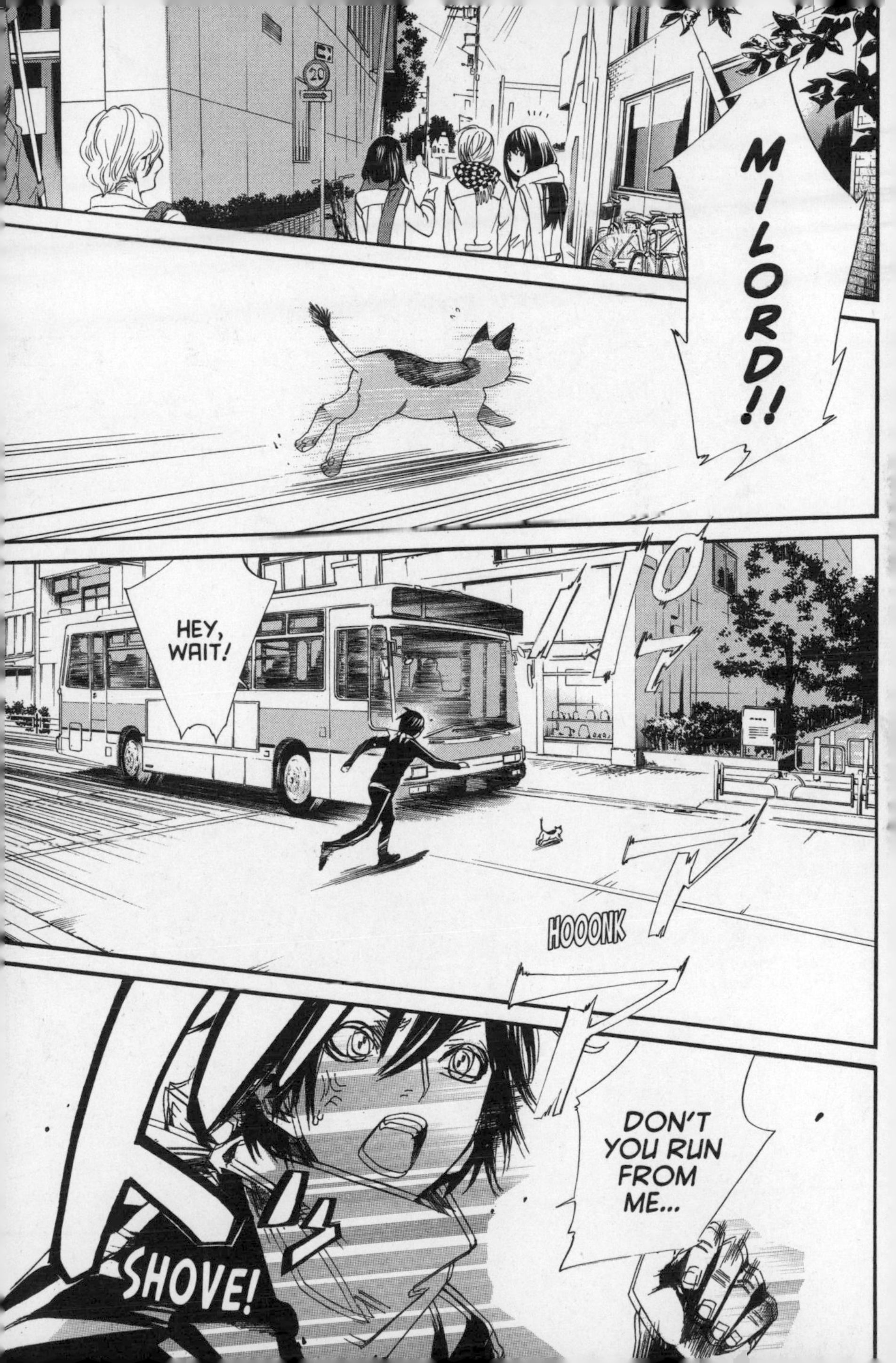
MILORD!!
HEY, WAIT!
HOOONK
DON'T YOU RUN FROM ME...
SHOVE!

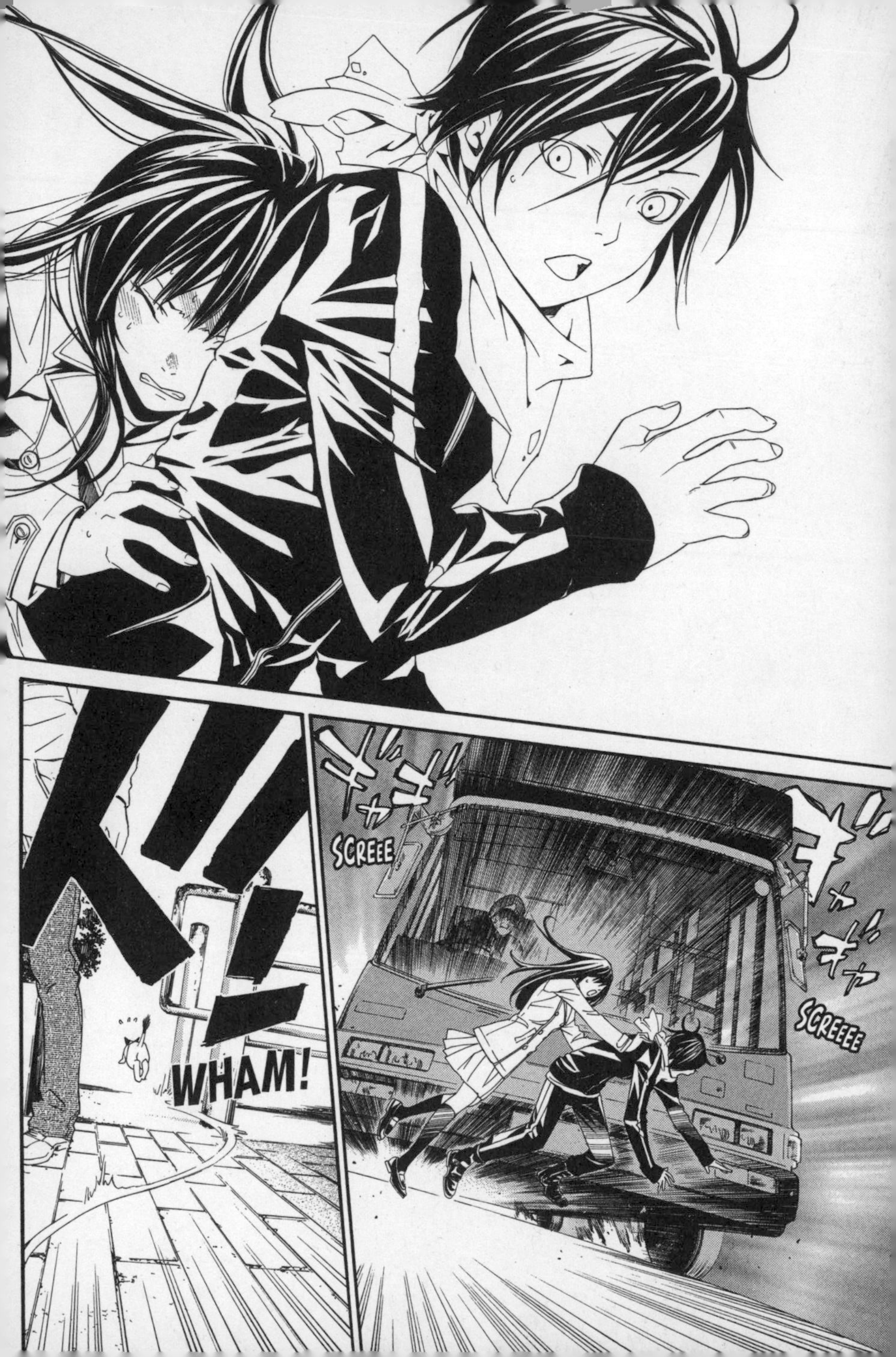
SCREEEE
SCREEE
WHAM!

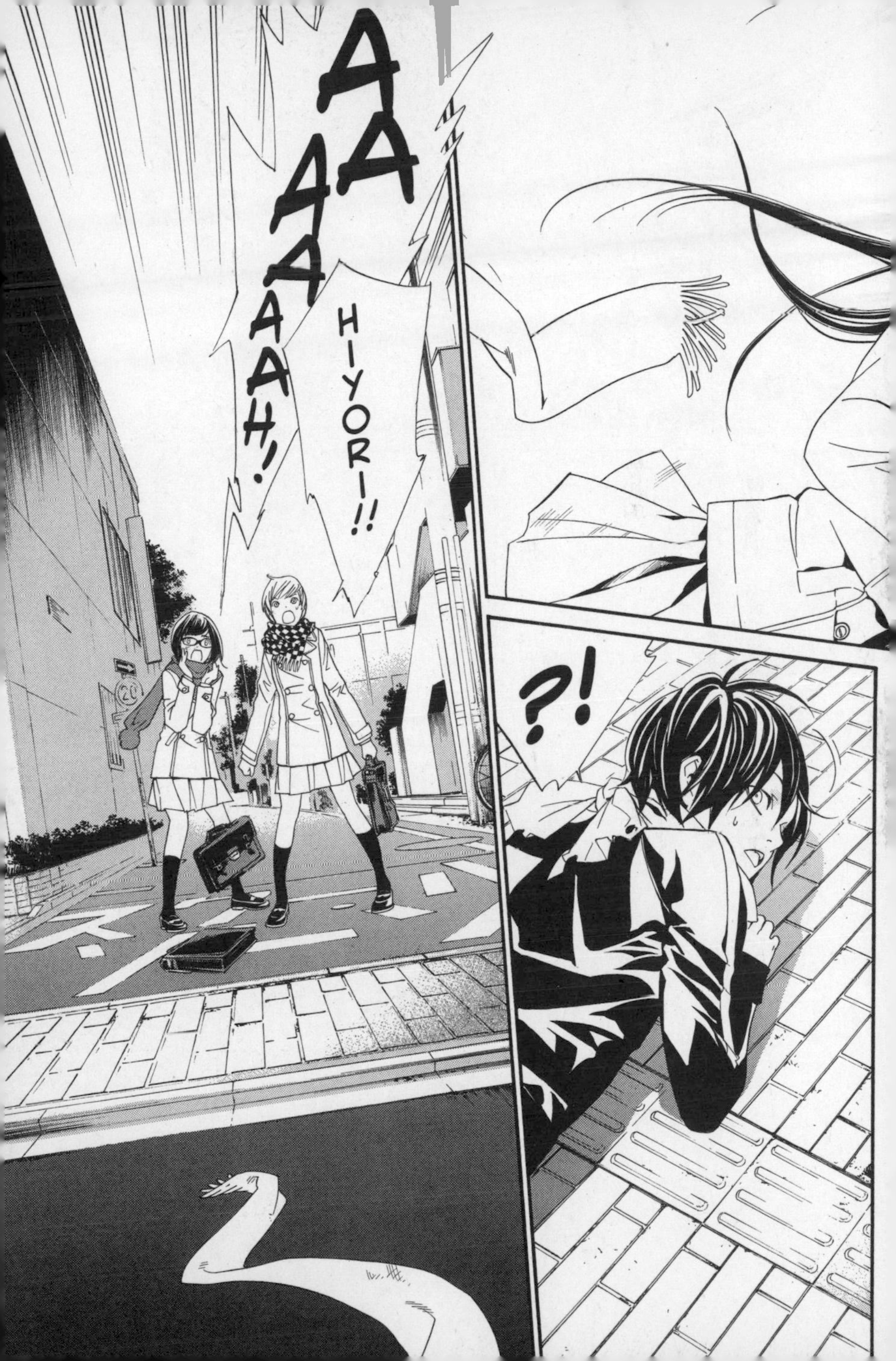
?!
AAAAAAH!
HIYORI!!

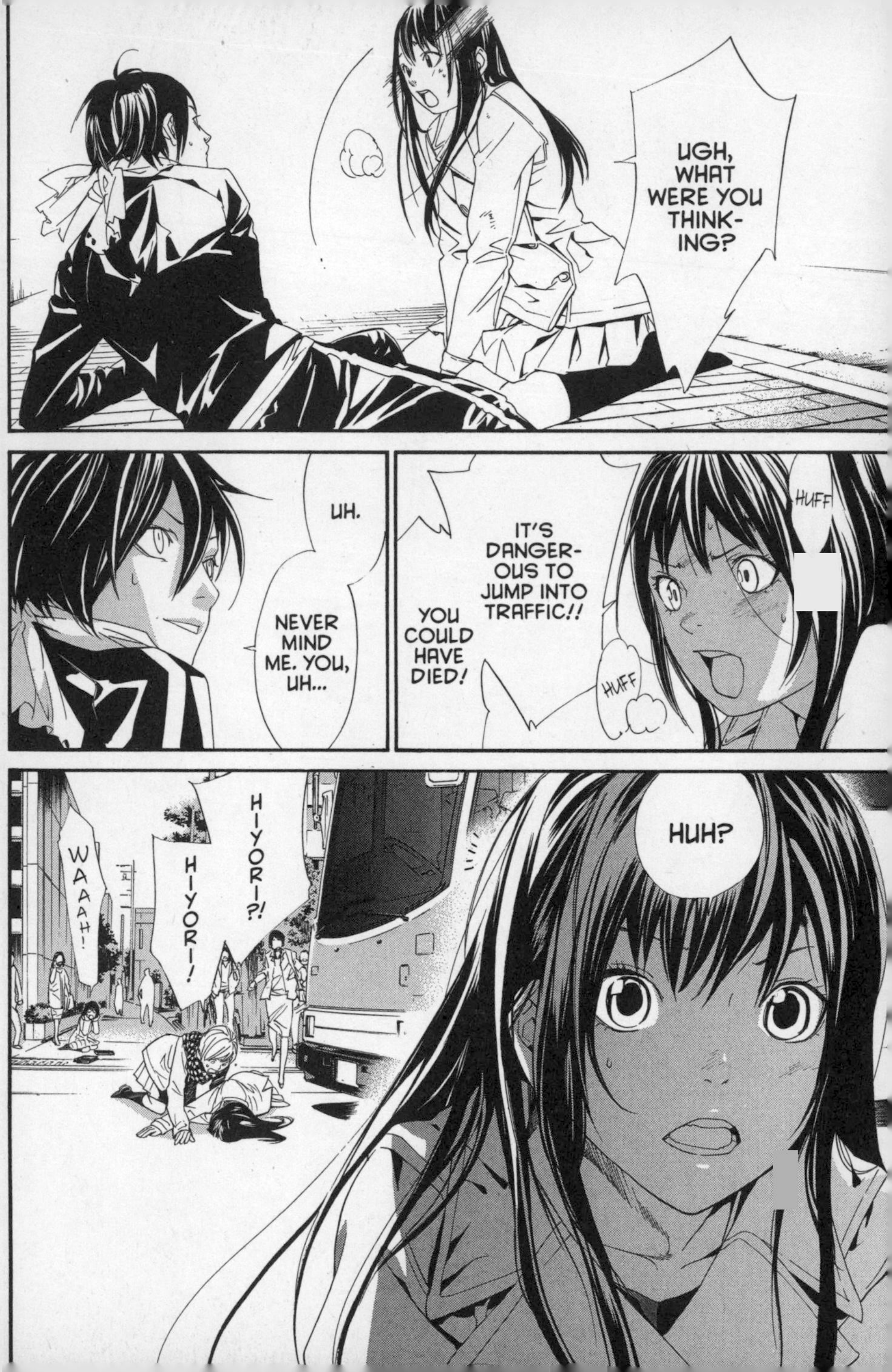
UGH, WHAT WERE YOU THINKING?
HUFF
IT'S DANGEROUS TO JUMP INTO TRAFFIC!!
YOU COULD HAVE DIED!
HUFF
UH.
NEVER MIND ME. YOU, UH...
HUH?
HIYORI?!
HIYORI!
WAAAH!

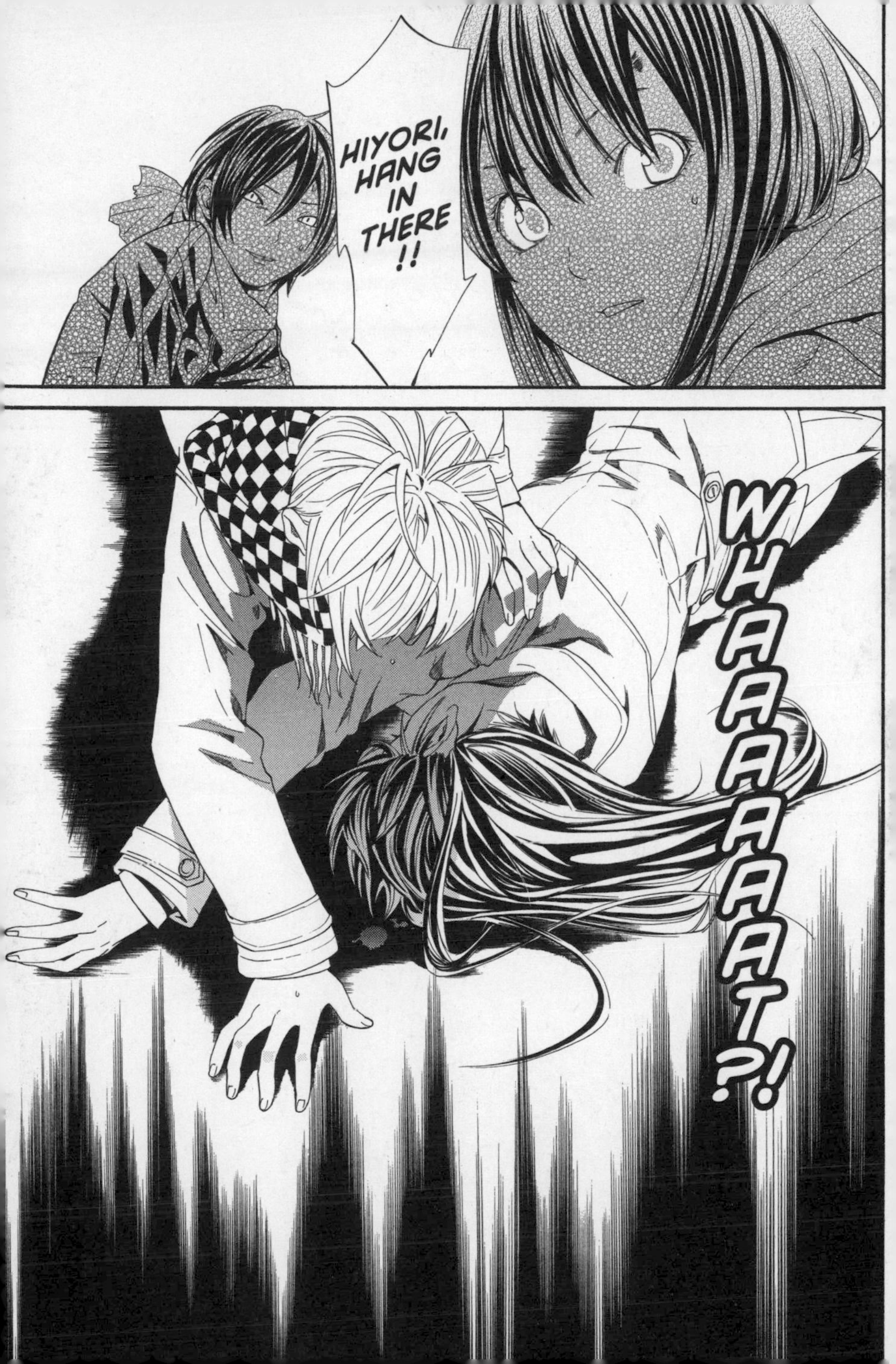
HIYORI, HANG IN THERE!!
WHAAAAAAAT?!

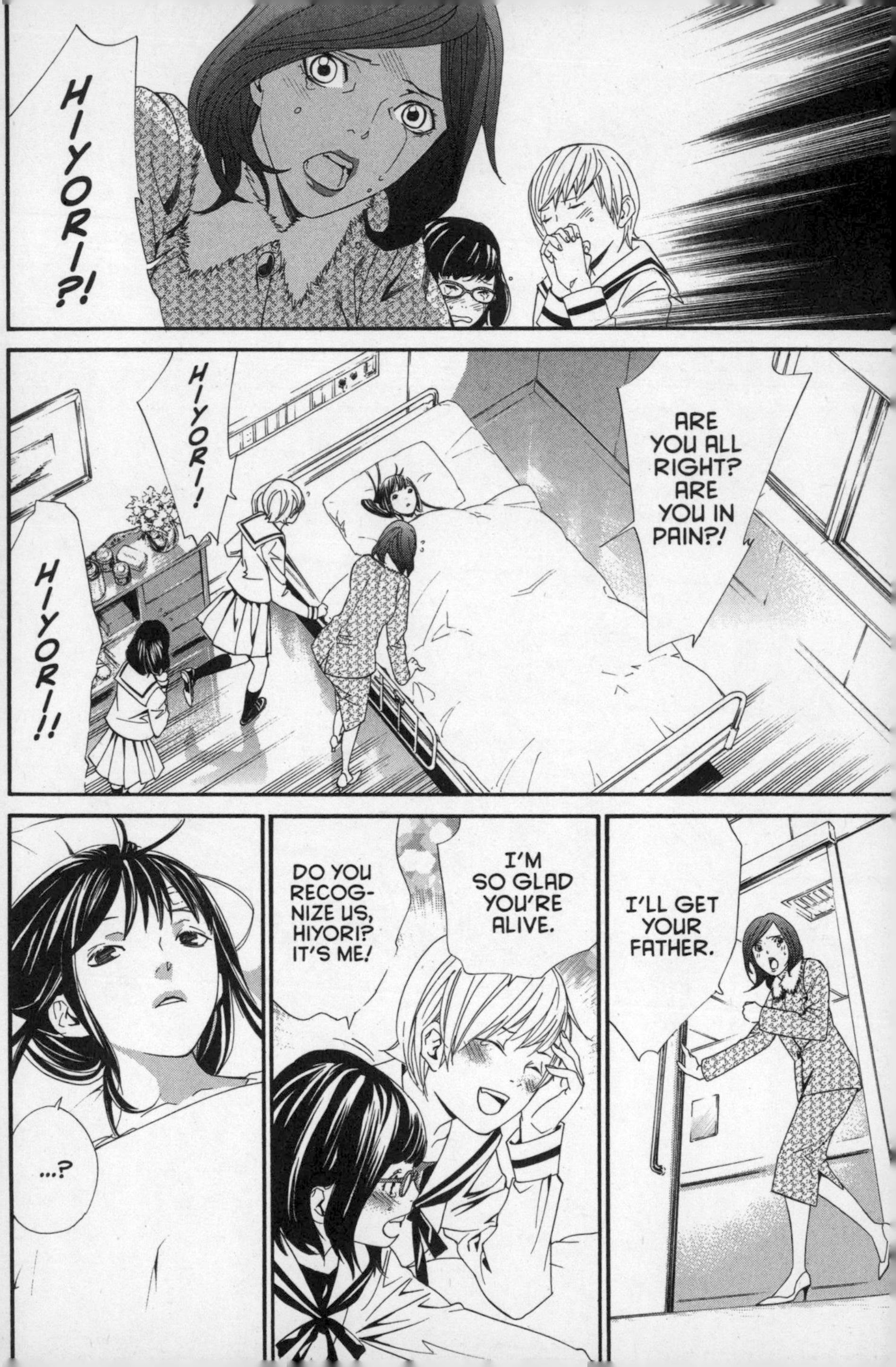
HIYORI?!
ARE YOU ALL RIGHT? ARE YOU IN PAIN?!
HIYORI!
HIYORI!!
I'LL GET YOUR FATHER.
I'M SO GLAD YOU'RE ALIVE.
DO YOU RECOG-NIZE US, HIYORI? IT'S ME!
...?

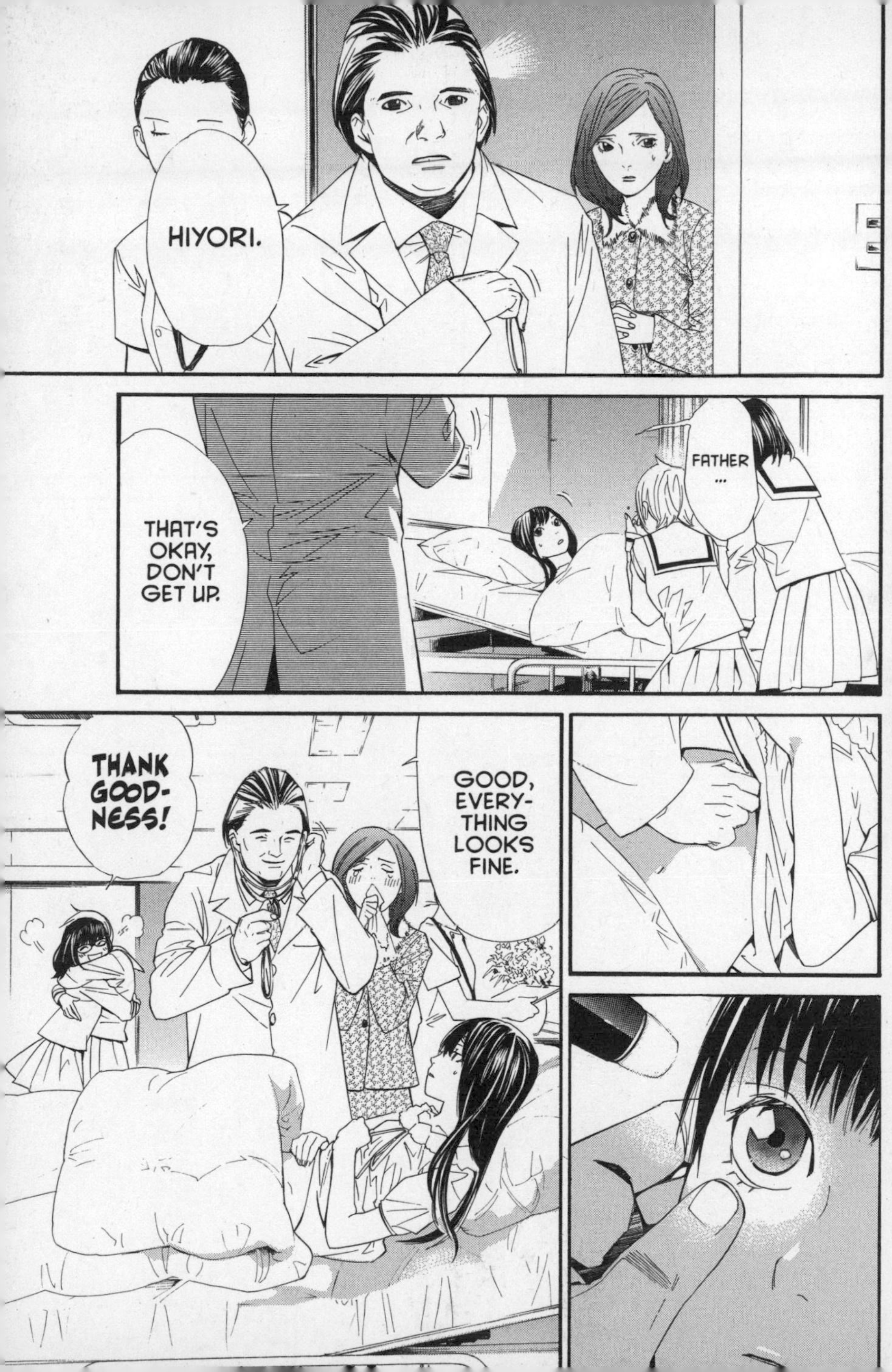
HIYORI.
FATHER ...
THAT'S OKAY, DON'T GET UP.
GOOD, EVERY-THING LOOKS FINE.
THANK GOOD-NESS!

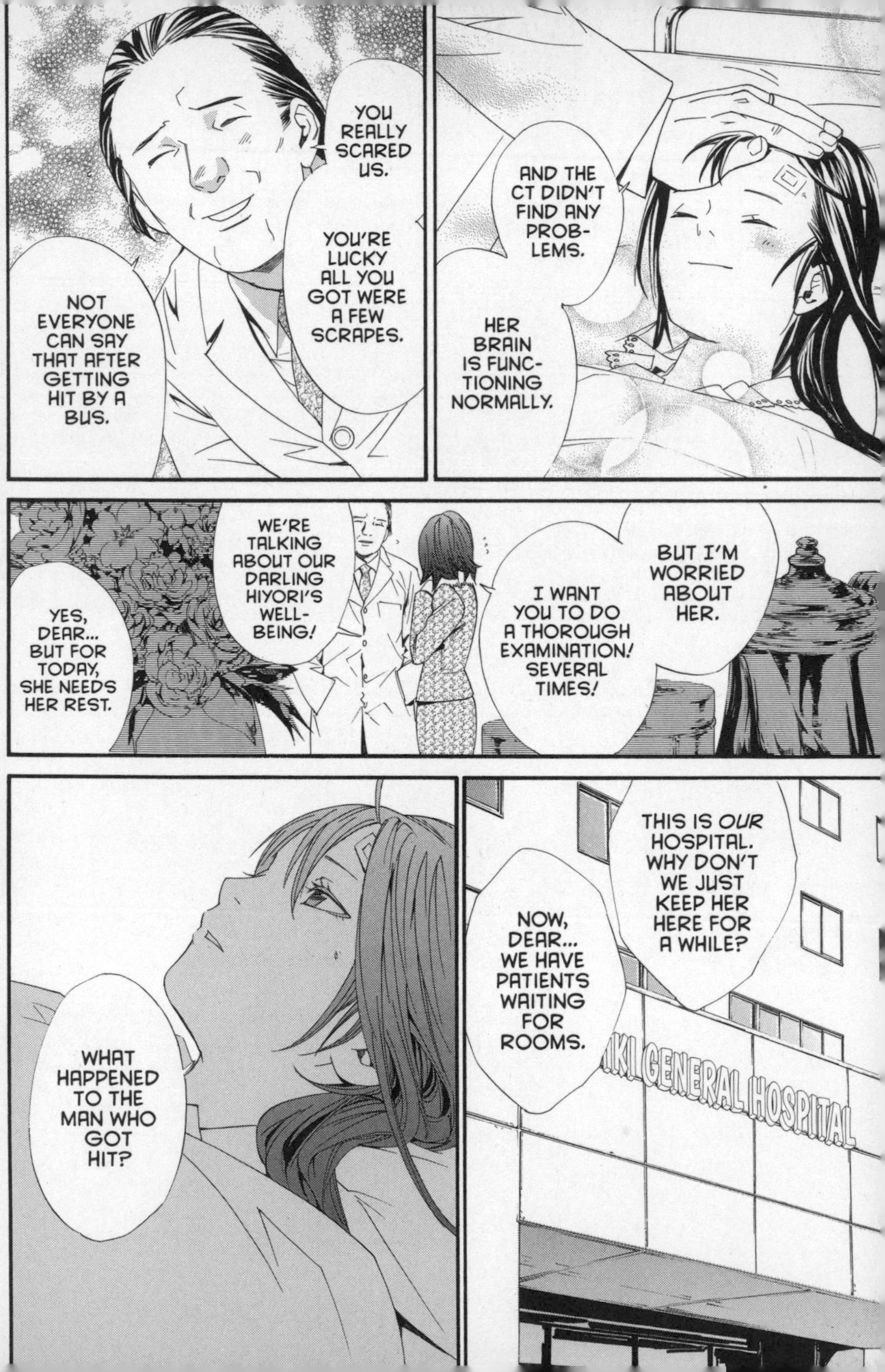

AND THE CT DIDN'T FIND ANY PROBLEMS.
HER BRAIN IS FUNCTIONING NORMALLY.
YOU REALLY SCARED US.
YOU'RE LUCKY ALL YOU GOT WERE A FEW SCRAPES.
NOT EVERYONE CAN SAY THAT AFTER GETTING HIT BY A BUS.
BUT I'M WORRIED ABOUT HER.
I WANT YOU TO DO A THOROUGH EXAMINATION! SEVERAL TIMES!
WE'RE TALKING ABOUT OUR DARLING HIYORI'S WELL-BEING!
YES, DEAR... BUT FOR TODAY, SHE NEEDS HER REST.
THIS IS *OUR* HOSPITAL. WHY DON'T WE JUST KEEP HER HERE FOR A WHILE?
NOW, DEAR... WE HAVE PATIENTS WAITING FOR ROOMS.
GENERAL HOSPITAL
WHAT HAPPENED TO THE MAN WHO GOT HIT?

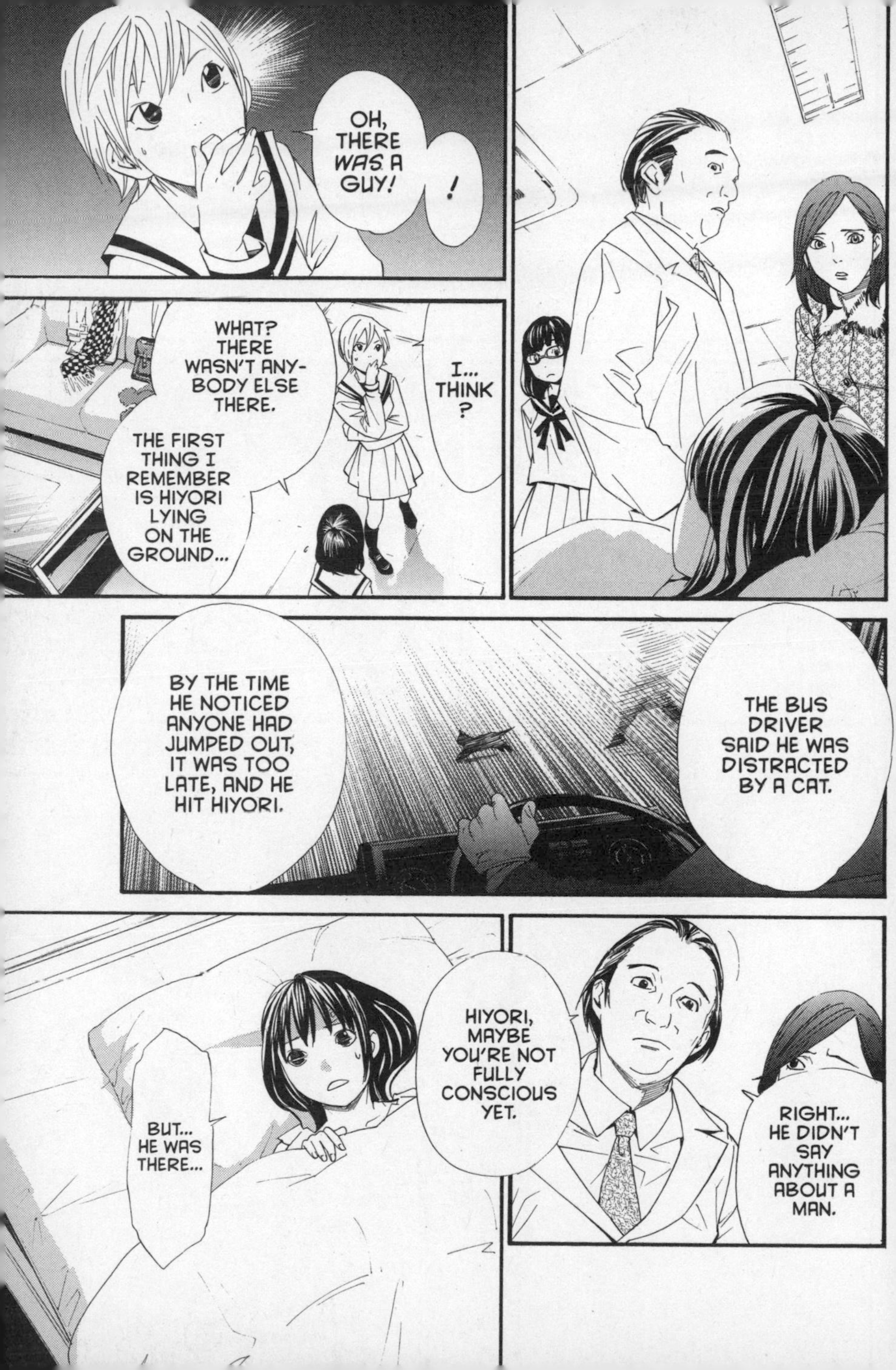
OH, THERE WAS A GUY!
!
I... THINK?
WHAT? THERE WASN'T ANYBODY ELSE THERE.
THE FIRST THING I REMEMBER IS HIYORI LYING ON THE GROUND...
THE BUS DRIVER SAID HE WAS DISTRACTED BY A CAT.
BY THE TIME HE NOTICED ANYONE HAD JUMPED OUT, IT WAS TOO LATE, AND HE HIT HIYORI.
RIGHT... HE DIDN'T SAY ANYTHING ABOUT A MAN.
HIYORI, MAYBE YOU'RE NOT FULLY CONSCIOUS YET.
BUT... HE WAS THERE...

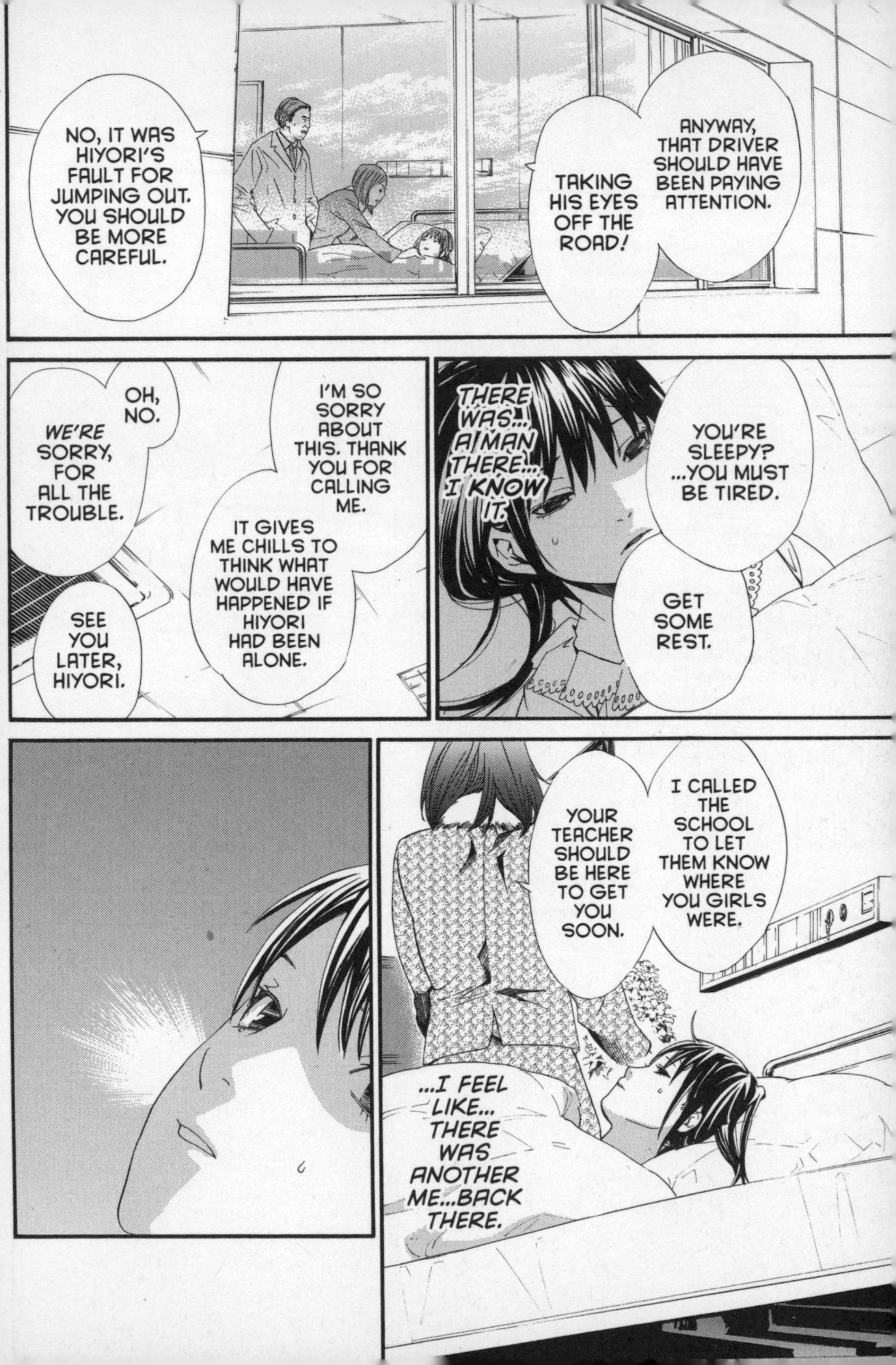
ANYWAY, THAT DRIVER SHOULD HAVE BEEN PAYING ATTENTION.
TAKING HIS EYES OFF THE ROAD!
NO, IT WAS HIYORI'S FAULT FOR JUMPING OUT. YOU SHOULD BE MORE CAREFUL.
YOU'RE SLEEPY? ...YOU MUST BE TIRED.
GET SOME REST.
THERE WAS... A MAN THERE... I KNOW IT.
I'M SO SORRY ABOUT THIS. THANK YOU FOR CALLING ME.
IT GIVES ME CHILLS TO THINK WHAT WOULD HAVE HAPPENED IF HIYORI HAD BEEN ALONE.
OH, NO. *WE'RE* SORRY, FOR ALL THE TROUBLE.
SEE YOU LATER, HIYORI.
I CALLED THE SCHOOL TO LET THEM KNOW WHERE YOU GIRLS WERE.
YOUR TEACHER SHOULD BE HERE TO GET YOU SOON.
...I FEEL LIKE... THERE WAS ANOTHER ME...BACK THERE.

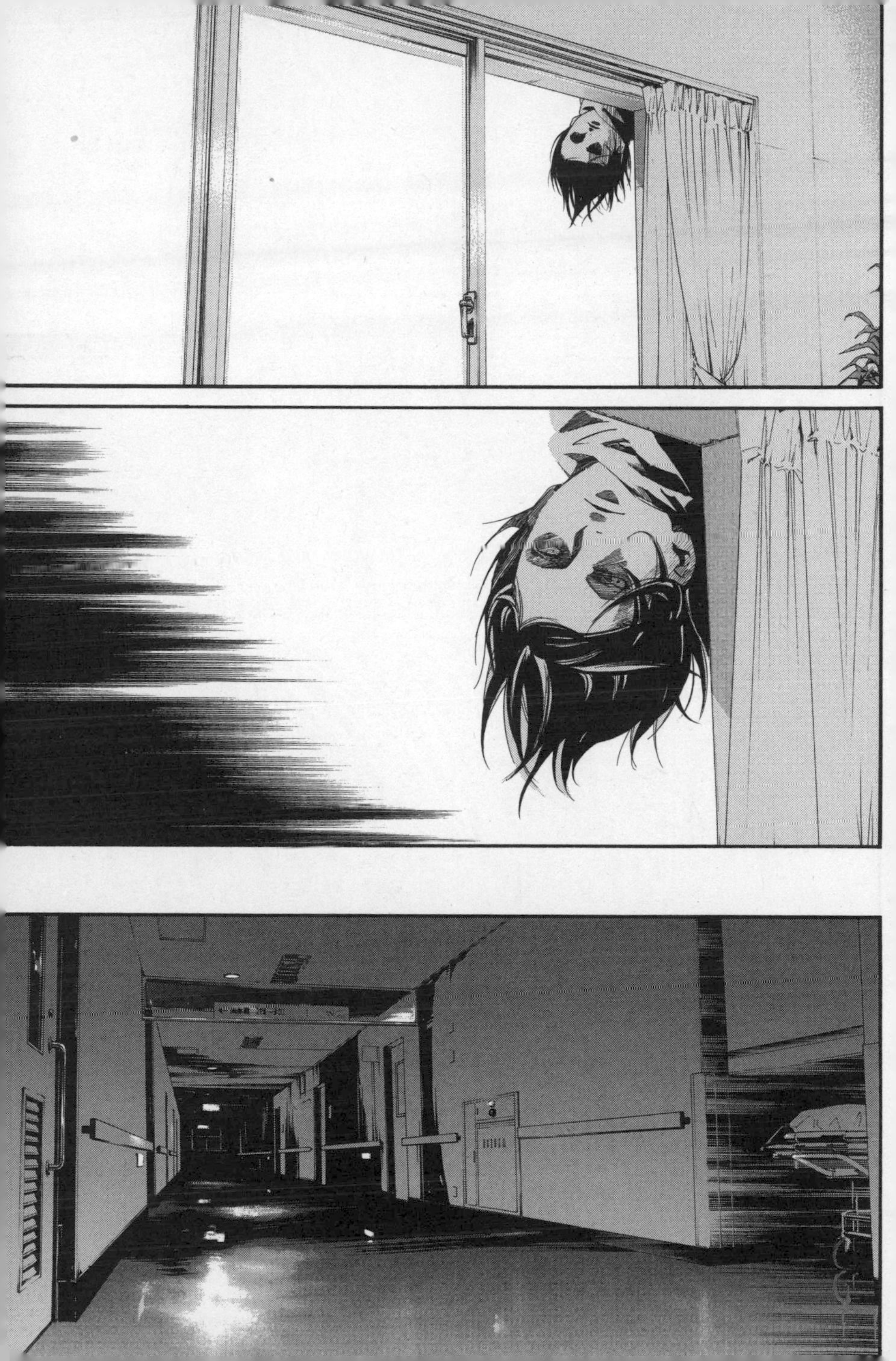

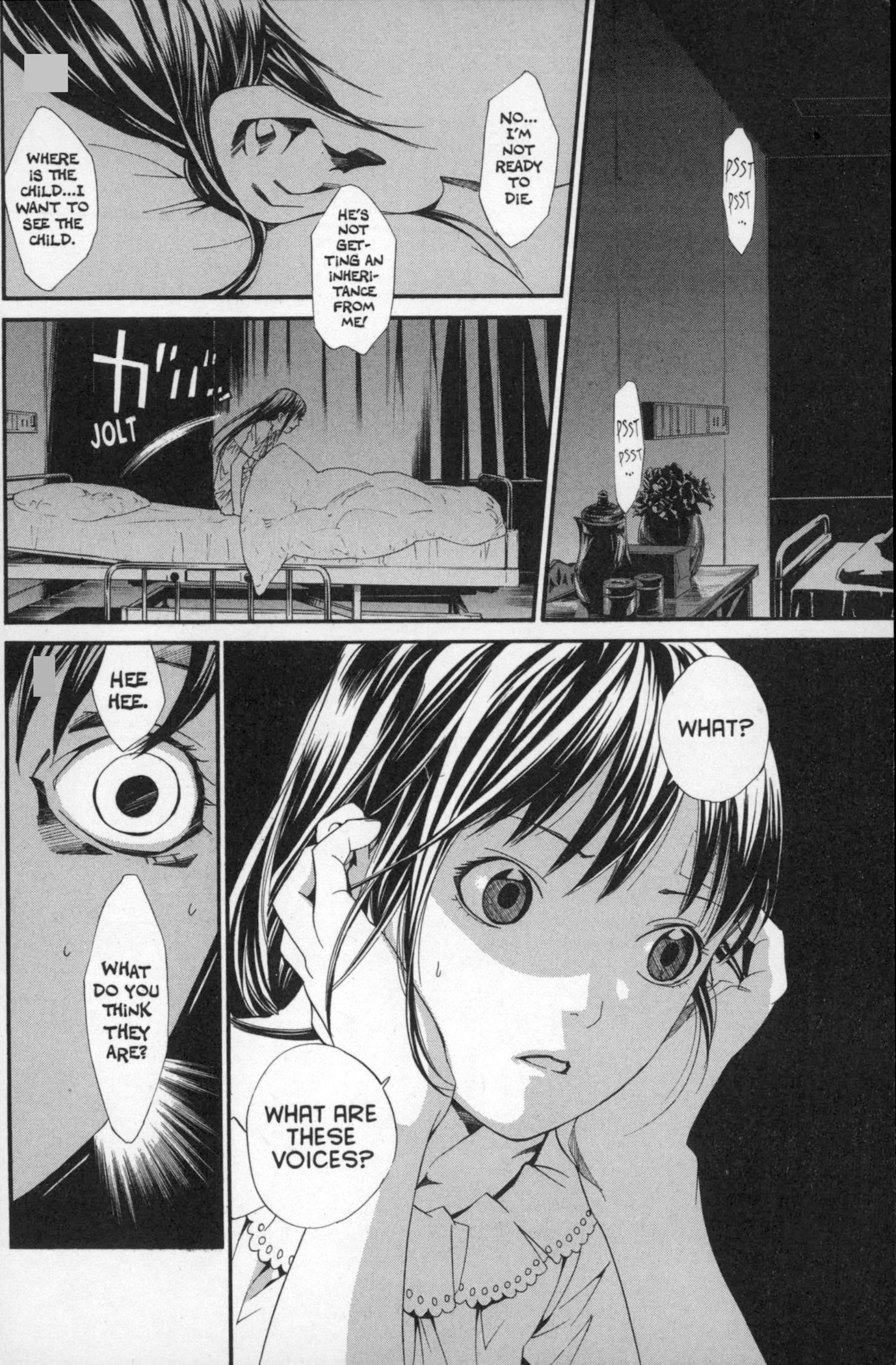
PSST PSST ...
PSST PSST ...
NO... I'M NOT READY TO DIE
HE'S NOT GETTING AN INHERITANCE FROM ME!
WHERE IS THE CHILD...I WANT TO SEE THE CHILD.
JOLT
WHAT?
WHAT ARE THESE VOICES?
HEE HEE.
WHAT DO YOU THINK THEY ARE?

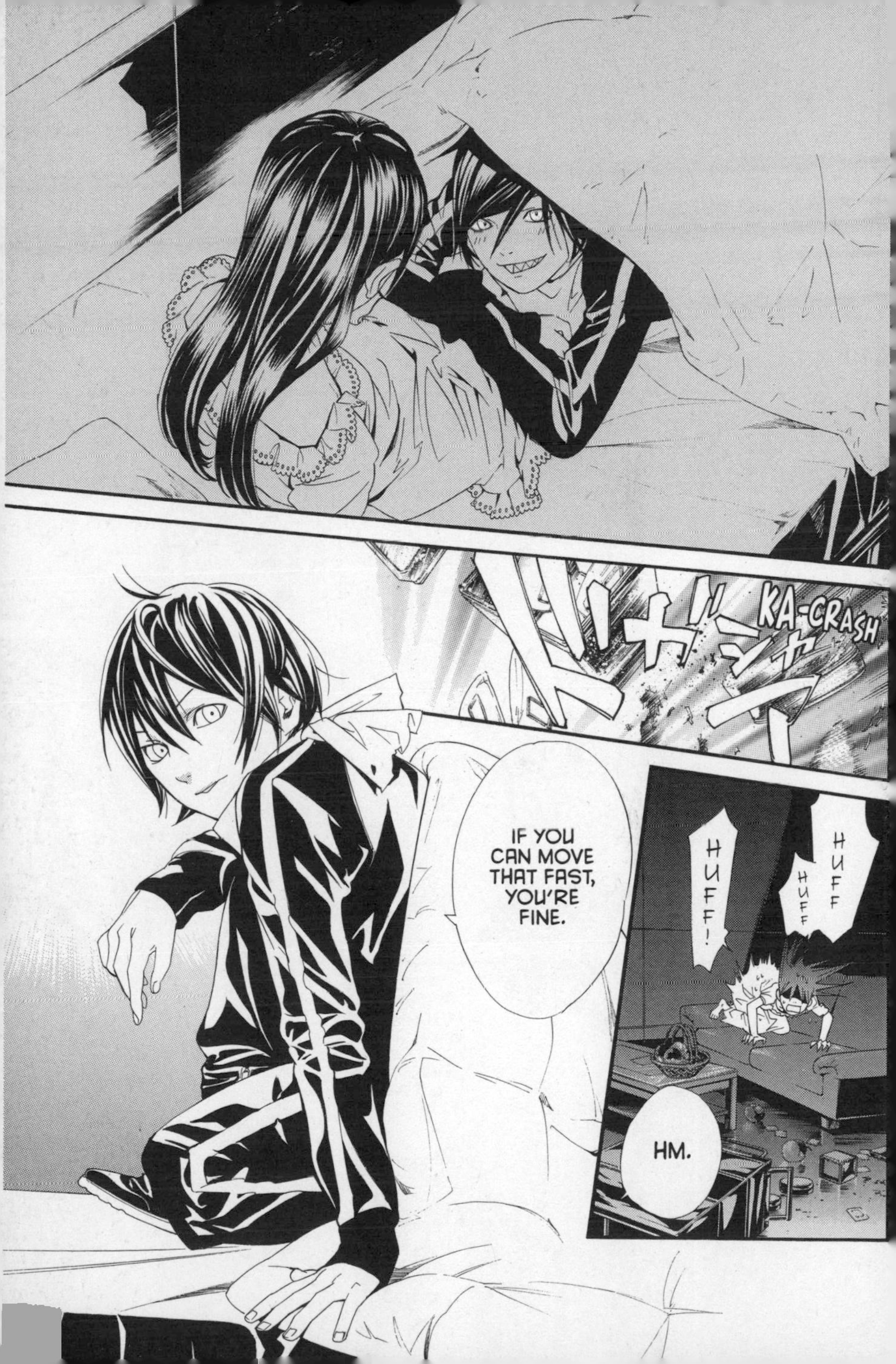
KA-CRASH
HUFF
HUFF
HUFF!
IF YOU CAN MOVE THAT FAST, YOU'RE FINE.
HM.

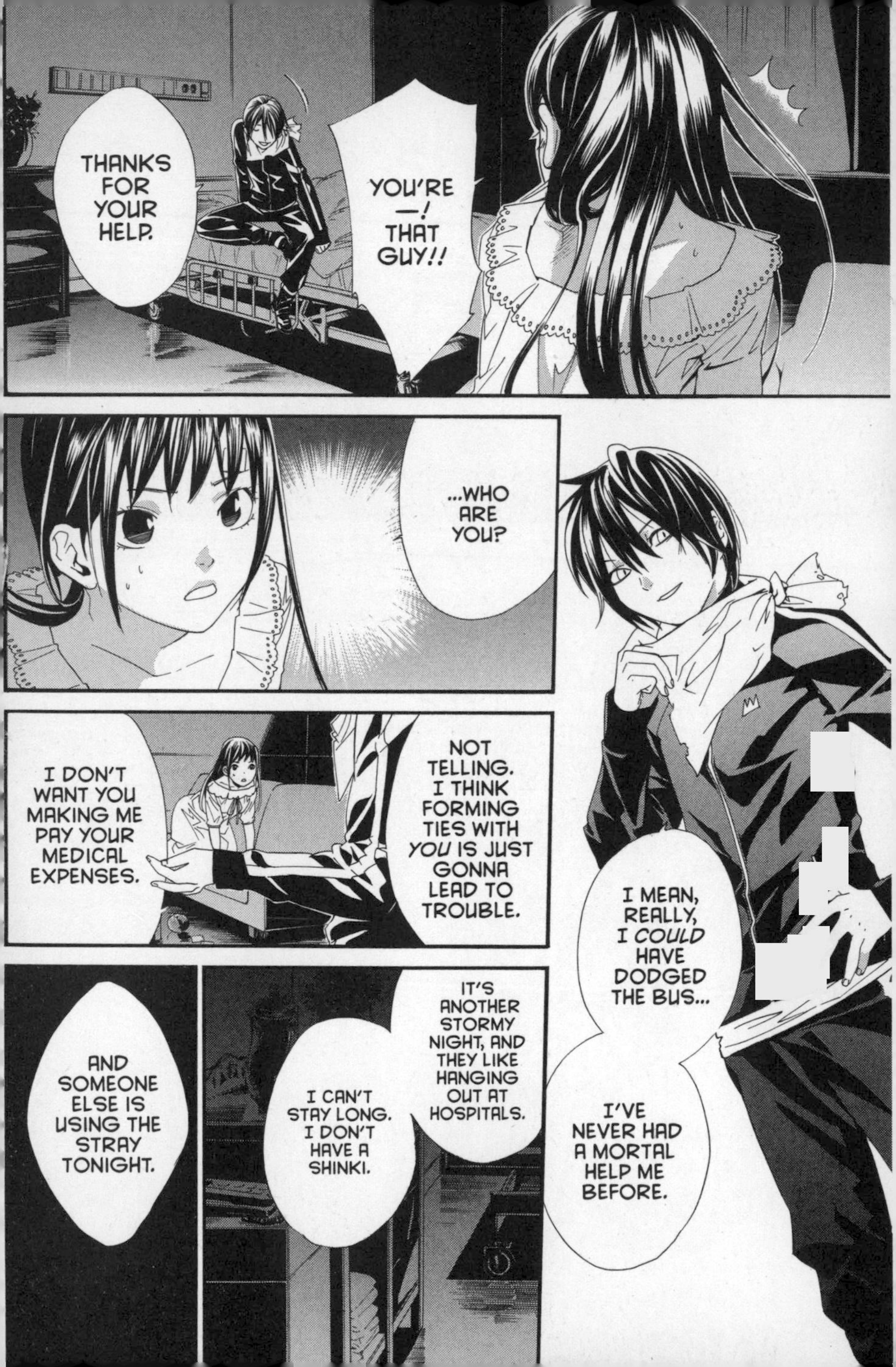
YOU'RE—! THAT GUY!!
THANKS FOR YOUR HELP.
I MEAN, REALLY, I *COULD* HAVE DODGED THE BUS...
I'VE NEVER HAD A MORTAL HELP ME BEFORE.
...WHO ARE YOU?
NOT TELLING. I THINK FORMING TIES WITH *YOU* IS JUST GONNA LEAD TO TROUBLE.
I DON'T WANT YOU MAKING ME PAY YOUR MEDICAL EXPENSES.
IT'S ANOTHER STORMY NIGHT, AND THEY LIKE HANGING OUT AT HOSPITALS.
I CAN'T STAY LONG. I DON'T HAVE A SHINKI.
AND SOMEONE ELSE IS USING THE STRAY TONIGHT.

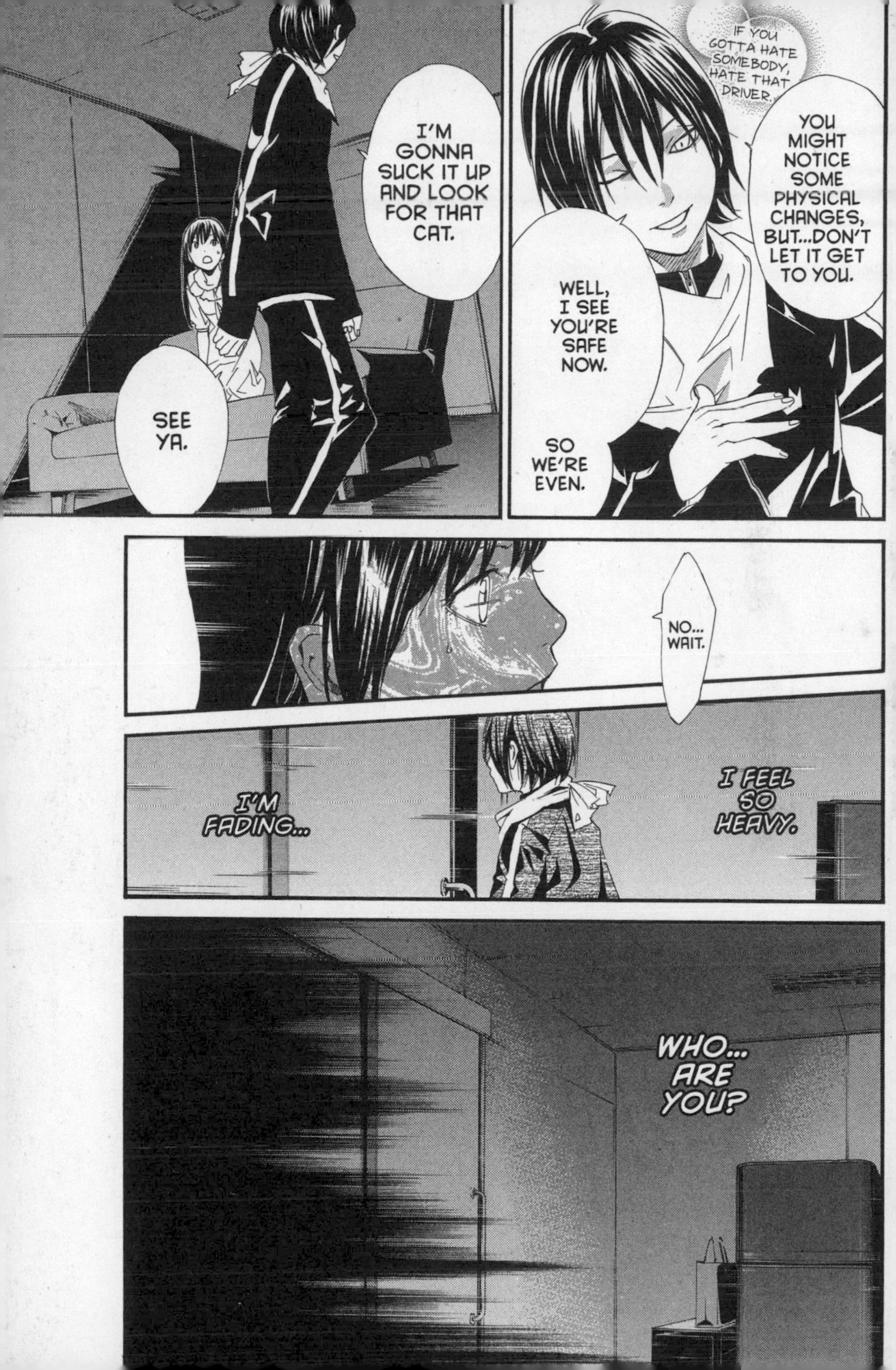
IF YOU GOTTA HATE SOMEBODY, HATE THAT DRIVER.
YOU MIGHT NOTICE SOME PHYSICAL CHANGES, BUT...DON'T LET IT GET TO YOU.
WELL, I SEE YOU'RE SAFE NOW.
SO WE'RE EVEN.
I'M GONNA SUCK IT UP AND LOOK FOR THAT CAT.
SEE YA.
NO... WAIT.
I FEEL SO HEAVY.
I'M FADING...
WHO... ARE YOU?

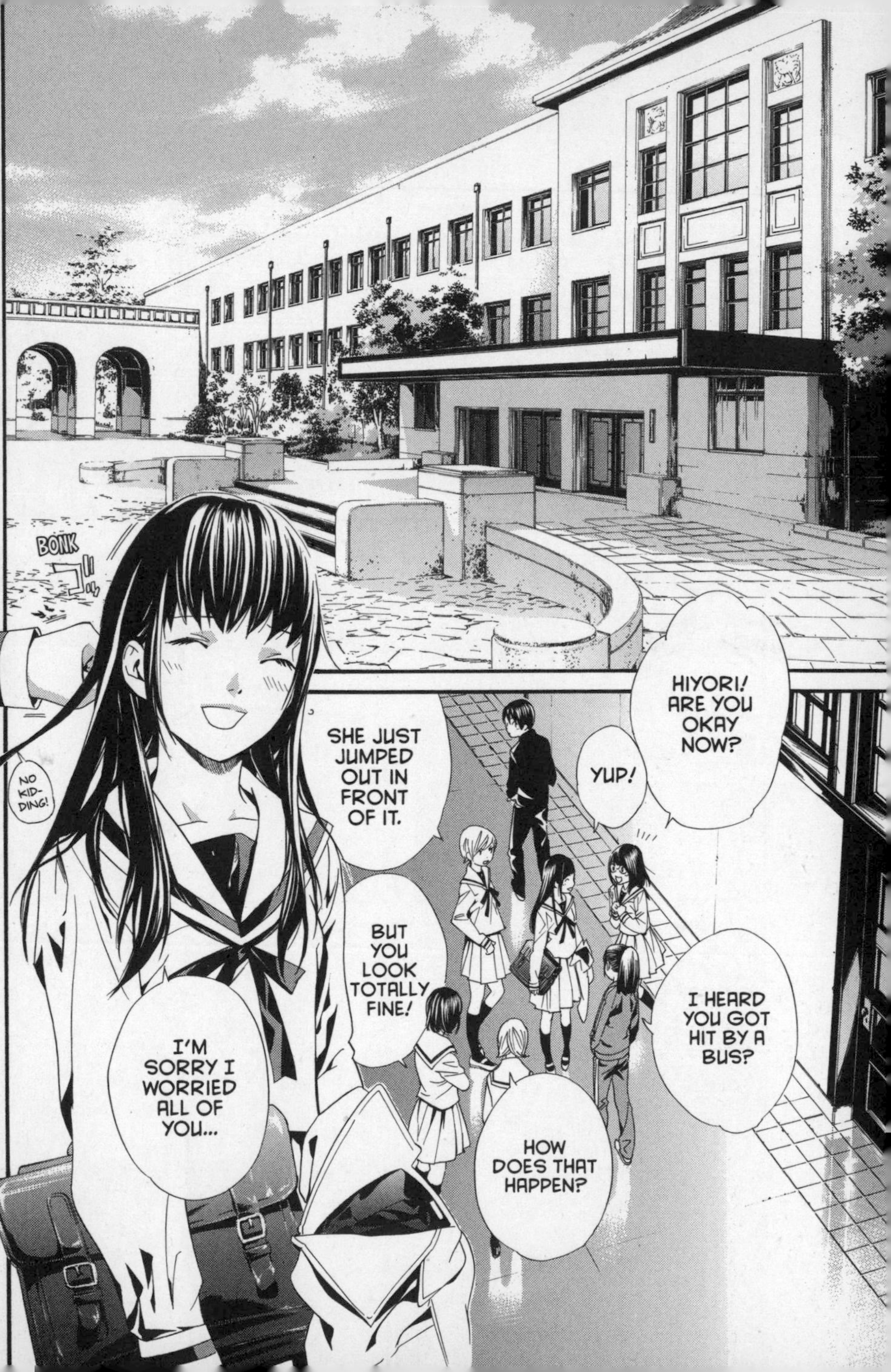
HIYORI! ARE YOU OKAY NOW?
YUP!
SHE JUST JUMPED OUT IN FRONT OF IT.
I HEARD YOU GOT HIT BY A BUS?
BUT YOU LOOK TOTALLY FINE!
HOW DOES THAT HAPPEN?
I'M SORRY I WORRIED ALL OF YOU...
NO KID-DING!
BONK

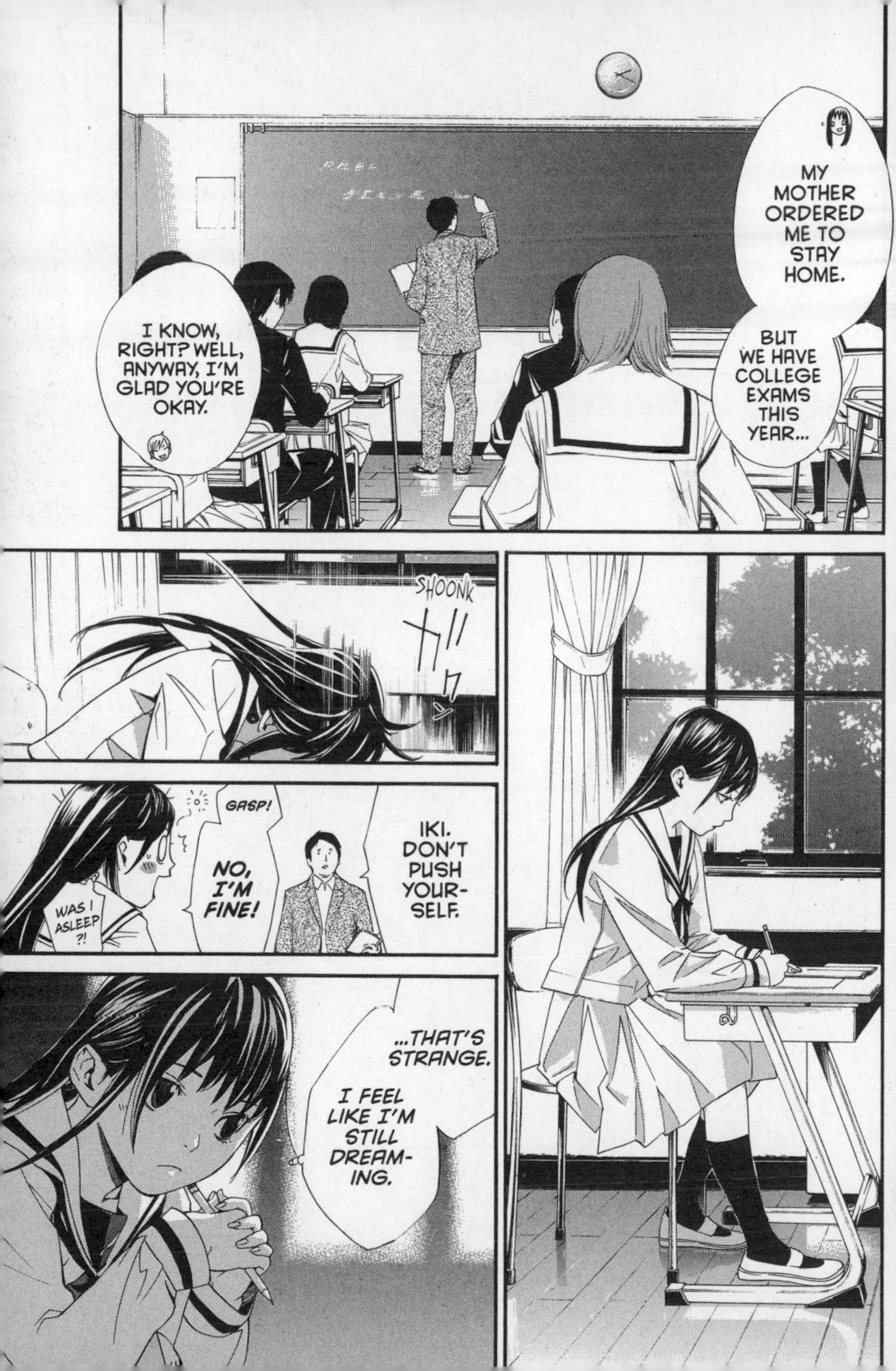
MY MOTHER ORDERED ME TO STAY HOME.
BUT WE HAVE COLLEGE EXAMS THIS YEAR...
I KNOW, RIGHT? WELL, ANYWAY, I'M GLAD YOU'RE OKAY.
SHOONK
ガタッ
IKI. DON'T PUSH YOURSELF.
NO, I'M FINE!
GASP!
WAS I ASLEEP?!
...THAT'S STRANGE.
I FEEL LIKE I'M STILL DREAMING.

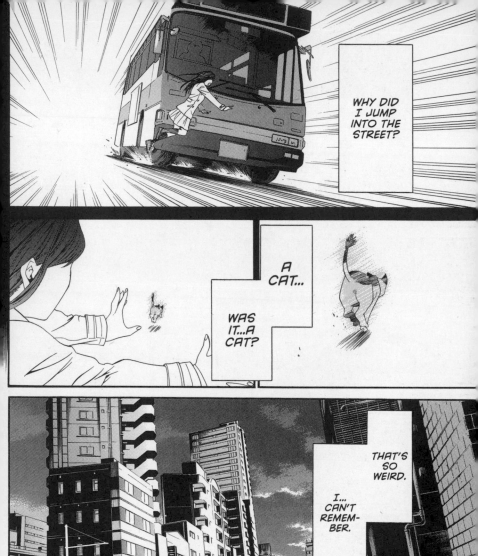

WHY DID I JUMP INTO THE STREET?

A CAT...

WAS IT...A CAT?

THAT'S SO WEIRD.

I... CAN'T REMEM-BER.

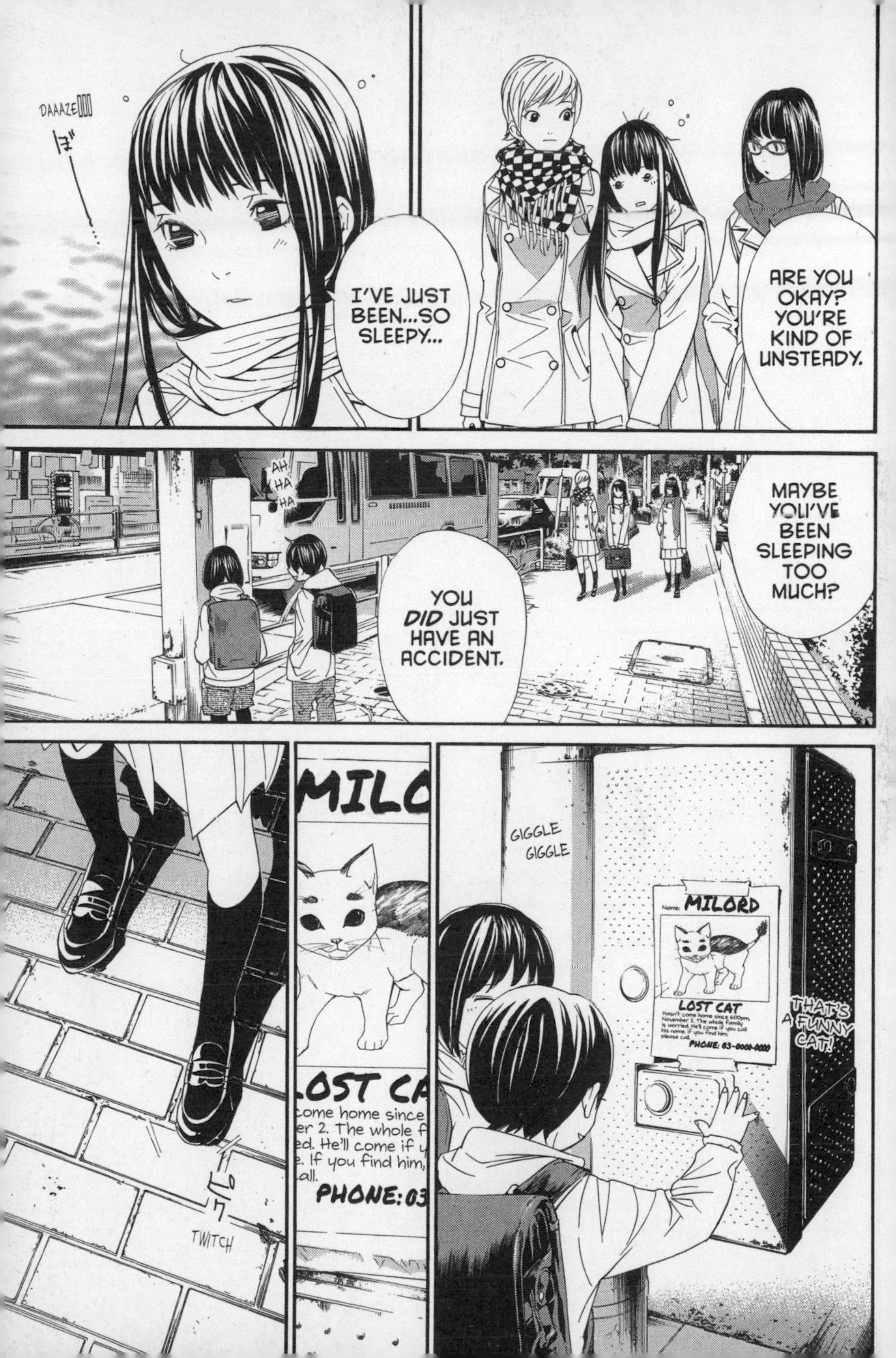
ARE YOU OKAY? YOU'RE KIND OF UNSTEADY.
DAAAZE
ぼー
I'VE JUST BEEN...SO SLEEPY...
MAYBE YOU'VE BEEN SLEEPING TOO MUCH?
YOU DID JUST HAVE AN ACCIDENT.
AH HA HA
GIGGLE GIGGLE
Name: MILORD
LOST CAT
Hasn't come home since 600pm, November 2. The whole family is worried. He'll come if you call his name. If you find him, please call.
PHONE: 03-0000-0000
THAT'S A FUNNY CAT!
MILO
LOST CA
come home since
er 2. The whole f
ed. He'll come if y
e. If you find him,
all.
PHONE:03
ピク
TWITCH

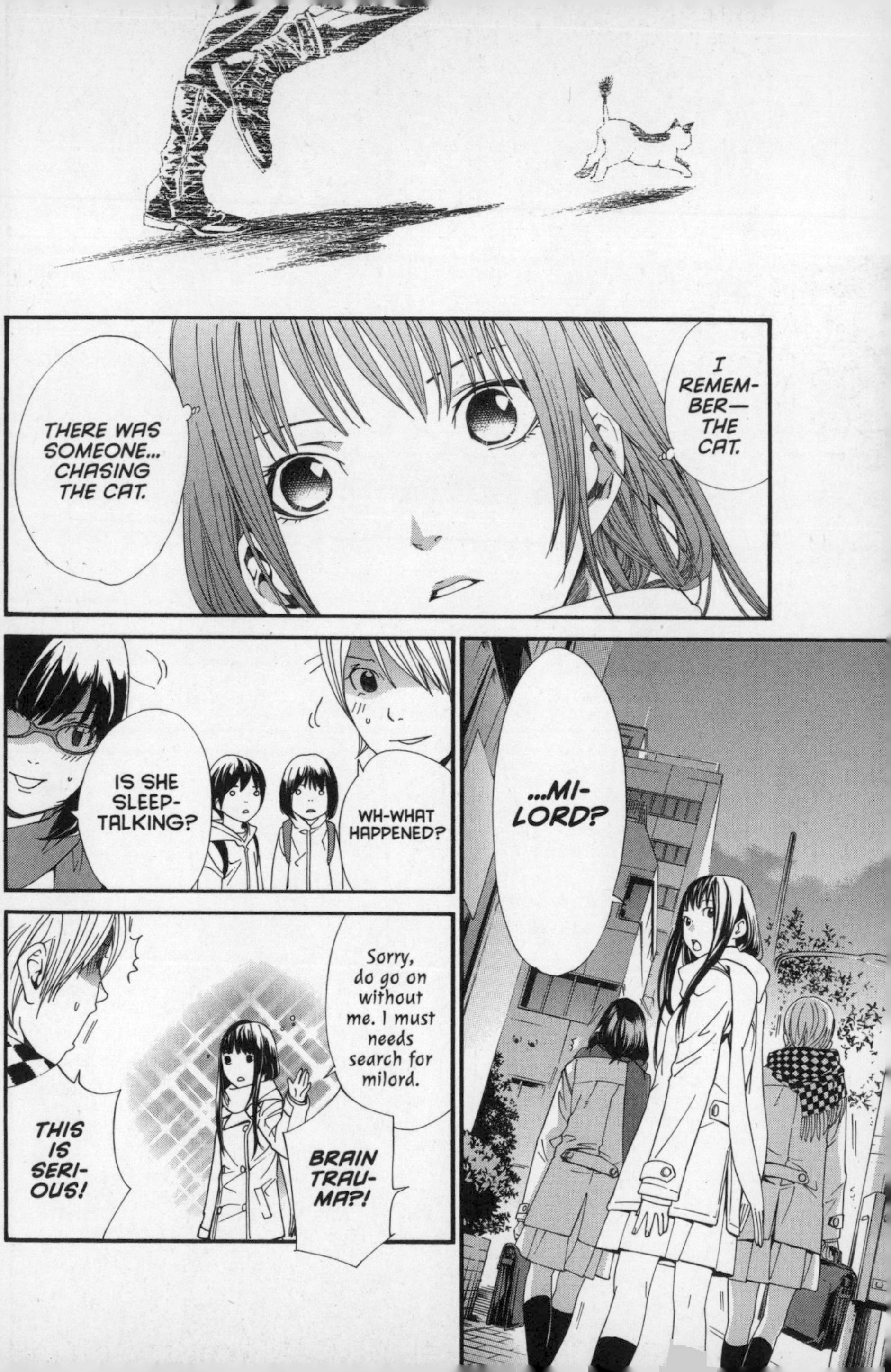

I REMEMBER—THE CAT.
THERE WAS SOMEONE... CHASING THE CAT.
...MILORD?
WH-WHAT HAPPENED?
IS SHE SLEEP-TALKING?
Sorry, do go on without me. I must needs search for milord.
BRAIN TRAUMA?!
THIS IS SERIOUS!

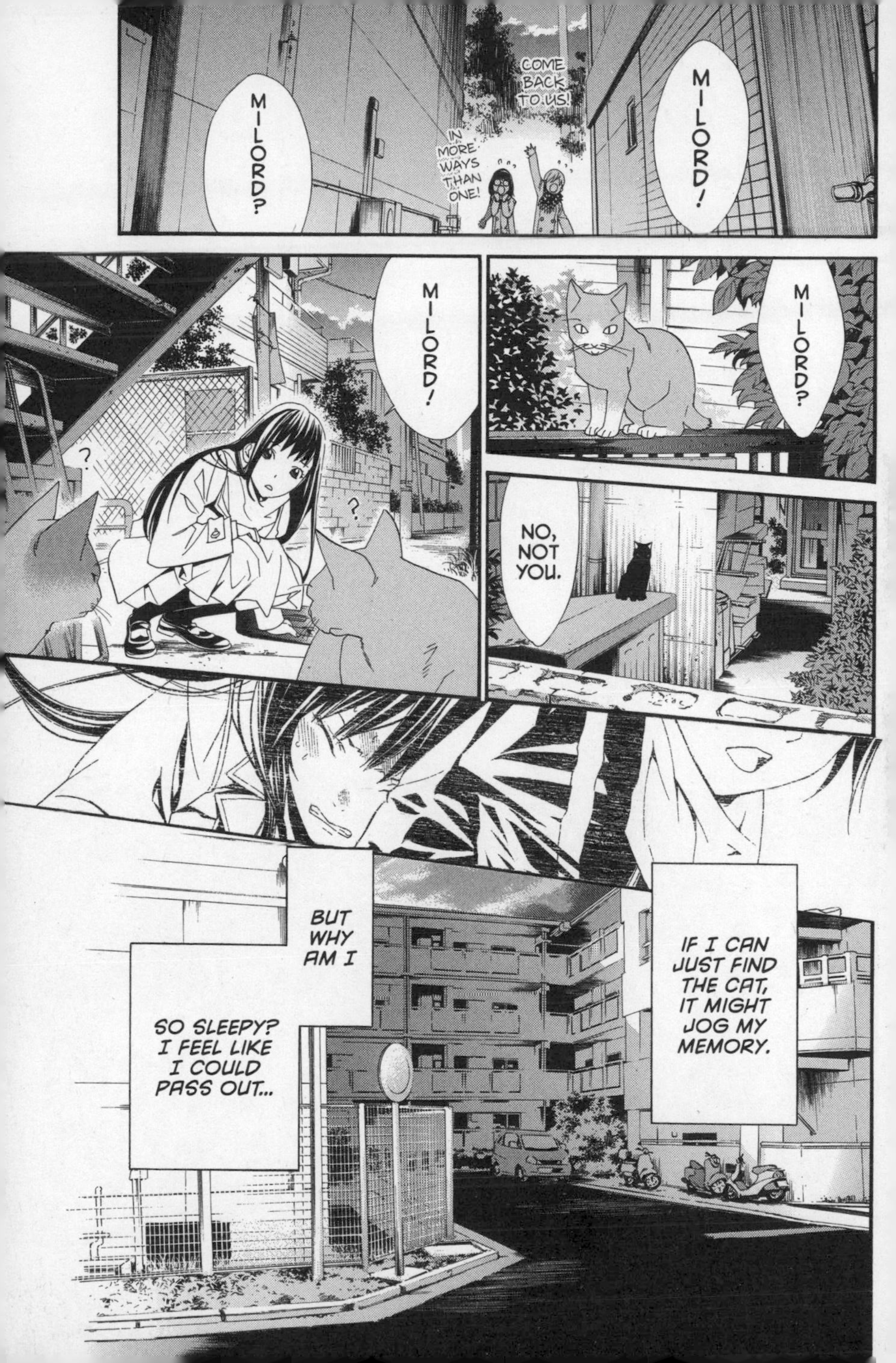
MILORD!
COME BACK TO US!
IN MORE WAYS THAN ONE!
MILORD?
MILORD?
NO, NOT YOU.
MILORD!
?
?
IF I CAN JUST FIND THE CAT, IT MIGHT JOG MY MEMORY.
BUT WHY AM I
SO SLEEPY? I FEEL LIKE I COULD PASS OUT...

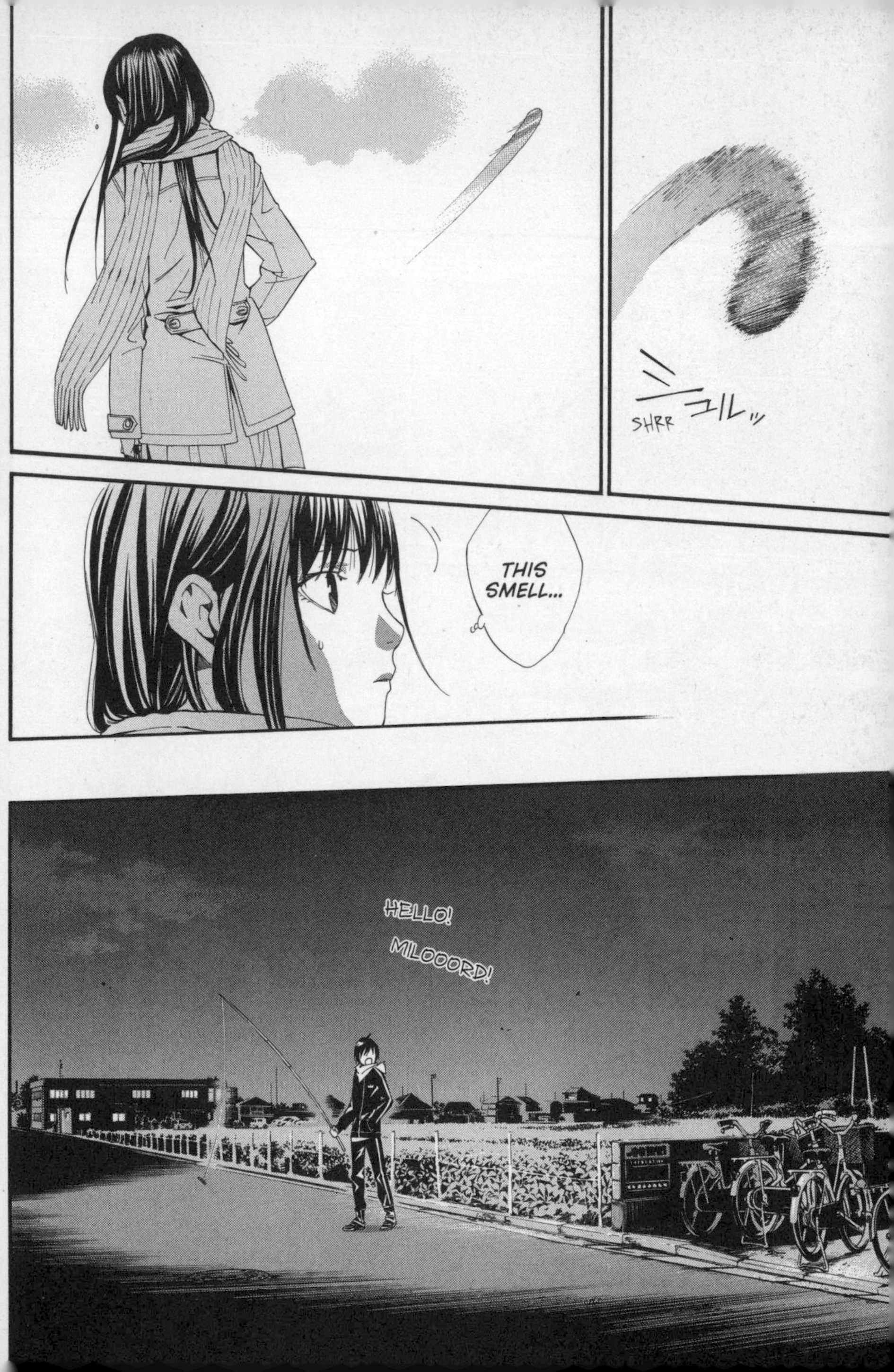

SHRR
シュルッ
THIS SMELL...
HELLO!
MILOOORD!

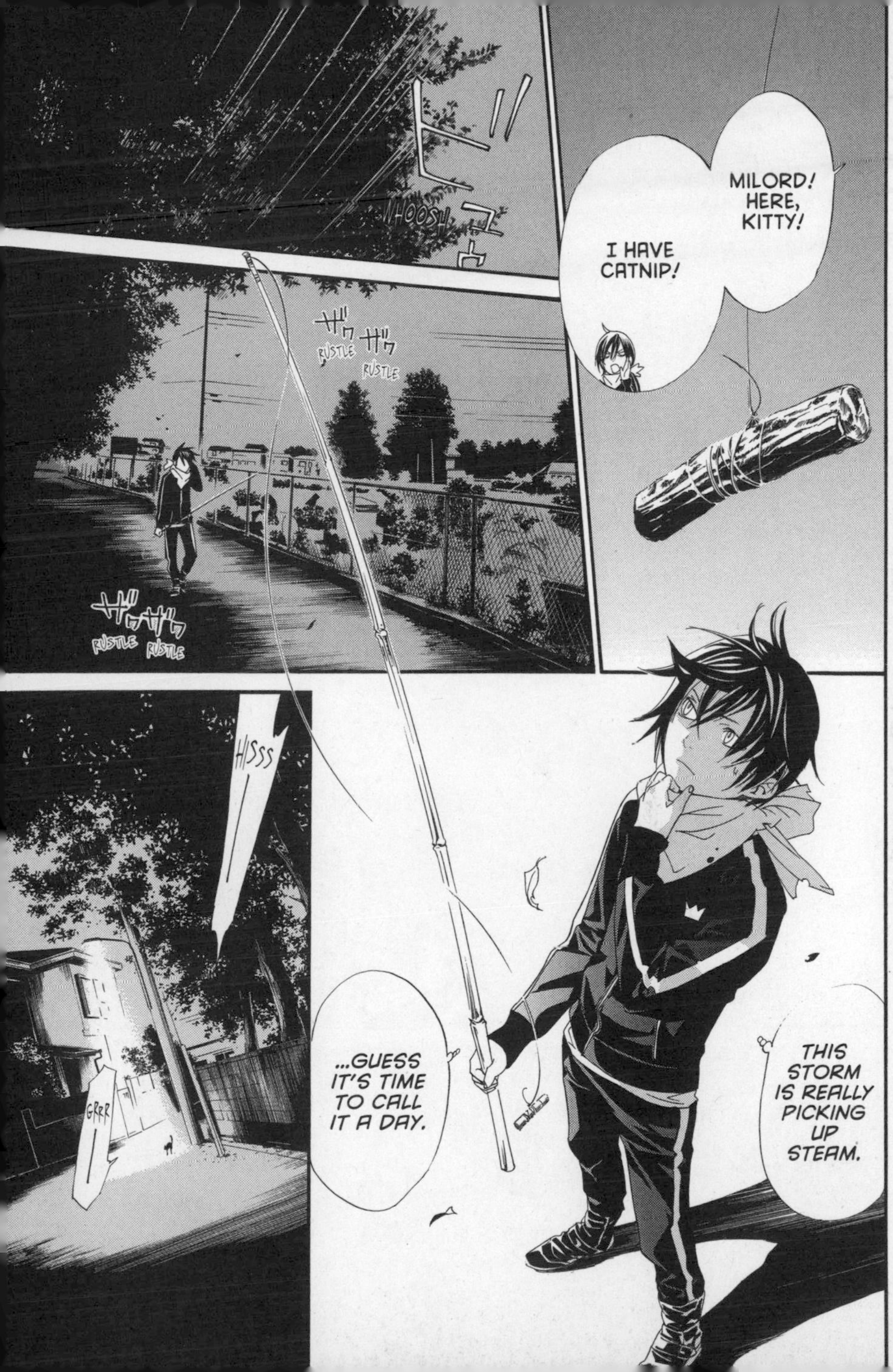
MILORD! HERE, KITTY!
I HAVE CATNIP!
WHOOSH
RUSTLE RUSTLE
RUSTLE RUSTLE
THIS STORM IS REALLY PICKING UP STEAM.
...GUESS IT'S TIME TO CALL IT A DAY.
HISSS
GRRR

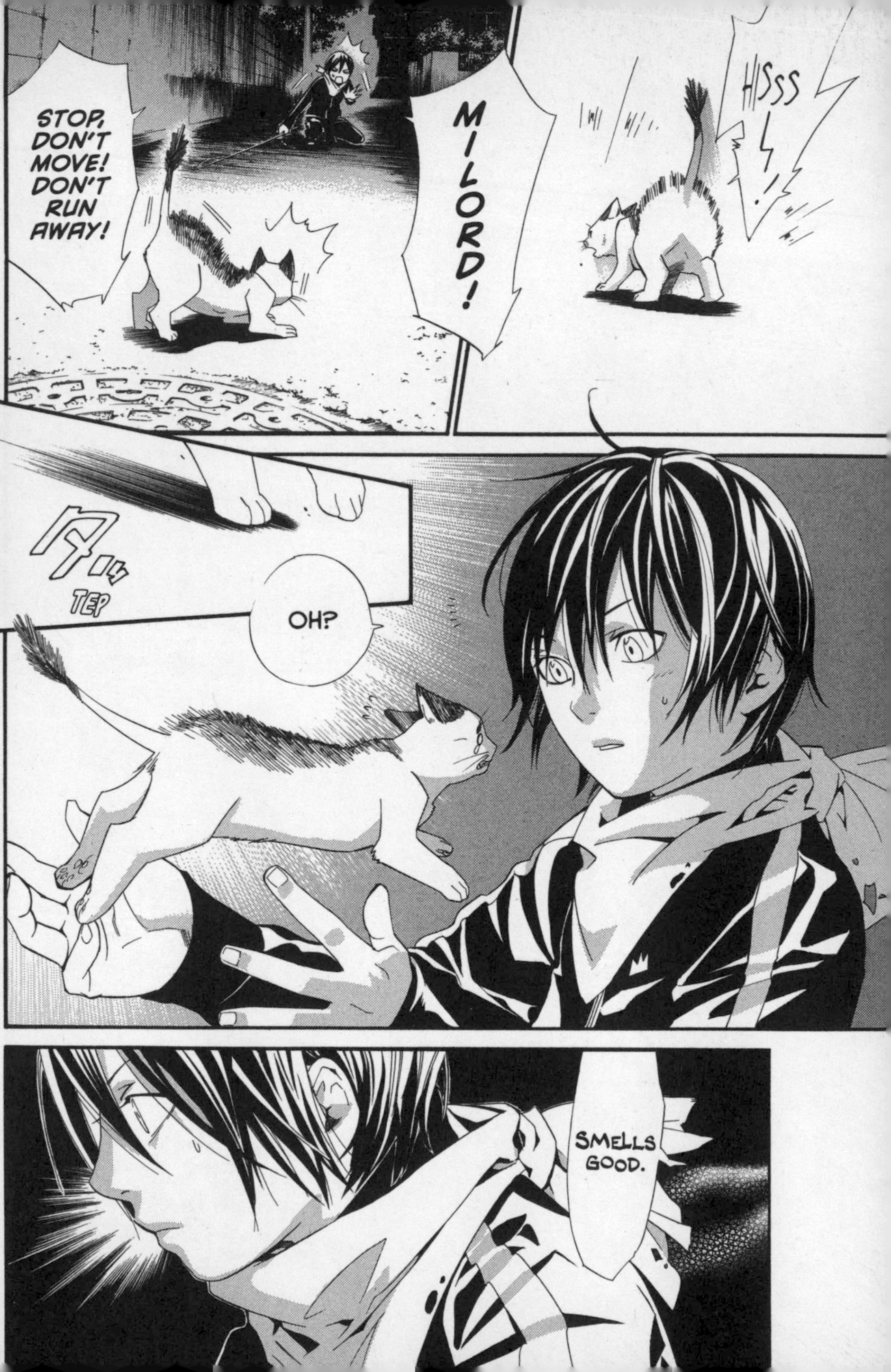
HISSS
MILORD!
STOP, DON'T MOVE! DON'T RUN AWAY!
タッ
TEP
OH?
SMELLS GOOD.

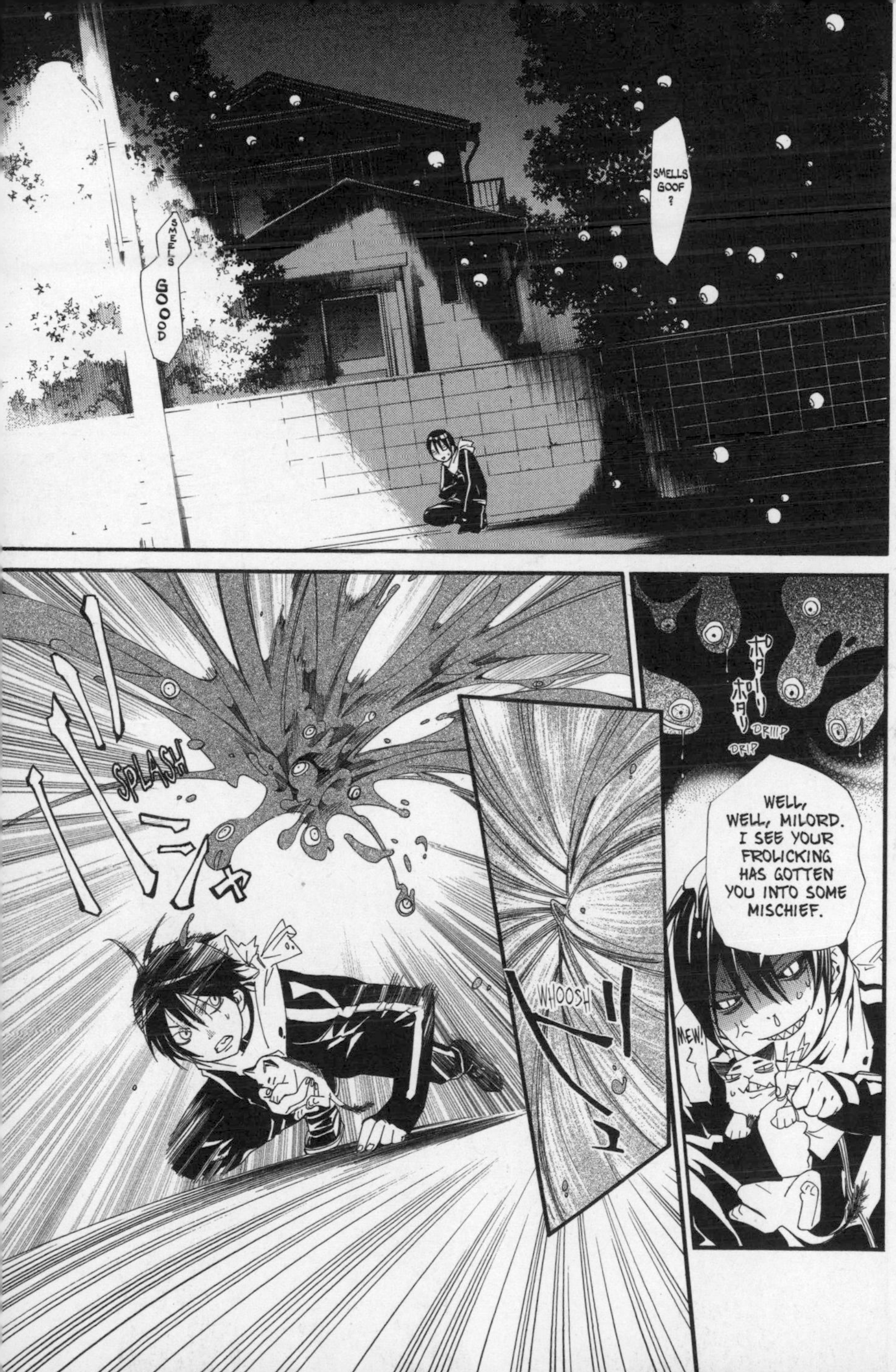
SMELLS GOOF?
SMELLS GOOOD
ポタリ ポタリ
DRIIIP
DRIP
WELL, WELL, MILORD. I SEE YOUR FROLICKING HAS GOTTEN YOU INTO SOME MISCHIEF.
MEW!
WHOOSH
SPLASH

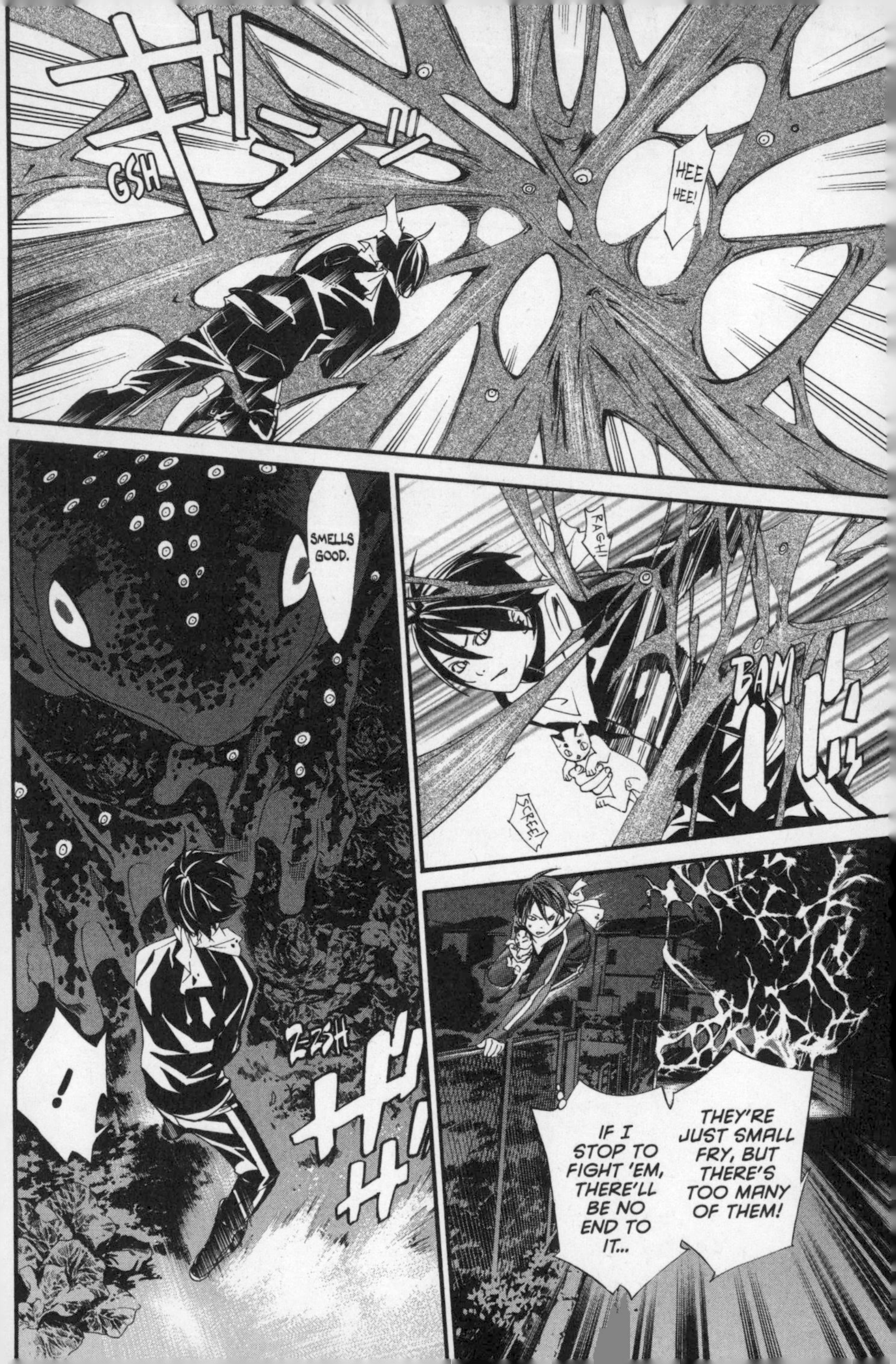
HEE HEE!
GSH
RAGH!
BAM
SCREE!
THEY'RE JUST SMALL FRY, BUT THERE'S TOO MANY OF THEM!
IF I STOP TO FIGHT 'EM, THERE'LL BE NO END TO IT...
SMELLS GOOD.
Z-ZSH
!

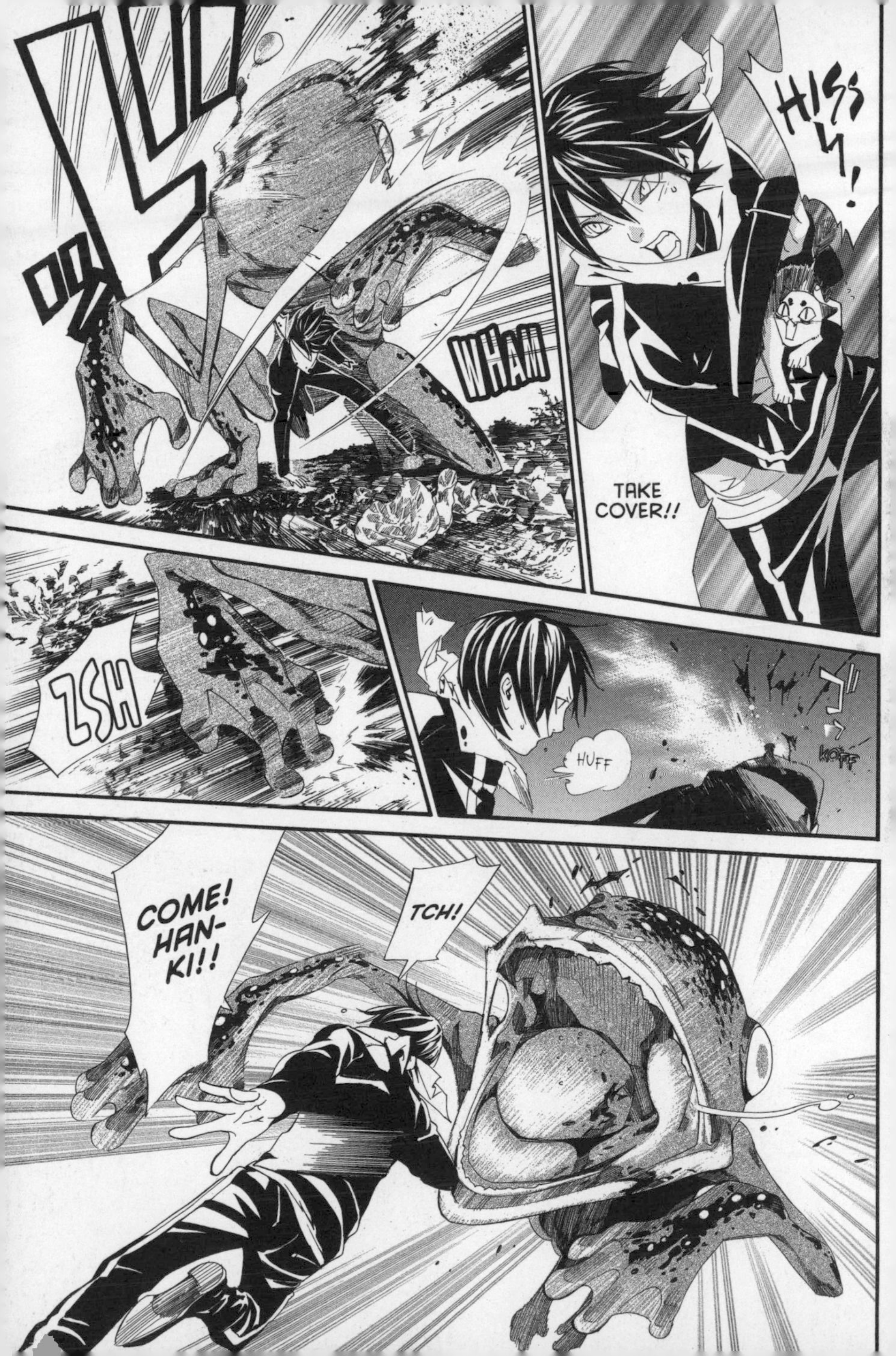
HISSS!
TAKE COVER!!
WHAM
HUFF
KOFF
ZSH
TCH!
COME! HAN-KI!!

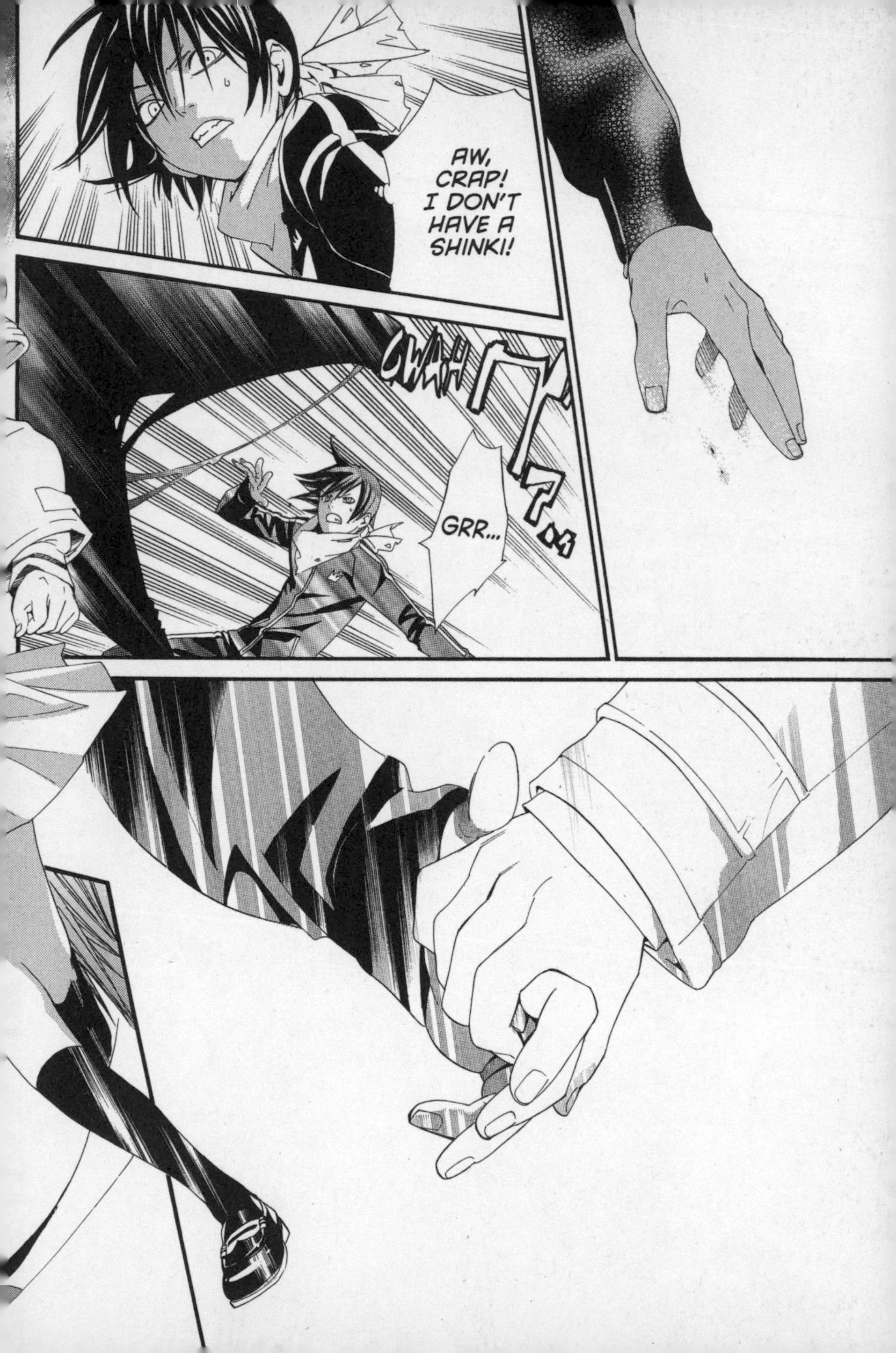
AW, CRAP! I DON'T HAVE A SHINKI!
GWAH
GRR...

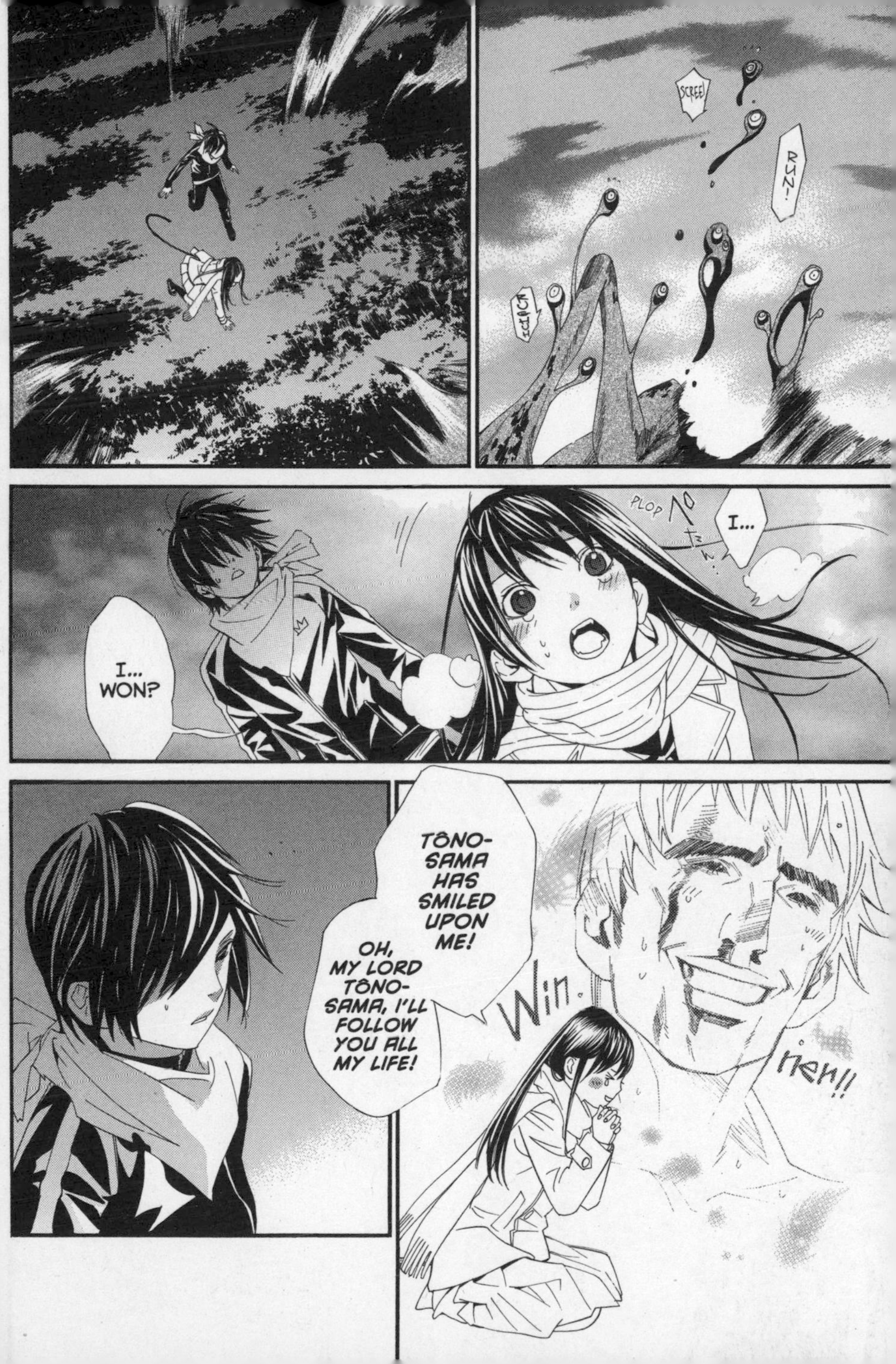
SCREE!
RUN!
PLOP
I...
I... WON?
TÔNO-SAMA HAS SMILED UPON ME!
OH, MY LORD TÔNO-SAMA, I'LL FOLLOW YOU ALL MY LIFE!
Win. nen!!

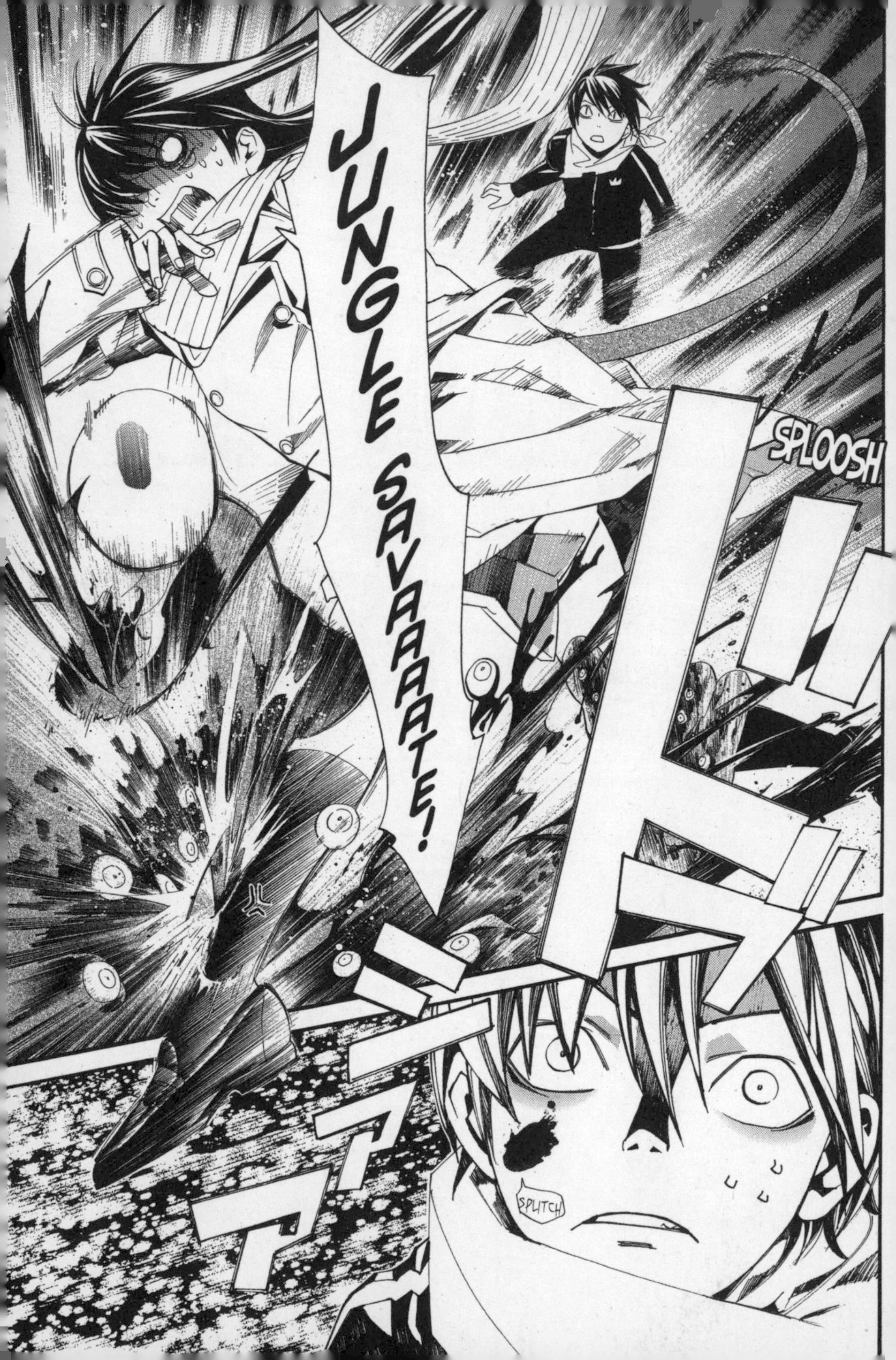
JUNGLE SAVAAAAATE!
SPLOOSH
SPLITCH

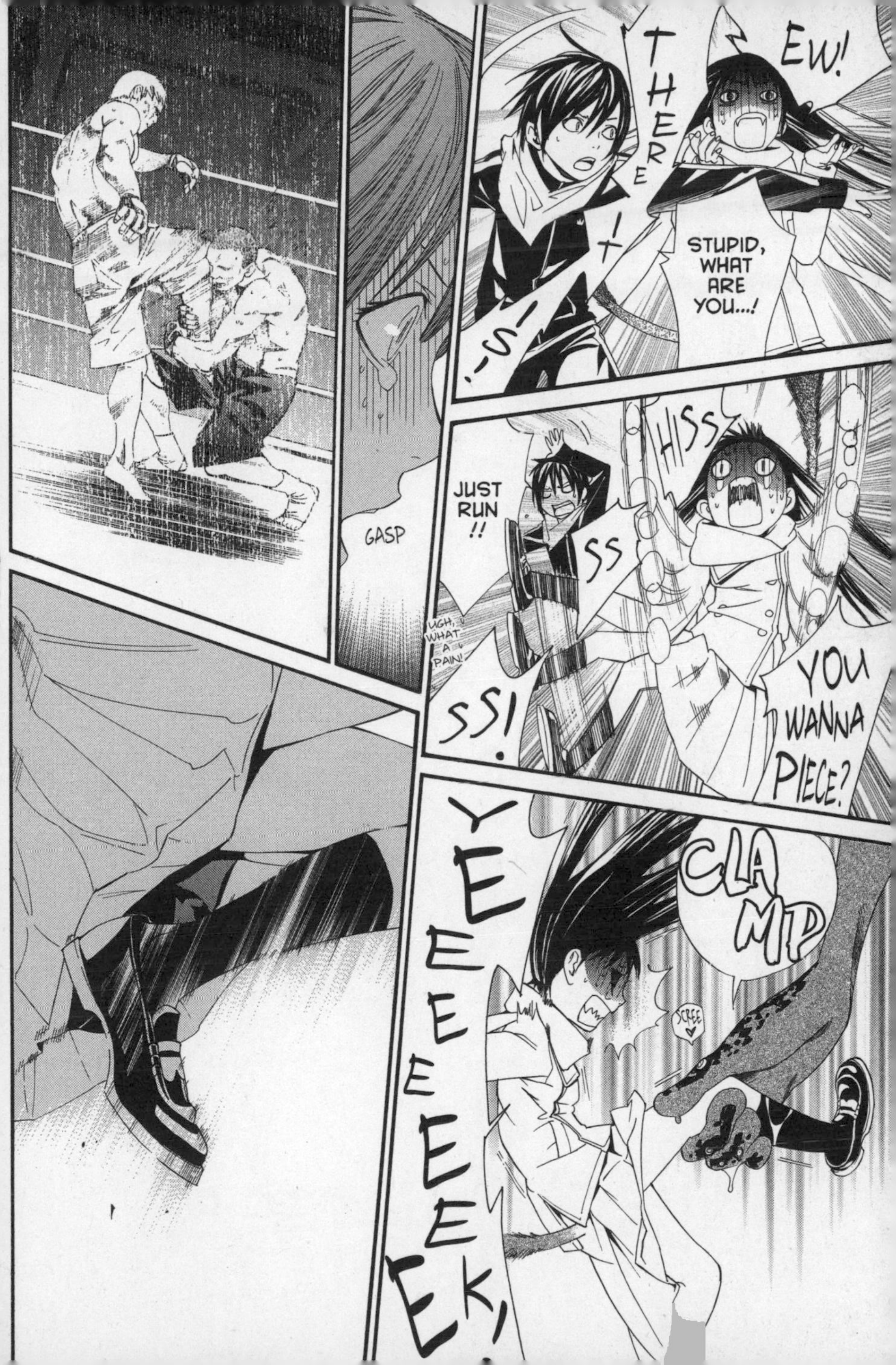
EW!
THERE IT IS!
STUPID, WHAT ARE YOU...!
HISS
JUST RUN!!
SS
UGH, WHAT A PAIN!
SSI!
YOU WANNA PIECE?
CLAMP
SCREE
YEEEEEEEK!
GASP

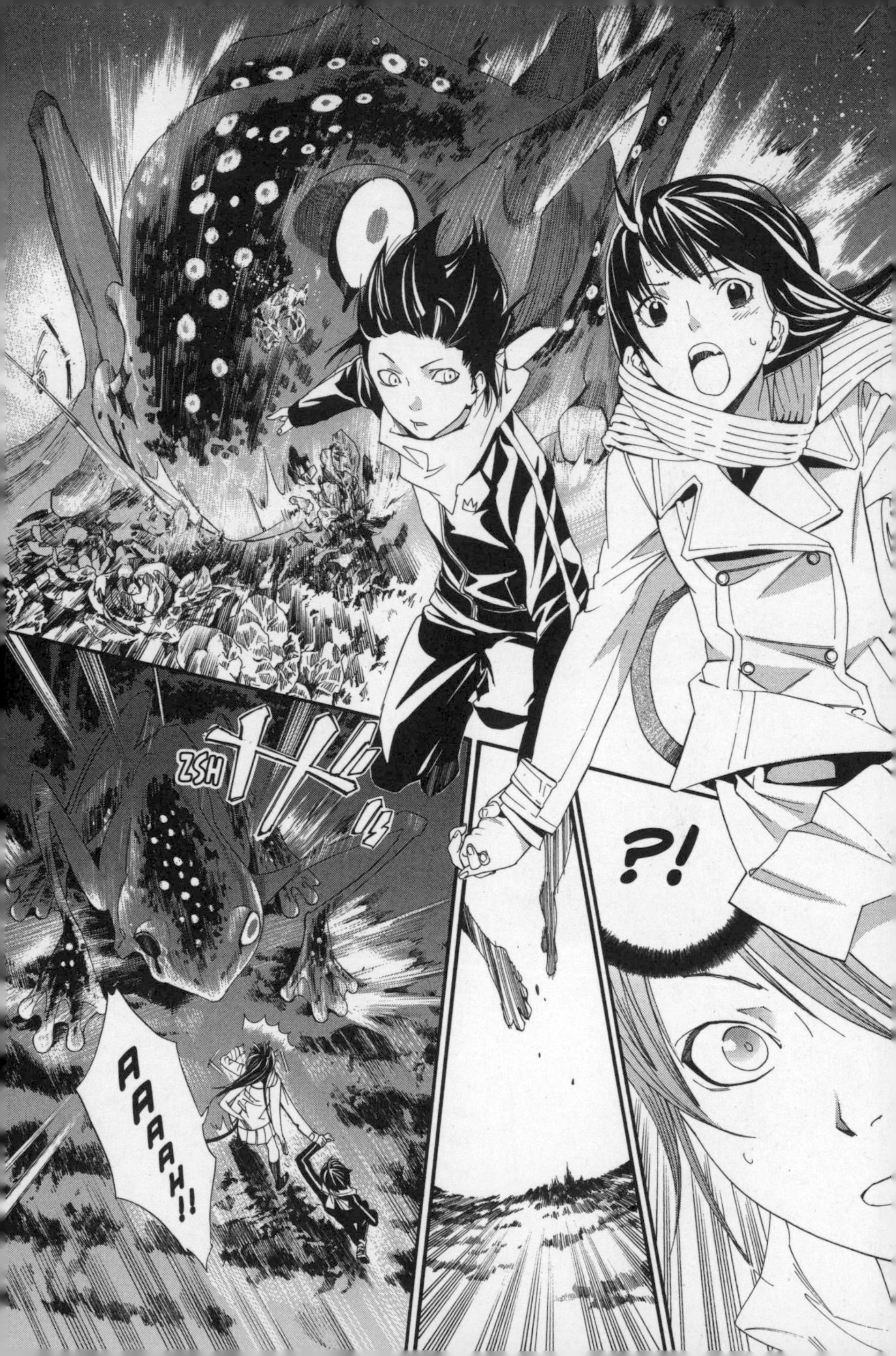
?!
ZSH
AAAAH!!

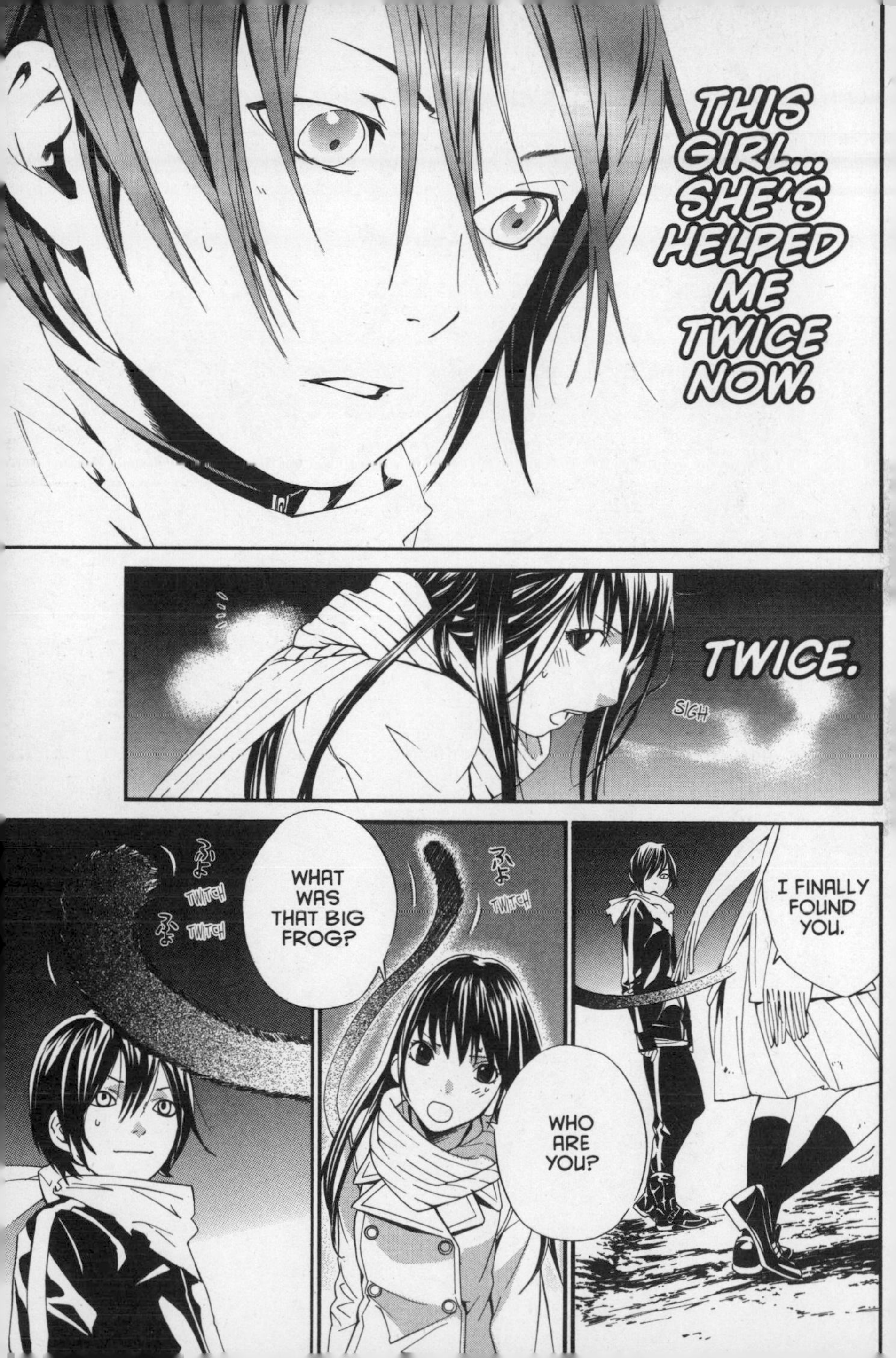
THIS GIRL... SHE'S HELPED ME TWICE NOW.
TWICE.
SIGH
I FINALLY FOUND YOU.
ふよ
TWITCH
WHO ARE YOU?
WHAT WAS THAT BIG FROG?
ふよ
TWITCH
ふよ
TWITCH

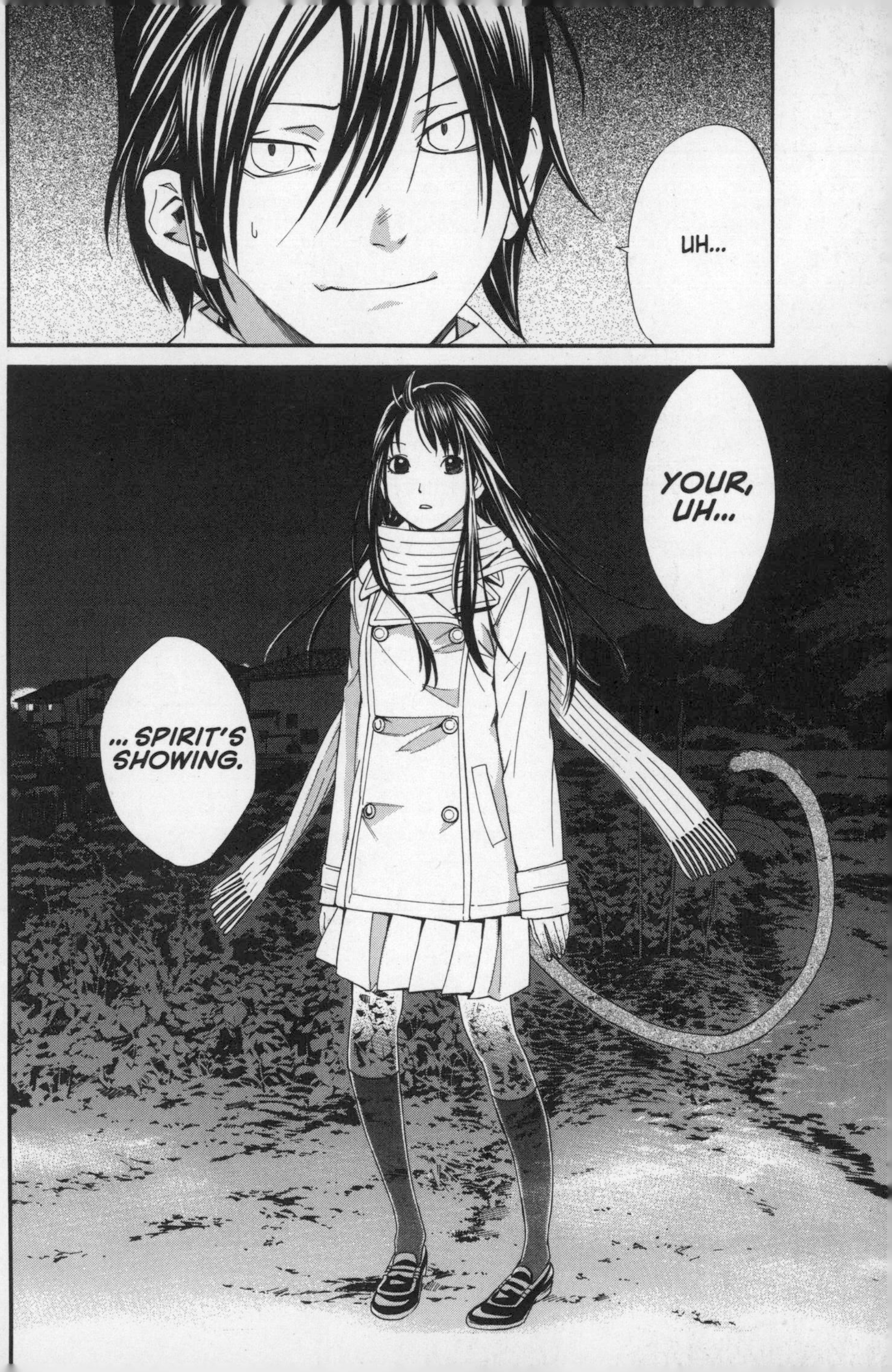
UH...
YOUR, UH...
...SPIRIT'S SHOWING.

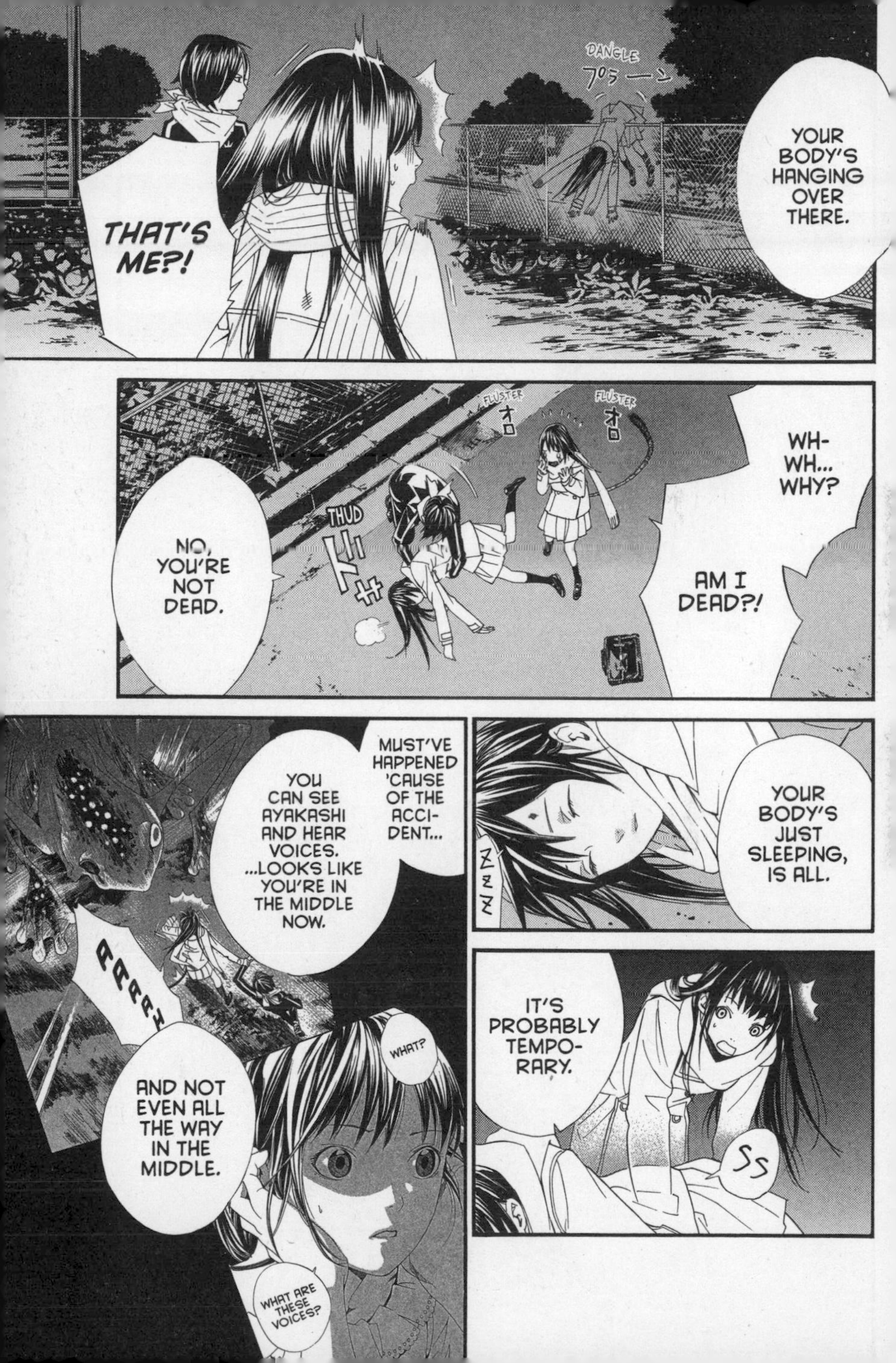
YOUR BODY'S HANGING OVER THERE.
DANGLE
THAT'S ME?!
WH-WH... WHY?
AM I DEAD?!
FLUSTER
FLUSTER
THUD
NO, YOU'RE NOT DEAD.
YOUR BODY'S JUST SLEEPING, IS ALL.
ZZZ
IT'S PROBABLY TEMPORARY.
SS
MUST'VE HAPPENED 'CAUSE OF THE ACCIDENT...
YOU CAN SEE AYAKASHI AND HEAR VOICES. ...LOOKS LIKE YOU'RE IN THE MIDDLE NOW.
AAAAH
WHAT?
AND NOT EVEN ALL THE WAY IN THE MIDDLE.
WHAT ARE THESE VOICES?

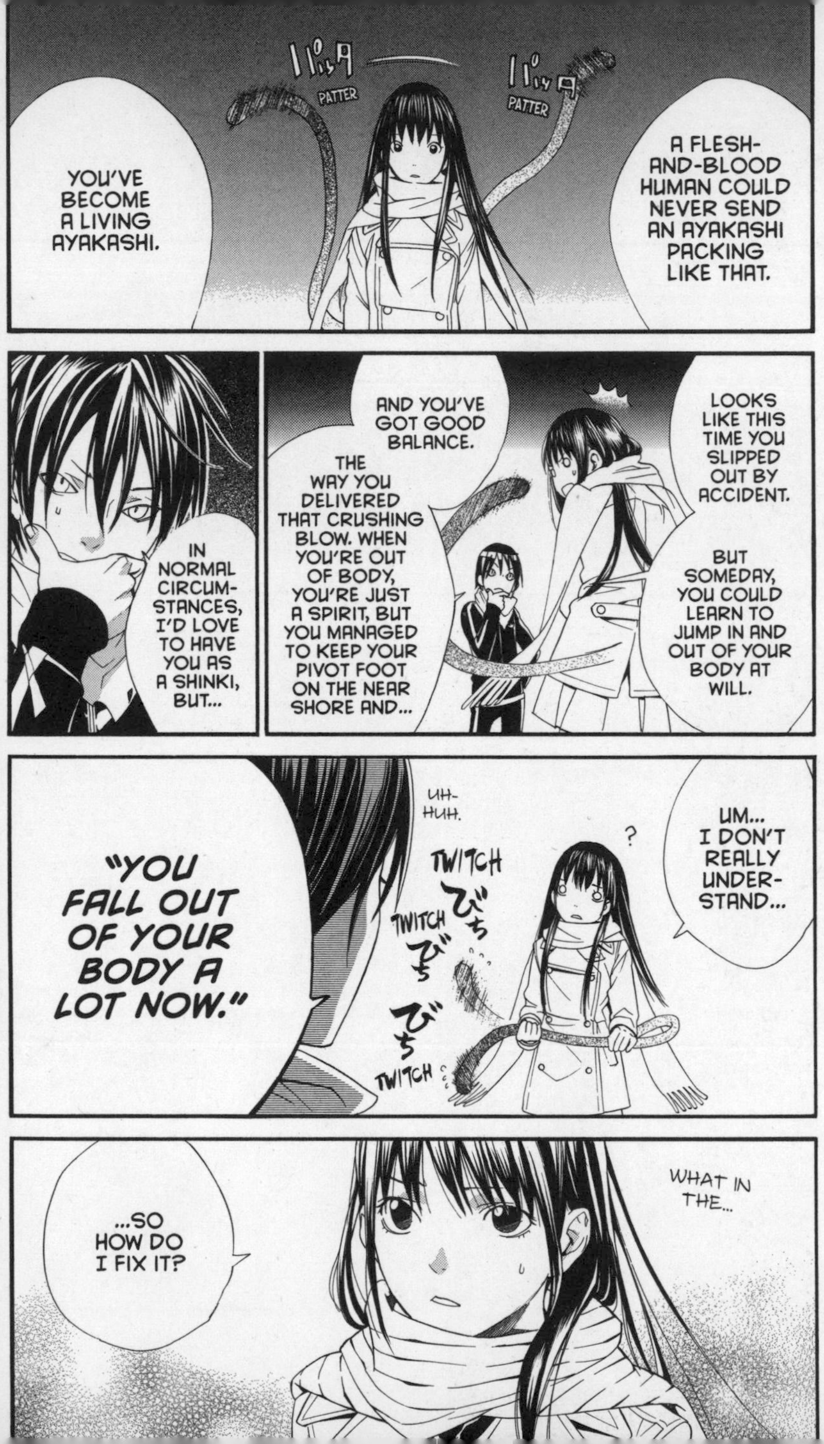
パッタ
PATTER
A FLESH-AND-BLOOD HUMAN COULD NEVER SEND AN AYAKASHI PACKING LIKE THAT.
パッタ
PATTER
YOU'VE BECOME A LIVING AYAKASHI.
LOOKS LIKE THIS TIME YOU SLIPPED OUT BY ACCIDENT.
BUT SOMEDAY, YOU COULD LEARN TO JUMP IN AND OUT OF YOUR BODY AT WILL.
AND YOU'VE GOT GOOD BALANCE.
THE WAY YOU DELIVERED THAT CRUSHING BLOW. WHEN YOU'RE OUT OF BODY, YOU'RE JUST A SPIRIT, BUT YOU MANAGED TO KEEP YOUR PIVOT FOOT ON THE NEAR SHORE AND...
IN NORMAL CIRCUMSTANCES, I'D LOVE TO HAVE YOU AS A SHINKI, BUT...
UM... I DON'T REALLY UNDERSTAND...
?
UH-HUH.
TWITCH
びち
TWITCH
びち
びち
TWITCH
"YOU FALL OUT OF YOUR BODY A LOT NOW."
WHAT IN THE...
...SO HOW DO I FIX IT?

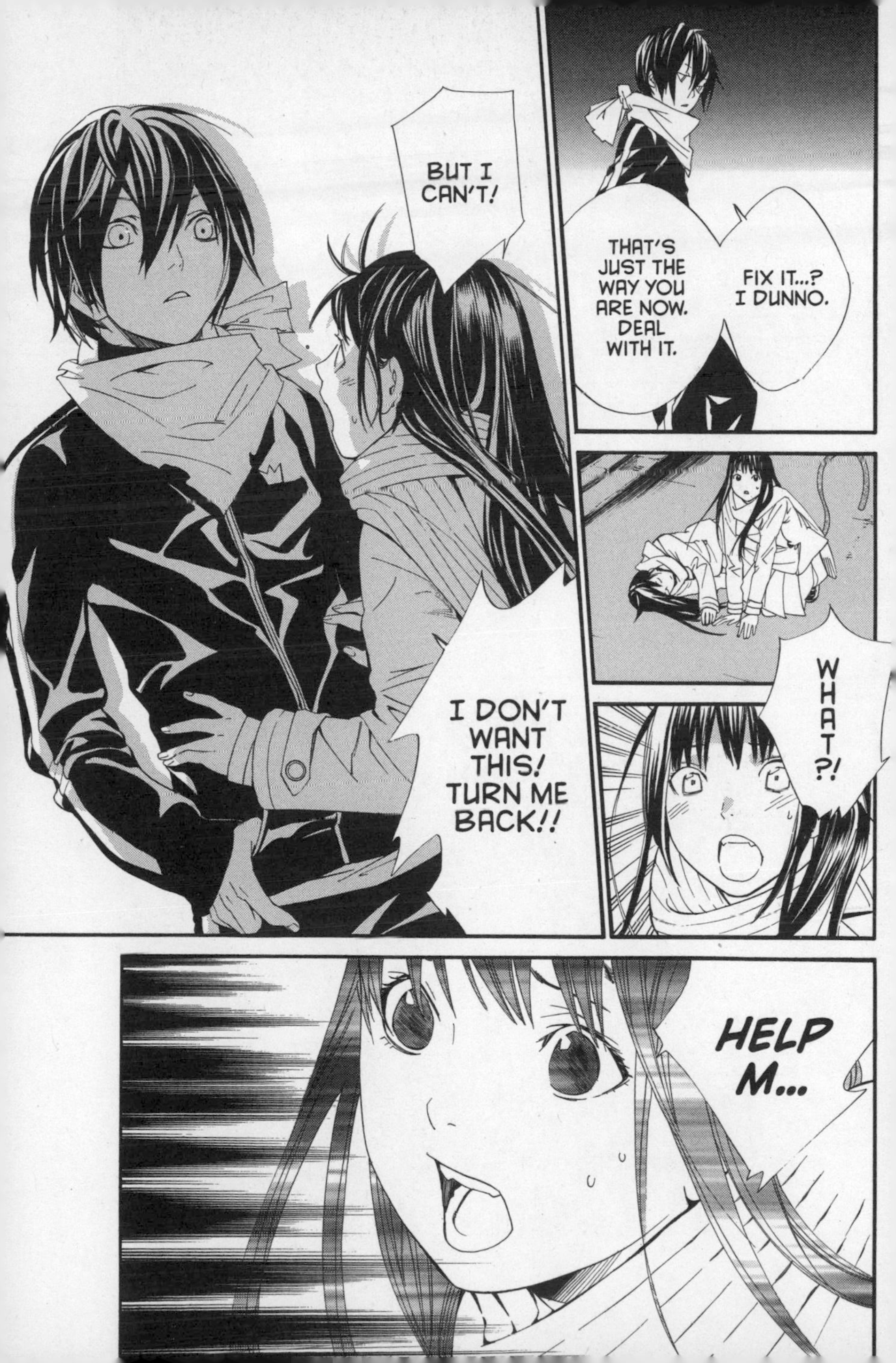
FIX IT...? I DUNNO.
THAT'S JUST THE WAY YOU ARE NOW. DEAL WITH IT.
WHAT?!
BUT I CAN'T!
I DON'T WANT THIS! TURN ME BACK!!
HELP M...

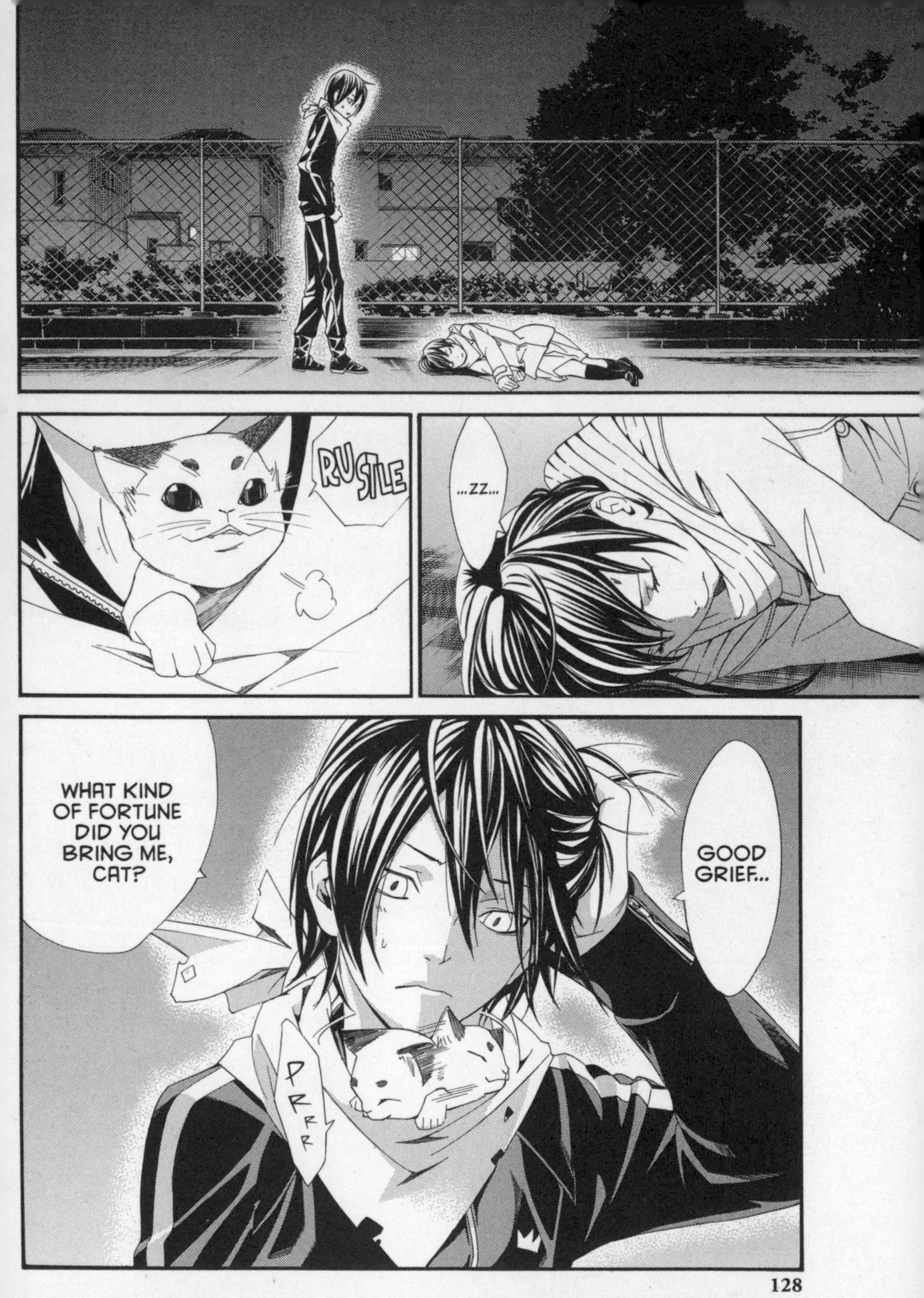
...ZZ...
RUSTLE
GOOD GRIEF...
WHAT KIND OF FORTUNE DID YOU BRING ME, CAT?
PRRR

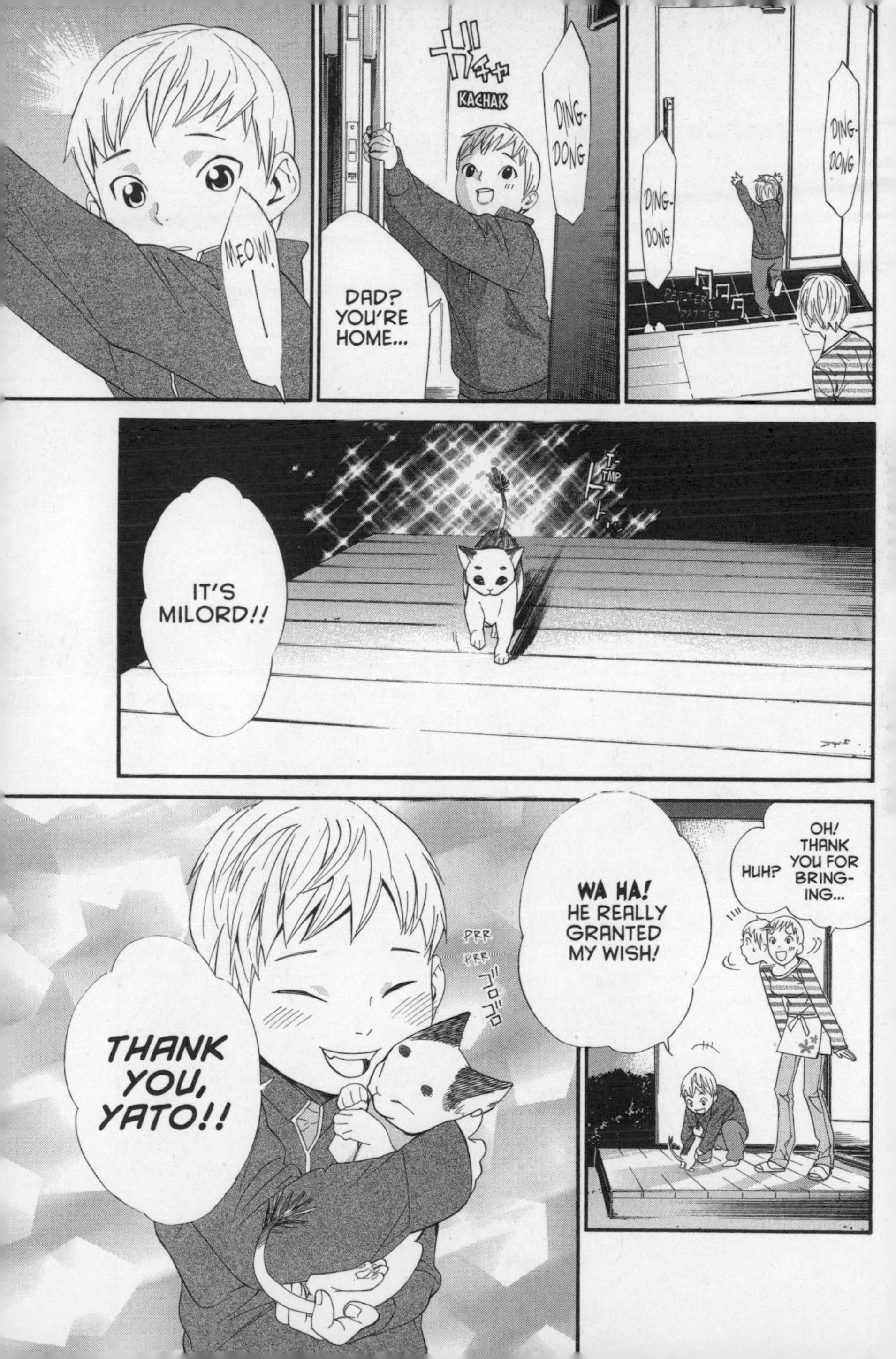
DING-DONG
DING-DONG
PATTER PATTER
KACHAK
DING-DONG
DAD? YOU'RE HOME...
MEOW!
T-TMP
IT'S MILORD!!
OH! THANK YOU FOR BRING-ING...
HUH?
WA HA! HE REALLY GRANTED MY WISH!
PRR PRR
THANK YOU, YATO!!

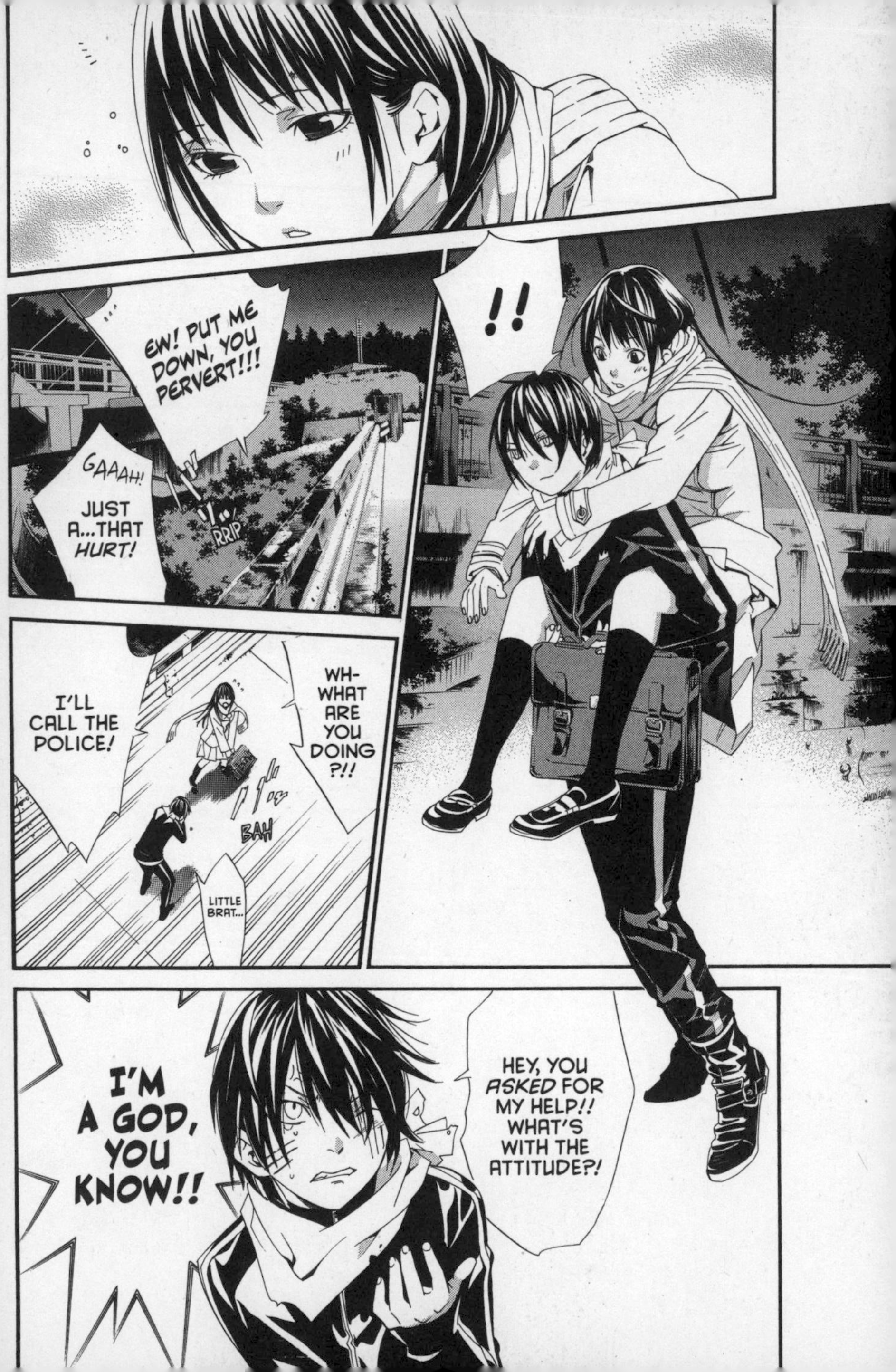
!!
EW! PUT ME DOWN, YOU PERVERT!!!
GAAAH!
RRIP
JUST A...THAT *HURT!*
WH-WHAT ARE YOU DOING?!!
I'LL CALL THE POLICE!
BAH
LITTLE BRAT...
HEY, YOU *ASKED* FOR MY HELP!! WHAT'S WITH THE ATTITUDE?!
I'M A GOD, YOU KNOW!!

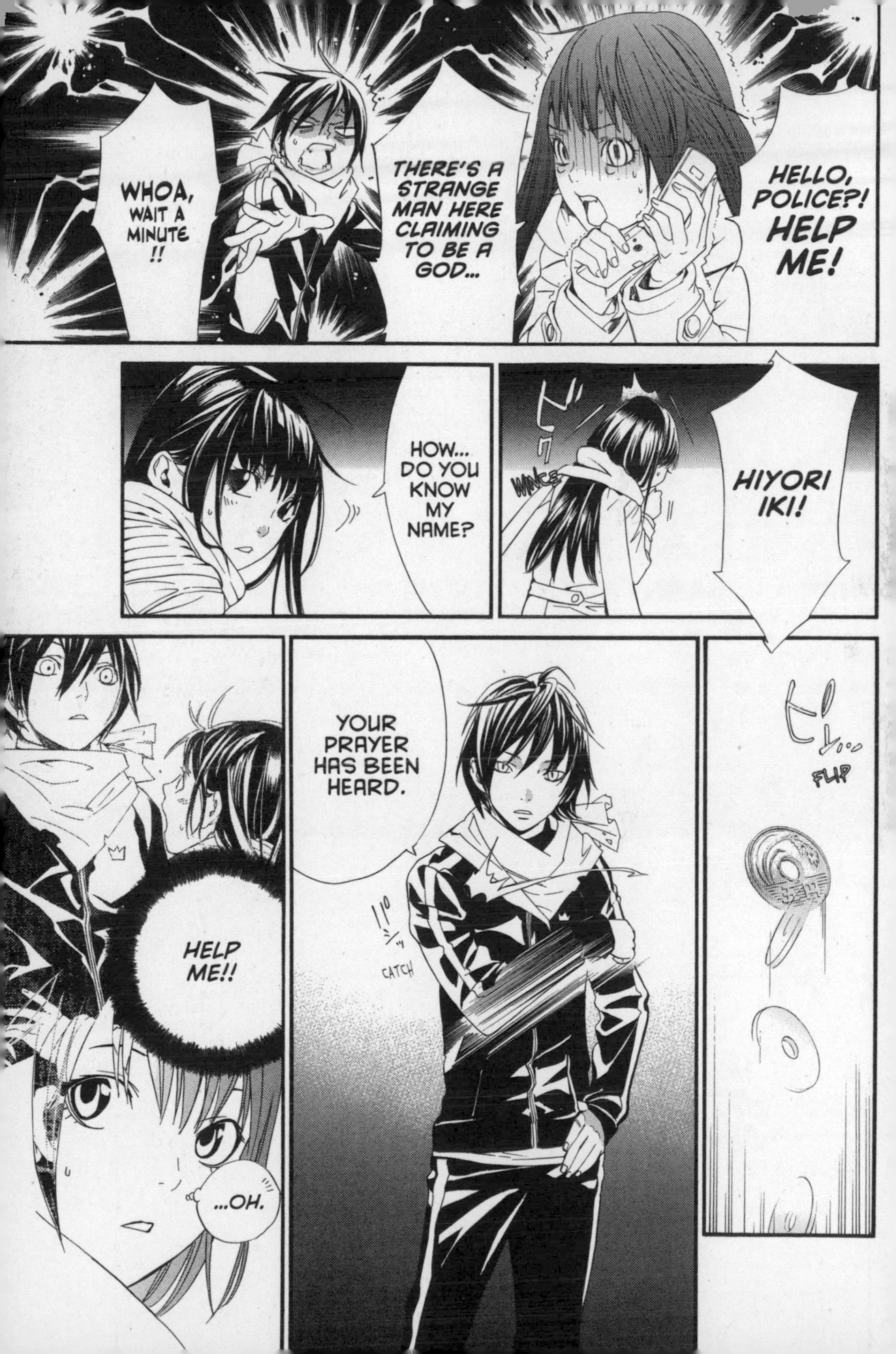
HELLO, POLICE?! HELP ME!
THERE'S A STRANGE MAN HERE CLAIMING TO BE A GOD...
WHOA, WAIT A MINUTE !!
HIYORI IKI!
WINCE
HOW... DO YOU KNOW MY NAME?
FLIP
YOUR PRAYER HAS BEEN HEARD.
CATCH
HELP ME!!
...OH.

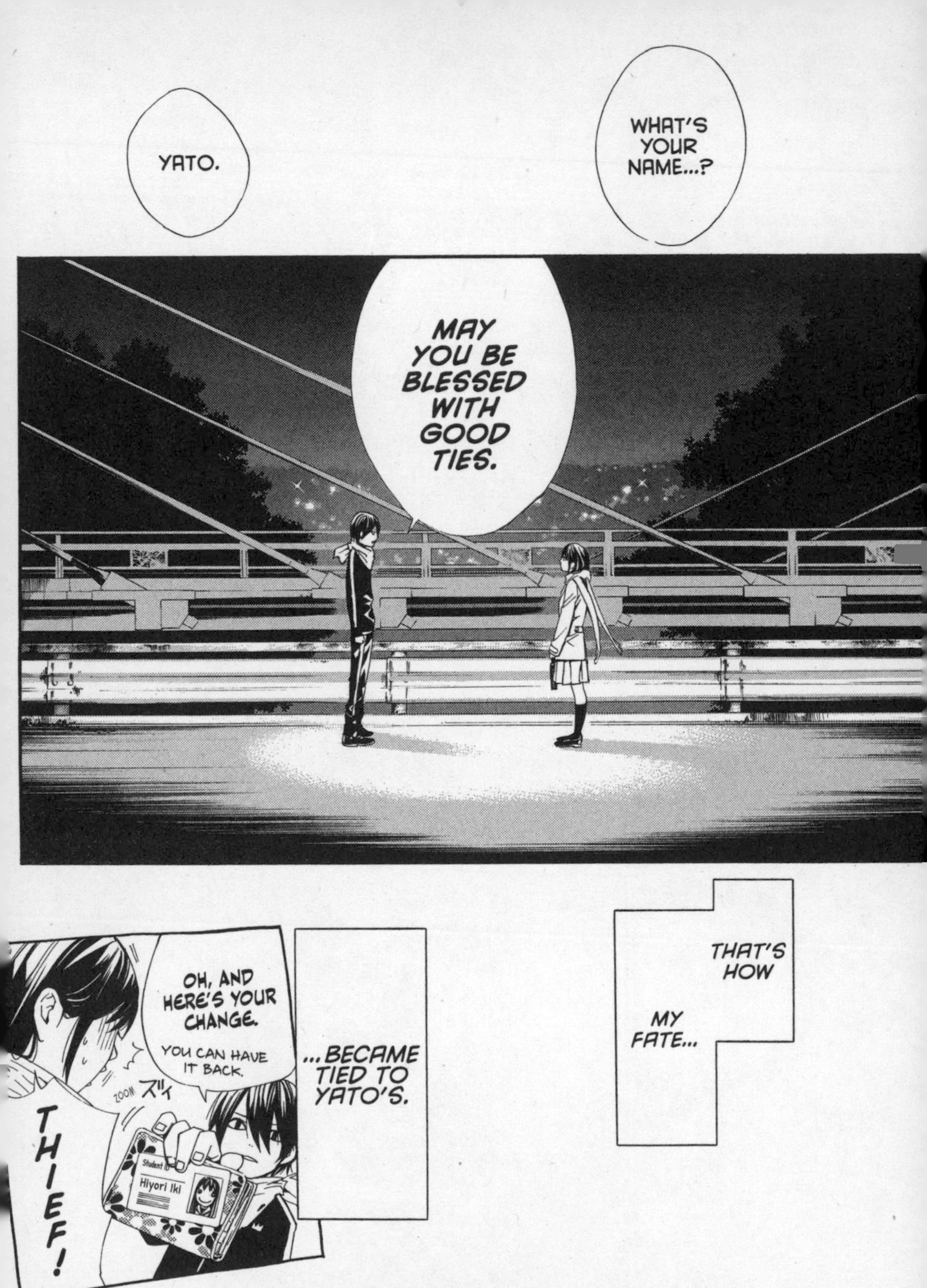
WHAT'S YOUR NAME...?
YATO.
MAY YOU BE BLESSED WITH GOOD TIES.
THAT'S HOW MY FATE...
...BECAME TIED TO YATO'S.
OH, AND HERE'S YOUR CHANGE.
YOU CAN HAVE IT BACK.
ZOOM ズイ
Student ID
Hiyori Iki
THIEF!

CHAPTER 2 / END

野

兑

神

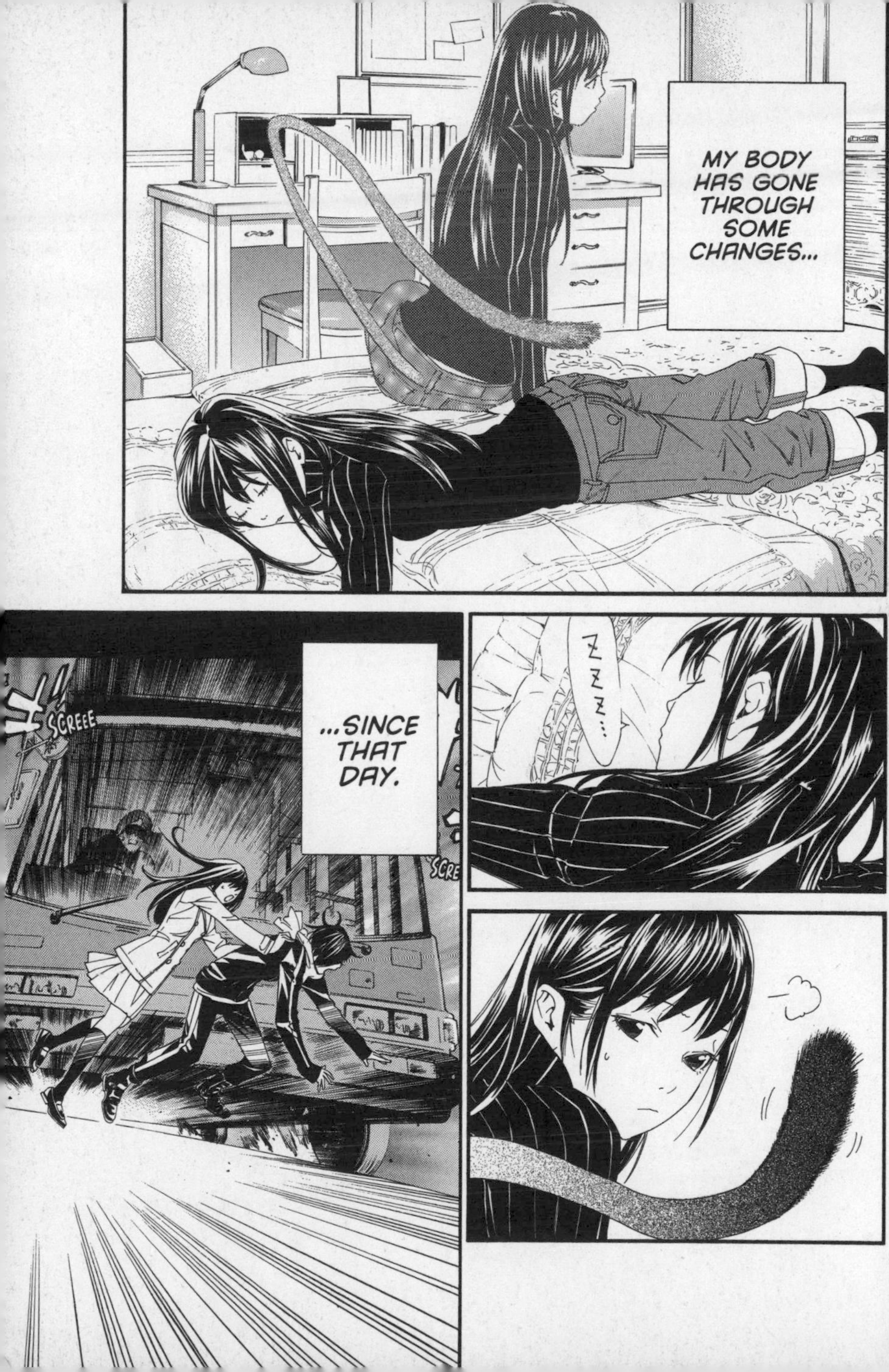
MY BODY HAS GONE THROUGH SOME CHANGES...
ZZZ...
...SINCE THAT DAY.
SCREEE
SCREE

CHAPTER 3: LIKE SNOW

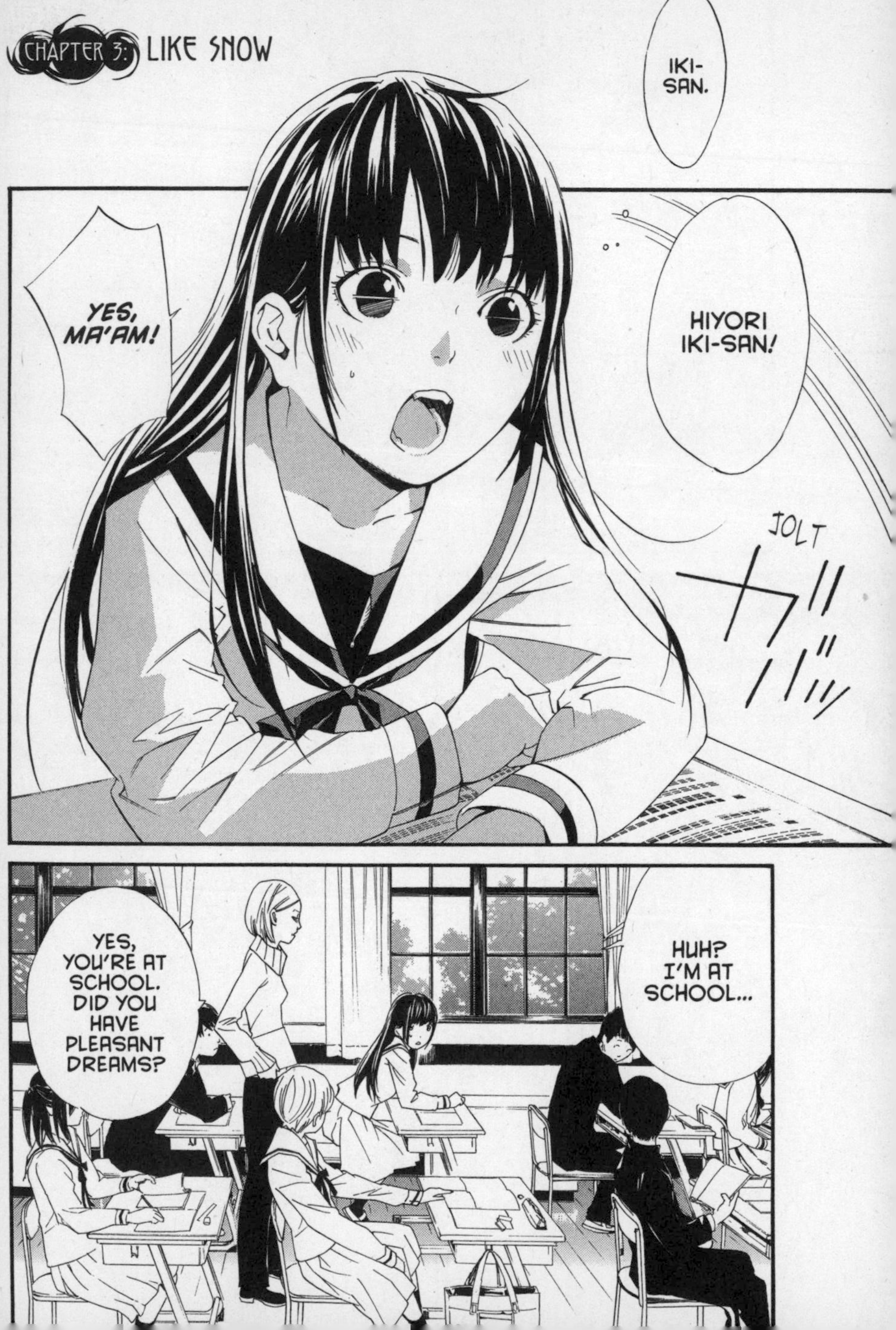
IKI-SAN.
HIYORI IKI-SAN!
JOLT
YES, MA'AM!
HUH? I'M AT SCHOOL...
YES, YOU'RE AT SCHOOL. DID YOU HAVE PLEASANT DREAMS?

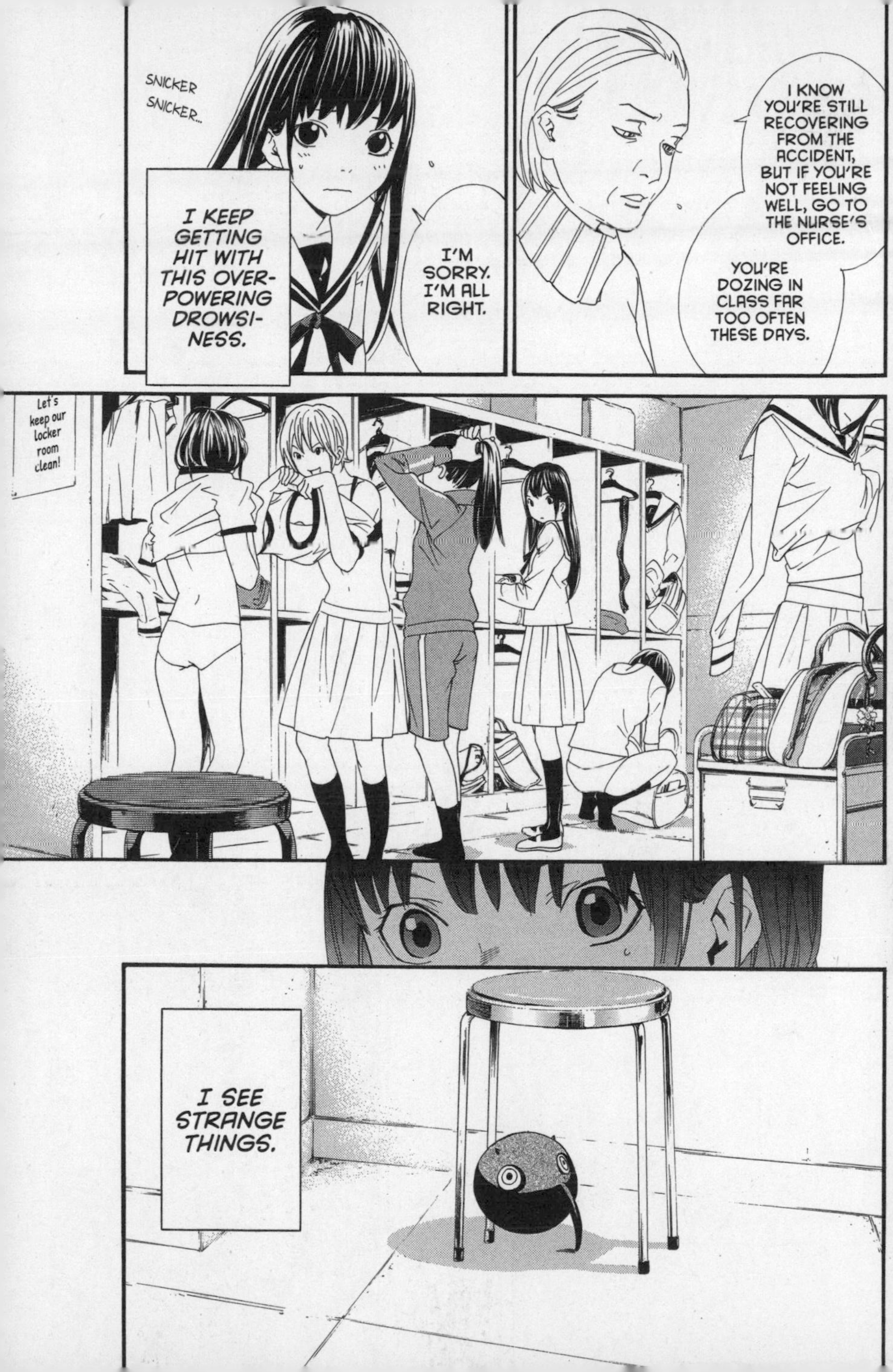
I KNOW YOU'RE STILL RECOVERING FROM THE ACCIDENT, BUT IF YOU'RE NOT FEELING WELL, GO TO THE NURSE'S OFFICE.
YOU'RE DOZING IN CLASS FAR TOO OFTEN THESE DAYS.
I'M SORRY. I'M ALL RIGHT.
SNICKER SNICKER...
I KEEP GETTING HIT WITH THIS OVER-POWERING DROWSI-NESS.
Let's keep our locker room clean!
I SEE STRANGE THINGS.

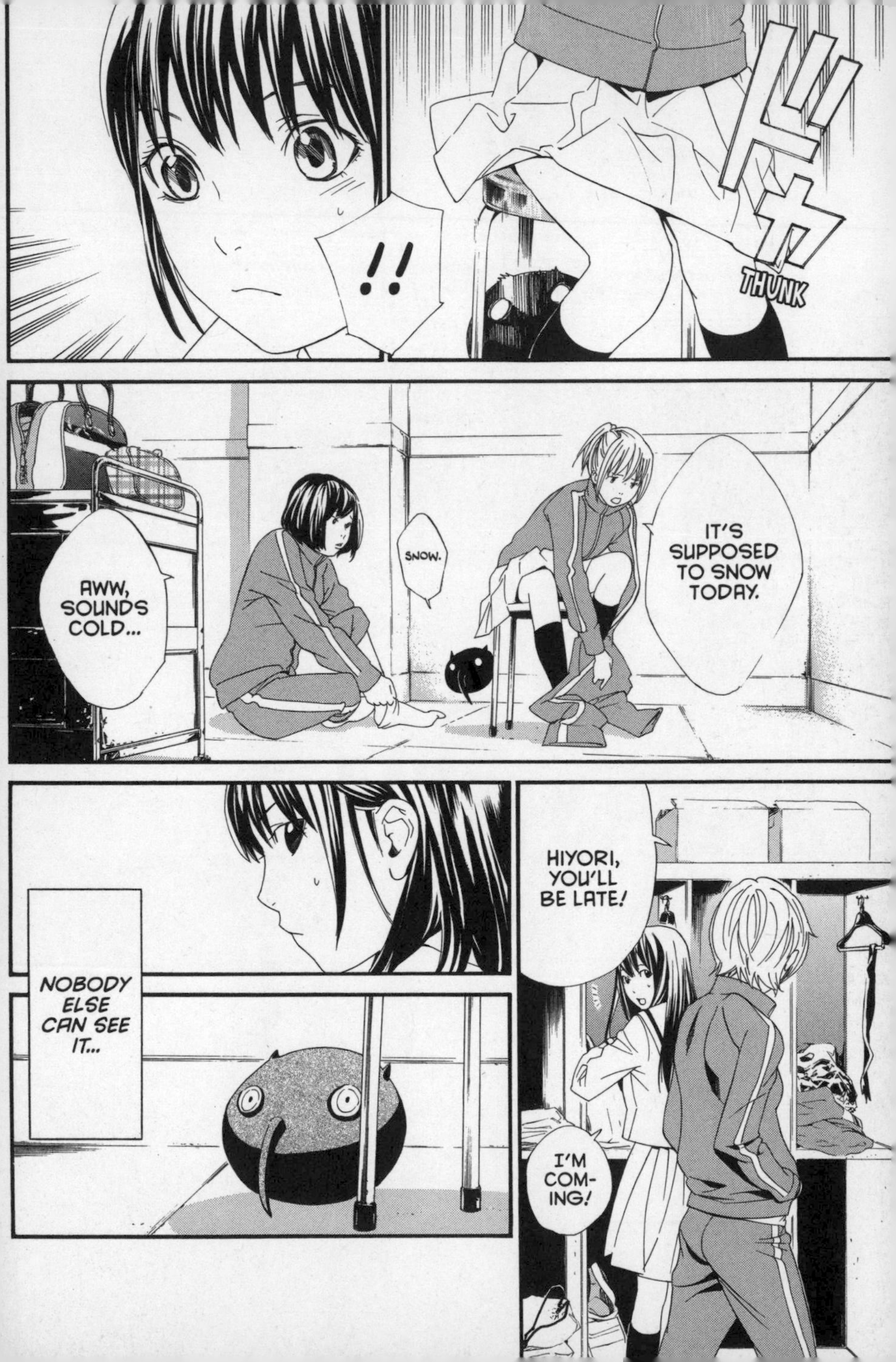
ドカ
THUNK
!!
IT'S SUPPOSED TO SNOW TODAY.
SNOW.
AWW, SOUNDS COLD...
HIYORI, YOU'LL BE LATE!
I'M COMING!
NOBODY ELSE CAN SEE IT...

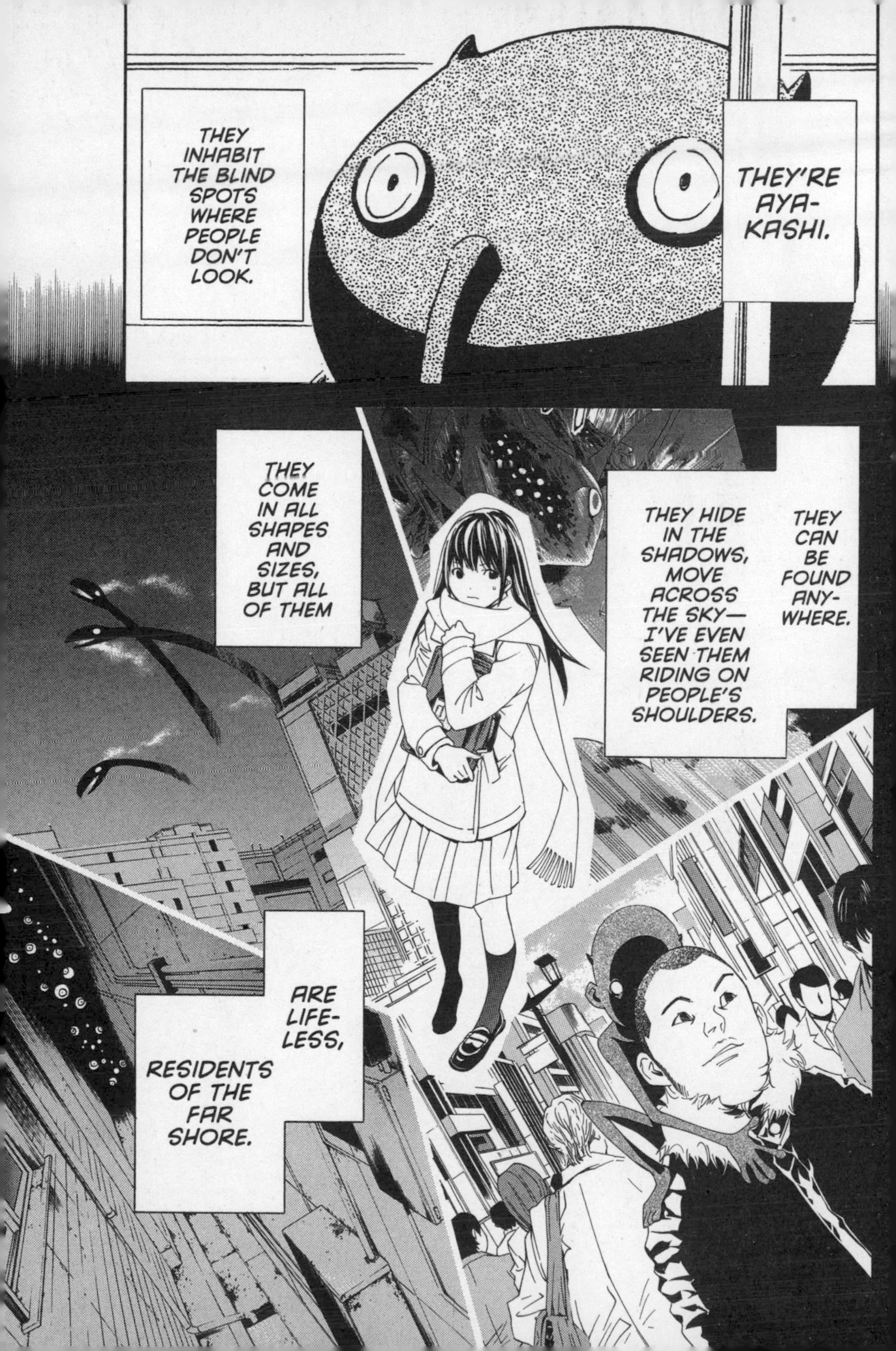
THEY'RE AYA-KASHI.
THEY INHABIT THE BLIND SPOTS WHERE PEOPLE DON'T LOOK.
THEY CAN BE FOUND ANY-WHERE.
THEY HIDE IN THE SHADOWS, MOVE ACROSS THE SKY—I'VE EVEN SEEN THEM RIDING ON PEOPLE'S SHOULDERS.
THEY COME IN ALL SHAPES AND SIZES, BUT ALL OF THEM
ARE LIFE-LESS,
RESIDENTS OF THE FAR SHORE.

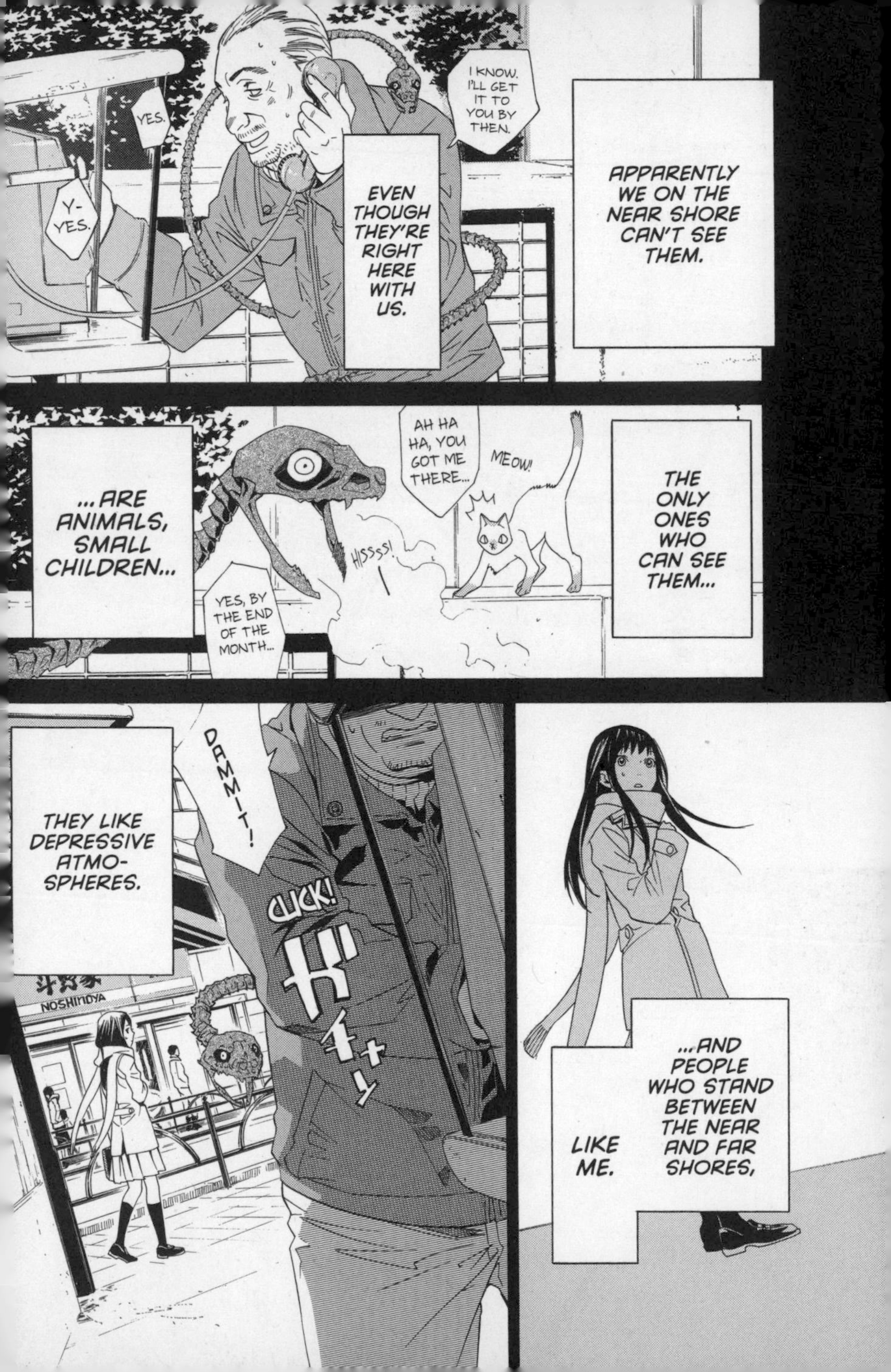
APPARENTLY WE ON THE NEAR SHORE CAN'T SEE THEM.
I KNOW. I'LL GET IT TO YOU BY THEN.
EVEN THOUGH THEY'RE RIGHT HERE WITH US.
YES.
Y-YES.
THE ONLY ONES WHO CAN SEE THEM...
MEOW!
AH HA HA, YOU GOT ME THERE...
HISSSS!
YES, BY THE END OF THE MONTH...
...ARE ANIMALS, SMALL CHILDREN...
...AND PEOPLE WHO STAND BETWEEN THE NEAR AND FAR SHORES,
LIKE ME.
DAMMIT!
CLICK!
THEY LIKE DEPRESSIVE ATMOSPHERES.
NOSHINOYA

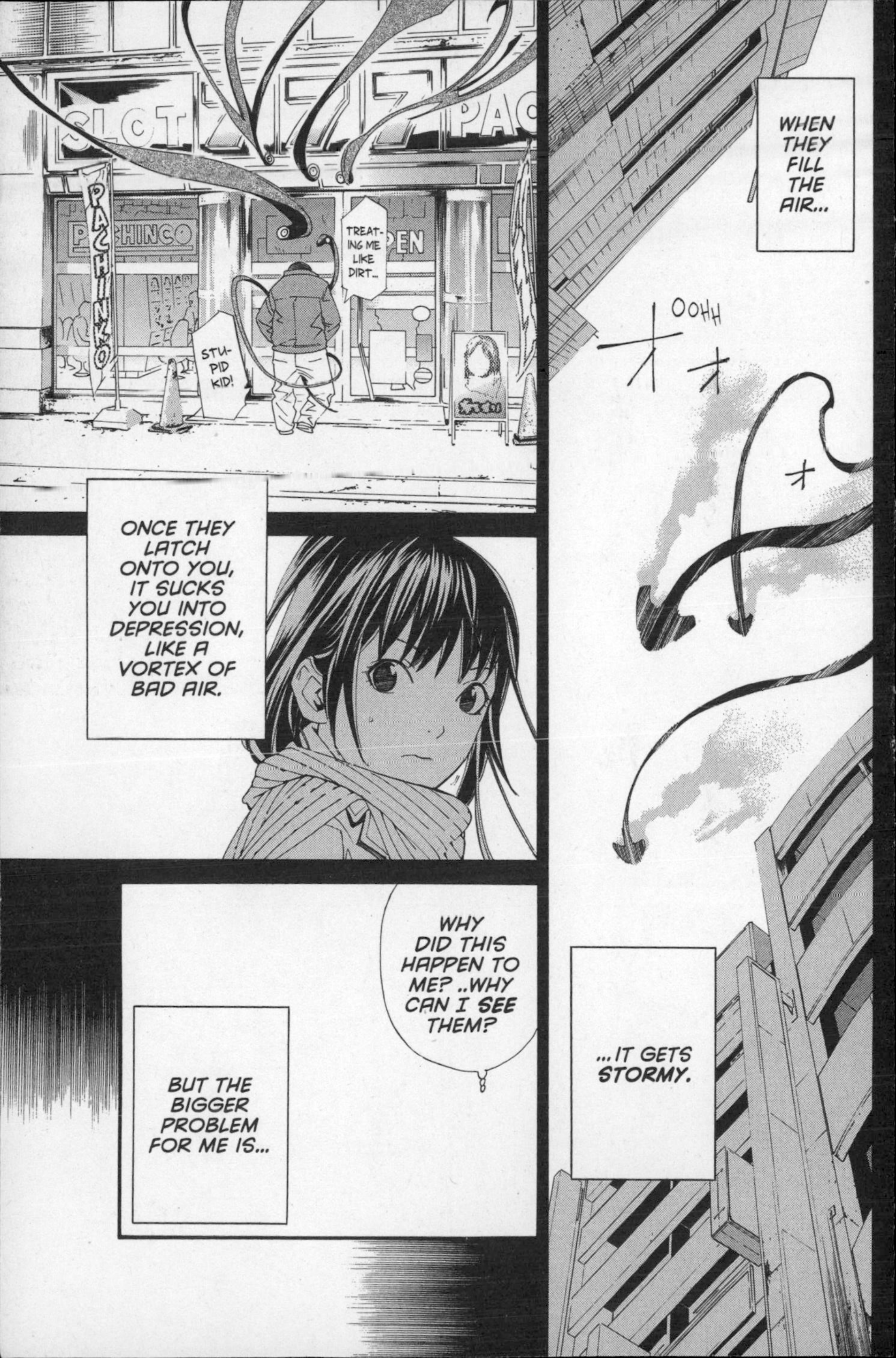
WHEN THEY FILL THE AIR...
OOHH
...IT GETS STORMY.
PACHINKO
PACHINCO
TREAT-ING ME LIKE DIRT...
STU-PID KID!
ONCE THEY LATCH ONTO YOU, IT SUCKS YOU INTO DEPRESSION, LIKE A VORTEX OF BAD AIR.
WHY DID THIS HAPPEN TO ME? ..WHY CAN I SEE THEM?
BUT THE BIGGER PROBLEM FOR ME IS...

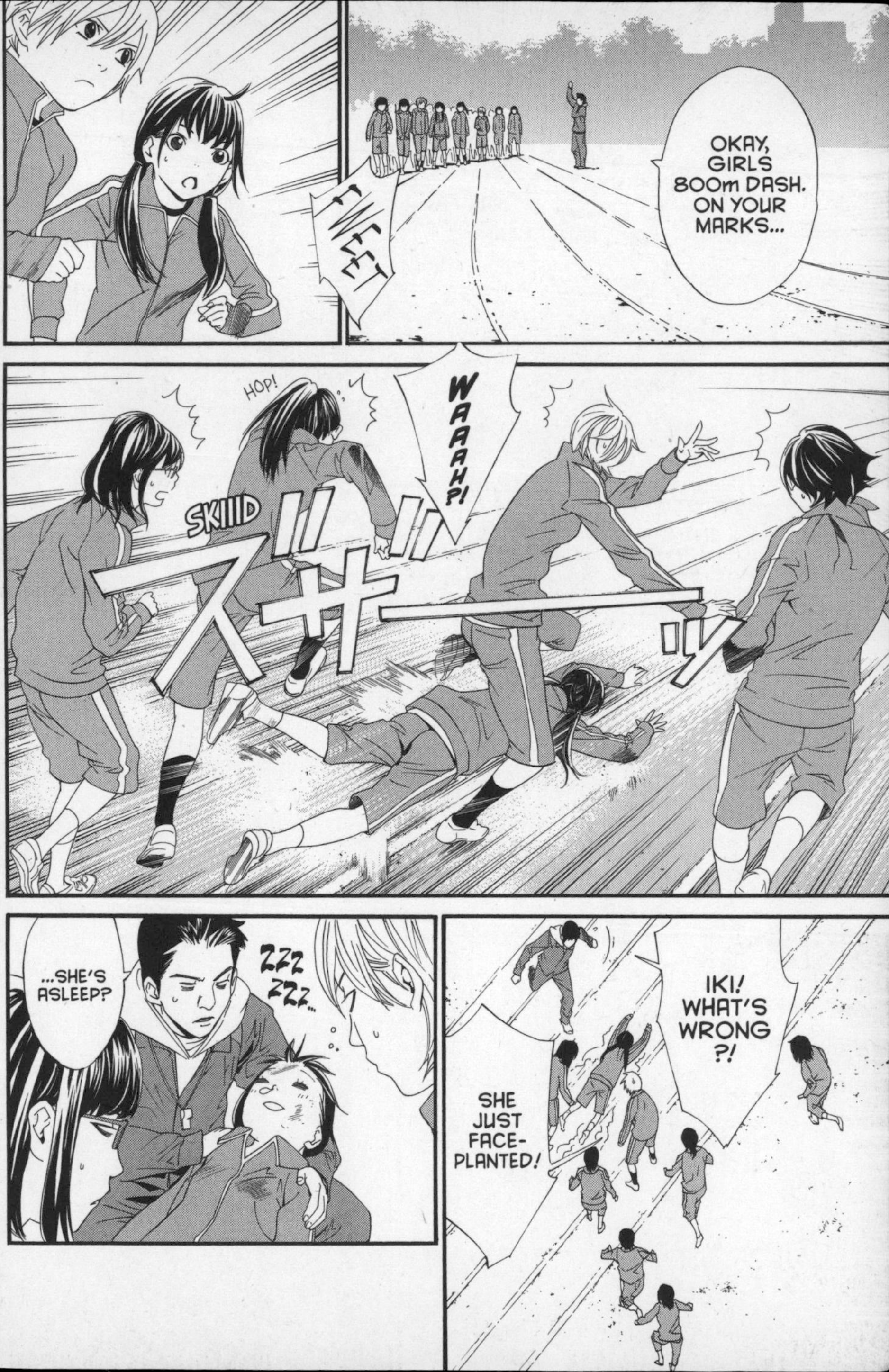
OKAY, GIRLS 800m DASH. ON YOUR MARKS...
FWEET
WAAAAHP?!
HOP!
SKIIID
ズザーッ
IKI! WHAT'S WRONG?!
SHE JUST FACE-PLANTED!
...SHE'S ASLEEP?
ZZZ ZZZ...

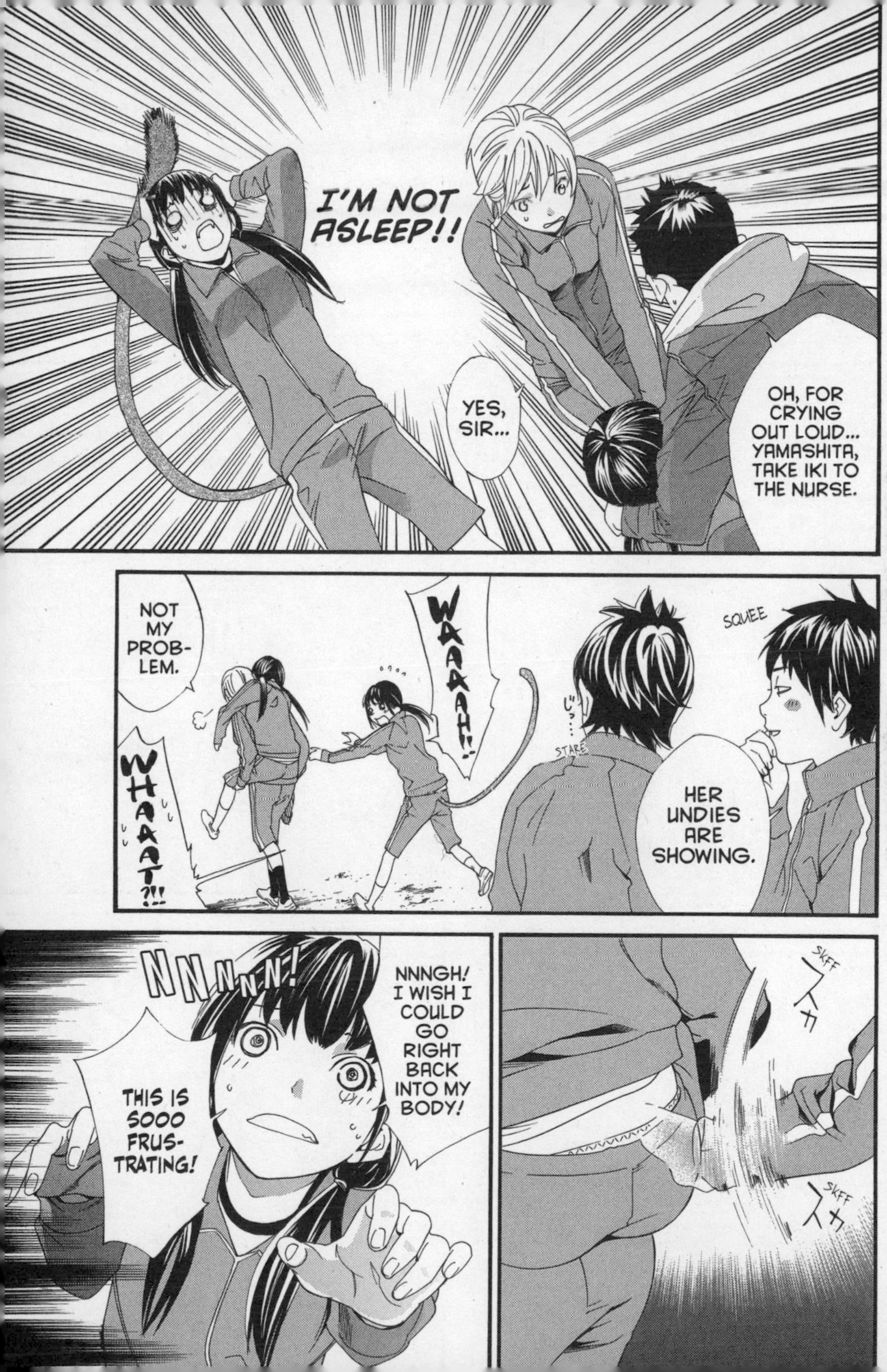
OH, FOR CRYING OUT LOUD... YAMASHITA, TAKE IKI TO THE NURSE.
YES, SIR...
I'M NOT ASLEEP!!
SQUEE
じっ…
STARE
HER UNDIES ARE SHOWING.
WAAAAH!!
NOT MY PROBLEM.
WHAAAT?!!
スカ
SKFF
スカ
SKFF
NNNNN!
NNNGH! I WISH I COULD GO RIGHT BACK INTO MY BODY!
THIS IS SOOO FRUSTRATING!

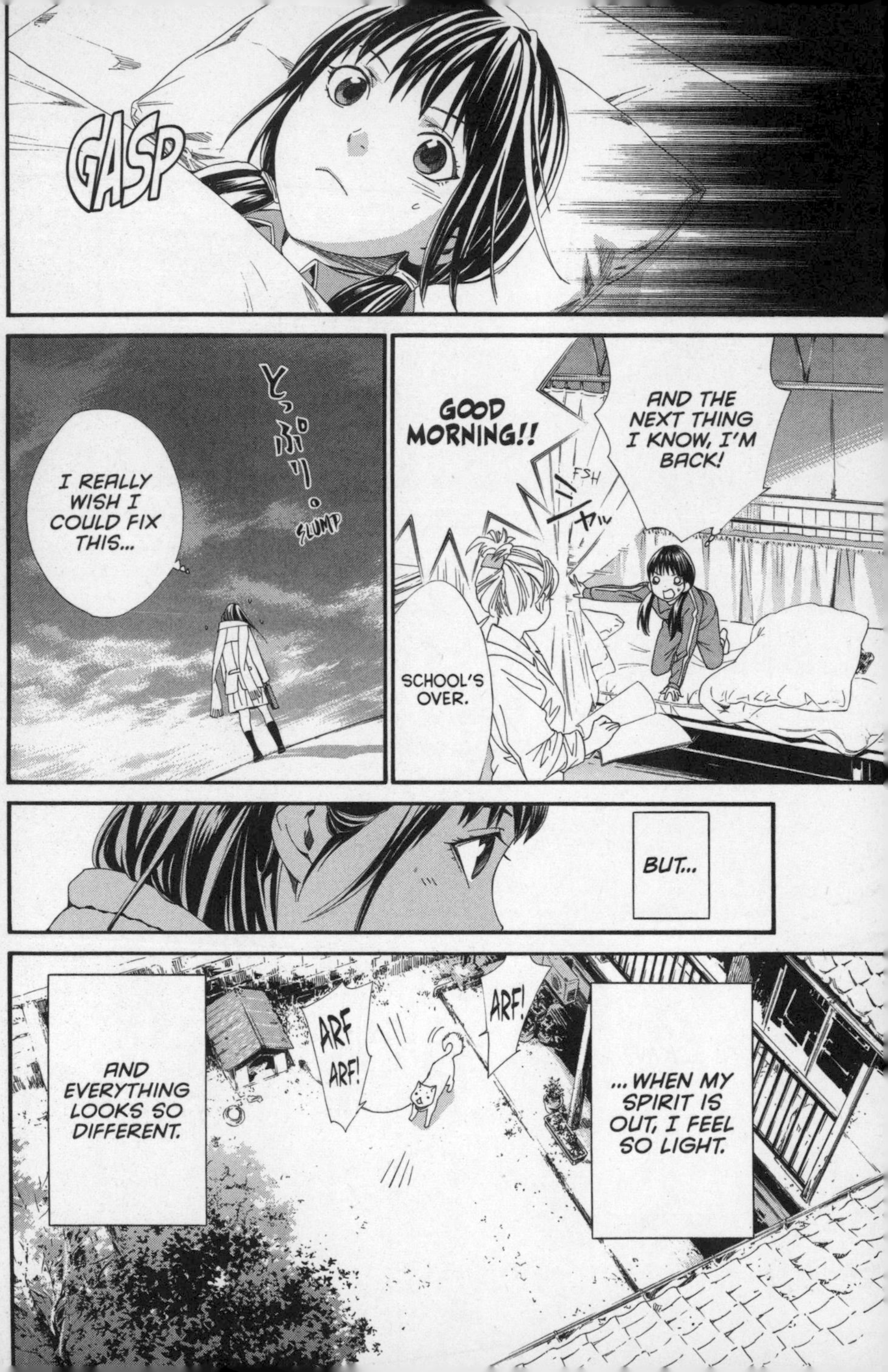
GASP
AND THE NEXT THING I KNOW, I'M BACK!
GOOD MORNING!!
FSH
SCHOOL'S OVER.
I REALLY WISH I COULD FIX THIS...
SLUMP
BUT...
...WHEN MY SPIRIT IS OUT, I FEEL SO LIGHT.
ARF!
ARF ARF!
AND EVERYTHING LOOKS SO DIFFERENT.

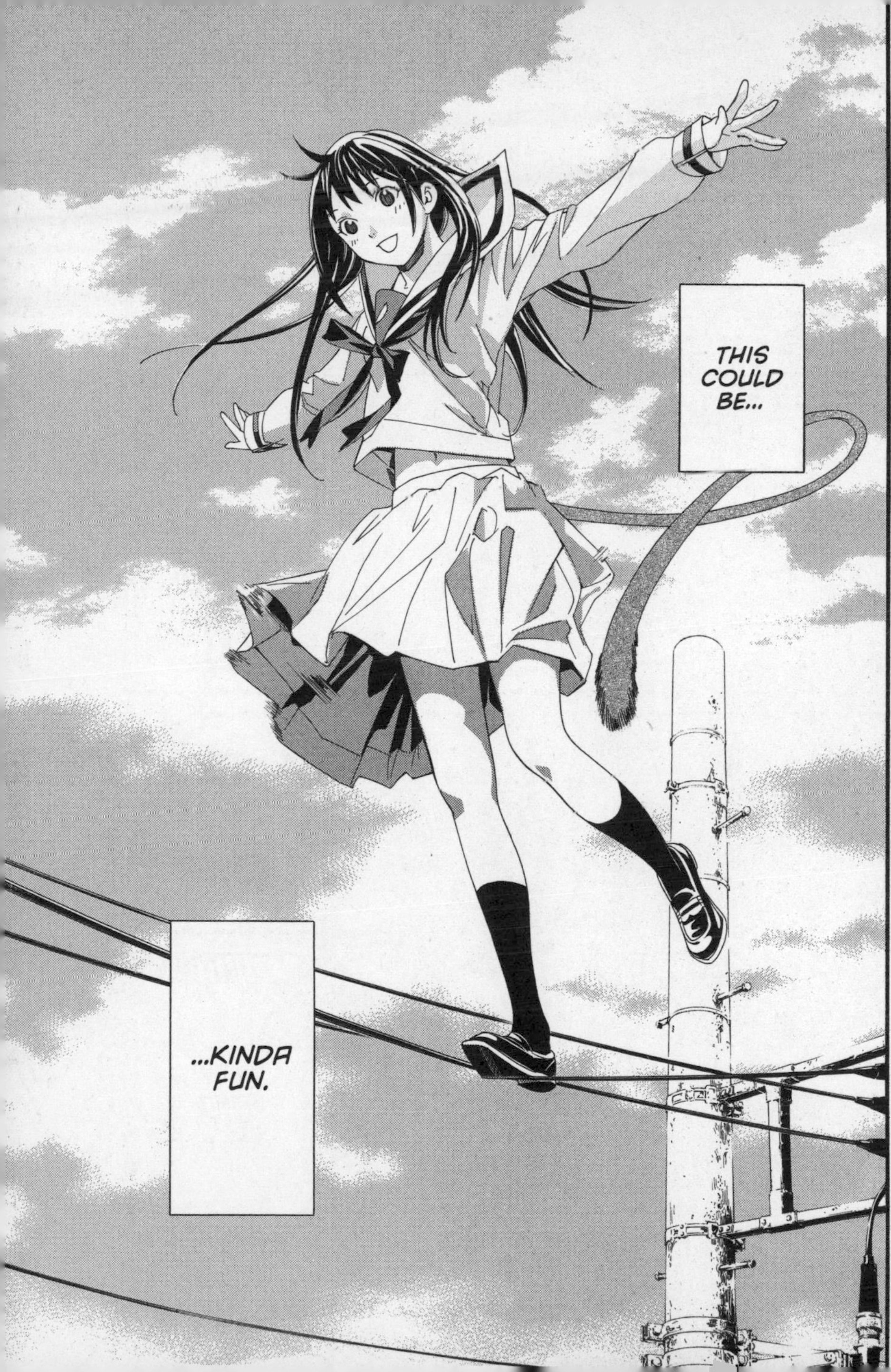
THIS COULD BE...
...KINDA FUN.

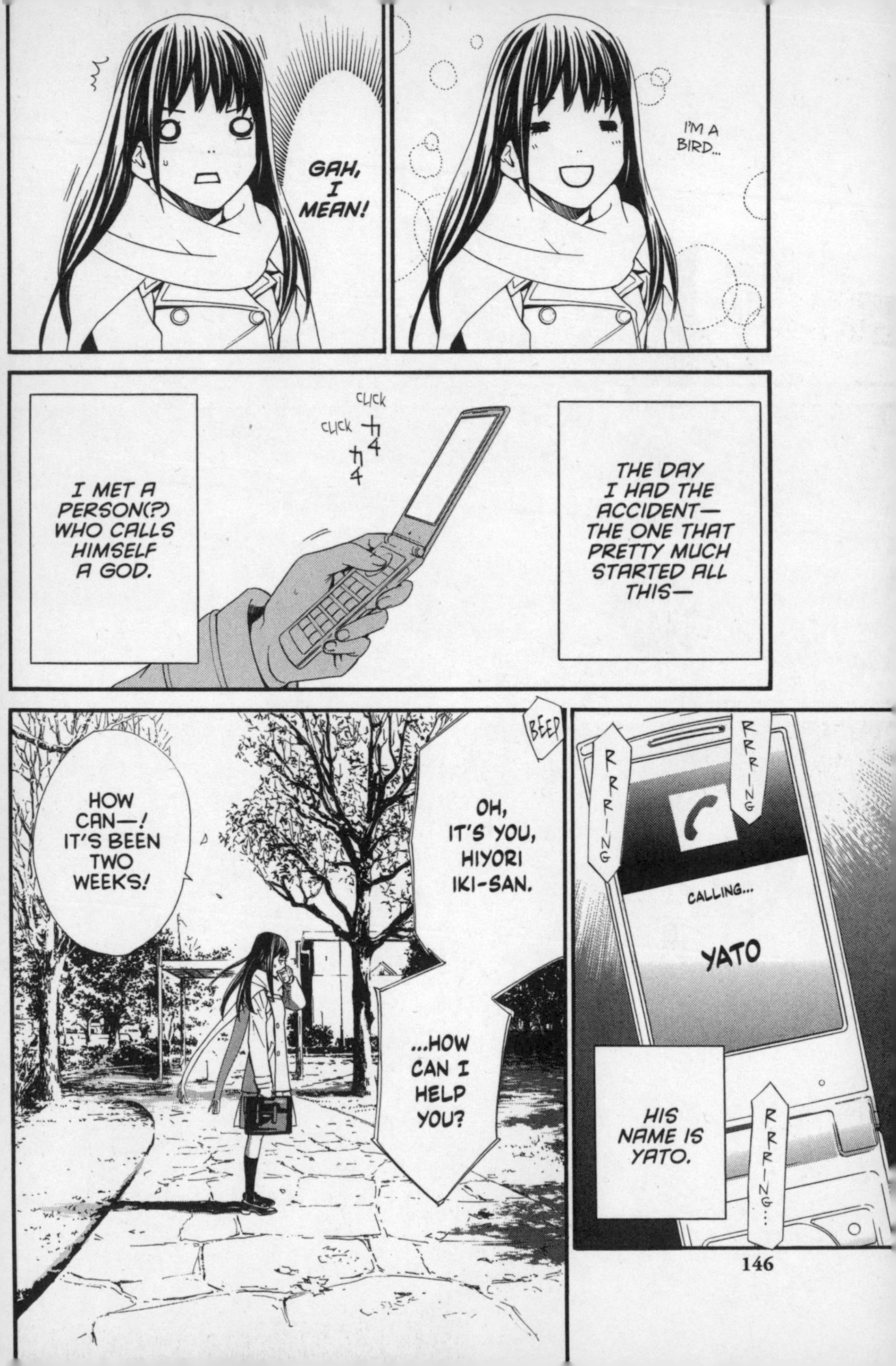
I'M A BIRD...
GAH, I MEAN!
THE DAY I HAD THE ACCIDENT—THE ONE THAT PRETTY MUCH STARTED ALL THIS—
CLICK
CLICK
I MET A PERSON(?) WHO CALLS HIMSELF A GOD.
RRRING
RRRING
CALLING...
YATO
HIS NAME IS YATO.
RRRING...
BEEP
OH, IT'S YOU, HIYORI IKI-SAN.
...HOW CAN I HELP YOU?
HOW CAN—! IT'S BEEN TWO WEEKS!

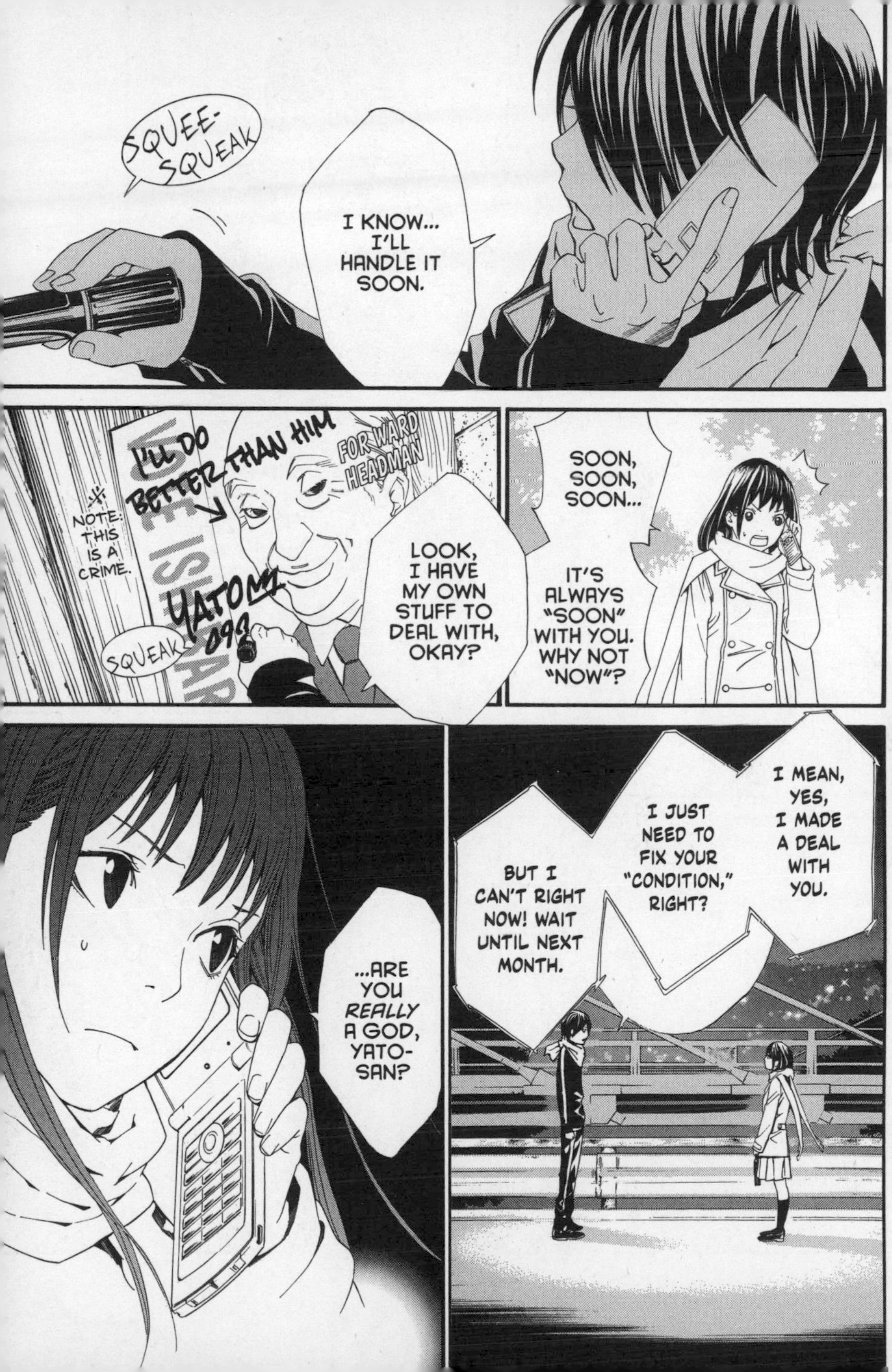
I KNOW... I'LL HANDLE IT SOON.
SQUEE-SQUEAK
SOON, SOON, SOON...
IT'S ALWAYS "SOON" WITH YOU. WHY NOT "NOW"?
LOOK, I HAVE MY OWN STUFF TO DEAL WITH, OKAY?
FOR WARD HEADMAN
I'LL DO BETTER THAN HIM
YATO
SQUEAK
※NOTE: THIS IS A CRIME.
I MEAN, YES, I MADE A DEAL WITH YOU.
I JUST NEED TO FIX YOUR "CONDITION," RIGHT?
BUT I CAN'T RIGHT NOW! WAIT UNTIL NEXT MONTH.
...ARE YOU *REALLY* A GOD, YATO-SAN?

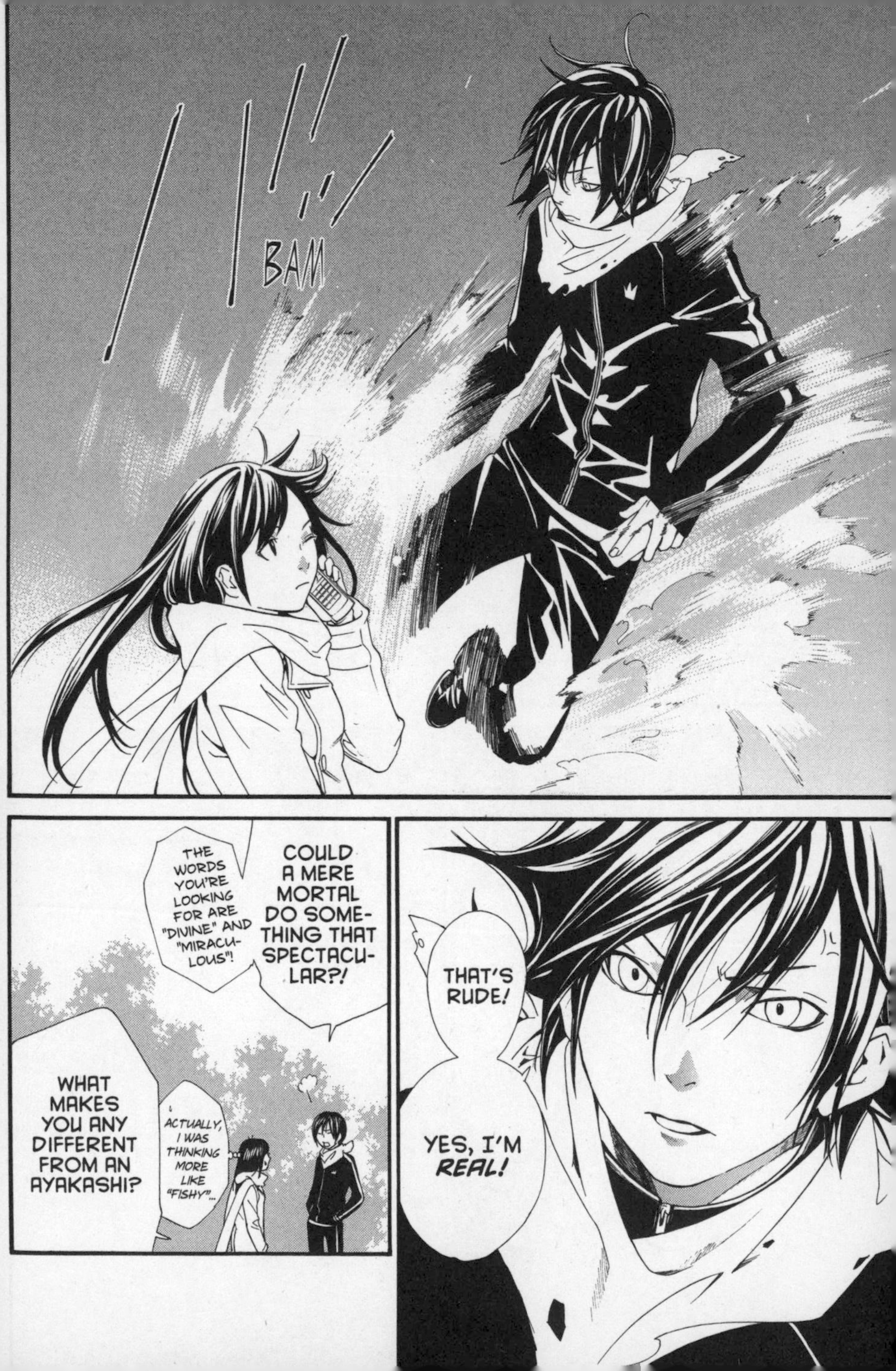
BAM
THAT'S RUDE!
YES, I'M *REAL!*
COULD A MERE MORTAL DO SOME-THING THAT SPECTACU-LAR?!
THE WORDS YOU'RE LOOKING FOR ARE "DIVINE" AND "MIRACU-LOUS"!
WHAT MAKES YOU ANY DIFFERENT FROM AN AYAKASHI?
ACTUALLY, I WAS THINKING MORE LIKE "FISHY"...

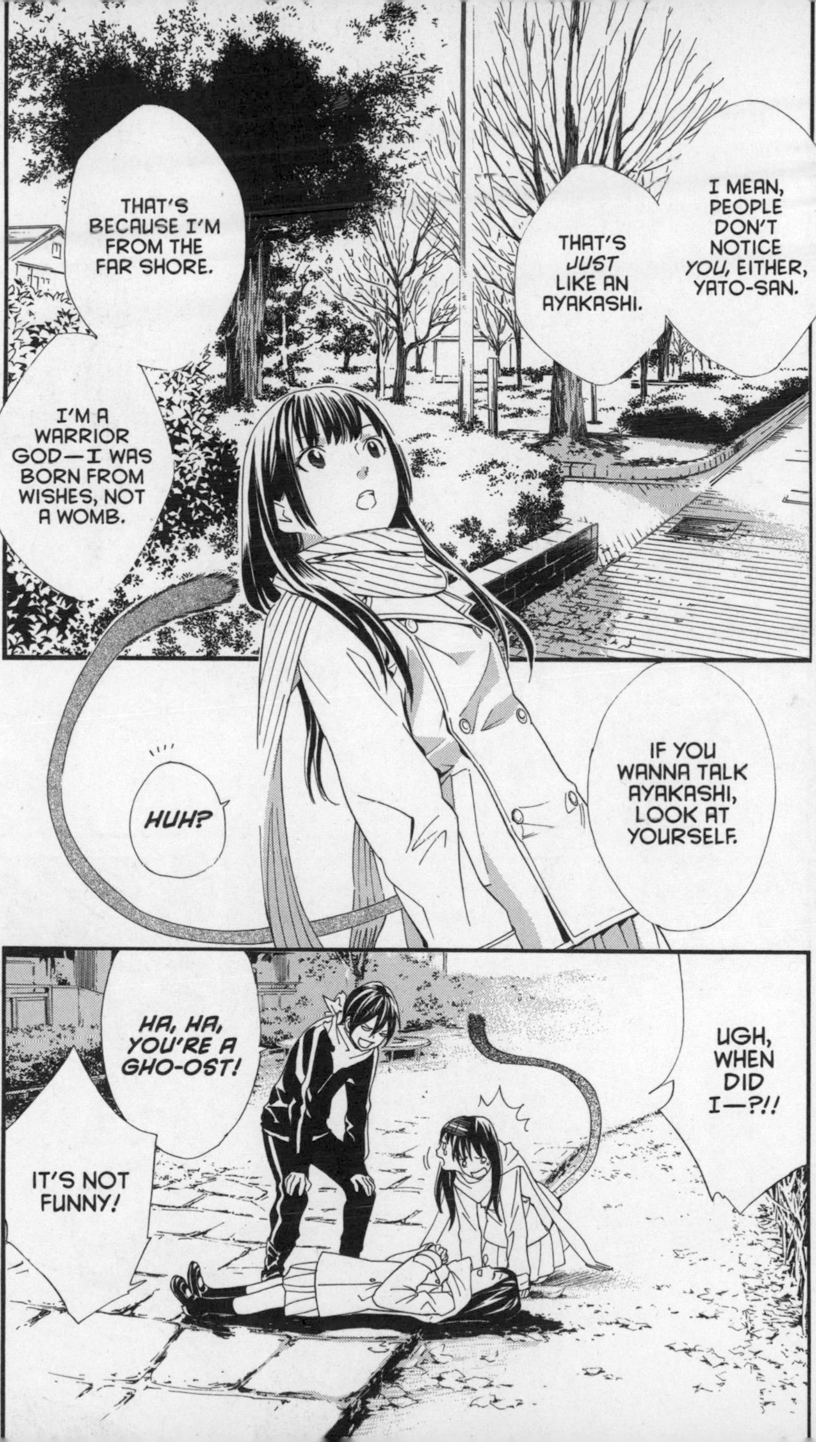
I MEAN, PEOPLE DON'T NOTICE *YOU*, EITHER, YATO-SAN.
THAT'S *JUST* LIKE AN AYAKASHI.
THAT'S BECAUSE I'M FROM THE FAR SHORE.
I'M A WARRIOR GOD—I WAS BORN FROM WISHES, NOT A WOMB.
IF YOU WANNA TALK AYAKASHI, LOOK AT YOURSELF.
HUH?
UGH, WHEN DID I—?!!
HA, HA, YOU'RE A GHO-OST!
IT'S NOT FUNNY!

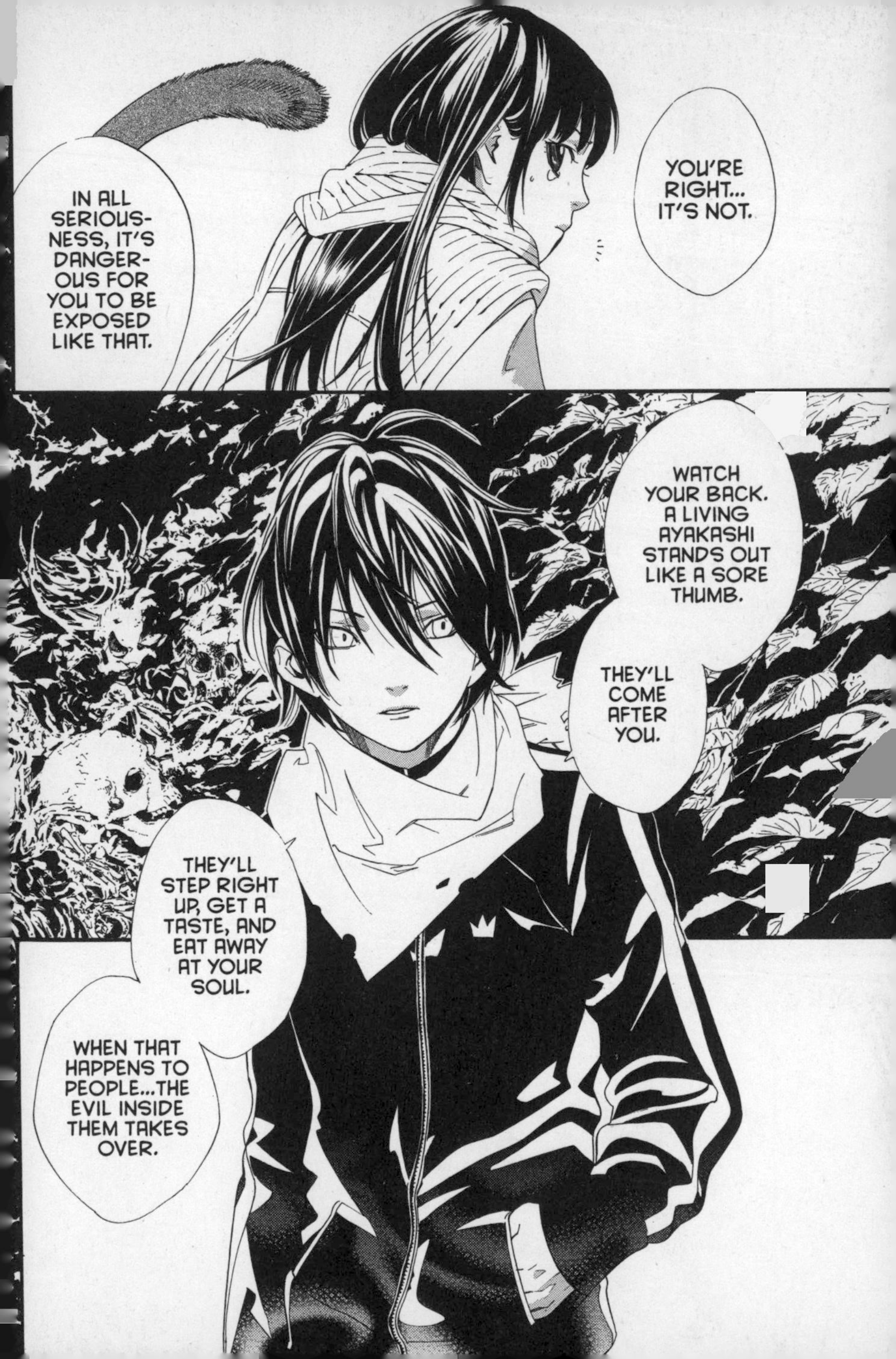
YOU'RE RIGHT... IT'S NOT.
IN ALL SERIOUSNESS, IT'S DANGEROUS FOR YOU TO BE EXPOSED LIKE THAT.
WATCH YOUR BACK. A LIVING AYAKASHI STANDS OUT LIKE A SORE THUMB.
THEY'LL COME AFTER YOU.
THEY'LL STEP RIGHT UP, GET A TASTE, AND EAT AWAY AT YOUR SOUL.
WHEN THAT HAPPENS TO PEOPLE...THE EVIL INSIDE THEM TAKES OVER.

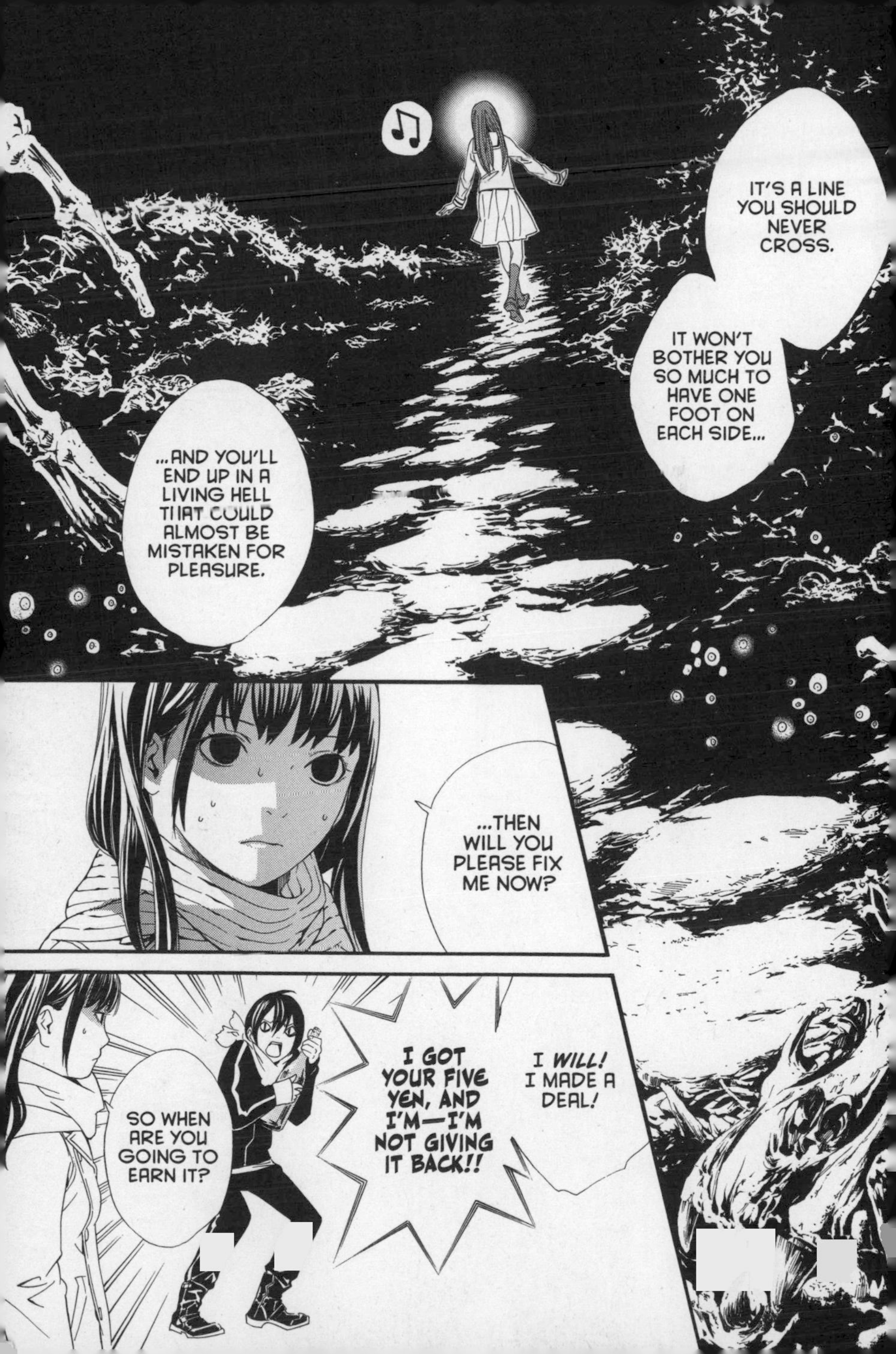

IT'S A LINE YOU SHOULD NEVER CROSS.
IT WON'T BOTHER YOU SO MUCH TO HAVE ONE FOOT ON EACH SIDE...
...AND YOU'LL END UP IN A LIVING HELL THAT COULD ALMOST BE MISTAKEN FOR PLEASURE.
...THEN WILL YOU PLEASE FIX ME NOW?
I *WILL!* I MADE A DEAL!
I GOT YOUR FIVE YEN, AND I'M—I'M NOT GIVING IT BACK!!
SO WHEN ARE YOU GOING TO EARN IT?

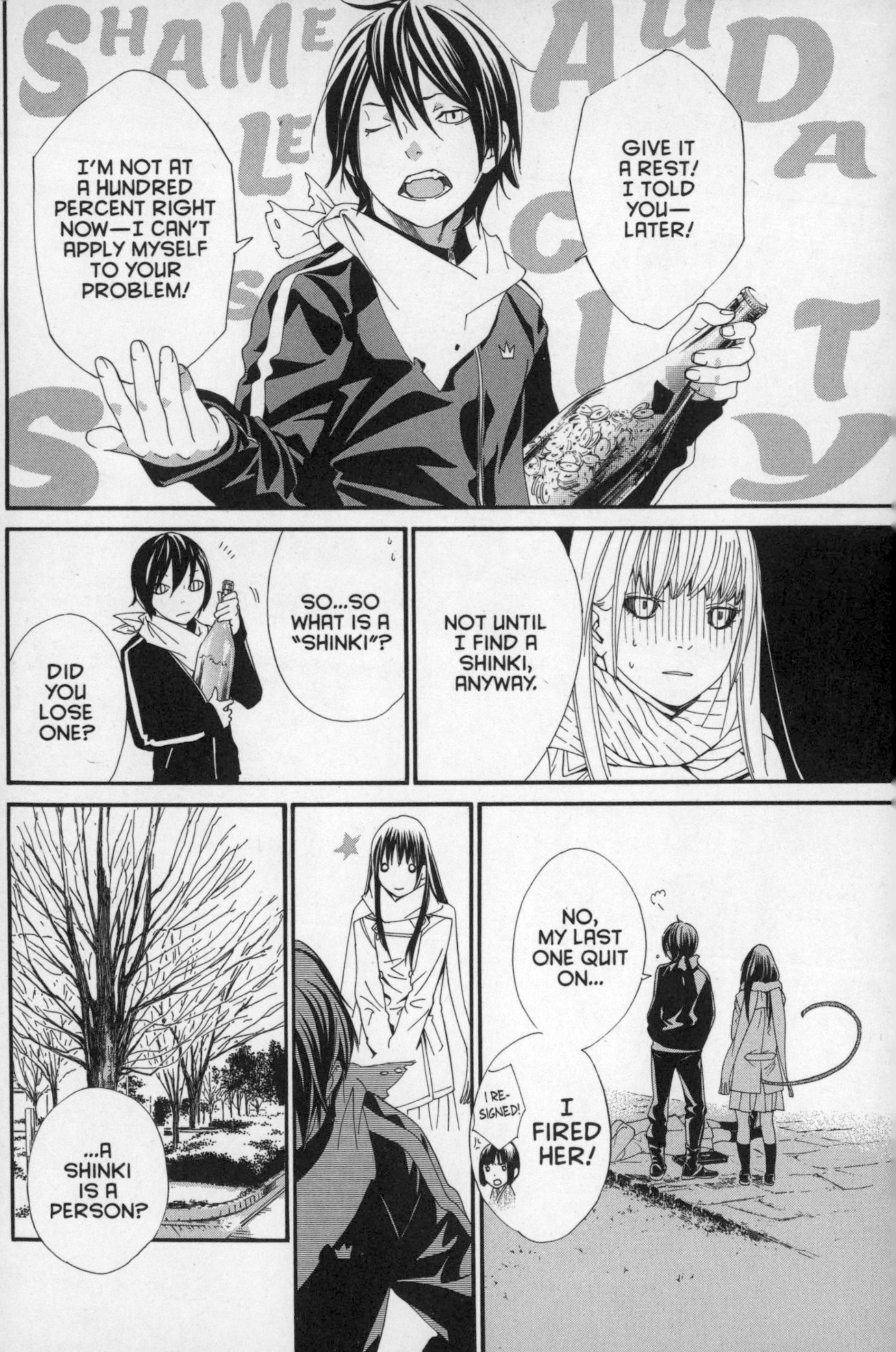
SHAMELESS
AUDACITY
GIVE IT A REST! I TOLD YOU—LATER!
I'M NOT AT A HUNDRED PERCENT RIGHT NOW—I CAN'T APPLY MYSELF TO YOUR PROBLEM!
NOT UNTIL I FIND A SHINKI, ANYWAY.
SO...SO WHAT IS A "SHINKI"?
DID YOU LOSE ONE?
NO, MY LAST ONE QUIT ON...
I FIRED HER!
I RE-SIGNED!
...A SHINKI IS A PERSON?

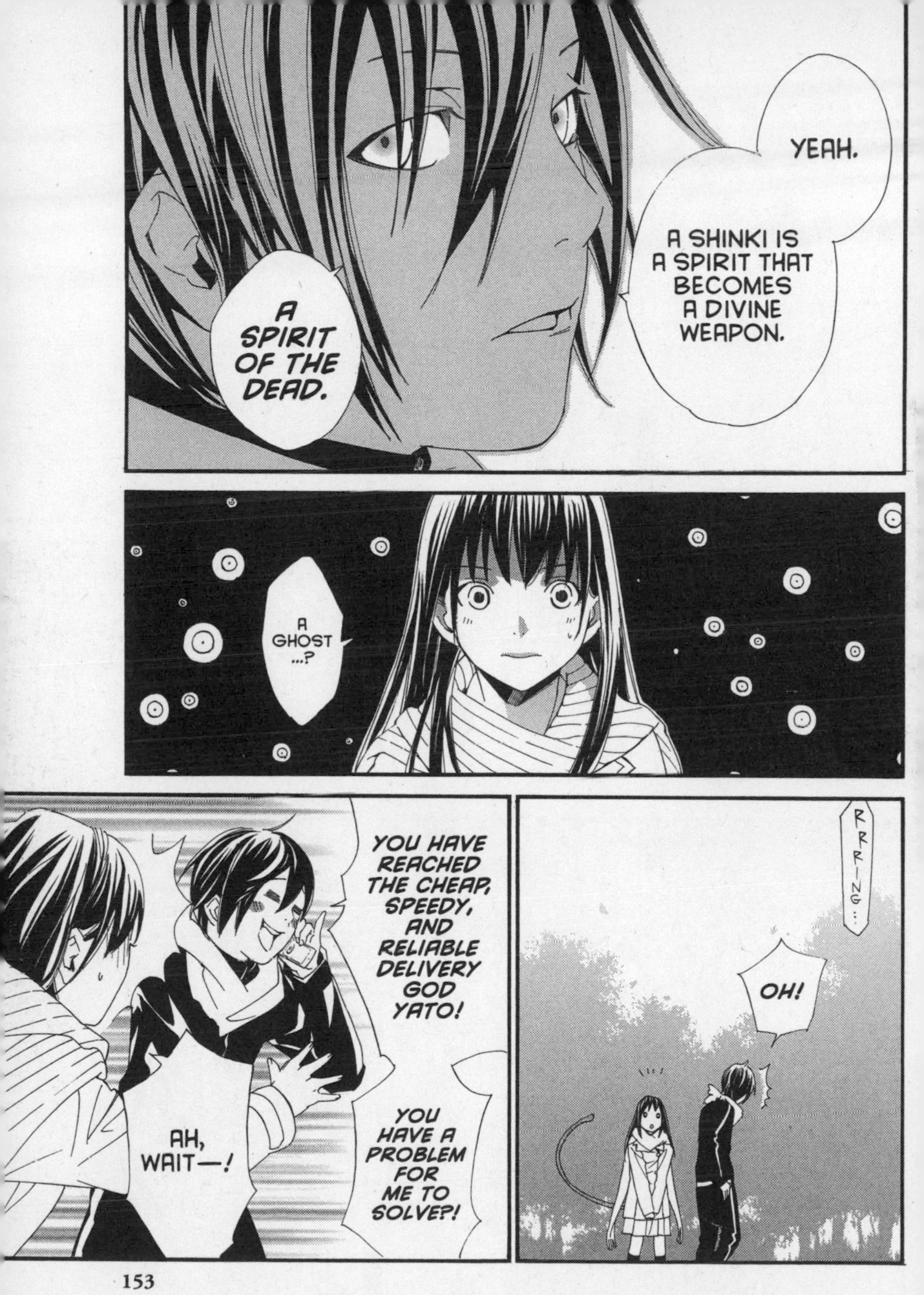
YEAH.
A SHINKI IS A SPIRIT THAT BECOMES A DIVINE WEAPON.
A SPIRIT OF THE DEAD.
A GHOST ...?
RRRING...
OH!
YOU HAVE REACHED THE CHEAP, SPEEDY, AND RELIABLE DELIVERY GOD YATO!
YOU HAVE A PROBLEM FOR ME TO SOLVE?!
AH, WAIT—!

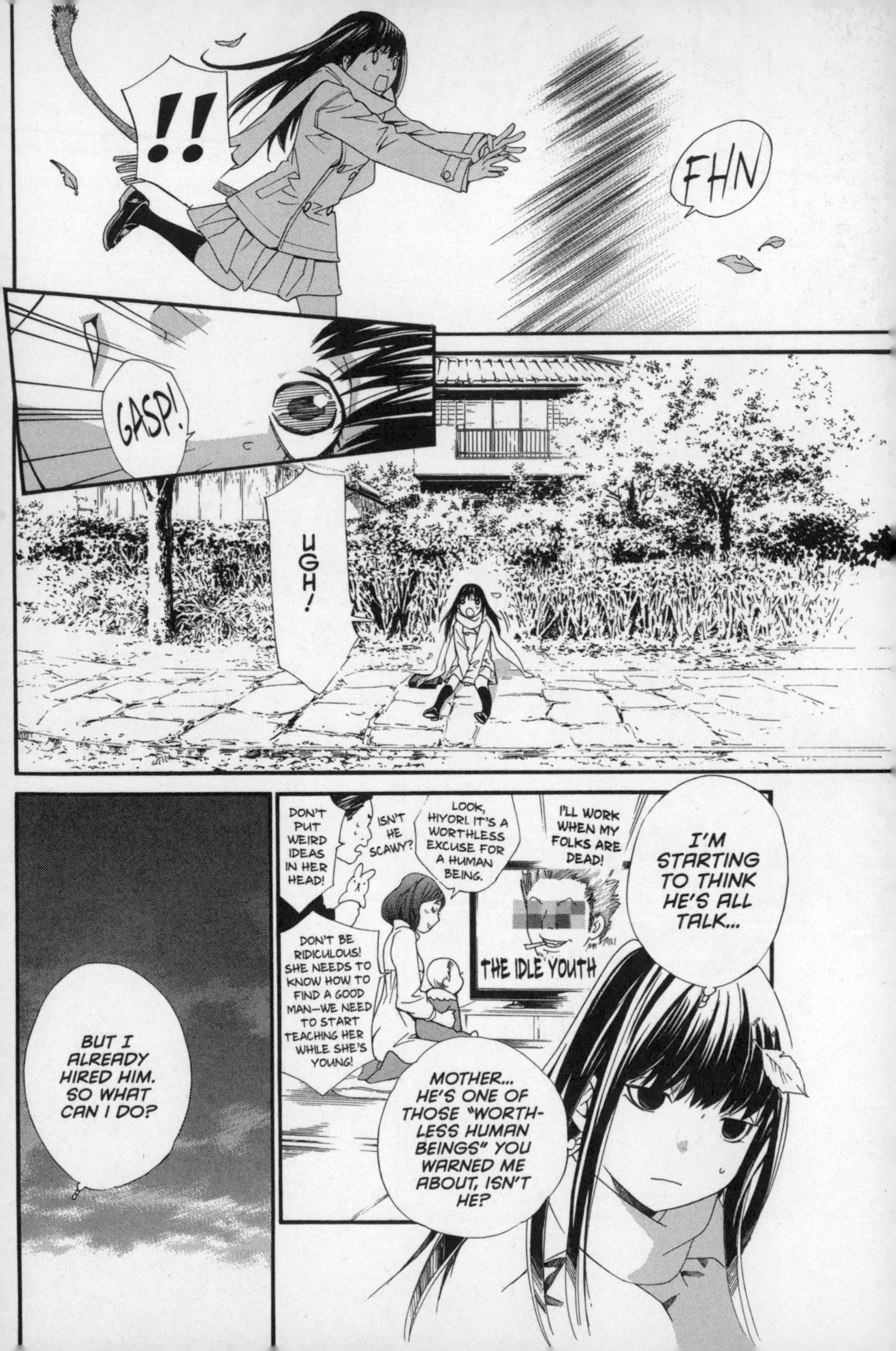
FHN
!!
GASP!
UGH!
I'M STARTING TO THINK HE'S ALL TALK...
I'LL WORK WHEN MY FOLKS ARE DEAD!
LOOK, HIYORI. IT'S A WORTHLESS EXCUSE FOR A HUMAN BEING.
ISN'T HE SCAWY?
DON'T PUT WEIRD IDEAS IN HER HEAD!
THE IDLE YOUTH
DON'T BE RIDICULOUS! SHE NEEDS TO KNOW HOW TO FIND A GOOD MAN—WE NEED TO START TEACHING HER WHILE SHE'S YOUNG!
MOTHER... HE'S ONE OF THOSE "WORTHLESS HUMAN BEINGS" YOU WARNED ME ABOUT, ISN'T HE?
BUT I ALREADY HIRED HIM. SO WHAT CAN I DO?

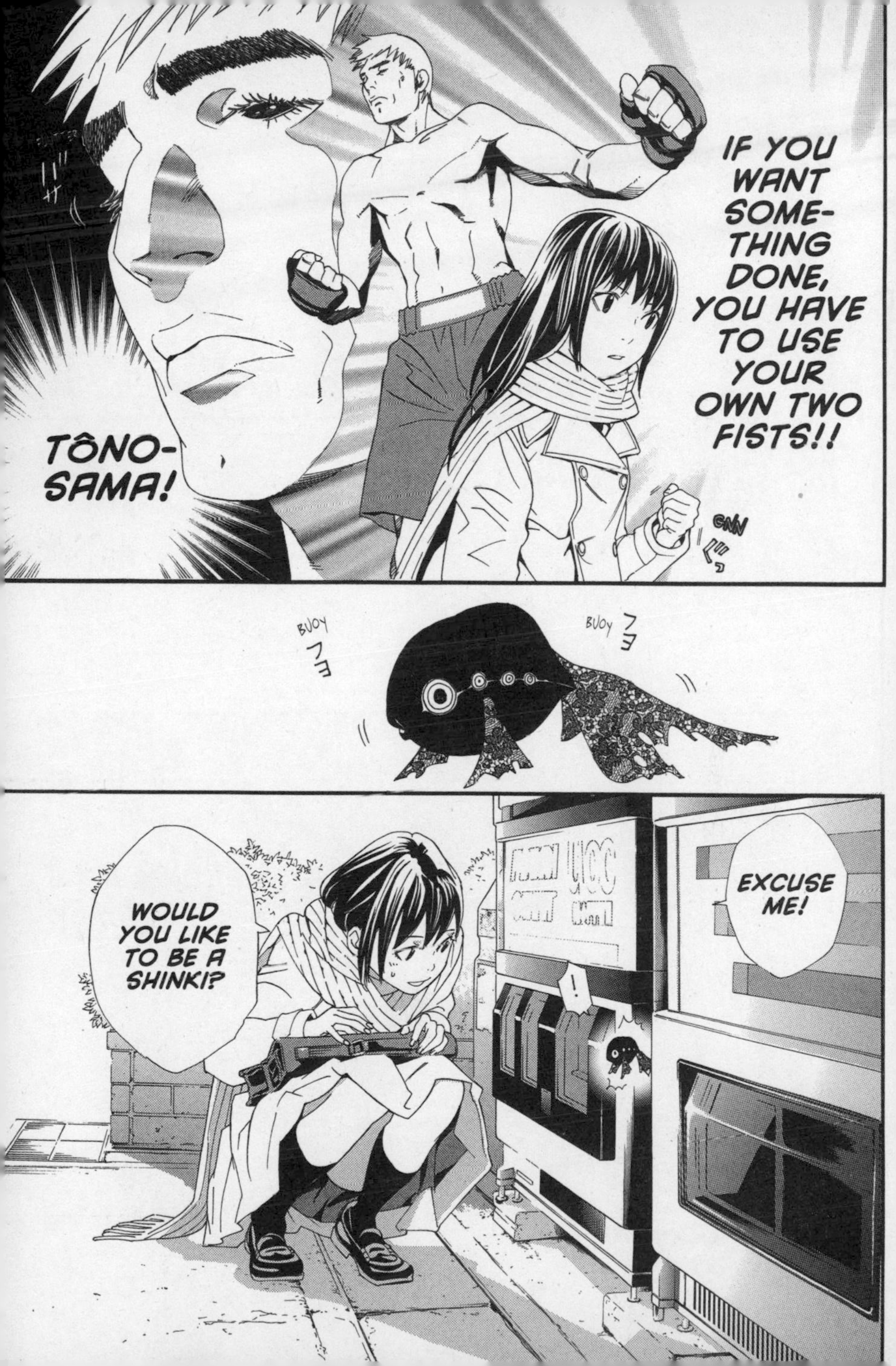
IF YOU WANT SOMETHING DONE, YOU HAVE TO USE YOUR OWN TWO FISTS!!
TÔNO-SAMA!
GNN
BUOY
BUOY
EXCUSE ME!
!
WOULD YOU LIKE TO BE A SHINKI?

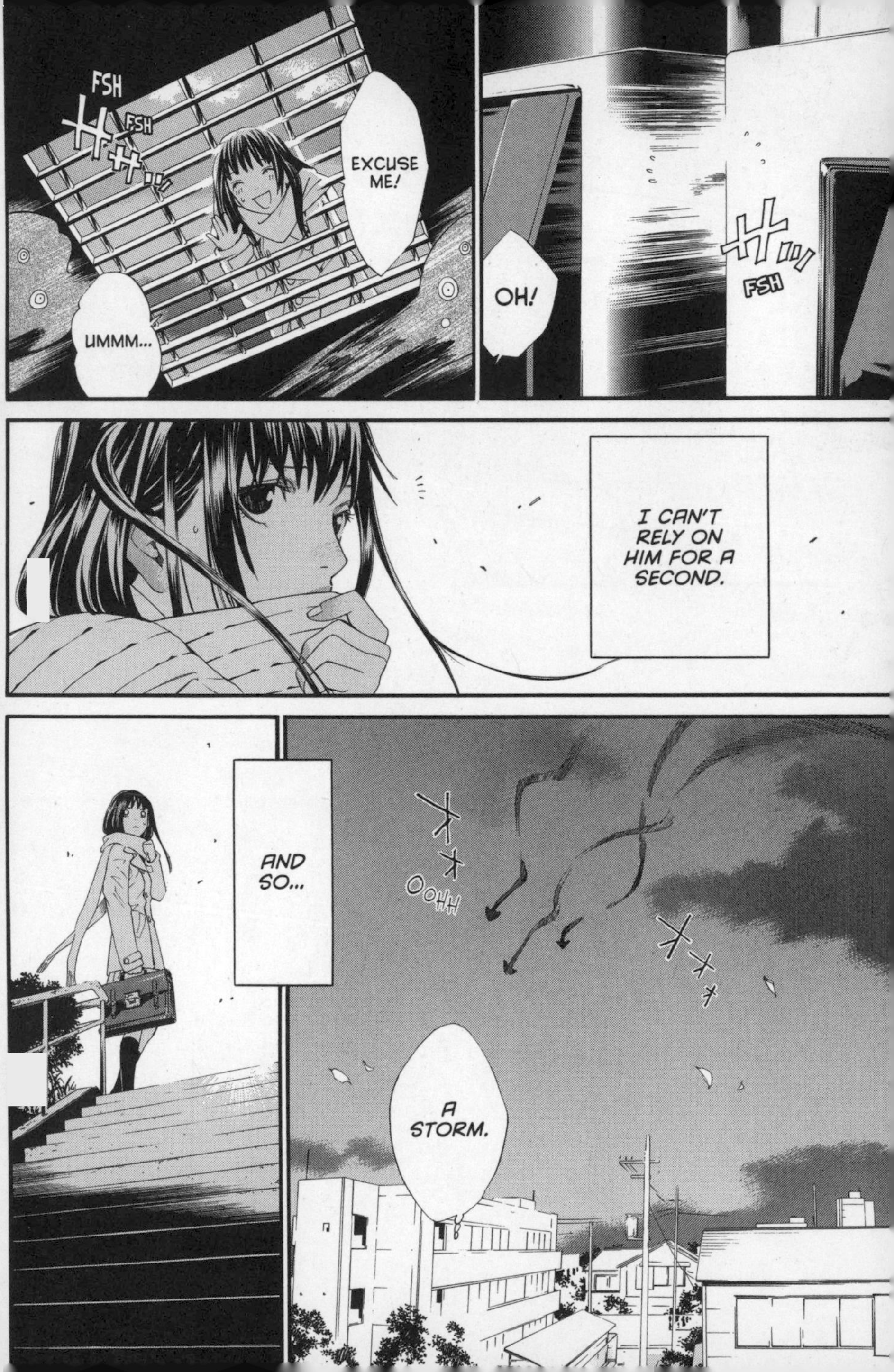
FSH
OH!
EXCUSE ME!
FSH
FSH
UMMM...
I CAN'T RELY ON HIM FOR A SECOND.
OOHH
A STORM.
AND SO...

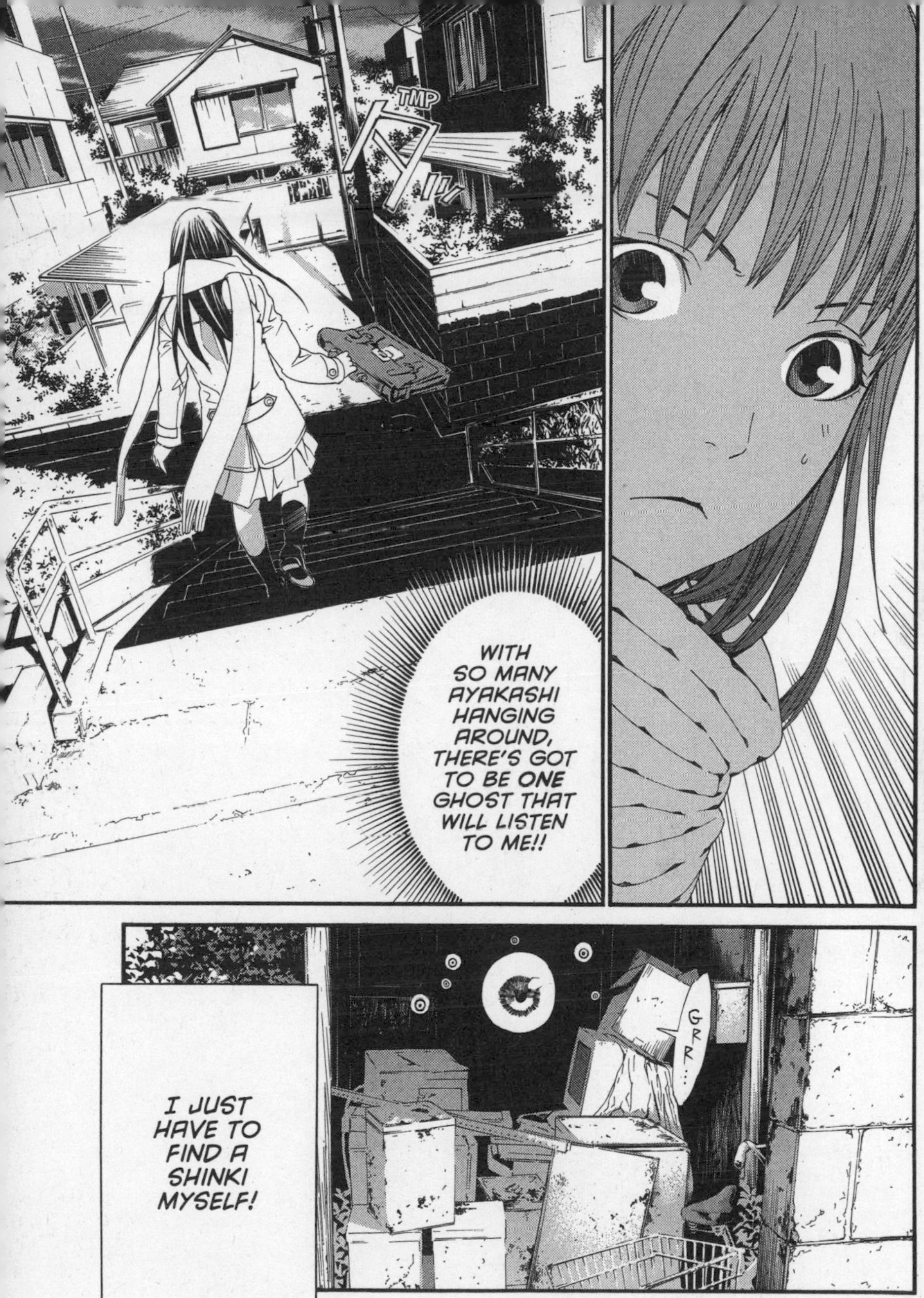
TMP
WITH SO MANY AYAKASHI HANGING AROUND, THERE'S GOT TO BE ONE GHOST THAT WILL LISTEN TO ME!!
GRR...
I JUST HAVE TO FIND A SHINKI MYSELF!

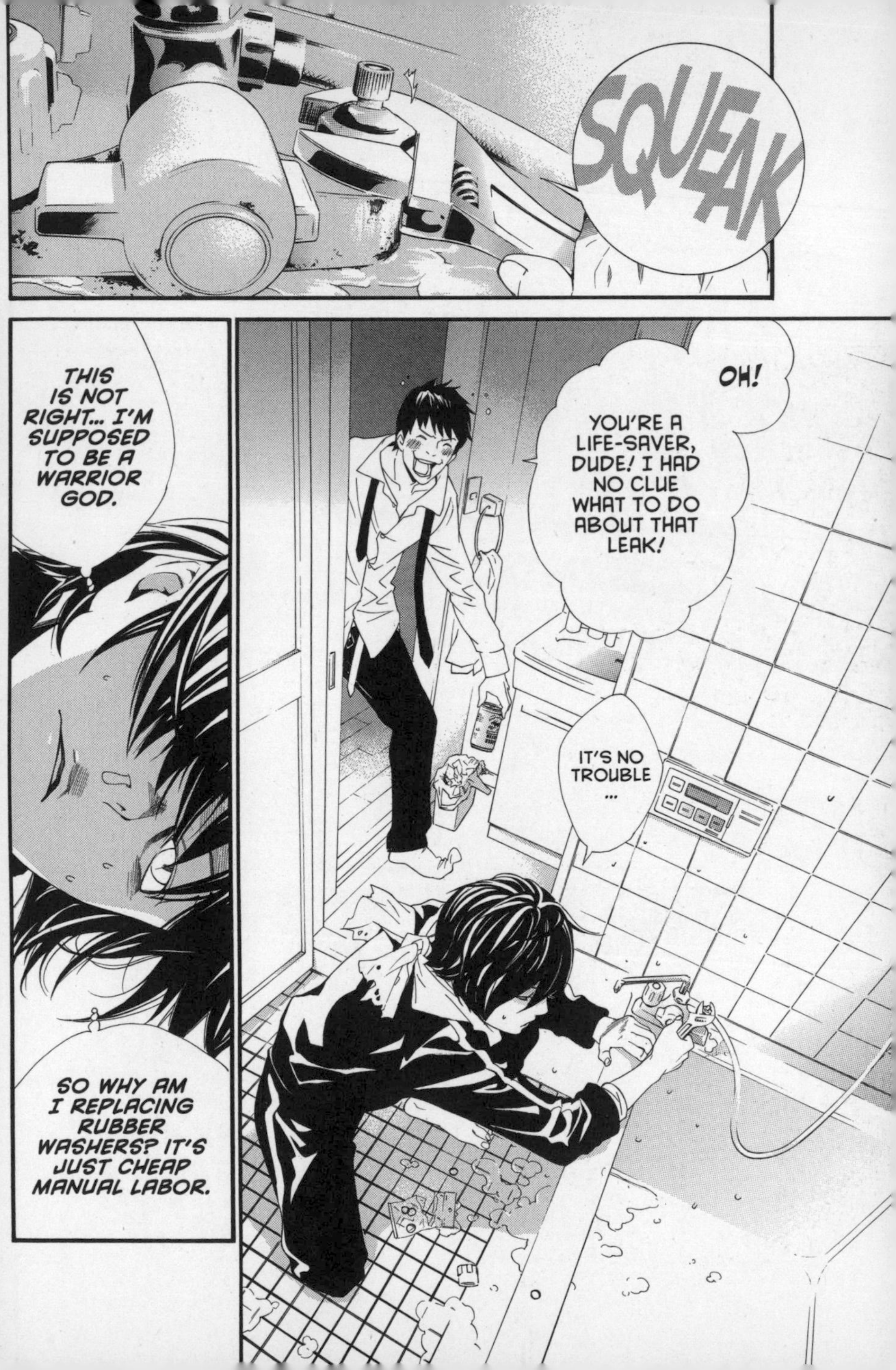
SQUEAK
OH!
YOU'RE A LIFE-SAVER, DUDE! I HAD NO CLUE WHAT TO DO ABOUT THAT LEAK!
IT'S NO TROUBLE ...
THIS IS NOT RIGHT... I'M SUPPOSED TO BE A WARRIOR GOD.
SO WHY AM I REPLACING RUBBER WASHERS? IT'S JUST CHEAP MANUAL LABOR.

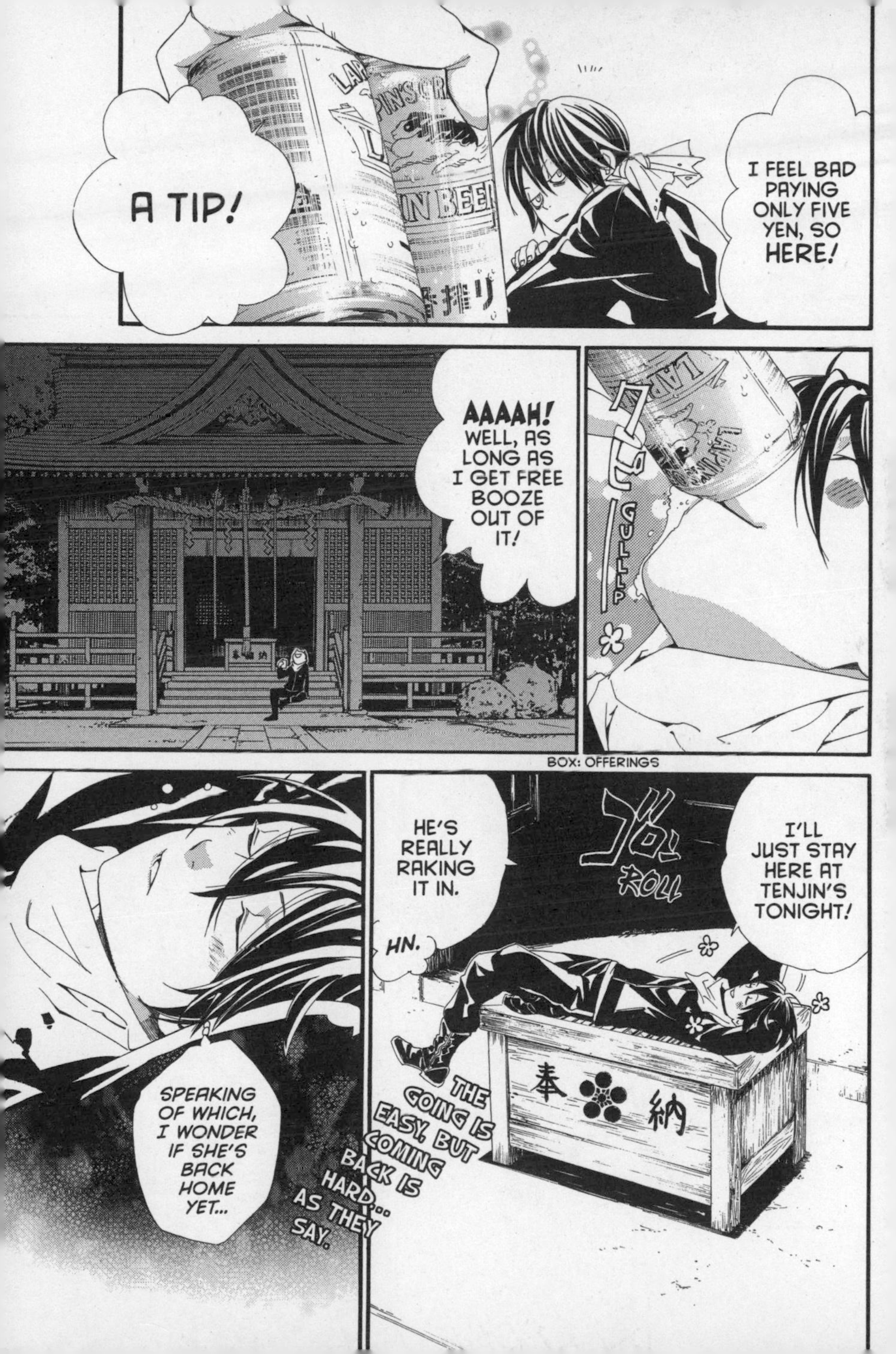
I FEEL BAD PAYING ONLY FIVE YEN, SO HERE!
A TIP!
GULLP
AAAAH! WELL, AS LONG AS I GET FREE BOOZE OUT OF IT!
BOX: OFFERINGS
I'LL JUST STAY HERE AT TENJIN'S TONIGHT!
ROLL
HE'S REALLY RAKING IT IN.
HN.
THE GOING IS EASY, BUT COMING BACK IS HARD... AS THEY SAY.
奉納
SPEAKING OF WHICH, I WONDER IF SHE'S BACK HOME YET...

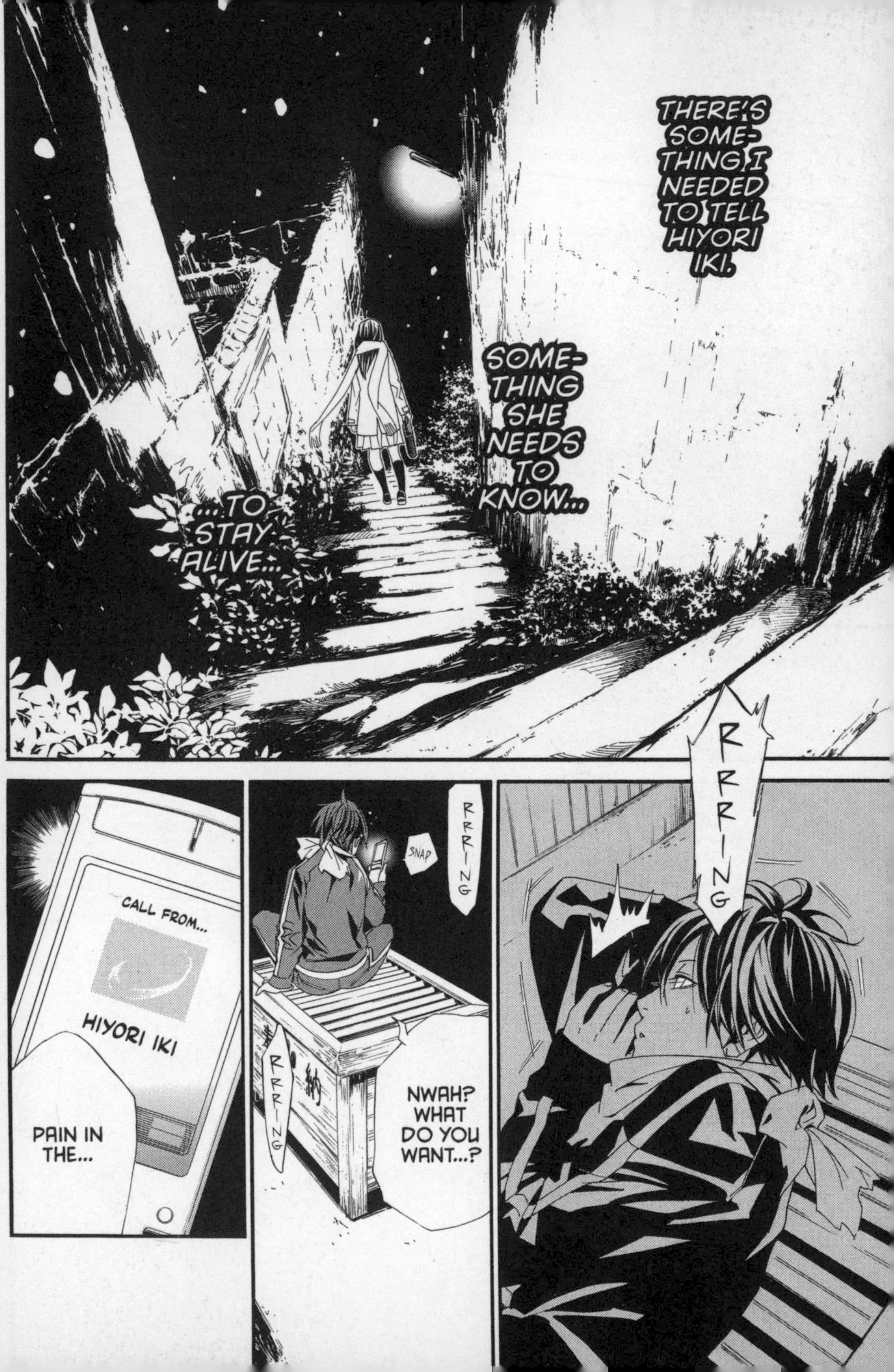
THERE'S SOME-THING I NEEDED TO TELL HIYORI IKI.
SOME-THING SHE NEEDS TO KNOW...
...TO STAY ALIVE...
RRRING
RRRING
SNAP
RRRING
NWAH? WHAT DO YOU WANT...?
CALL FROM...
HIYORI IKI
PAIN IN THE...

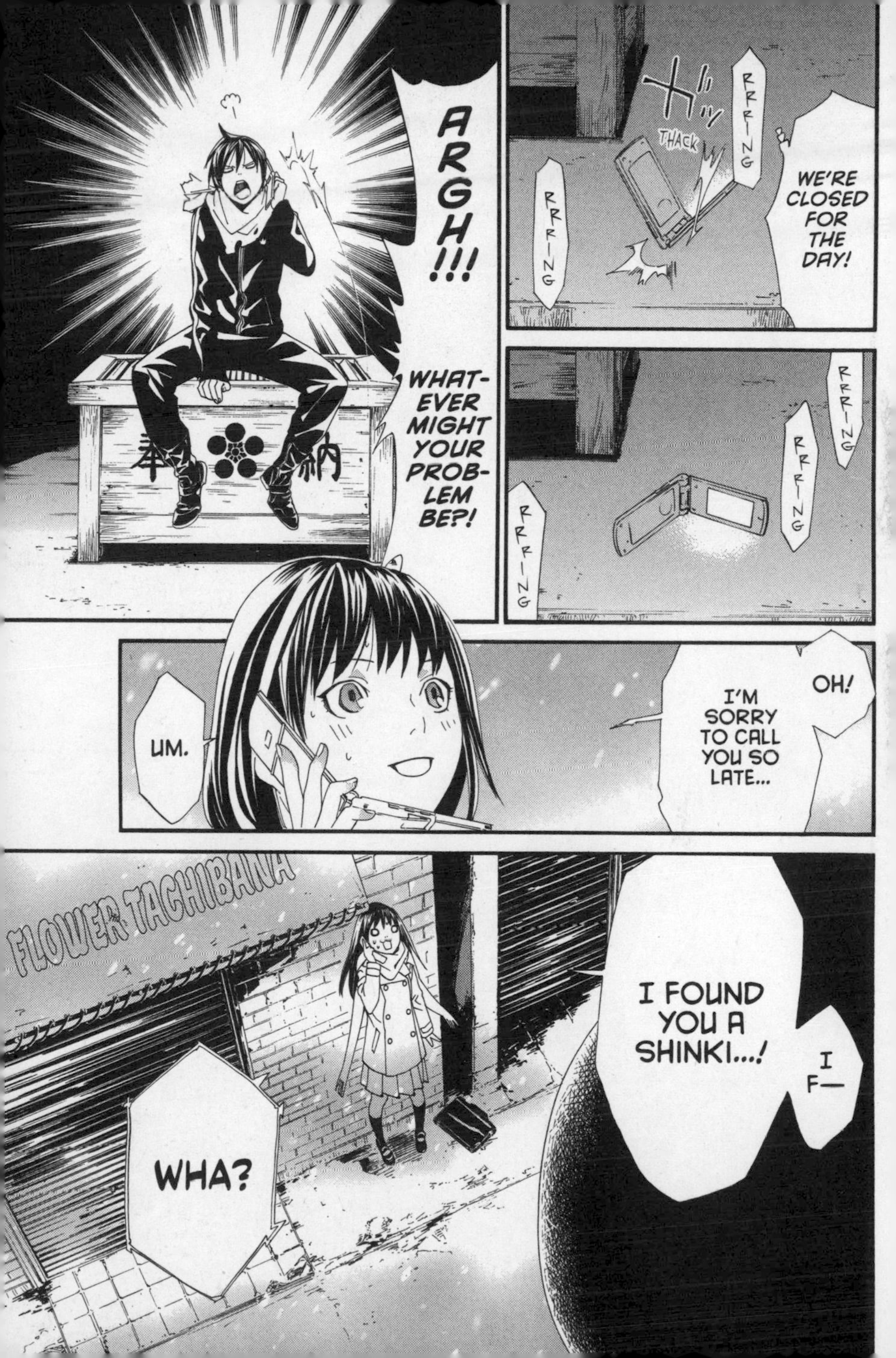
WE'RE CLOSED FOR THE DAY!
RRRING
THACK
RRRING
RRRING
RRRING
RRRING
ARGH!!!
WHATEVER MIGHT YOUR PROBLEM BE?!
奉納
OH!
I'M SORRY TO CALL YOU SO LATE...
UM.
I FOUND YOU A SHINKI...!
I F—
FLOWER TACHIBANA
WHA?

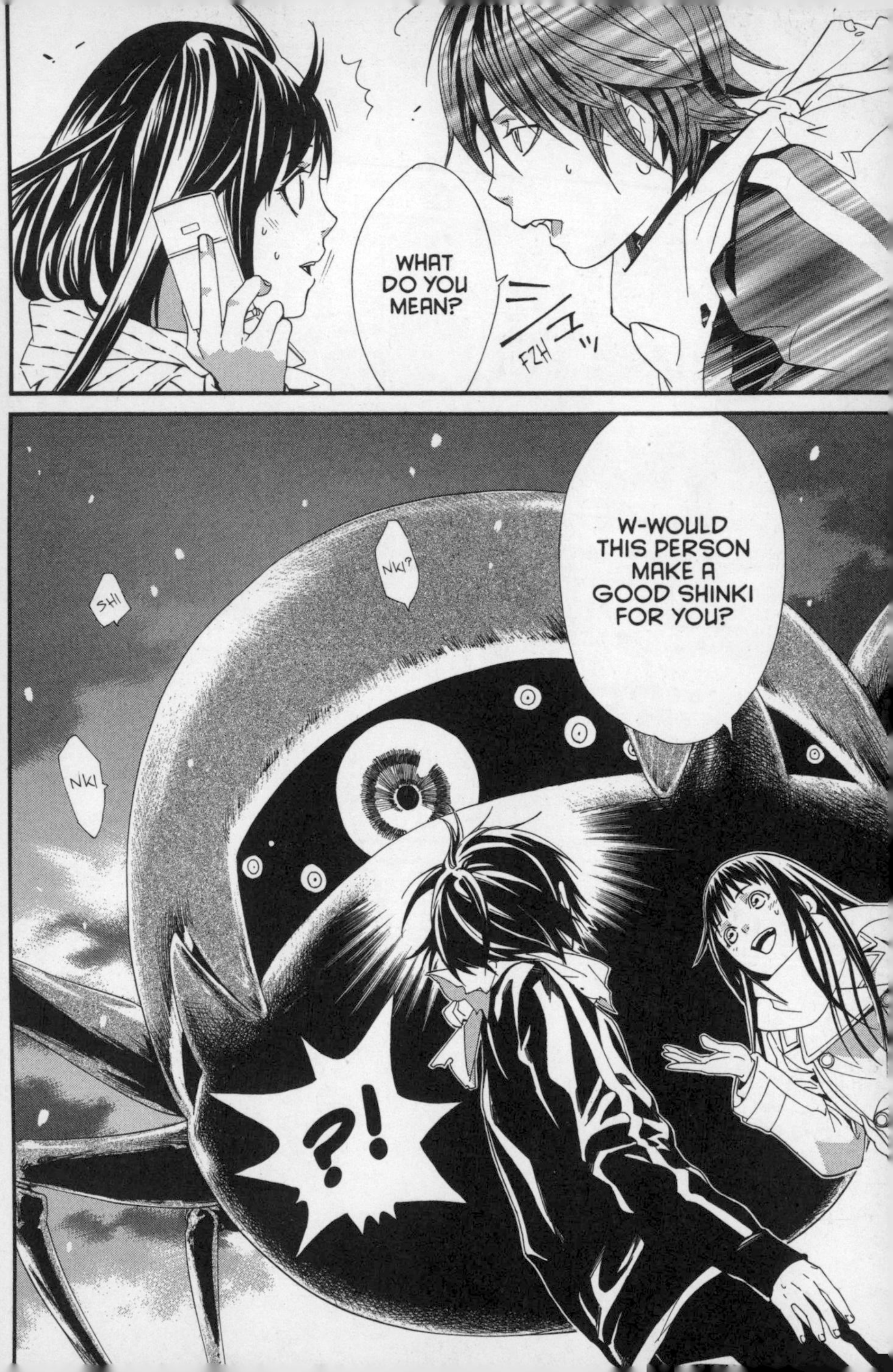
WHAT DO YOU MEAN?
FZH
W-WOULD THIS PERSON MAKE A GOOD SHINKI FOR YOU?
SHI
NKI?
NKI
?!

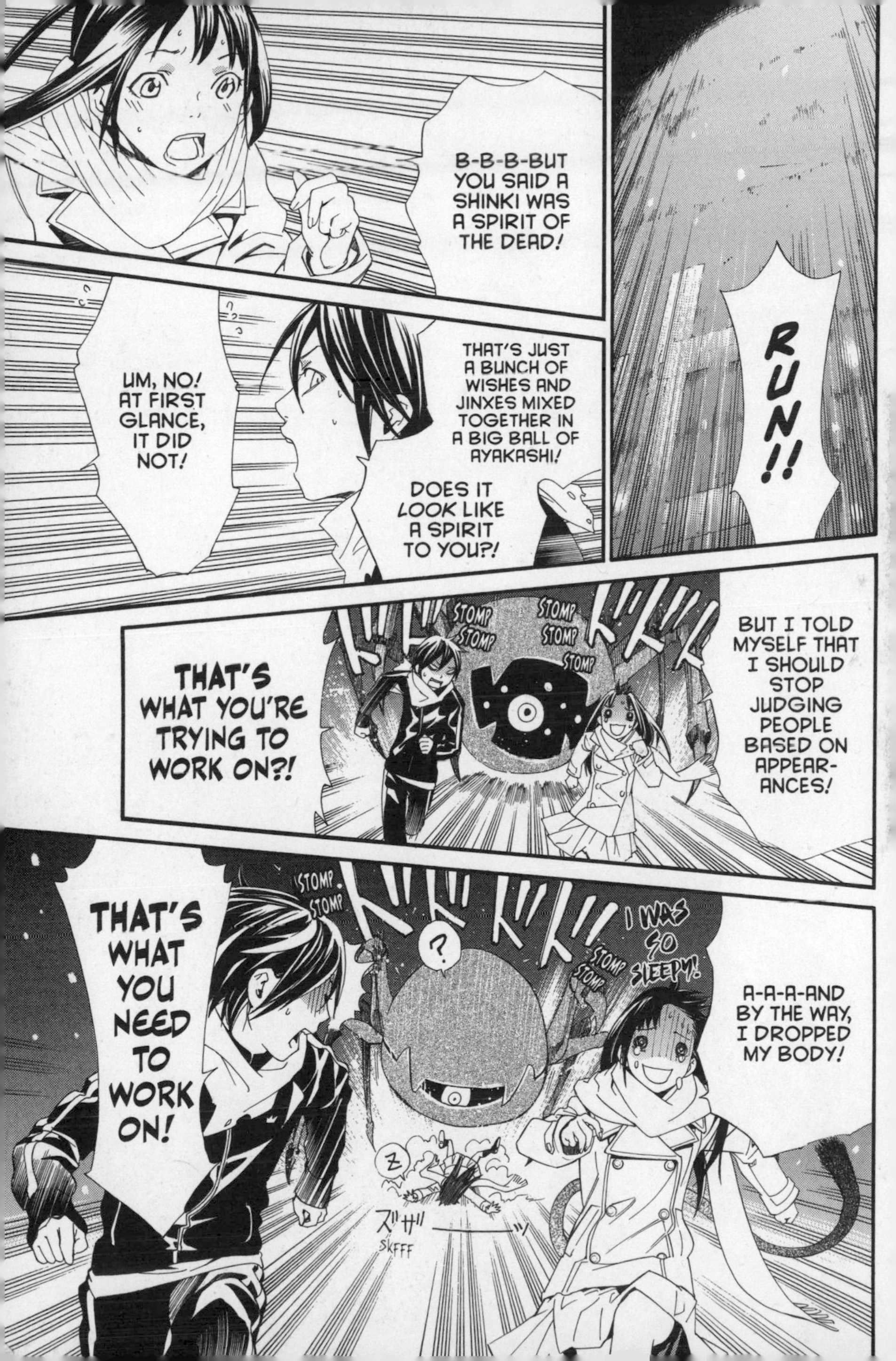
RUN!!
B-B-B-BUT YOU SAID A SHINKI WAS A SPIRIT OF THE DEAD!
THAT'S JUST A BUNCH OF WISHES AND JINXES MIXED TOGETHER IN A BIG BALL OF AYAKASHI!
DOES IT LOOK LIKE A SPIRIT TO YOU?!
UM, NO! AT FIRST GLANCE, IT DID NOT!
BUT I TOLD MYSELF THAT I SHOULD STOP JUDGING PEOPLE BASED ON APPEAR-ANCES!
STOMP STOMP
STOMP STOMP STOMP
STOMP STOMP
THAT'S WHAT YOU'RE TRYING TO WORK ON?!
A-A-A-AND BY THE WAY, I DROPPED MY BODY!
I WAS SO SLEEPY!
STOMP STOMP
?
STOMP STOMP
THAT'S WHAT YOU NEED TO WORK ON!
Z
SKFFF

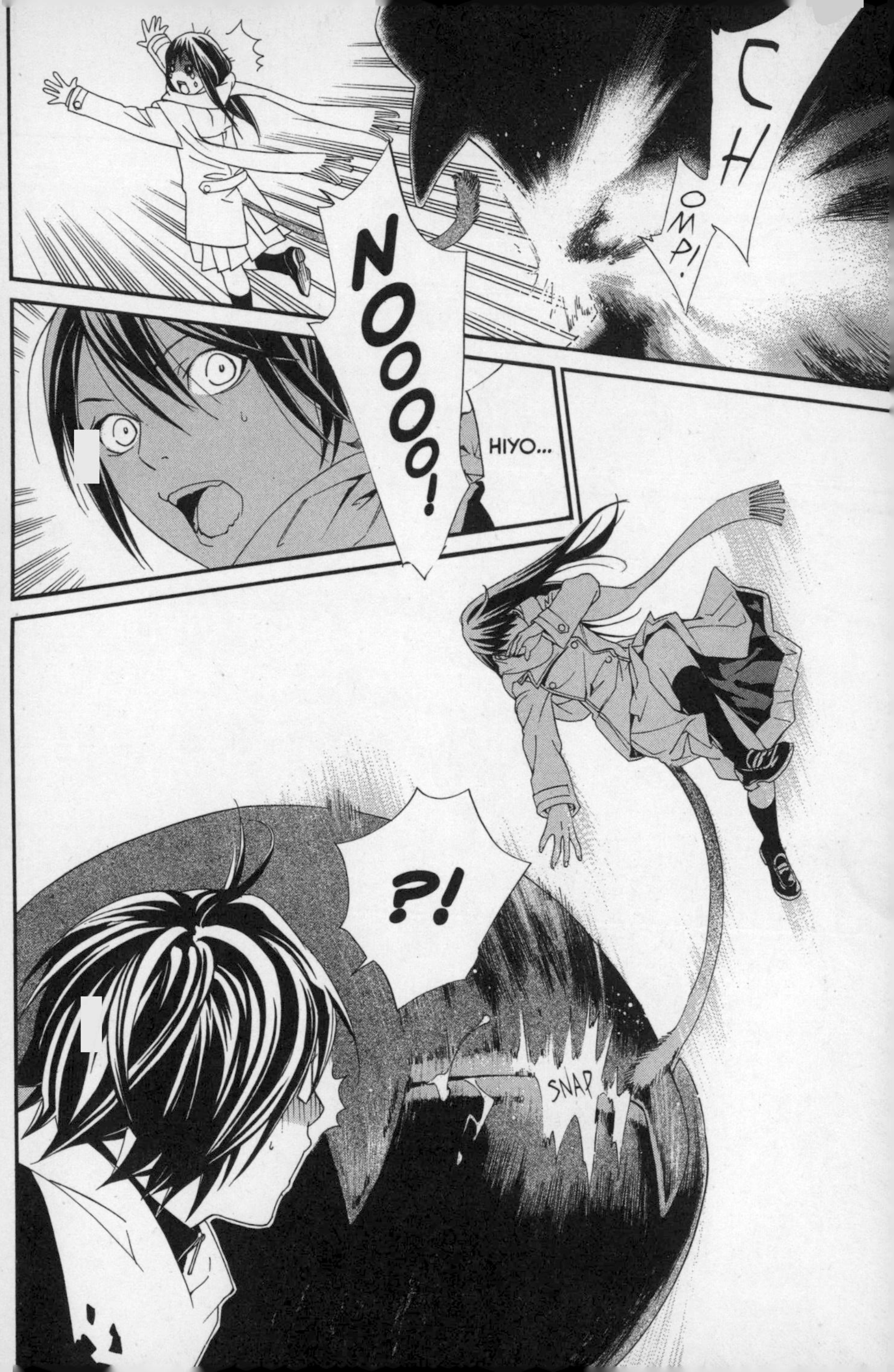
CHOMP!
HIYO...
NOOOOO!
?!
SNAP

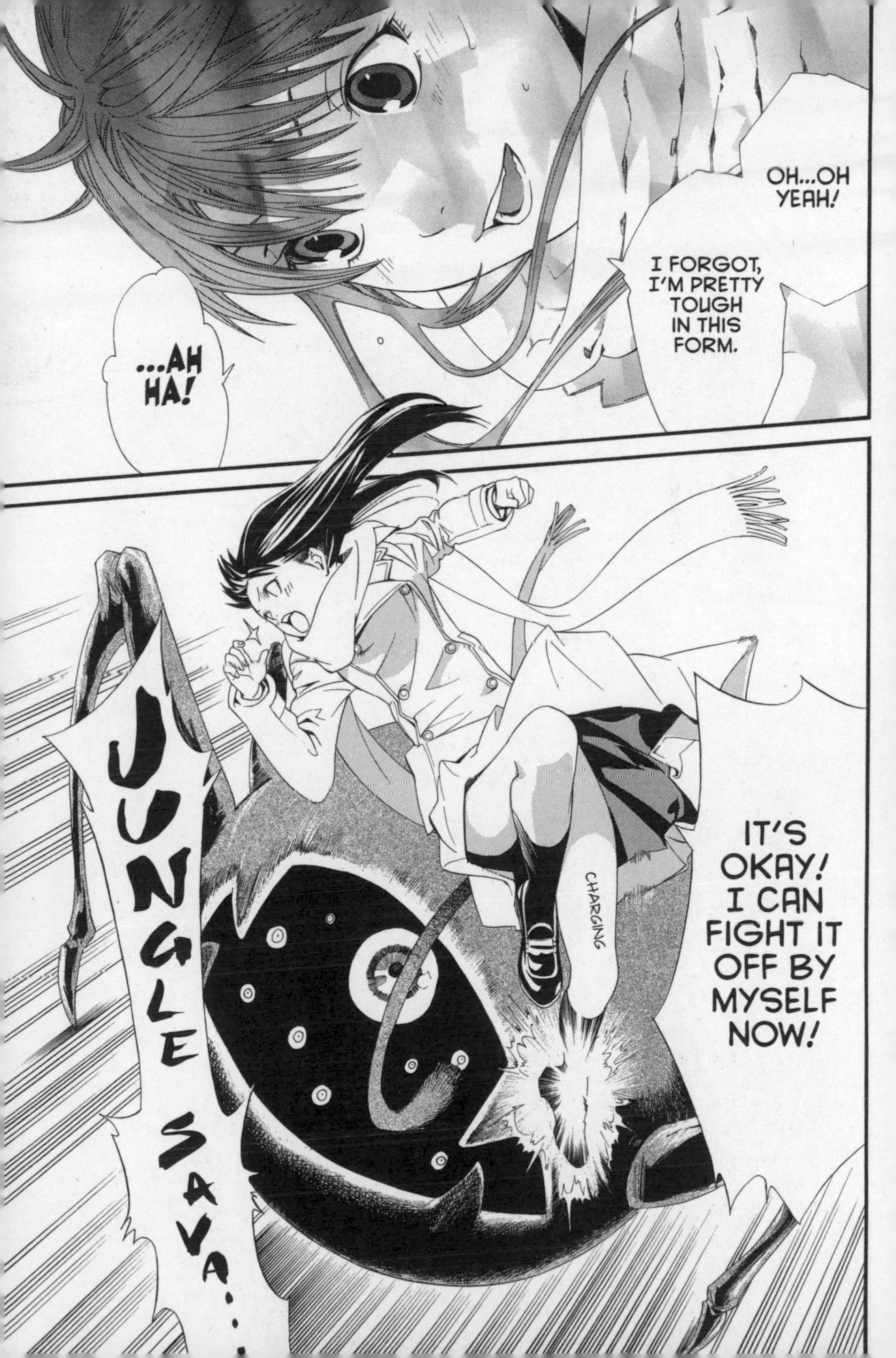

OH...OH YEAH!
I FORGOT, I'M PRETTY TOUGH IN THIS FORM.
...AH HA!
IT'S OKAY! I CAN FIGHT IT OFF BY MYSELF NOW!
CHARGING
JUNGLE SAVA...

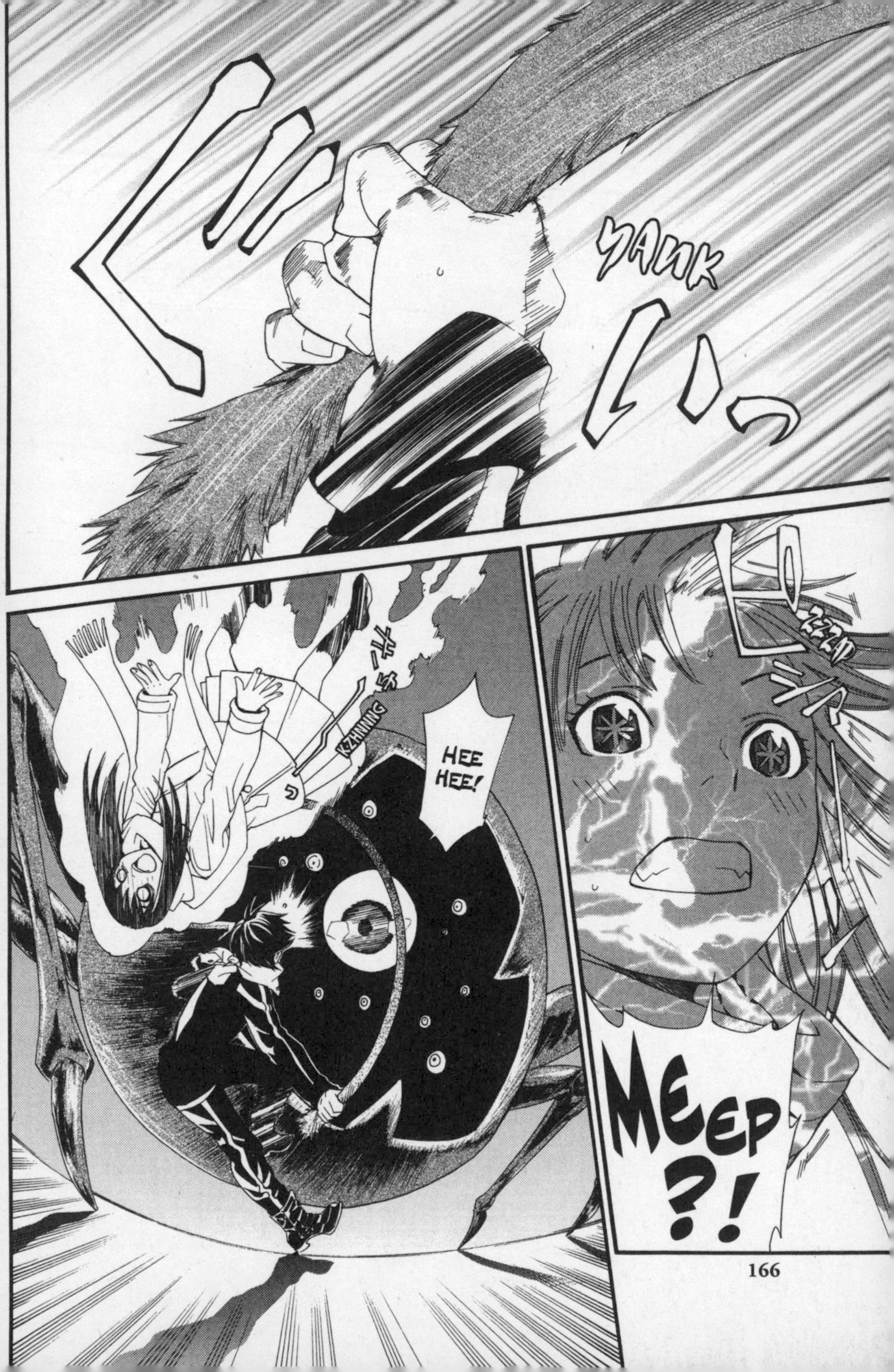
YANK
ZZZAP
MEEP ?!
HEE HEE!
KZHNNNG

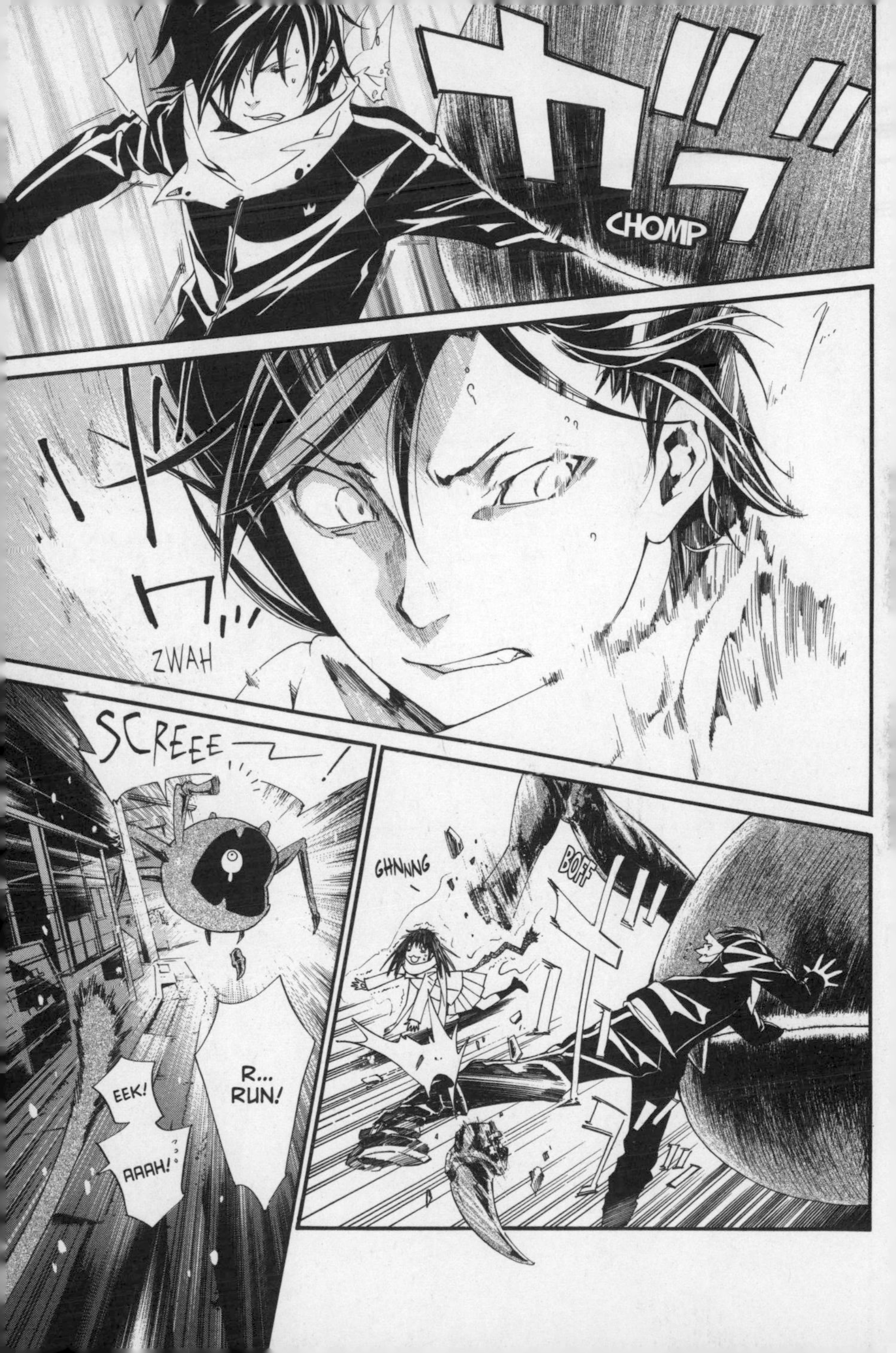
CHOMP
ZWAH
BOFF
GHNNNG
SCREEE—
R... RUN!
EEK!
AAAH!

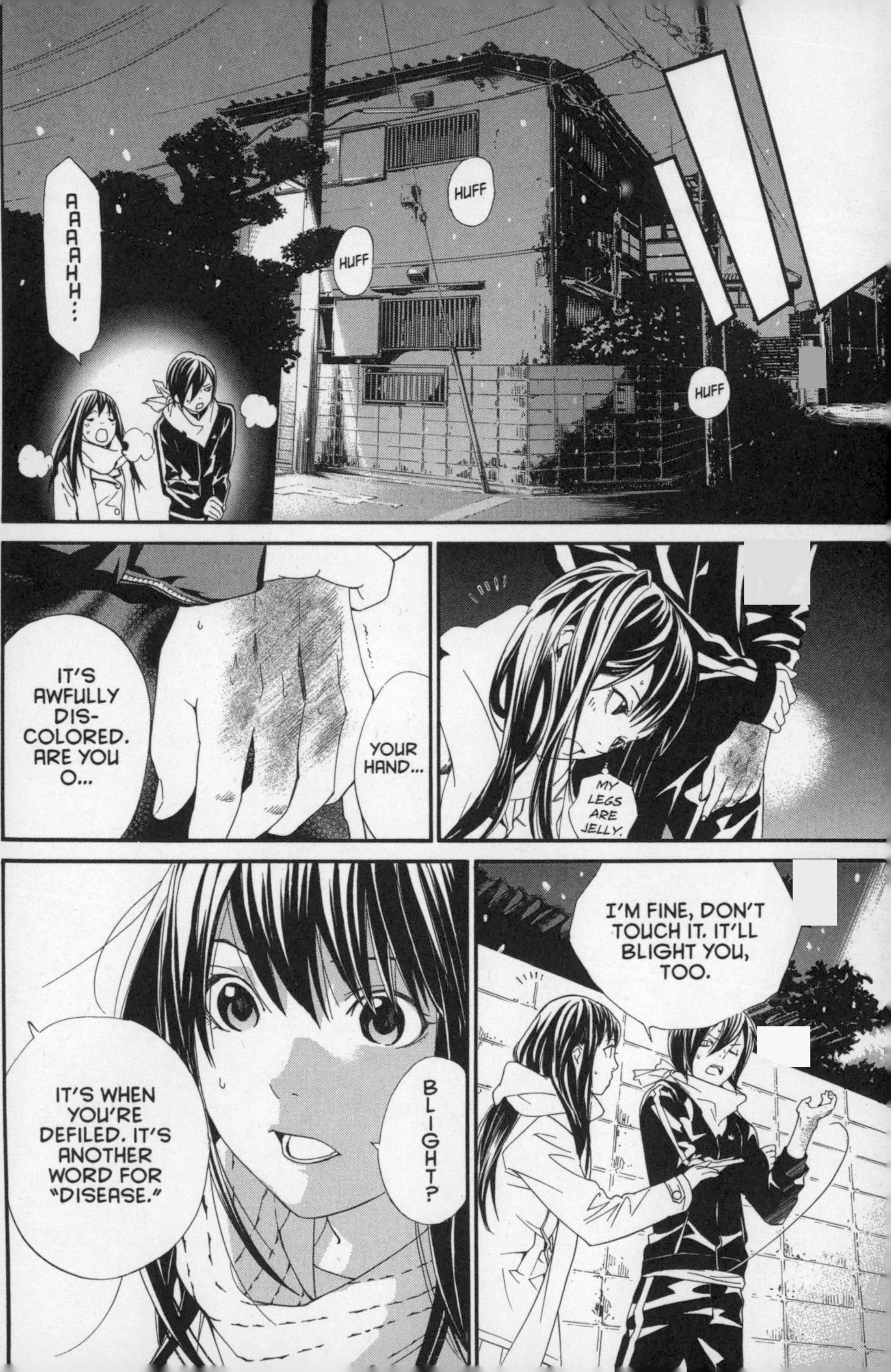
HUFF
HUFF
HUFF
AAAAHH...
MY LEGS ARE JELLY.
YOUR HAND...
IT'S AWFULLY DIS-COLORED. ARE YOU O...
I'M FINE, DON'T TOUCH IT. IT'LL BLIGHT YOU, TOO.
BLIGHT?
IT'S WHEN YOU'RE DEFILED. IT'S ANOTHER WORD FOR "DISEASE."

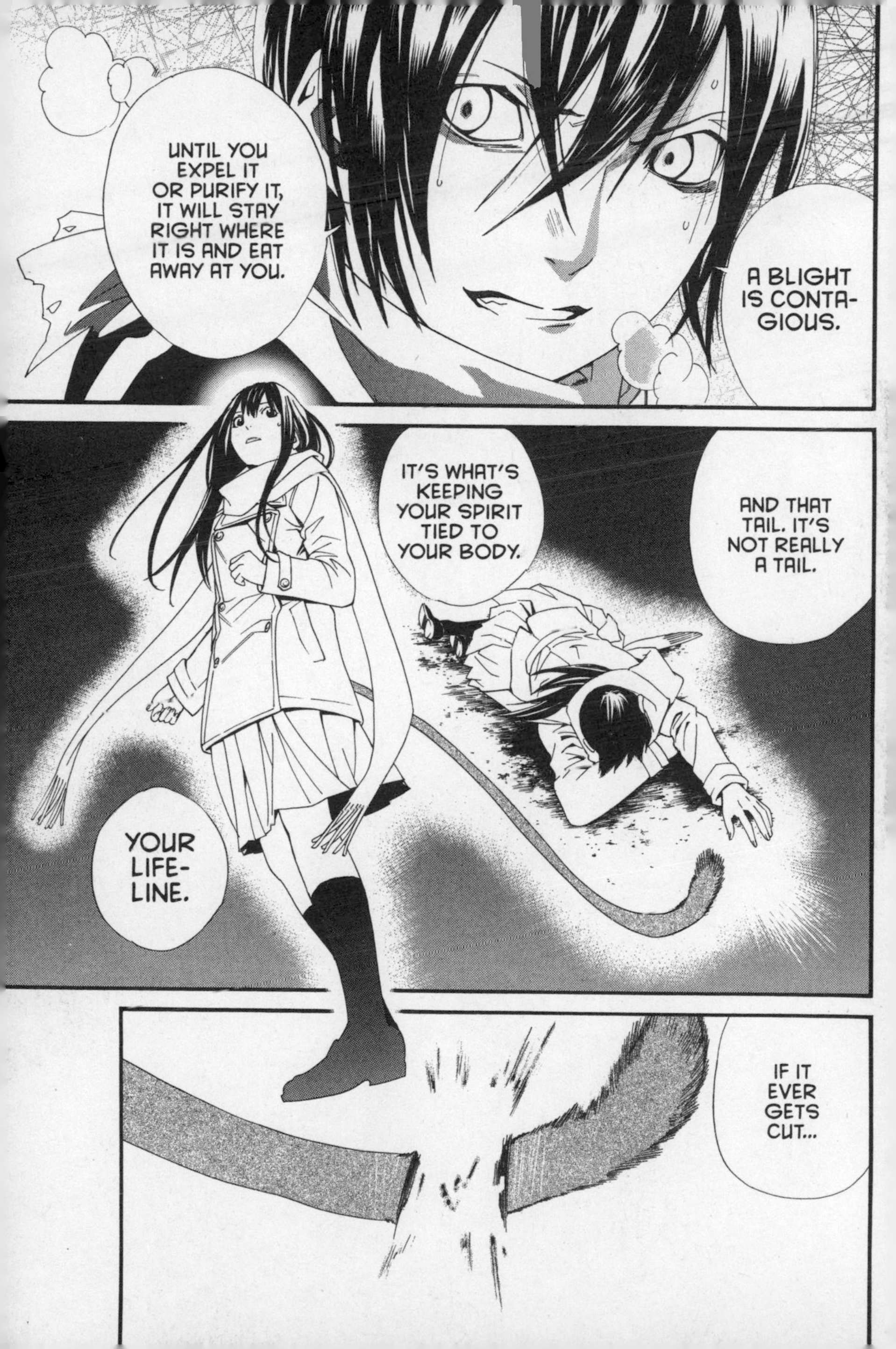
A BLIGHT IS CONTAGIOUS.
UNTIL YOU EXPEL IT OR PURIFY IT, IT WILL STAY RIGHT WHERE IT IS AND EAT AWAY AT YOU.
AND THAT TAIL. IT'S NOT REALLY A TAIL.
IT'S WHAT'S KEEPING YOUR SPIRIT TIED TO YOUR BODY.
YOUR LIFE-LINE.
IF IT EVER GETS CUT...

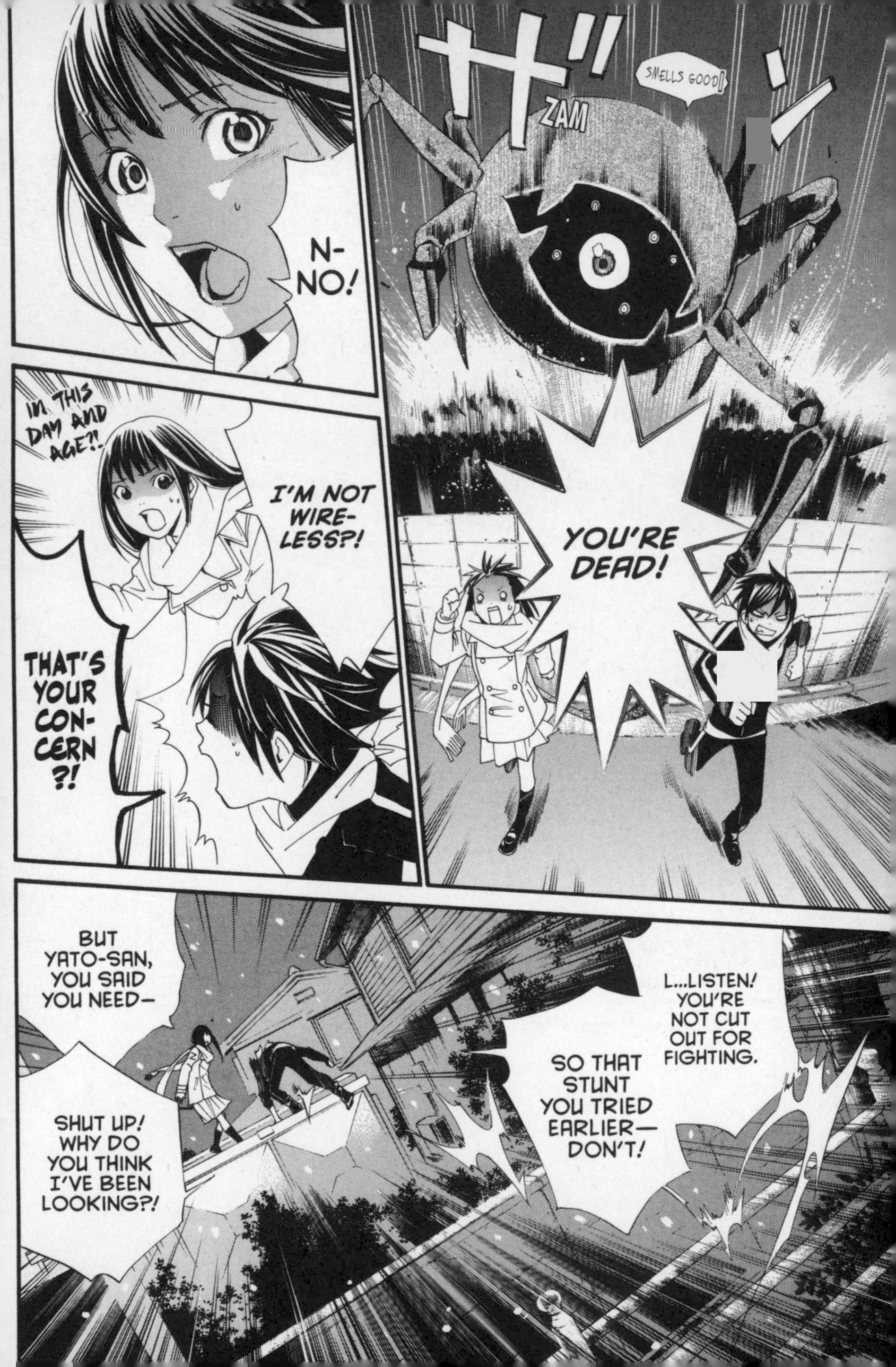
SMELLS GOOD
ZAM
N-NO!
YOU'RE DEAD!
I'M NOT WIRELESS?!
IN THIS DAY AND AGE?!
THAT'S YOUR CONCERN?!
L...LISTEN! YOU'RE NOT CUT OUT FOR FIGHTING.
SO THAT STUNT YOU TRIED EARLIER— DON'T!
BUT YATO-SAN, YOU SAID YOU NEED—
SHUT UP! WHY DO YOU THINK I'VE BEEN LOOKING?!

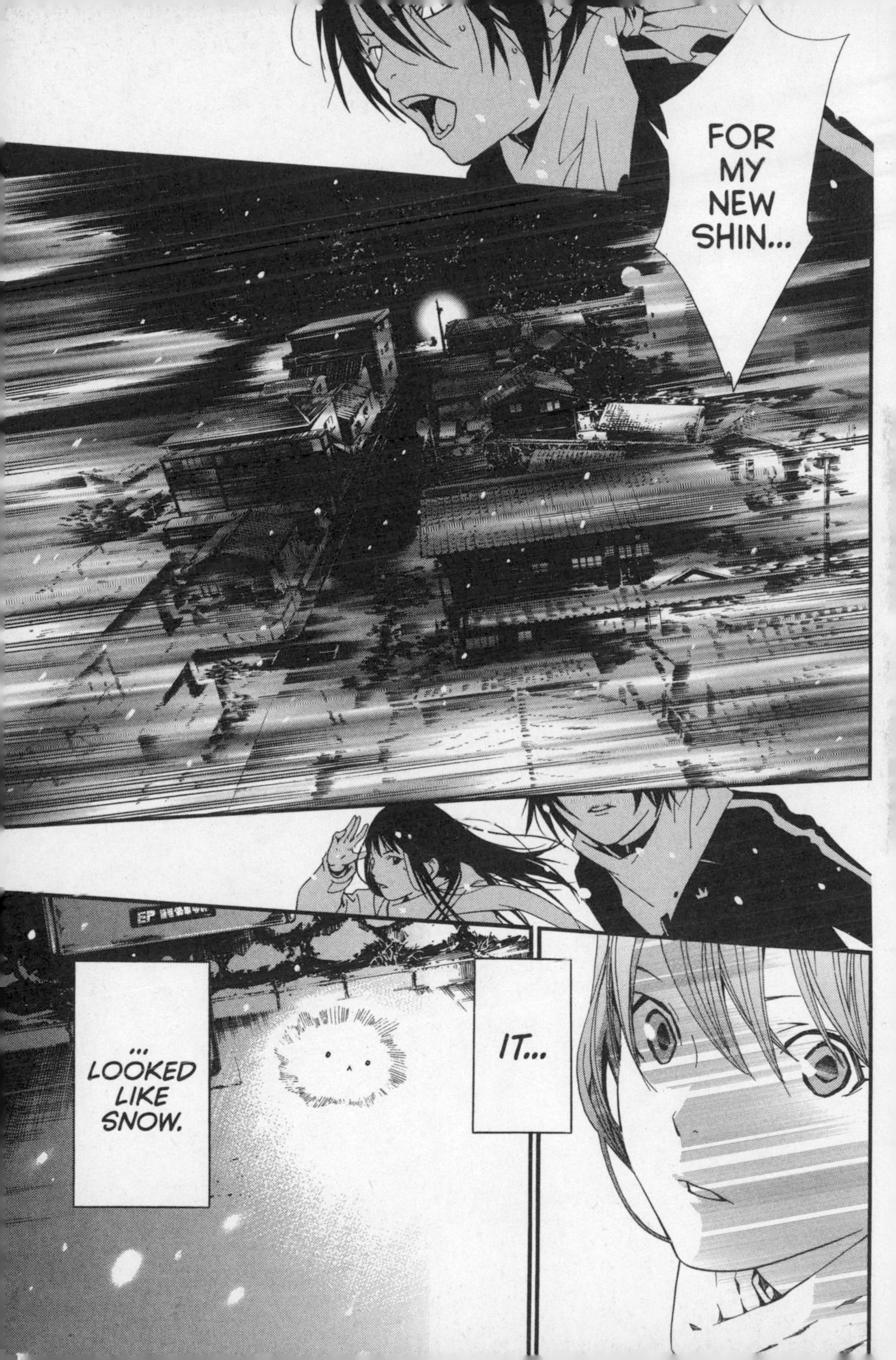
FOR MY NEW SHIN...
IT...
...LOOKED LIKE SNOW.

...A BOY.

KA-CHUNK

YATO-SAN?!

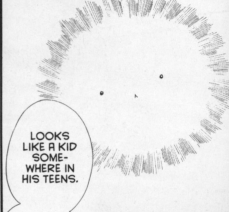

LOOKS LIKE A KID SOMEWHERE IN HIS TEENS.

THAT'S AN OBNOXIOUS AGE TO DEAL WITH...

HUFF

HUFF

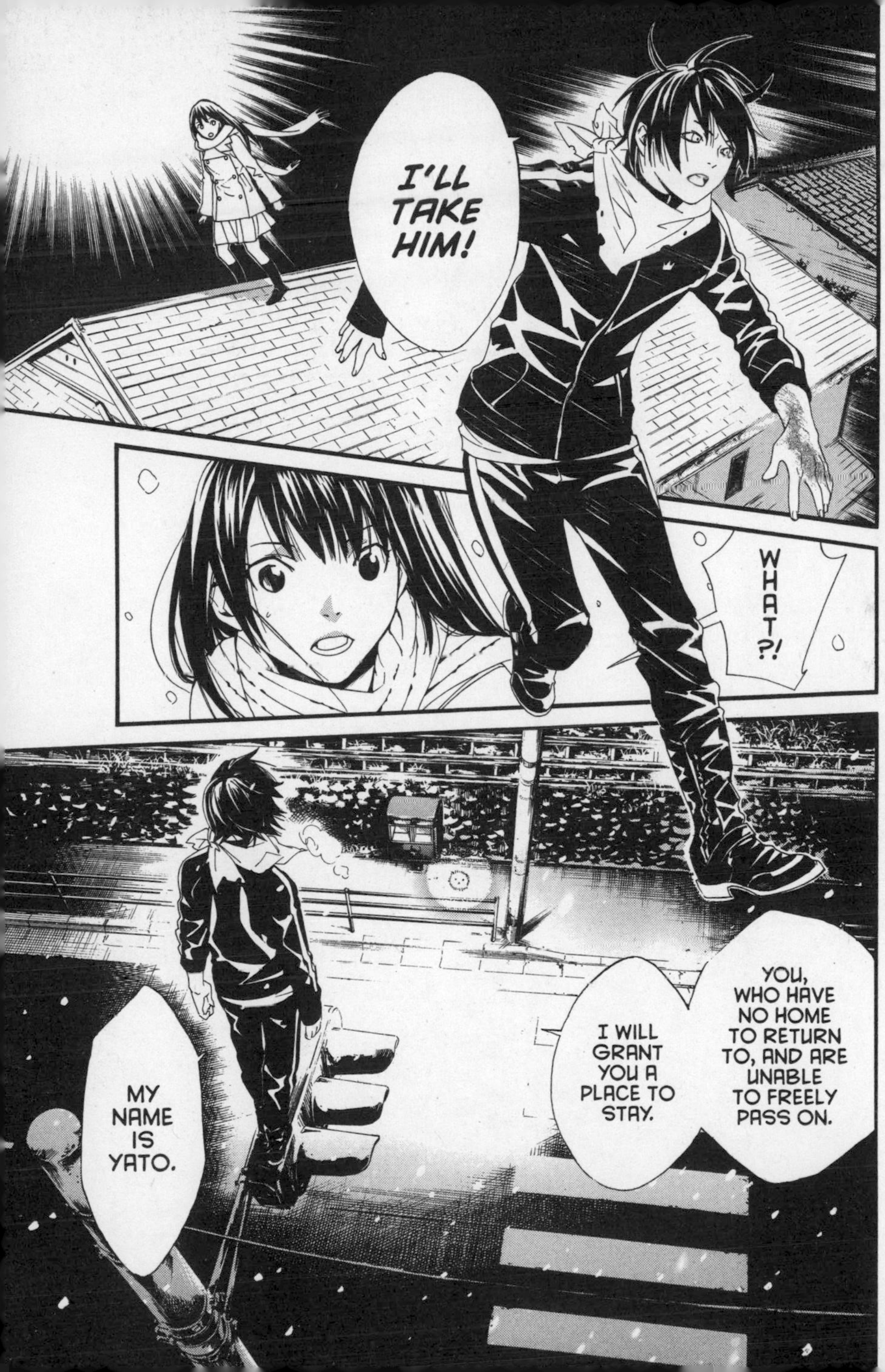
I'LL TAKE HIM!
WHAT?!
YOU, WHO HAVE NO HOME TO RETURN TO, AND ARE UNABLE TO FREELY PASS ON.
I WILL GRANT YOU A PLACE TO STAY.
MY NAME IS YATO.

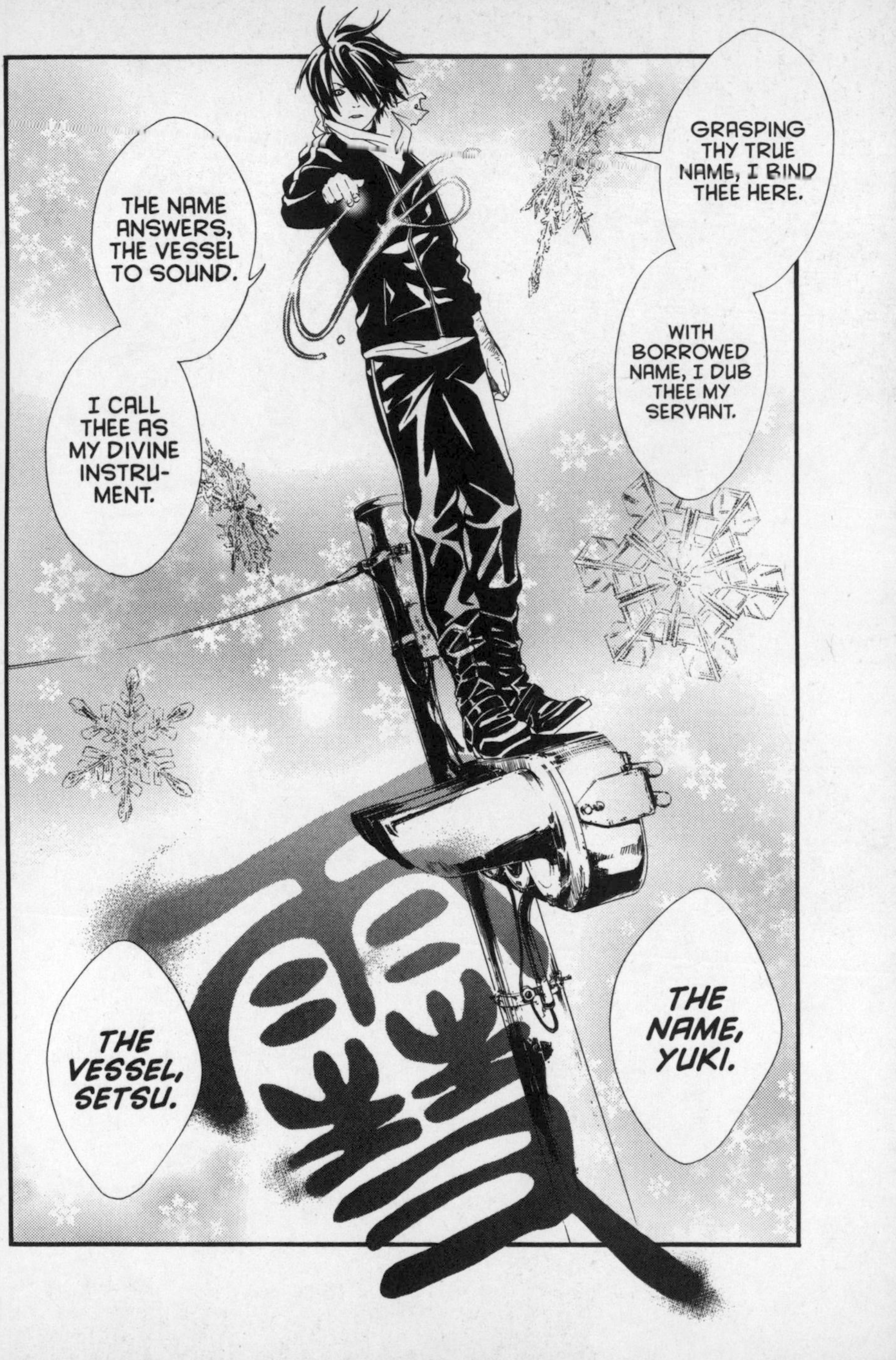
GRASPING THY TRUE NAME, I BIND THEE HERE.
WITH BORROWED NAME, I DUB THEE MY SERVANT.
THE NAME ANSWERS, THE VESSEL TO SOUND.
I CALL THEE AS MY DIVINE INSTRU-MENT.
THE NAME, YUKI.
THE VESSEL, SETSU.

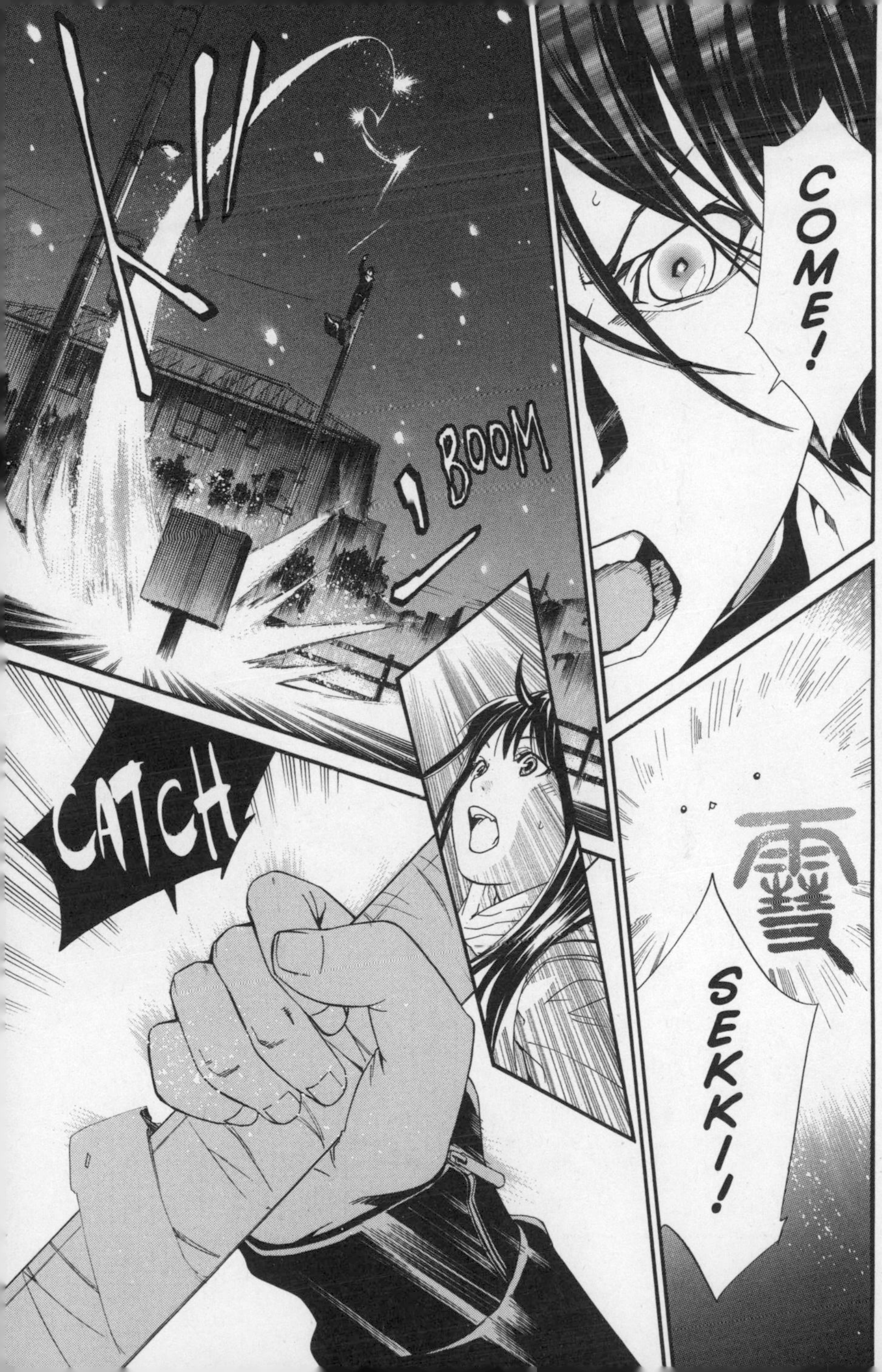

COME!
BOOM
SEKKI!!
CATCH

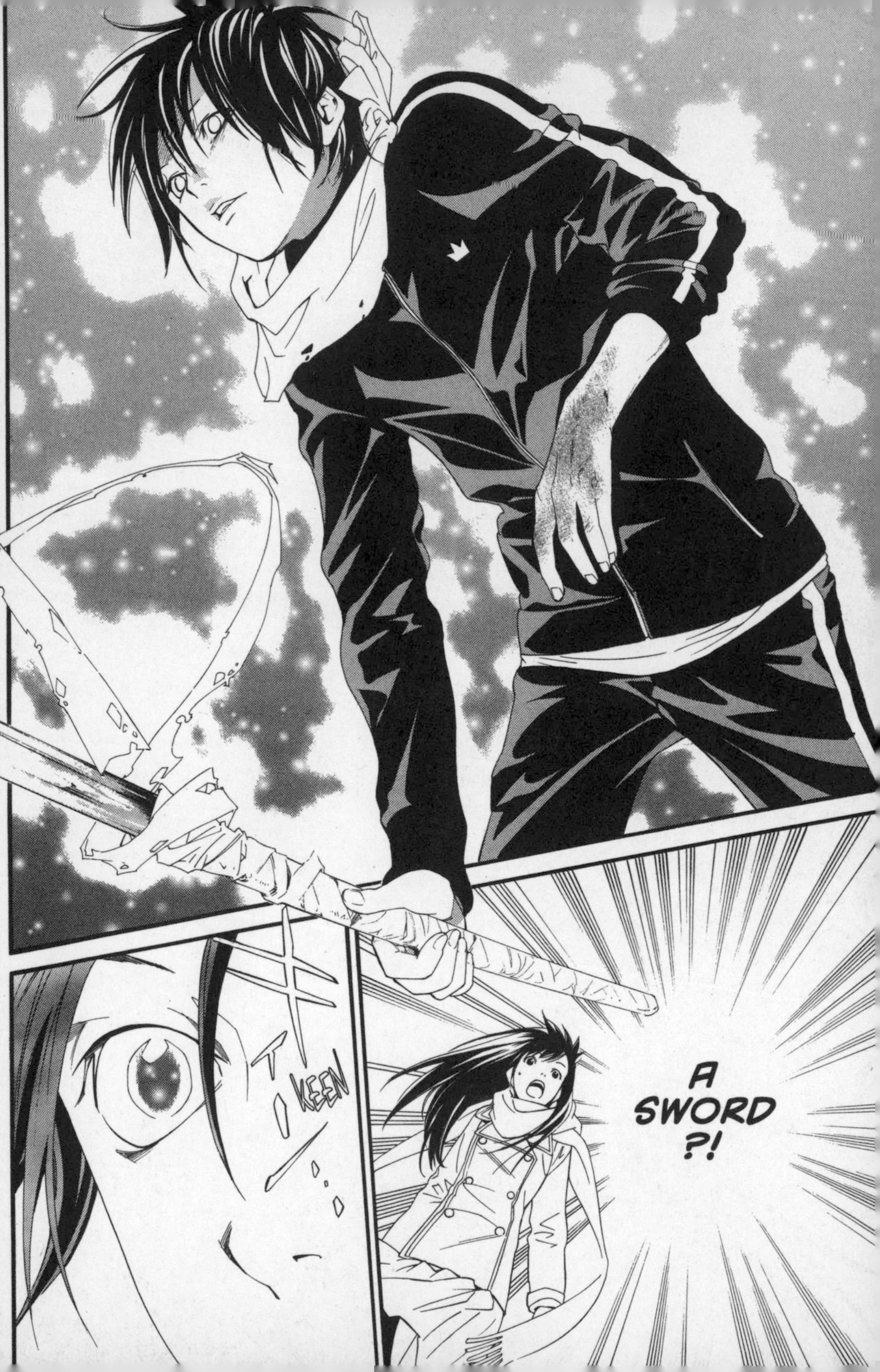
A SWORD ?!
KEEN

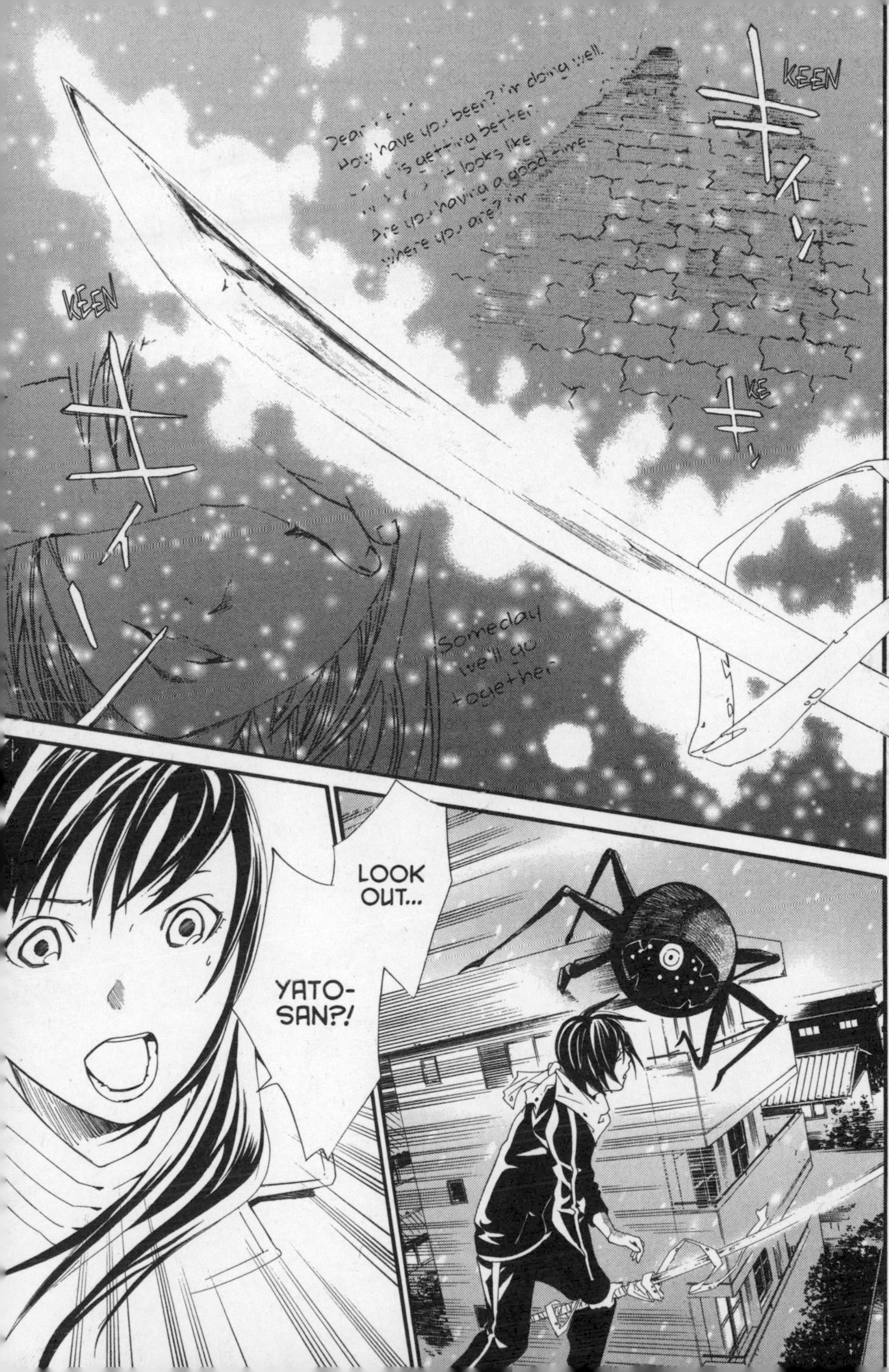
KEEN
KE
KEEN
Dear
How have you been? I'm doing well.
is getting better.
it looks like.
Are you having a good time
where you are? I'm
Someday
we'll go
together.
LOOK OUT...
YATO-SAN?!

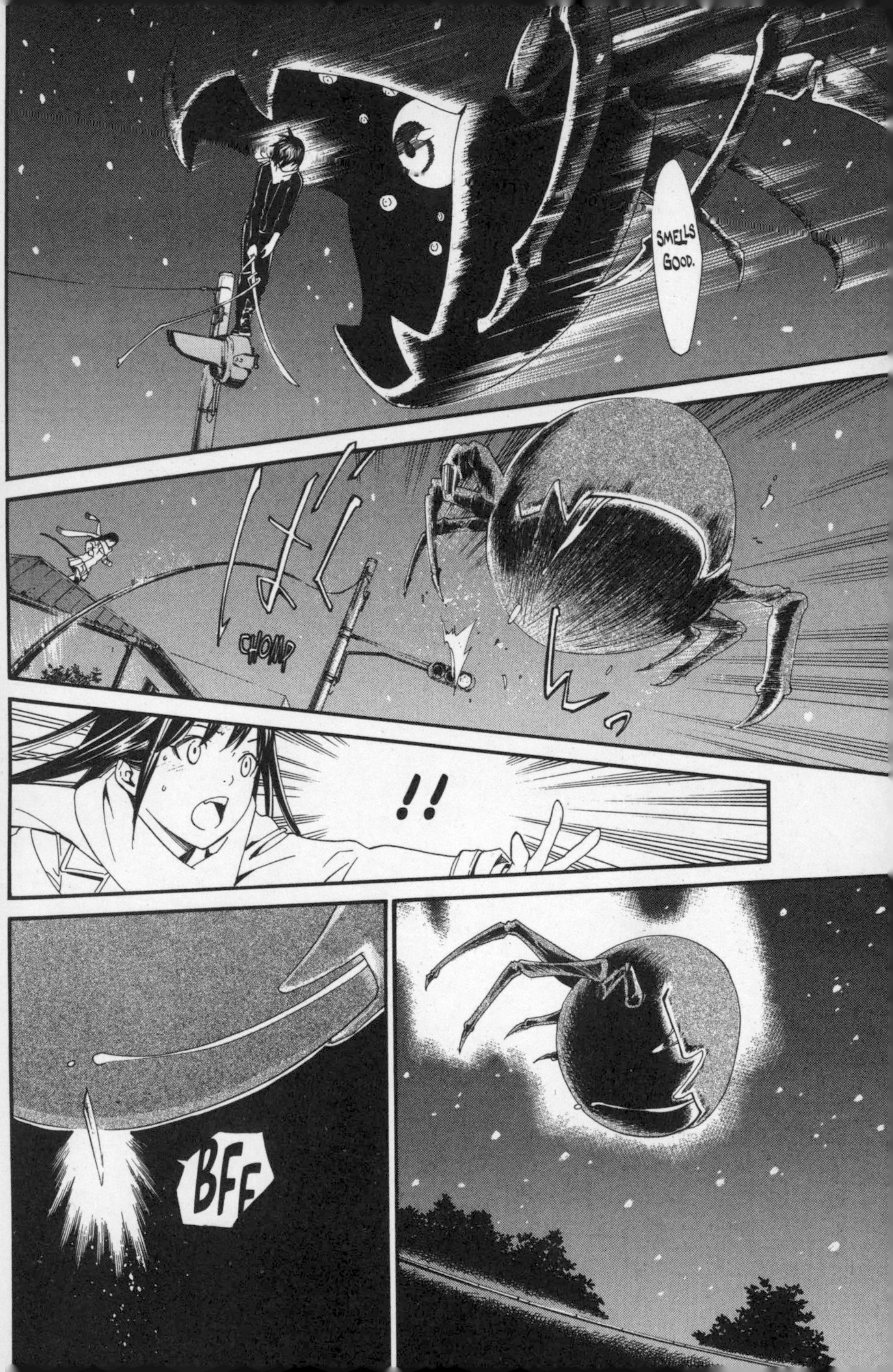
SMELLS GOOD.
CHOMP
!!
BFF

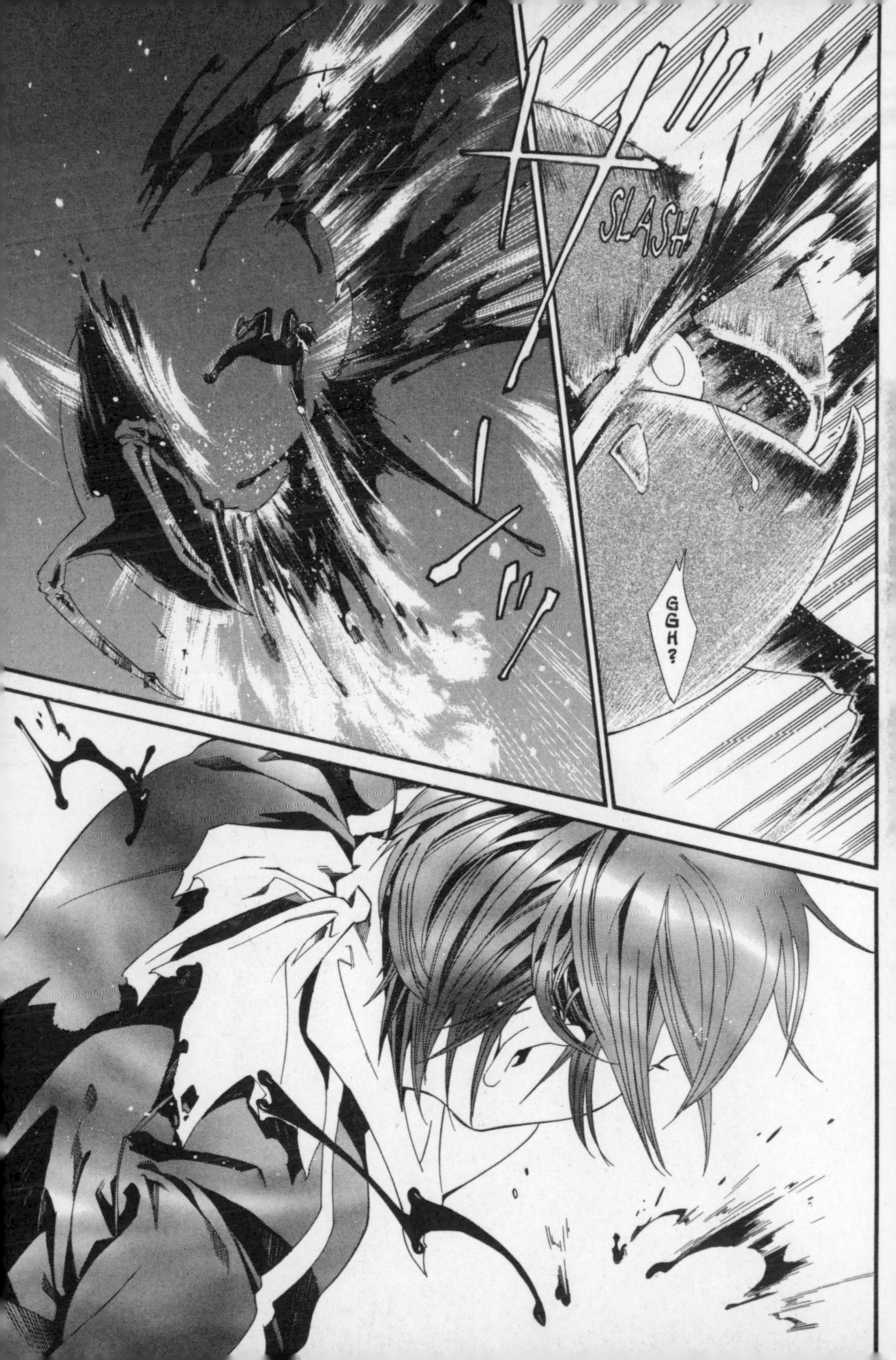
SLASH
GGH?

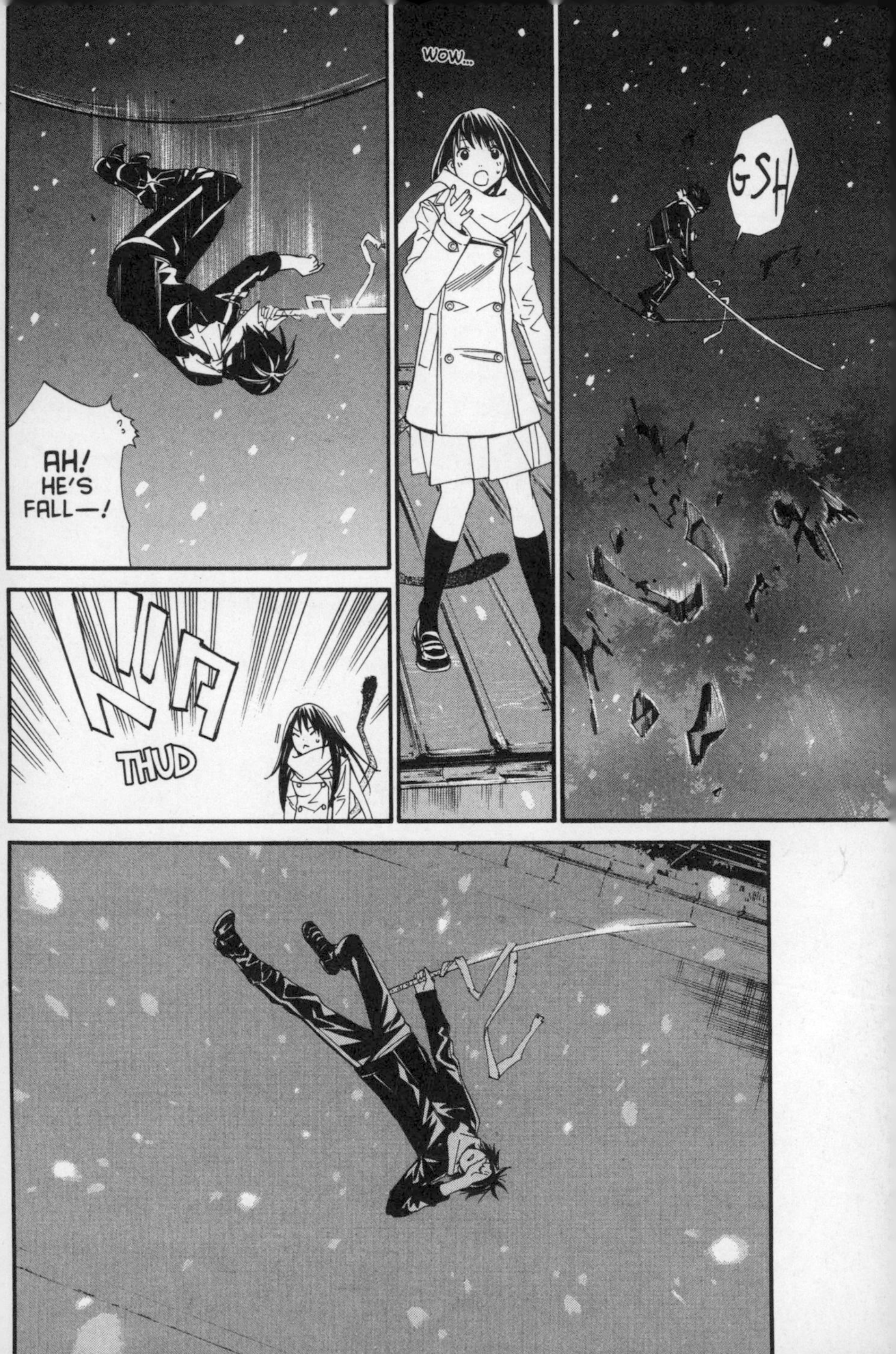
GSH
WOW...
AH! HE'S FALL—!
THUD

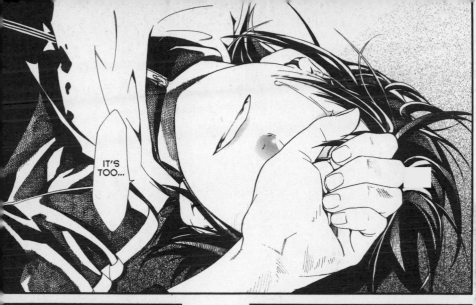

IT'S TOO...

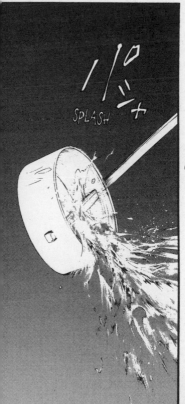

SPLASH

...WAS HE CRYING...?

FIP
FIP
FIP
FIP
FIP

...IS IT MY IMAGINATION?

OR...

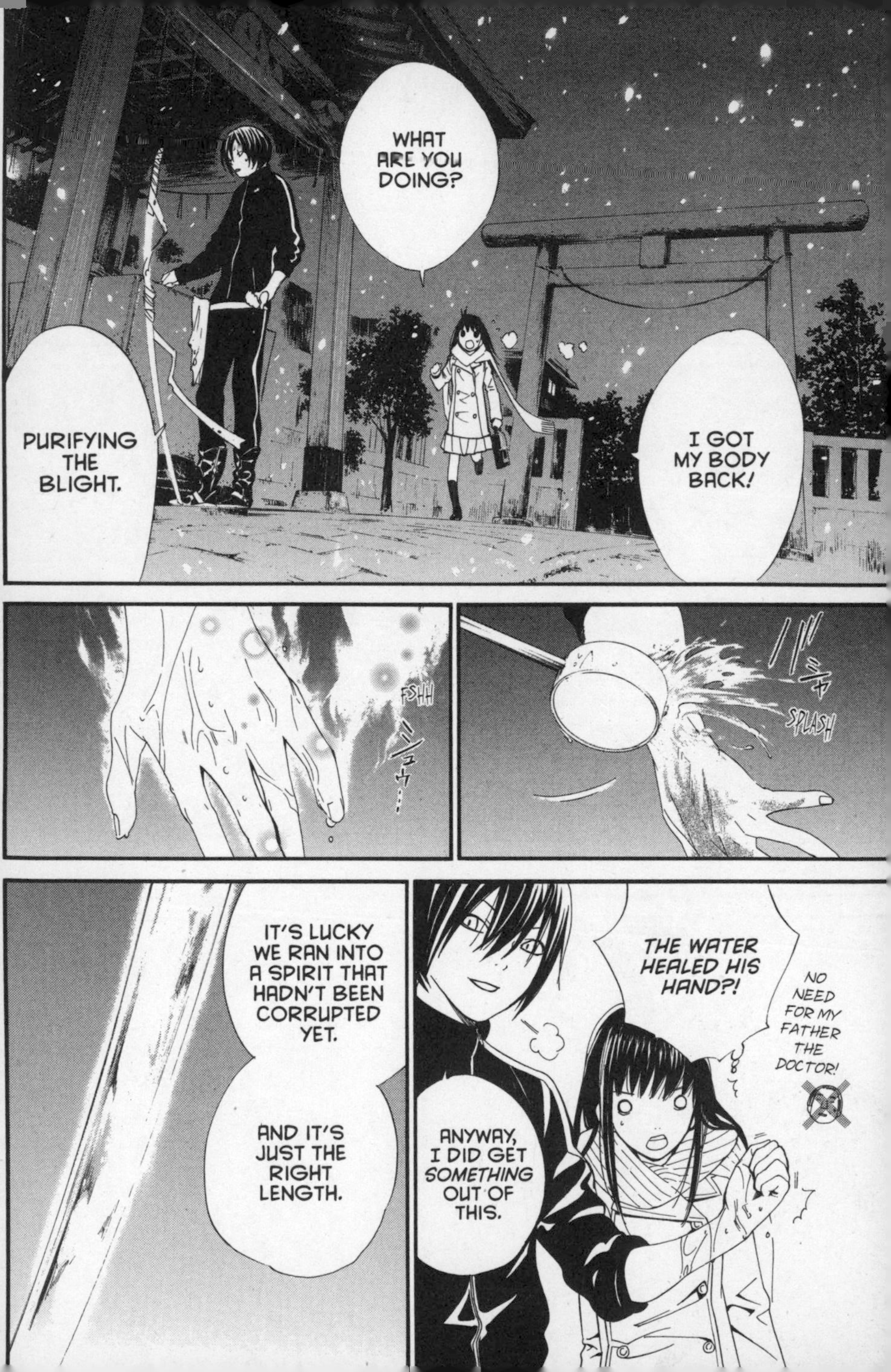
I GOT MY BODY BACK!
WHAT ARE YOU DOING?
PURIFYING THE BLIGHT.
SPLASH
FSHH
THE WATER HEALED HIS HAND?!
NO NEED FOR MY FATHER THE DOCTOR!
ANYWAY, I DID GET SOMETHING OUT OF THIS.
IT'S LUCKY WE RAN INTO A SPIRIT THAT HADN'T BEEN CORRUPTED YET.
AND IT'S JUST THE RIGHT LENGTH.

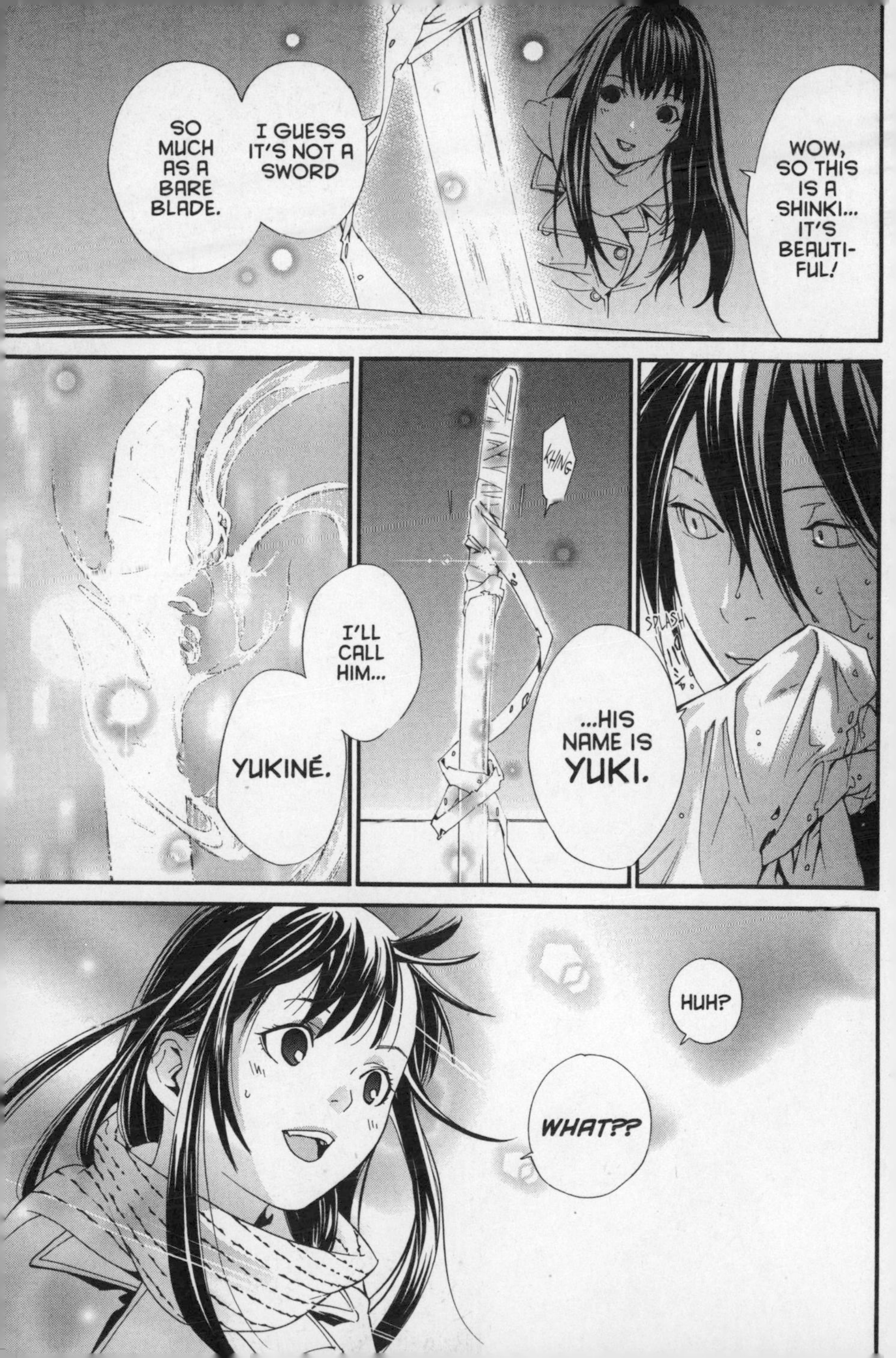
WOW, SO THIS IS A SHINKI... IT'S BEAUTI-FUL!
I GUESS IT'S NOT A SWORD
SO MUCH AS A BARE BLADE.
SPLASH
...HIS NAME IS YUKI.
KHING
I'LL CALL HIM...
YUKINÉ.
HUH?
WHAT??

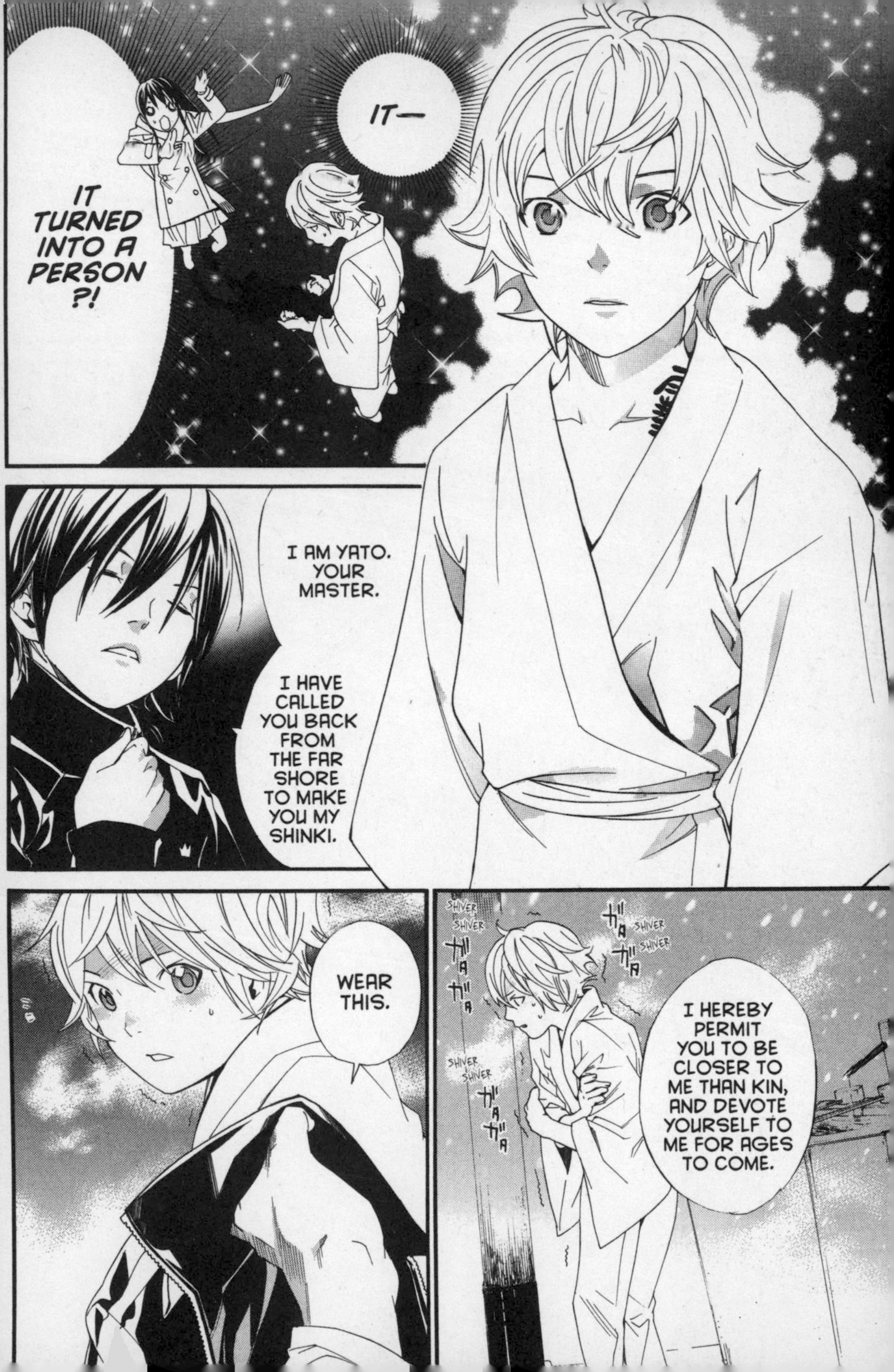
IT—
IT TURNED INTO A PERSON?!
I AM YATO. YOUR MASTER.
I HAVE CALLED YOU BACK FROM THE FAR SHORE TO MAKE YOU MY SHINKI.
SHIVER SHIVER
SHIVER SHIVER
SHIVER SHIVER
I HEREBY PERMIT YOU TO BE CLOSER TO ME THAN KIN, AND DEVOTE YOURSELF TO ME FOR AGES TO COME.
WEAR THIS.

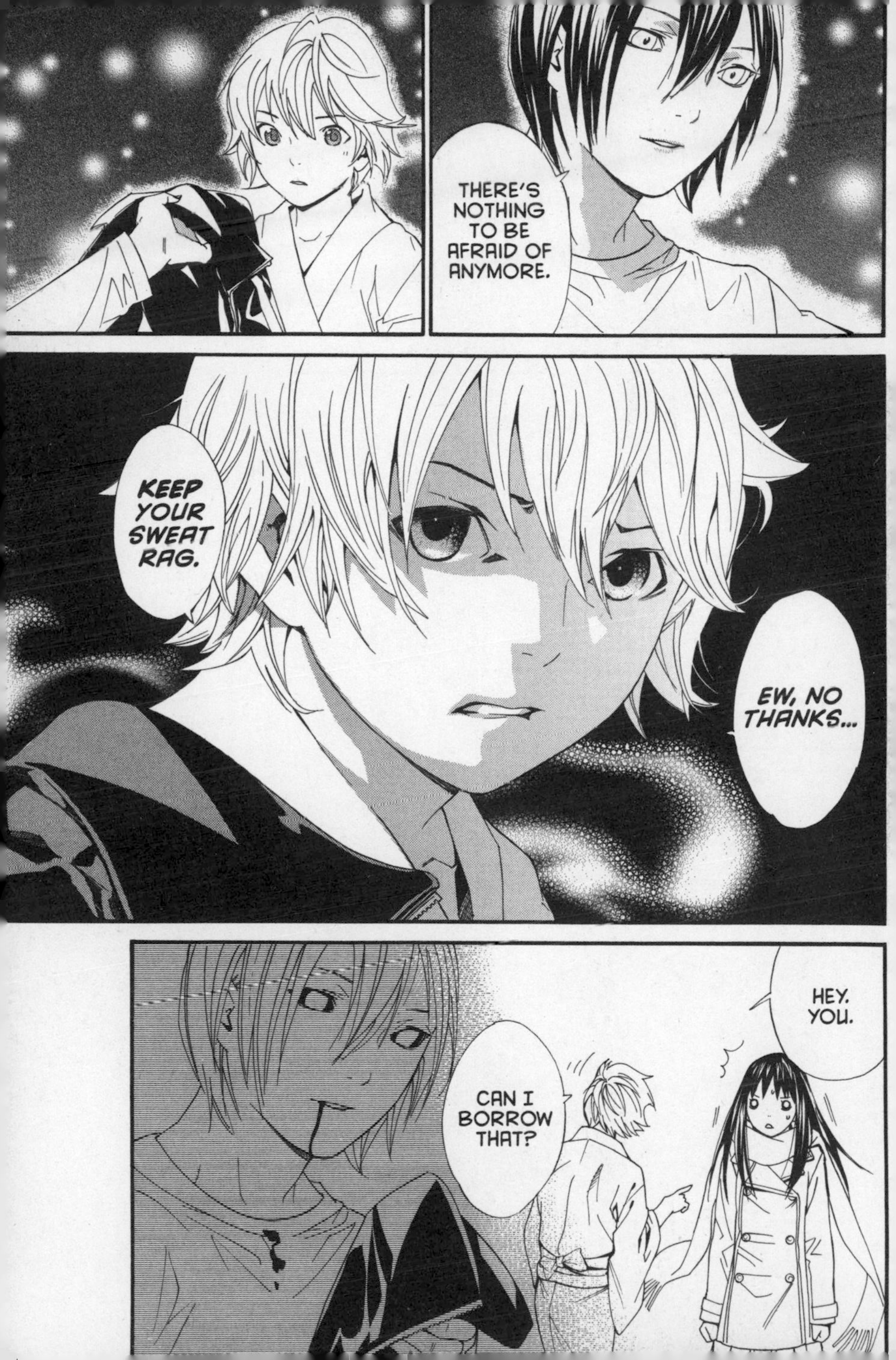
THERE'S NOTHING TO BE AFRAID OF ANYMORE.
KEEP YOUR SWEAT RAG.
EW, NO THANKS...
HEY. YOU.
CAN I BORROW THAT?

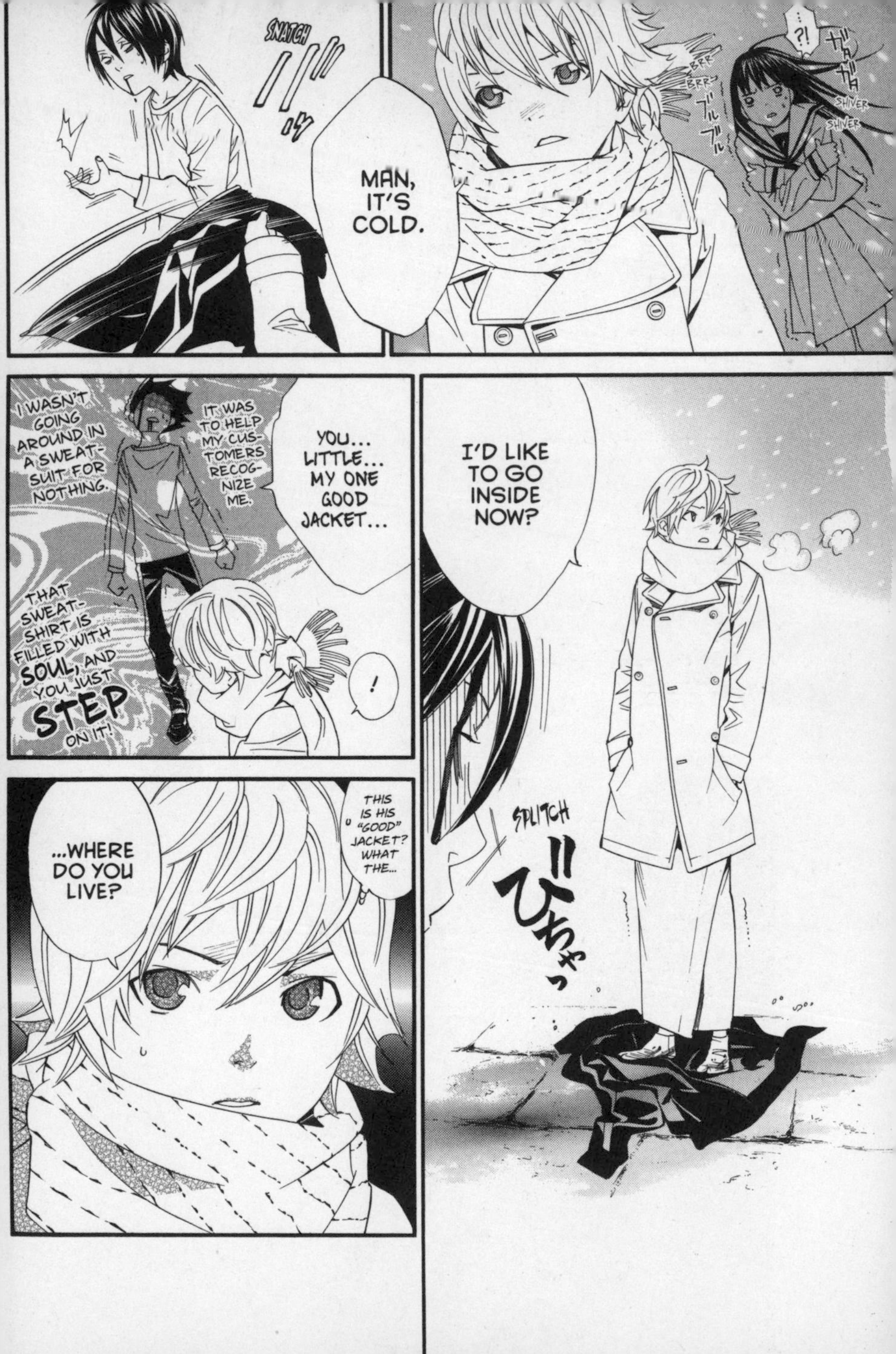

...?!
ガタガタ
SHIVER
SHIVER
BRR
BRR
ブルブル
MAN, IT'S COLD.
SNATCH
I'D LIKE TO GO INSIDE NOW?
SPLITCH
ぴちゃっ
YOU... LITTLE... MY ONE GOOD JACKET...
IT WAS TO HELP MY CUSTOMERS RECOGNIZE ME.
I WASN'T GOING AROUND IN A SWEATSUIT FOR NOTHING.
!
THAT SWEATSHIRT IS FILLED WITH SOUL, AND YOU JUST STEP ON IT!
THIS IS HIS "GOOD" JACKET? WHAT THE...
...WHERE DO YOU LIVE?

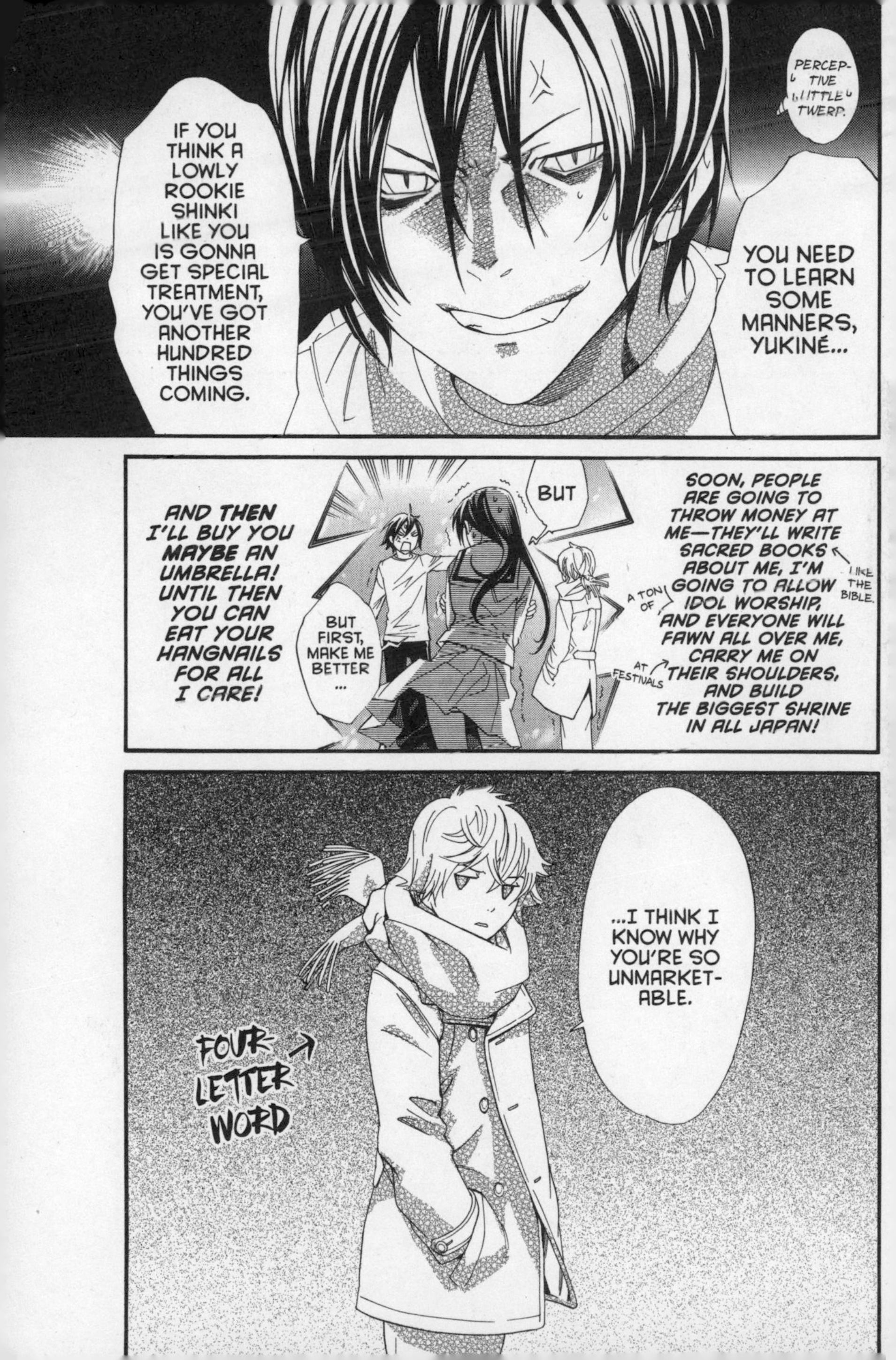
PERCEP-TIVE LITTLE TWERP.
YOU NEED TO LEARN SOME MANNERS, YUKINÉ...
IF YOU THINK A LOWLY ROOKIE SHINKI LIKE YOU IS GONNA GET SPECIAL TREATMENT, YOU'VE GOT ANOTHER HUNDRED THINGS COMING.
SOON, PEOPLE ARE GOING TO THROW MONEY AT ME—THEY'LL WRITE SACRED BOOKS ABOUT ME, I'M GOING TO ALLOW IDOL WORSHIP, AND EVERYONE WILL FAWN ALL OVER ME, CARRY ME ON THEIR SHOULDERS, AND BUILD THE BIGGEST SHRINE IN ALL JAPAN!
LIKE THE BIBLE.
A TON OF
AT FESTIVALS
BUT
AND THEN I'LL BUY YOU MAYBE AN UMBRELLA! UNTIL THEN YOU CAN EAT YOUR HANGNAILS FOR ALL I CARE!
BUT FIRST, MAKE ME BETTER ...
...I THINK I KNOW WHY YOU'RE SO UNMARKET-ABLE.
FOUR LETTER WORD

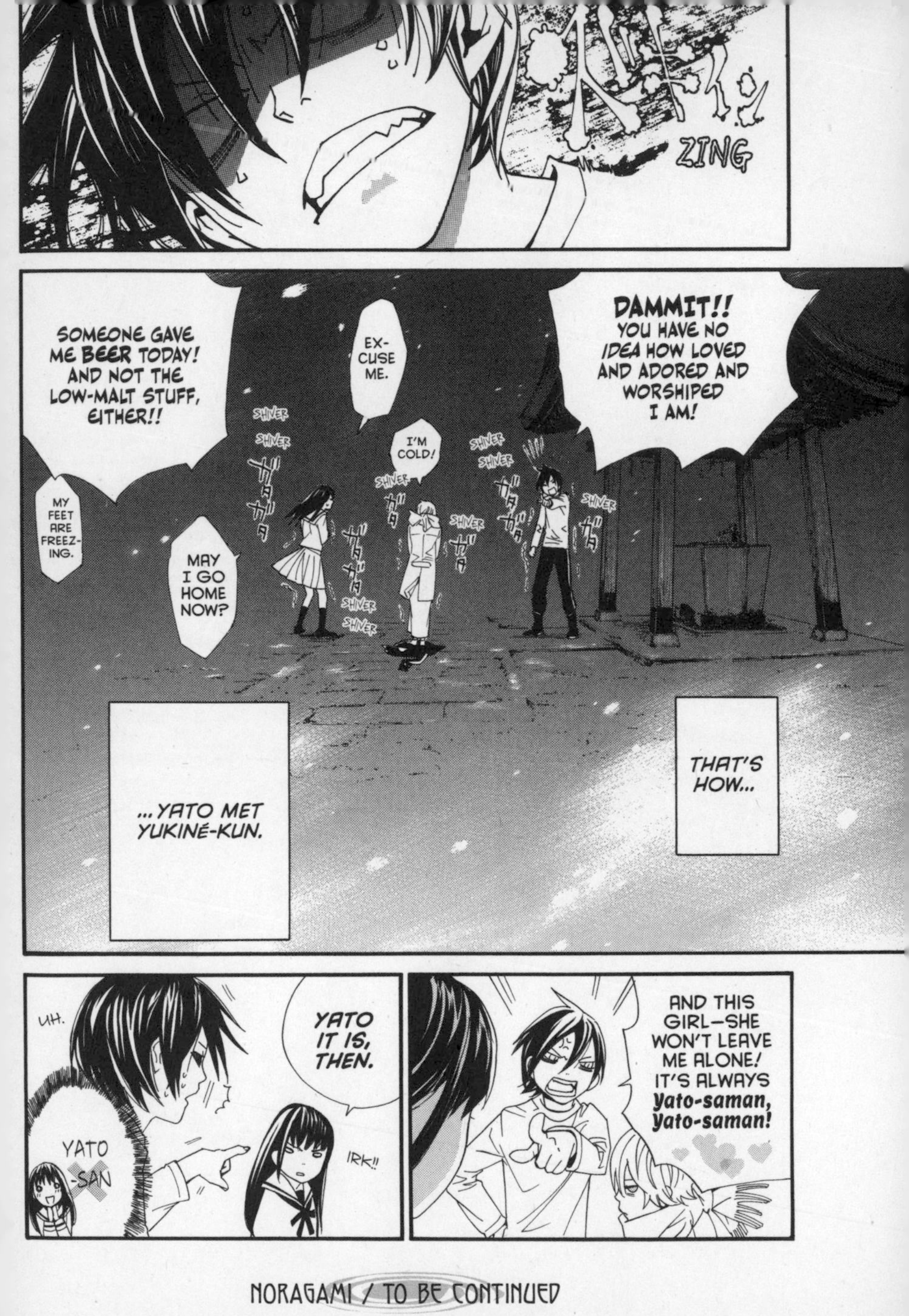
ZING
DAMMIT!! YOU HAVE NO IDEA HOW LOVED AND ADORED AND WORSHIPED I AM!
SHIVER SHIVER
SHIVER
I'M COLD!
SHIVER SHIVER
SHIVER
EX-CUSE ME.
SOMEONE GAVE ME BEER TODAY! AND NOT THE LOW-MALT STUFF, EITHER!!
SHIVER SHIVER
SHIVER SHIVER
MY FEET ARE FREEZ-ING.
MAY I GO HOME NOW?
THAT'S HOW...
...YATO MET YUKINÉ-KUN.
AND THIS GIRL—SHE WON'T LEAVE ME ALONE! IT'S ALWAYS Yato-saman, Yato-saman!
YATO IT IS, THEN.
UH.
IRK!!
YATO -SAN

NORAGAMI / TO BE CONTINUED

This work
is dedicated
to Tadashi
Kawashima-sensei
up in heaven.

Adachitoka

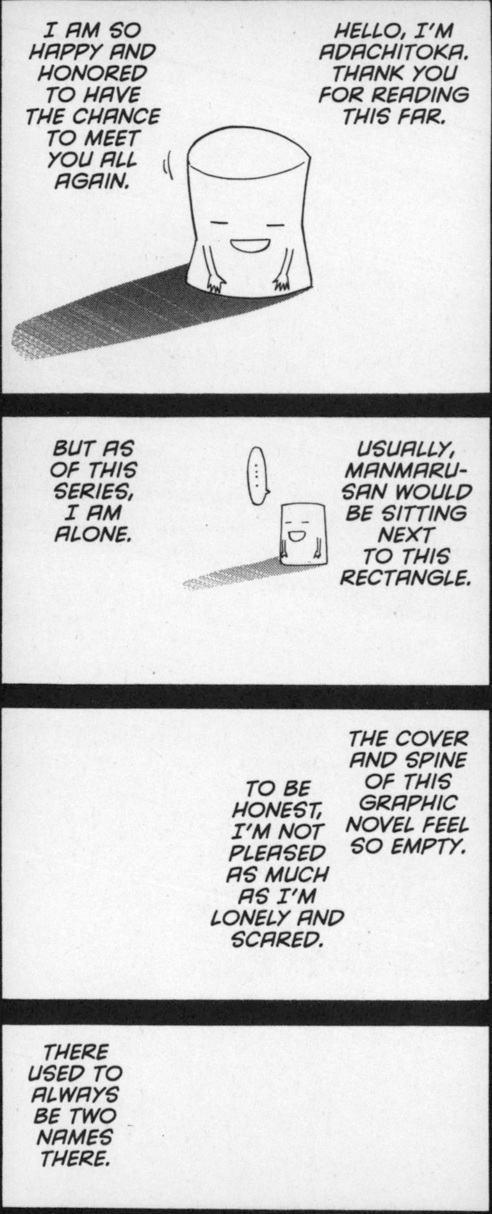
HELLO, I'M ADACHITOKA. THANK YOU FOR READING THIS FAR.
I AM SO HAPPY AND HONORED TO HAVE THE CHANCE TO MEET YOU ALL AGAIN.
USUALLY, MANMARU-SAN WOULD BE SITTING NEXT TO THIS RECTANGLE.
...
BUT AS OF THIS SERIES, I AM ALONE.
THE COVER AND SPINE OF THIS GRAPHIC NOVEL FEEL SO EMPTY.
TO BE HONEST, I'M NOT PLEASED AS MUCH AS I'M LONELY AND SCARED.
THERE USED TO ALWAYS BE TWO NAMES THERE.

A FEW PAGES PLEASE...

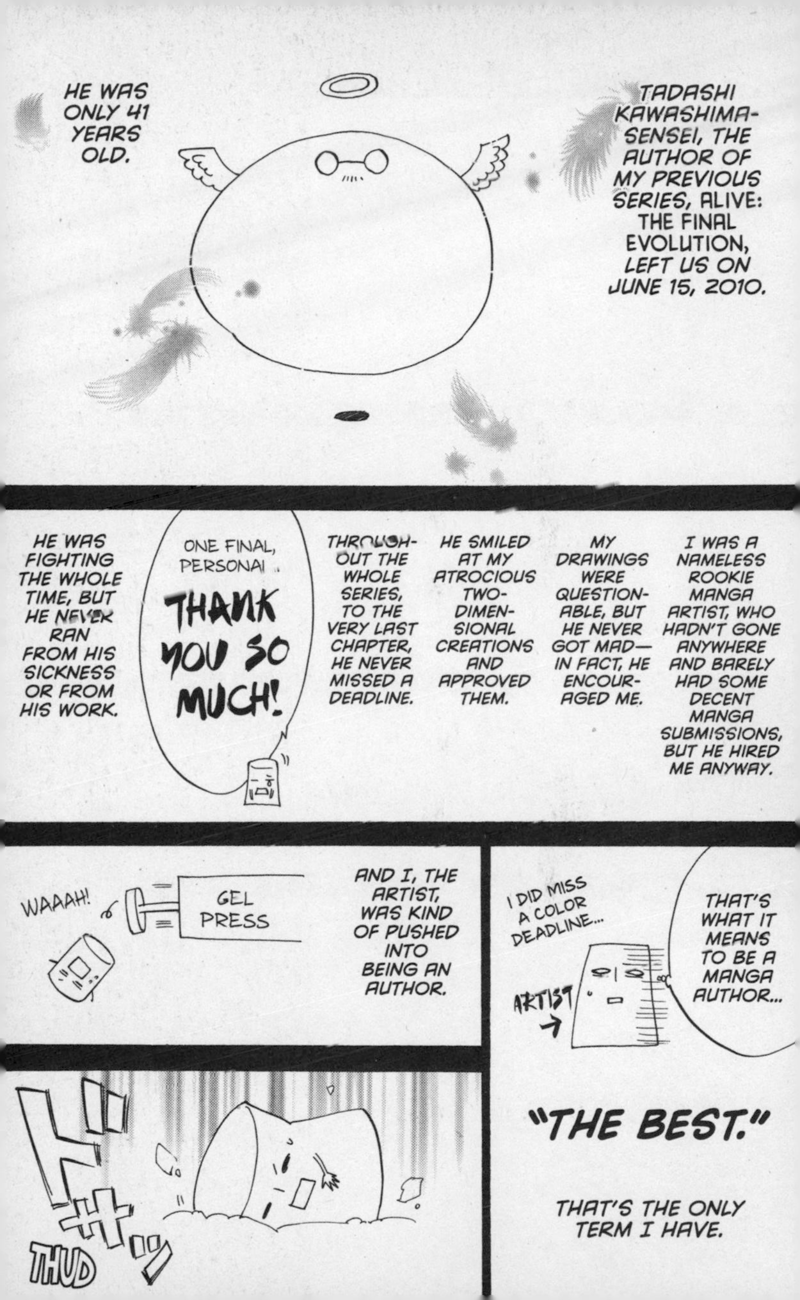
TADASHI KAWASHIMA-SENSEI, THE AUTHOR OF MY PREVIOUS SERIES, ALIVE: THE FINAL EVOLUTION, LEFT US ON JUNE 15, 2010.
HE WAS ONLY 41 YEARS OLD.
I WAS A NAMELESS ROOKIE MANGA ARTIST, WHO HADN'T GONE ANYWHERE AND BARELY HAD SOME DECENT MANGA SUBMISSIONS, BUT HE HIRED ME ANYWAY.
MY DRAWINGS WERE QUESTION-ABLE, BUT HE NEVER GOT MAD—IN FACT, HE ENCOUR-AGED ME.
HE SMILED AT MY ATROCIOUS TWO-DIMEN-SIONAL CREATIONS AND APPROVED THEM.
THROUGH-OUT THE WHOLE SERIES, TO THE VERY LAST CHAPTER, HE NEVER MISSED A DEADLINE.
ONE FINAL, PERSONAL
THANK YOU SO MUCH!
HE WAS FIGHTING THE WHOLE TIME, BUT HE NEVER RAN FROM HIS SICKNESS OR FROM HIS WORK.
I DID MISS A COLOR DEADLINE...
ARTIST
THAT'S WHAT IT MEANS TO BE A MANGA AUTHOR...
"THE BEST."
THAT'S THE ONLY TERM I HAVE.
AND I, THE ARTIST, WAS KIND OF PUSHED INTO BEING AN AUTHOR.
GEL PRESS
WAAAH!
THUD

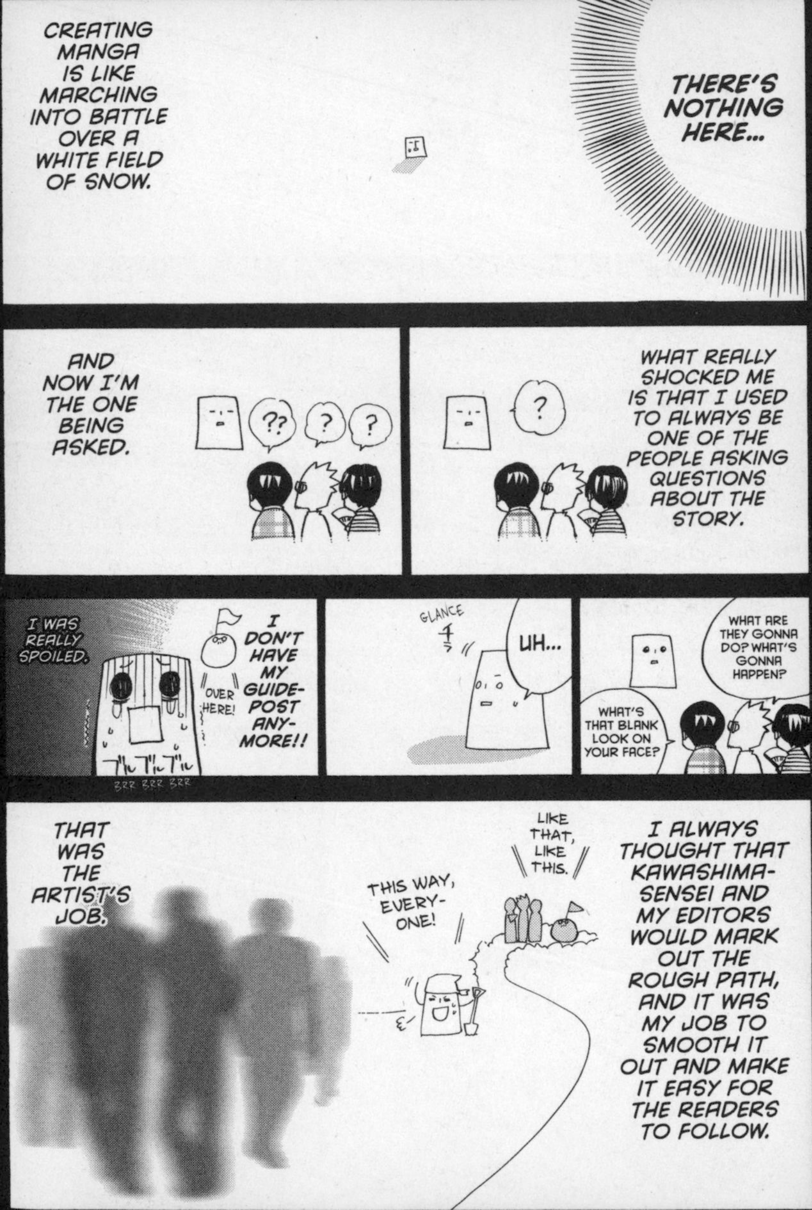
THERE'S NOTHING HERE...
CREATING MANGA IS LIKE MARCHING INTO BATTLE OVER A WHITE FIELD OF SNOW.
WHAT REALLY SHOCKED ME IS THAT I USED TO ALWAYS BE ONE OF THE PEOPLE ASKING QUESTIONS ABOUT THE STORY.
?
AND NOW I'M THE ONE BEING ASKED.
??
?
?
WHAT ARE THEY GONNA DO? WHAT'S GONNA HAPPEN?
WHAT'S THAT BLANK LOOK ON YOUR FACE?
GLANCE
UH...
I DON'T HAVE MY GUIDE-POST ANY-MORE!!
OVER HERE!
I WAS REALLY SPOILED.
BRR BRR BRR
I ALWAYS THOUGHT THAT KAWASHIMA-SENSEI AND MY EDITORS WOULD MARK OUT THE ROUGH PATH, AND IT WAS MY JOB TO SMOOTH IT OUT AND MAKE IT EASY FOR THE READERS TO FOLLOW.
LIKE THAT, LIKE THIS.
THIS WAY, EVERY-ONE!
THAT WAS THE ARTIST'S JOB.

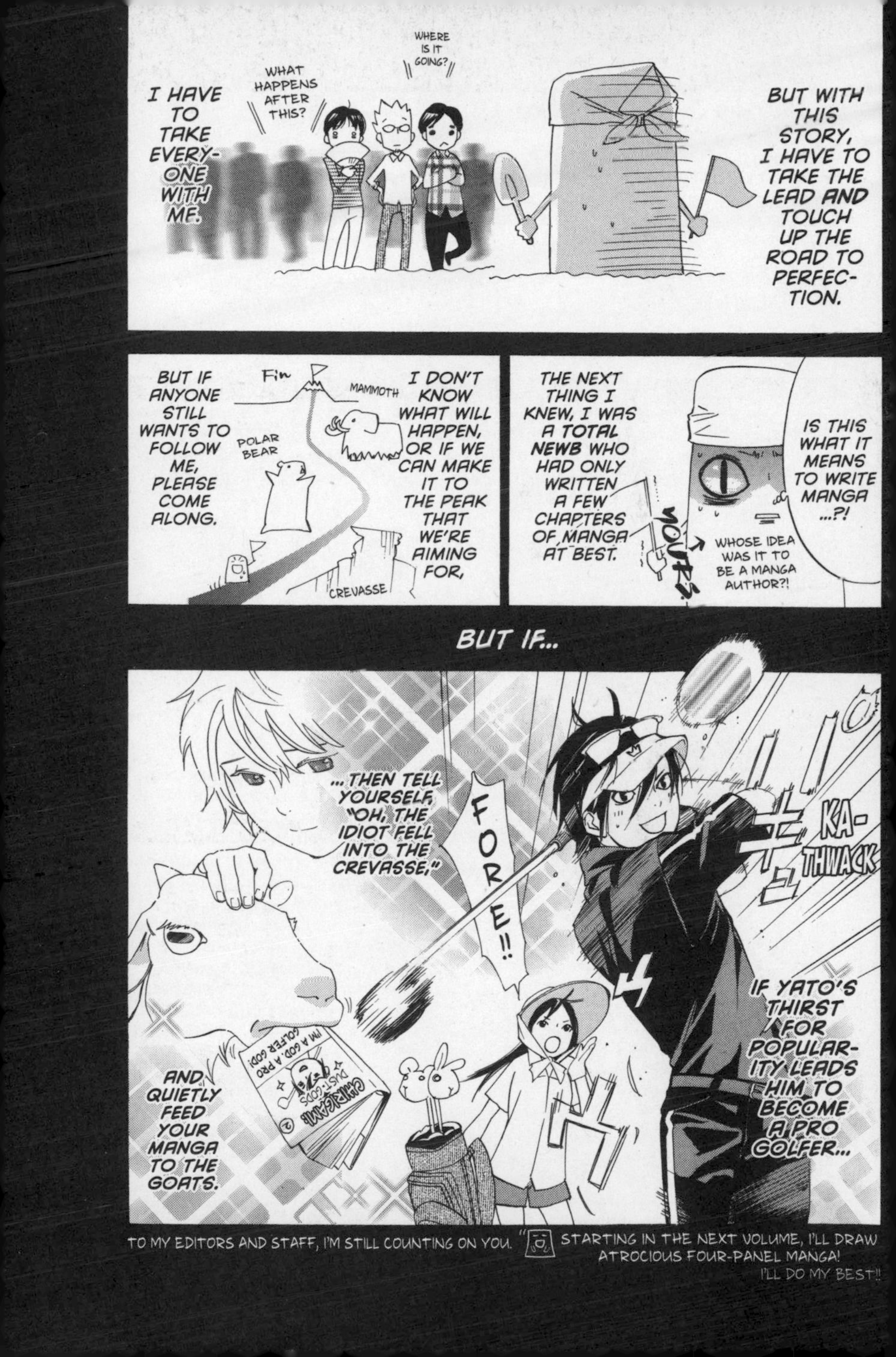
BUT WITH THIS STORY, I HAVE TO TAKE THE LEAD AND TOUCH UP THE ROAD TO PERFECTION.
WHERE IS IT GOING?
WHAT HAPPENS AFTER THIS?
I HAVE TO TAKE EVERYONE WITH ME.
THE NEXT THING I KNEW, I WAS A TOTAL NEWB WHO HAD ONLY WRITTEN A FEW CHAPTERS OF MANGA AT BEST.
IS THIS WHAT IT MEANS TO WRITE MANGA ...?!
YOURS.
WHOSE IDEA WAS IT TO BE A MANGA AUTHOR?!
I DON'T KNOW WHAT WILL HAPPEN, OR IF WE CAN MAKE IT TO THE PEAK THAT WE'RE AIMING FOR,
Fin
MAMMOTH
POLAR BEAR
CREVASSE
BUT IF ANYONE STILL WANTS TO FOLLOW ME, PLEASE COME ALONG.
BUT IF...
IF YATO'S THIRST FOR POPULARITY LEADS HIM TO BECOME A PRO GOLFER...
KA-THWACK
FORE!!
...THEN TELL YOURSELF, "OH, THE IDIOT FELL INTO THE CREVASSE,"
CHIRIGAMI: DUST-GODS
I'M A GOD, A PRO GOLFER GOD!
AND QUIETLY FEED YOUR MANGA TO THE GOATS.

STARTING IN THE NEXT VOLUME, I'LL DRAW ATROCIOUS FOUR-PANEL MANGA! I'LL DO MY BEST!!

TO MY EDITORS AND STAFF, I'M STILL COUNTING ON YOU.

TRANSLATION NOTES

Japanese is a tricky language for most Westerners, and translation is often more art than science. For your edification and reading pleasure, here are notes on some of the places where we could have gone in a different direction in our translation of the work, or where a Japanese cultural reference is used.

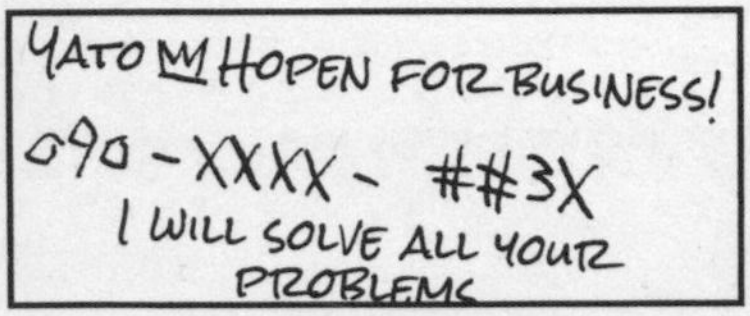
YATO HOPEN FOR BUSINESS!
090-XXXX-##3X
I WILL SOLVE ALL YOUR PROBLEMS

Hopen for business, page 4

In the original Japanese, Yato used a clever play on the Japanese written word. He writes the *kanji* characters for spring, summer, and winter. Because the seasons listed don't include autumn, the three together read *akinai*, which means "no autumn," but is also a word for "business." He follows it up with a *kanji* that means "in process of." So together, they mean "open for business." The translators attempted to replicate the cuteness of pun in English by using a slogan they've seen on a billboard. The success of this attempt is open for debate.

Subsi-date, page 6

A subsidized date. Mutsumi is afraid that the man she has just called is going to offer to "solve her problems" by paying her to date him.

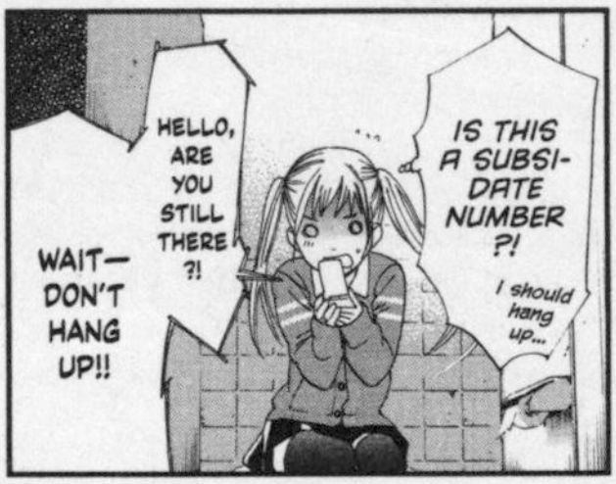
IS THIS A SUBSI-DATE NUMBER?!
I should hang up...
...
HELLO, ARE YOU STILL THERE?!
WAIT— DON'T HANG UP!!

The divine hierarchy, page 11

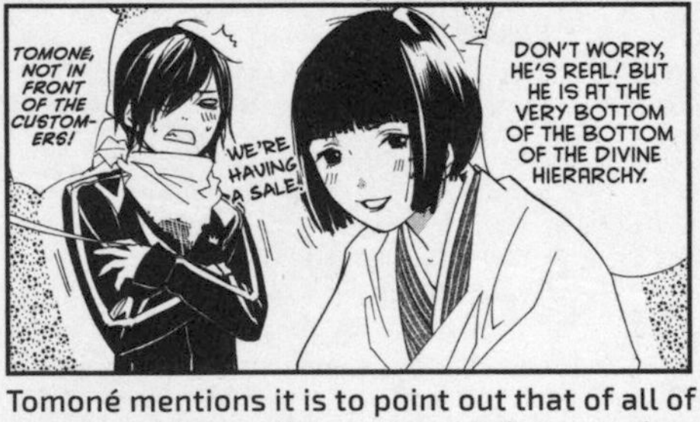
DON'T WORRY, HE'S REAL! BUT HE IS AT THE VERY BOTTOM OF THE BOTTOM OF THE DIVINE HIERARCHY.
WE'RE HAVING A SALE!
TOMONE, NOT IN FRONT OF THE CUSTOMERS!

In Japan, there's a concept called the *yaoyorozu no kami*, which literally means eight million *kami*, or gods or spirits. The number "eight million" is used figuratively to mean, roughly, "lots and lots and lots." The general idea of this concept is that everything has a spirit, or in other words, there's a god of everything. But the reason Tomoné mentions it is to point out that of all of those millions upon millions of gods in existence, Yato is the absolute very least among them.

Crider, page 19

Also known as a "cricket spider." This particular type of insect likes damp places and so can often be found crying in restrooms. In fact, one Japanese name for it translates to "bathroom cricket," which is what Yato compares Mutsumi to, because she, too, cries in a bathroom.

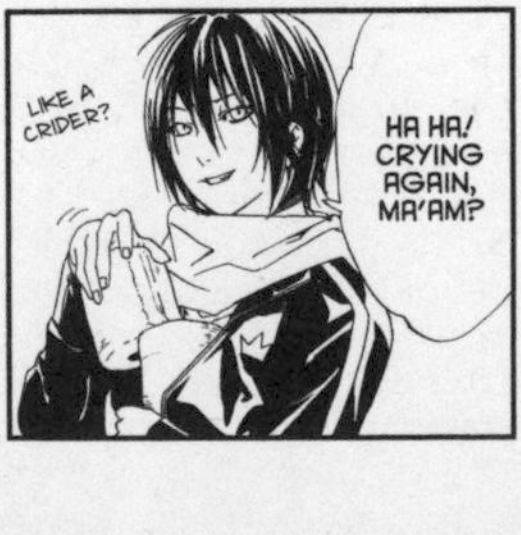
HA HA! CRYING AGAIN, MA'AM?
LIKE A CRIDER?

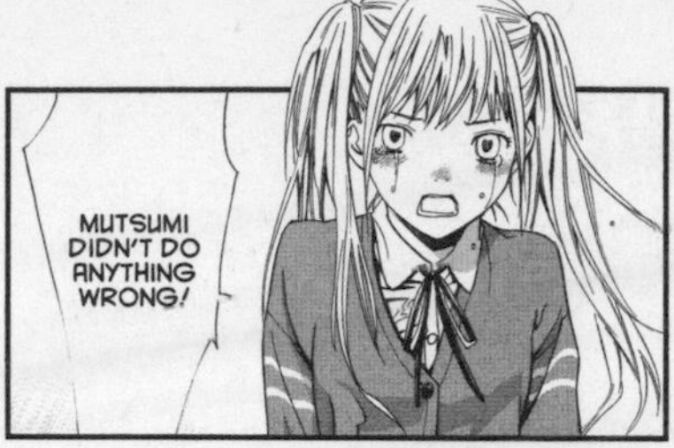
MUTSUMI DIDN'T DO ANYTHING WRONG!

Talking about yourself in the third person, page 20

In the Japanese language, it's very easy to talk about yourself in the third person, because all you have to do is use your name instead of "I" or "me"—other than that, the grammar stays exactly the same. For this reason, it's a relatively common practice for young children, who haven't yet learned to use first-person pronouns. That being the case, girls will sometimes speak of themselves in the third person in an attempt to seem cute and childlike. The attempt often backfires, because it also comes across as self-absorption.

Ayakashi, page 21

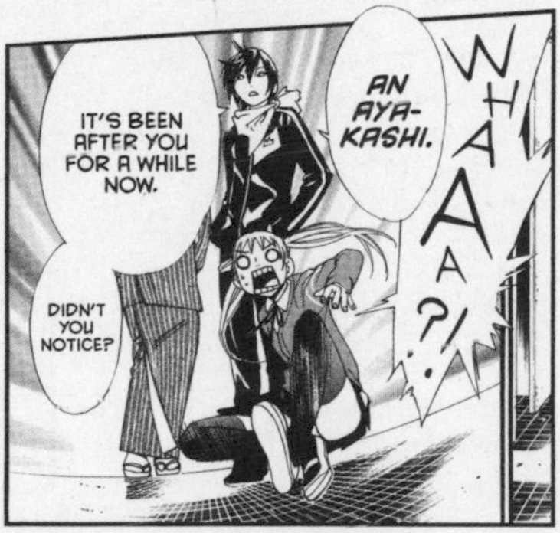
WHAAAA?!
AN AYA-KASHI.
IT'S BEEN AFTER YOU FOR A WHILE NOW.
DIDN'T YOU NOTICE?

Ayakashi is one of a few blanket terms used to describe supernatural phenomena and/or creatures. This word and related terms (such as *yōkai*) have been translated many different ways, including ghost, phantom, demon, ghoul, etc., but all of those seem to be a little too specific for the purposes of *Noragami*. A close English equivalent might be *fairy*, which, in European folklore, is actually used to describe many different magical creatures, both good and evil. But because the term *fairy* is most commonly used in reference to specific types of sprites that don't match the image of the *ayakashi* in this series, and because the series takes place in Japan, the translators have opted to use the Japanese term.

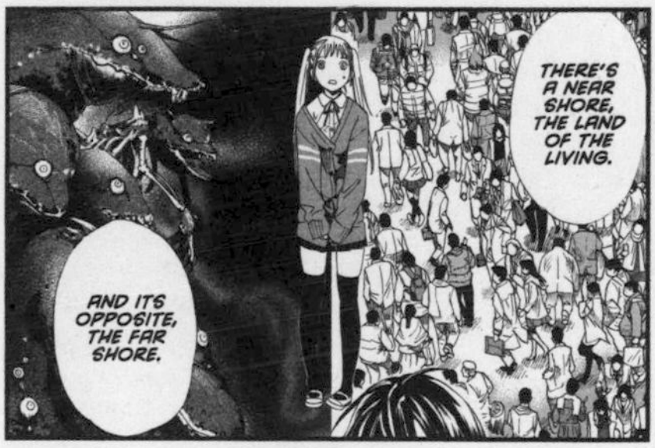
THERE'S A NEAR SHORE, THE LAND OF THE LIVING.
AND ITS OPPOSITE, THE FAR SHORE.

The Near Shore and the Far Shore, page 23

In many cultures, the land of the living and the land of the dead are believed to be separated by a river. Thus, the two different worlds are referred to as "shores," describing their relationship to that river—the border between life and death.

Five thousand, page 36

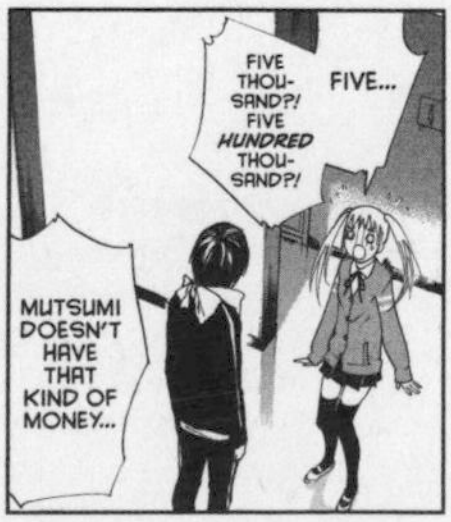
FIVE...
FIVE THOU-SAND?! FIVE *HUNDRED* THOU-SAND?!
MUTSUMI DOESN'T HAVE THAT KIND OF MONEY...

Fans of math and linguistic accuracy will be interested to know that Mutsumi's first guess as to Yato's asking price was not five thousand, but five *man*, where *man* means "ten thousand." In other words, five ten thousands, or fifty thousand. The translators brought the number down to five thousand because, seeing five fingers, an English speaker would be more likely to say "five [something]" than "fifty [something]." Her second guess really was five hundred thousand.

Five yen offering, page 37

When it comes to making monetary offerings at a Japanese shrine (or to delivery gods making house calls), the five yen coin is standard because of its symbolic meaning. The word for five yen, *goen*, is a homonym—*goen* can also refer to what has been translated in this series as "good ties," or good relationships, or encounters with people who will become good relations. The word *en* is closely connected to "fate," because even seemingly random encounters can have a profound effect on those involved. The offering of five yen then becomes a prayer: may I be blessed with good ties. Thus, when Yato makes a contract with a customer, he finalizes it by saying, "May you be blessed with good ties."
As a point of interest, the Chinese character for en can also be pronounced *fuchi*, which refers to the hilt of a sword.

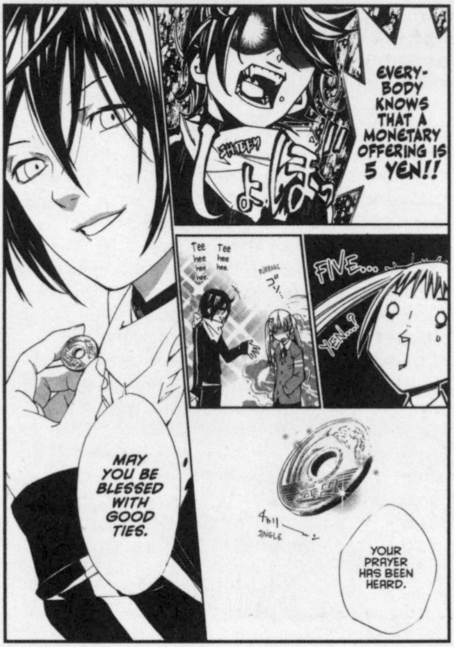
EVERY-BODY KNOWS THAT A MONETARY OFFERING IS 5 YEN!!
FIVE...
YEN...?
Tee hee hee hee.
Tee hee hee.
JINGLE
YOUR PRAYER HAS BEEN HEARD.
MAY YOU BE BLESSED WITH GOOD TIES.

Shinki, page 39

As Yato will explain later, a *shinki* is a divine weapon. Shin means "god" or "divine," and *ki* means "vessel" or "instrument." Just as a *buki* (weapon) is the instrument (*ki*) of a warrior (*bu*), or a *gakki* is a musical (*gaku*) instrument, a *shinki* is the instrument of a god. The term is sometimes translated as "regalia," because the most famous *shinki* are known as the Imperial Regalia of Japan—the sword, the mirror, and the jewel. In this case, the word is pronounced *jingi*.

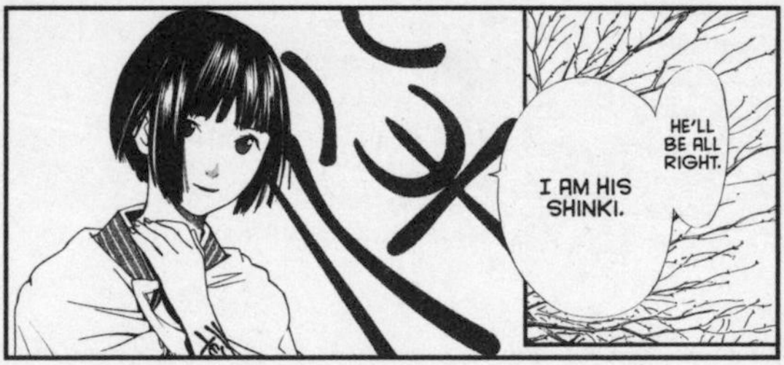
HE'LL BE ALL RIGHT.
I AM HIS SHINKI.

Kaki-pea, page 73

Kaki-pea, meaning roughly "persimmons and peanuts," is a type of Japanese junk food. It consists of peanuts and pieces of *senbei* rice crackers cut to look like persimmon seeds.

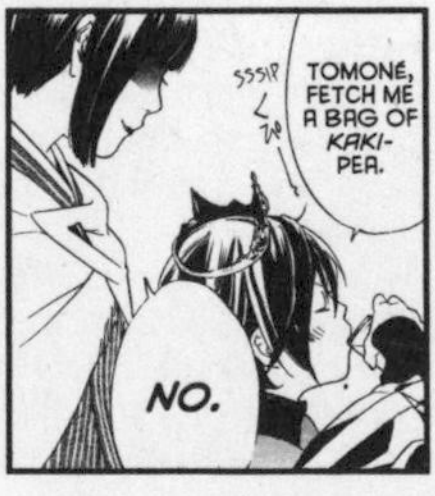
TOMONÉ, FETCH ME A BAG OF KAKI-PEA.
NO.

Milord, Jenny's, Hyakki Yakō, and Tōno-sama, pages 83, 85

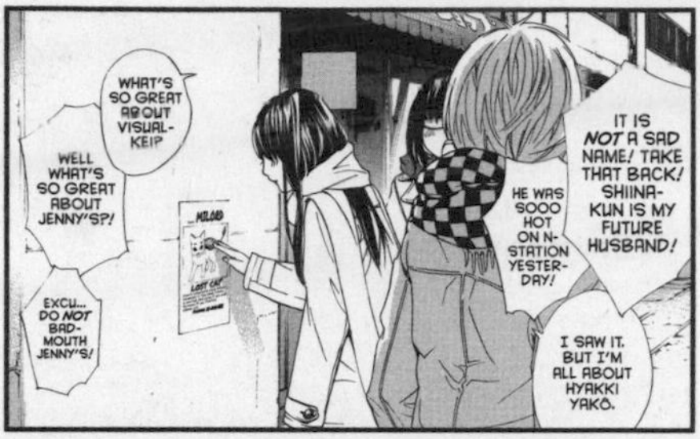
IT IS NOT A SAD NAME! TAKE THAT BACK! SHIINA-KUN IS MY FUTURE HUSBAND!
HE WAS SOOO HOT ON N-STATION YESTERDAY!
I SAW IT. BUT I'M ALL ABOUT HYAKKI YAKŌ.
WHAT'S SO GREAT ABOUT VISUAL-KEI?
WELL WHAT'S SO GREAT ABOUT JENNY'S?!
EXCU... DO NOT BAD-MOUTH JENNY'S!
LOST CAT

The various idols worshiped by the characters in this chapter. Milord may not be worshiped so much, but he's definitely sought after and beloved. His name in Japanese is Ue-sama, which means, roughly, Milord. Jenny's are the *Noragami* version of Johnny's, a collection of male pop star idols represented by Johnny & Associates. Hyakki Yakō is the name of a visual kei band, taken from the Japanese term meaning roughly "100 demons on a night parade." Visual kei, meaning roughly "of the visual persuasion," is more a genre of musical performance fashion than of music. Visual kei bands are known for their heavy makeup and flamboyant costumes. Tōno-sama doesn't need much of an explanation, but it's worth noting that his name is very similar to the Japanese word *tono*, which also means, roughly, my lord (usually in reference to the feudal lords of Medieval Japan).

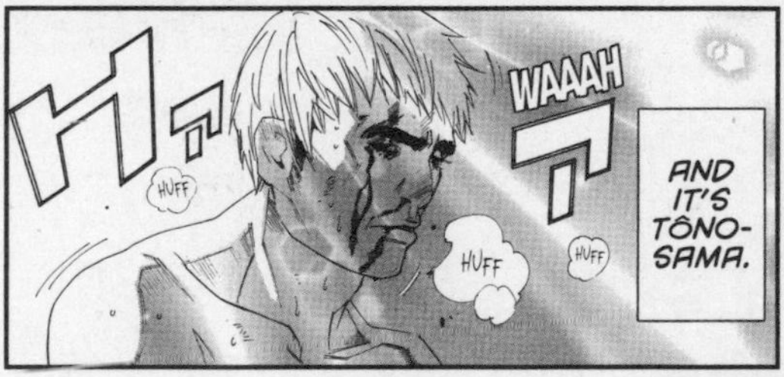
AND IT'S TÔNO-SAMA.
WAAAH
HUFF
HUFF
HUFF

The Stray, page 104

The word for "stray" is *nora*, and like many terms in this series, it has a myriad of meanings. In this particular case, "stray" is probably the most applicable, but when used in the case of the "stray god" Yato, some of the other meanings work well, too. It can refer to a lazy person, or someone who spends all their time and money in pursuit of worldly pleasures. Another interesting meaning of the term comes from ancient times and applies when it is used as a name suffix like -san or -chan—it is a term of endearment, expressing love and affection for the person to whose name it is attached.

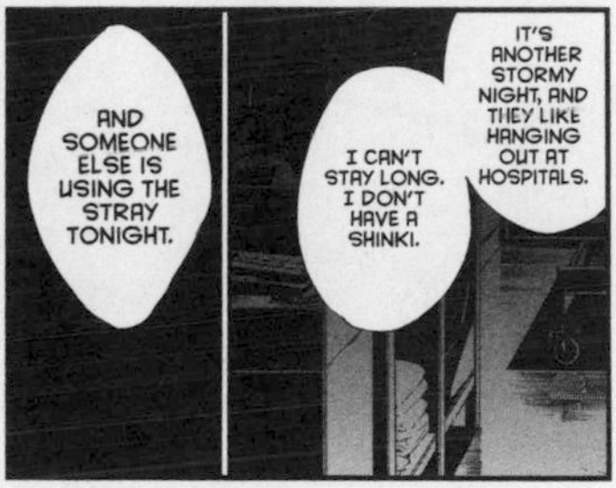
IT'S ANOTHER STORMY NIGHT, AND THEY LIKE HANGING OUT AT HOSPITALS.
I CAN'T STAY LONG. I DON'T HAVE A SHINKI.
AND SOMEONE ELSE IS USING THE STRAY TONIGHT.

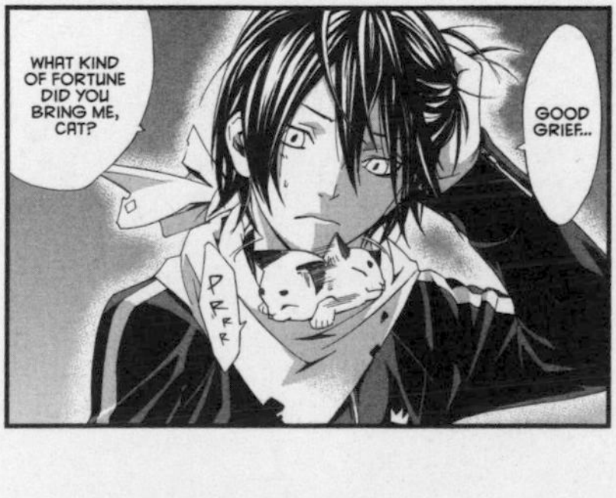
GOOD GRIEF...
WHAT KIND OF FORTUNE DID YOU BRING ME, CAT?
PRRR

What kind of fortune did you bring me, cat?, page 128

In this line, Yato suggests that Milord is a *maneki-neko*, or "beckoning cat." A beckoning cat is usually a figurine of a cat with a paw held up in a welcoming position, often placed at the entrance of a business to attract customers and, ideally, good fortune. In this case, Yato isn't so sure the fortune brought by the cat is a good one.

You're a ghost, page 149

Specifically, Yato teases Hiyori for being a "living ghost" or *ikiryō*. In Japanese folklore, there is a belief that if a living person feels strongly enough about something or someone, usually in a negative way, their spirit will leave their body to do something about those feelings—for example, curse a love rival, or spend time with loved ones.

UGH, WHEN DID I—?!!
HA, HA, YOU'RE A GHO-OST!
IT'S NOT FUNNY!

The going is easy, but coming back is hard, page 159

Here Yato starts singing to himself a Japanese children's song called Tōryanse, which can be heard frequently in Japan as the tune played at traffic lights when it's safe to cross the street. The song is about going along the path to a Shinto shrine, and in it, the god of the shrine is referred to as Tenjin (a term that can refer to a specific deity, or to a category of deities). Since Yato is staying at Tenjin's shrine for the night, it stands to reason that this song would come to mind.

I'LL JUST STAY HERE AT TENJIN'S TONIGHT!
ROLL
HE'S REALLY RAKING IT IN.
HN.
奉納
THE GOING IS EASY, BUT COMING BACK IS HARD... AS THEY SAY.

Blight, page 168

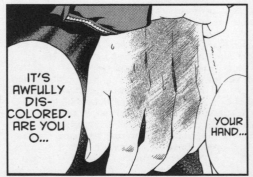

The Japanese word Yato uses here is *yasumu*, or in noun form, *yasumi*. Shinto priestesses that served the Ise Shrine were not allowed to say certain words because those words would bring defilement. One of those words was *yamai*, meaning sickness. So instead of saying *yamai*, when they needed to talk about illness, they would use the word *yasumi*, which sounds just like the Japanese word for "rest."

YOUR HAND...
IT'S AWFULLY DIS-COLORED. ARE YOU O...

Grasping thy true name, I bind thee here, page 174

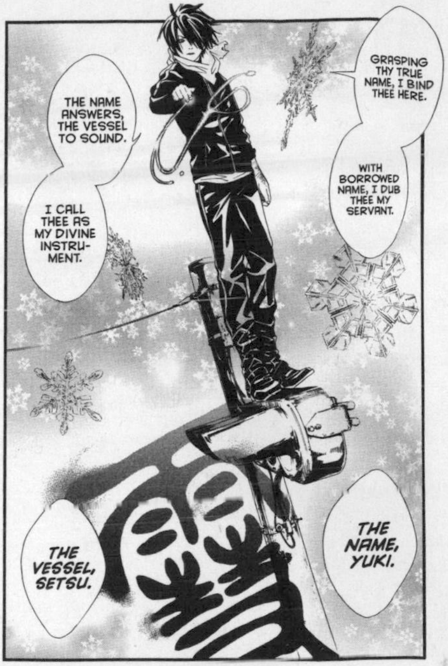
GRASPING THY TRUE NAME, I BIND THEE HERE.
WITH BORROWED NAME, I DUB THEE MY SERVANT.
THE NAME ANSWERS, THE VESSEL TO SOUND.
I CALL THEE AS MY DIVINE INSTRUMENT.
THE NAME, YUKI.
THE VESSEL, SETSU.

The words that Yato uses to summon his shinki are fraught with multiple meanings, many of them having to do with the Japanese language. First, Yato mentions the shinki's "true name," or *imina*. The word *imina* can mean, loosely, "avoided name," based on the idea that knowledge of someone's true name gives you power over them—therefore the name is rarely spoken, to prevent the knowledge of it from falling into the wrong hands, and another name is used instead. Another word for *imina* is *mana*, which means "true name" but is also a word for the Chinese characters, or *kanji*, used in the Japanese writing system.

Next, Yato mentions a borrowed name—a name provided by himself to the shinki. In this case, the word is *karina*, but the *kanji* can also be pronounced *kana*, which is the word for the Japanese phonetic characters used in conjunction with the kanji. This becomes significant because of the next line, "The name answers, the vessel to sound." The kanji used for "answer," or more literally "obey," usually means "reading," and applies to the Japanese pronunciation of a *kanji* character. The *kanji* for "sound" is used to refer to the phonetic reading of the character, based on Chinese. Most *kanji* have at least two different pronunciations: the Japanese "native reading (*kun-yomi*)" and the Chinese-based "sound reading (*on-yomi*)."

Thus, when Yato gives his shinki a name, he actually gives it two: the native reading of the *kanji*, which becomes part of the shinki's human-form name; and the sound reading, which becomes part of the shinki's instrument-form name. For example, in the case of Tomoné, he used for her name 伴, which you can see on her left arm, and means companion (Yato would appear to lack creativity in naming). The native reading is *tomo*, and sound reading is *han*. For the curious, the *ne* in Tomoné means "sound," and the *ki* in Hanki means "vessel" or "instrument." In the case of Yukiné and Sekki, the character means snow and can be pronounced *yuki* (native reading) or *setsu* (sound reading). Often when a word ending in *tsu* is followed by a voiceless consonant like K, then the *tsu* is swallowed and it becomes a double consonant, hence *sekki* (pronounced sek-ki).

Finally, Yato gives the order and the shinki becomes his weapon. The first part of the line can also be rendered as "at my command." The word he uses for "command," translated in the manga as "call," is *mei*, which full of potential meanings. The first, of course, is order, comand, etc. Second, it can mean "life" or "destiny." Whether either of these meanings has any application to Yato's ties with his shinki has yet to be revealed. However, with a different *kanji*, the word *mei* can mean "name," bringing it back to the main theme of this speech.

A Kodansha Comics Trade Paperback Original.

Noragami: Stray God volume 1 copyright © 2011 Adachitoka
English translation copyright © 2014 Adachitoka

Published in the United States by Kodansha Comics, an imprint of Kodansha USA Publishing, LLC, New York.

Publication rights for this English edition arranged through Kodansha Ltd., Tokyo.

First published in Japan in 2011 by Kodansha Ltd., Tokyo.

ISBN 978-1-61262-906-3

Printed in the United States of America.

www.kodanshacomics.com

9 8 7 6 5

Translator: Alethea Nibley & Athena Nibley
Lettering: Lys Blakeslee